Java Security Handbook

Jamie Jaworski
Paul Perrone
Venkata S. R. Krishna Chaganti

A Division of Macmillan USA
201 West 103rd St., Indianapolis, Indiana, 46290 USA

Java Security Handbook

Copyright © 2000 by Sams Publishing

International Standard Book Number: 0-672-31602-1

Library of Congress Catalog Card Number: 99-62250

Printed in the United States of America

First Printing: September, 2000

02   01   00   4   3   2   1

Trademarks

Warning and Disclaimer

ASSOCIATE PUBLISHER
Michael Stephens

ACQUISITIONS EDITOR
Steve Anglin

DEVELOPMENT EDITOR
Tiffany Taylor

MANAGING EDITORS
Matt Purcell
Lisa Wilson

PROJECT EDITOR
Natalie F. Harris

COPY EDITOR
Mary Lagu

INDEXER
Sandy Henselmeier

PROOFREADERS
Candice Hightower
Jill Mazurczyk
Tony Reitz
Andrew Simmons
Matt Wynalda

TECHNICAL EDITOR
Krishna Sankar

TEAM COORDINATORS
Pamalee Nelsen
Karen Opal

MEDIA DEVELOPER
Adam Swetnam

INTERIOR DESIGNER
Dan Armstrong

COVER DESIGNER
Alan Clements

PRODUCTION
Darin Crone

Contents at a Glance

Table of Contents

About the Authors

Jamie Jaworski is the president of JSPWare.com, where he advises Fortune 100 companies on approaches to building secure Java-based Web applications. He is also a professional Java developer and Sun-certified programmer, developer, and architect. Mr. Jaworski has written several best-selling books on Java and JavaScript, including *Java 2 Platform Unleashed* and *Mastering JavaScript and JScript*. He also writes the SuperScripter column for CNET's popular Web site for Web developers, `Builder.com`.

Paul J. Perrone is the founder, the president, and a senior software consultant for Assured Technologies, Inc. Through Assured Technologies (`http://www.assuredtech.com`), Paul provides software consulting, training, products, and research for companies interested in highly secure, highly intelligent, economical, scalable, and Internet-enabled distributed enterprise systems used for e-commerce, business-to-business (B2B) transactions, and general enterprise-wide application. Paul has enabled his specialized background in high-intelligence and high-assurance (for example, security) systems to be reflected in Assured Technologies' business practice and pursuits. Paul has been a key player in the architecture, design, and development of numerous large-scale n-tier distributed systems and products for both Fortune 500 and medium-sized organizations. Paul's key technology and training expertise areas are enterprise Java and the J2EE, EJB, embedded-enterprise system connectivity, CORBA, XML, UML, and object-oriented and component-based software. In addition to this book, Paul has written *Building Java Enterprise Systems with J2EE*, has been a speaker at the JavaOne conference, and publishes his work in various trade journals. He has an MSEE from the University of Virginia and a BSEE from Rutgers University. He is a member of the IEEE and ACM and is active in the Northern Virginia technology community. Paul can be reached at `pperrone@assuredtech.com` or (703)728-0115.

Venkata S. R. Krishna Chaganti has developed many of the code examples used in Chapters 3, 9, and 13 of this book. Krishna is a senior software engineering consultant and has been developing distributed computing software for the past seven years using Java and C++ programming environments. Krishna has been working with Fortune 500 companies to develop EJB, CORBA, and DCE software for their distributed computing needs. Krishna has also been teaching Java and related technologies for two years. He has an MSEE in Computer Engineering and an MSEE in Electrical Engineering from the University of Alabama in Huntsville. He also has a B.Tech in Electronics and Communications Engineering from Nagarjuna University, A.P., India. He can be reached at `chaganti@erols.com`.

Dedication

This book is dedicated to Fred Neal, Ralph Seay, and all of the great folks at HQ USAFE INSA. Thanks for showing me a good time.

Jamie Jaworski

To my wife and parents.

Paul Perrone

Acknowledgments

I'd like to thank everyone who helped to see this book through to completion. In particular, I'd like to thank Margot Maley Hutchison of Waterside Productions for making the book possible; Paul Perrone for rescuing it and bringing it to completion, Steve Anglin, Dawn Pearson, Tiffany Taylor, Mary Lagu, and the entire Macmillan team for their numerous, valuable suggestions; Tim Ryan for getting me started; and Krishna Sankar for the numerous technical suggestions that improved the overall quality of this book. Finally, I'd like to thank Lisa, Emily, and Jason for their patience, love, and understanding.

—*Jamie Jaworski*

Familial and friendly culture shapes who we are and helps drive how we approach solving problems. Thus, I always owe thanks to my large and extended family for being there throughout the years and being supportive during my current software development and writing efforts. I always am grateful for having a wife like Janie Perrone for love, understanding, and support. Of course, I also owe many thanks to my parents, Don and Judy Perrone, my brother and family, Don, Denise, Allison, and Julia Perrone, Catherine Stiles, the Vances, the Heilmanns, the Izzos, the Lawlesses; the rather lengthy family list goes on and on. I am also always grateful to the late Anthony Perrone and Louis Perrone for everything they've brought into my life.

Aside from family, many friends and colleagues help shape my mental processes and insight, including Anup Ghosh, Andy Stauffer, Jim Wamsley, Paul Kirkitelos, Jeff Ebert, Charles Choi, Doug Szajda, Geoff Hoekstra, Rick Hatch, Steve Wynne, Mike Carr, Catherine Longo, Ben Collingsworth, Barry Johnson, Steven Sandler, the PRC folks, the Copper Key folks, and Cappy. Last, but not least, Krishna Chaganti deserves many kudos for developing many of the code examples strewn throughout Chapters 3, 9, and 13.

—*Paul Perrone*

Tell Us What You Think!

As the reader of this book, *you* are our most important critic and commentator. We value your opinion and want to know what we're doing right, what we could do better, what areas you'd like to see us publish in, and any other words of wisdom you're willing to pass our way.

As a Publisher for Sams, I welcome your comments. You can fax, email, or write me directly to let me know what you did or didn't like about this book—as well as what we can do to make our books stronger.

Please note that I cannot help you with technical problems related to the topic of this book and that, due to the high volume of mail I receive, I might not be able to reply to every message.

When you write, please be sure to include this book's title and author as well as your name and phone or fax number. I will carefully review your comments and share them with the author and editors who worked on the book.

Fax:	317-581-4770
Email:	java@mcp.com
Mail:	Michael Stephens
	Sams Publishing
	201 West 103rd Street
	Indianapolis, IN 46290 USA

Introduction

To many programmers, Java is the language of choice for developing Web-based applications and Enterprise services. Java's initial appeal stemmed from its support of applets and the extensive API provided with version 1.0 of the Java Development Kit (JDK). This appeal was extended by Netscape's LiveConnect, which allows applets to be scripted using JavaScript, by language improvements in the version 1.1 JDK, and by numerous features that were added in the version 1.1 API. These improvements include JavaBeans, which provides a mechanism for developing both GUI and non-GUI components, Java remote method invocation (RMI), which provides a foundation for distributed object communication, and JDBC, which adds database connectivity to Java applets and applications.

JDK 1.2 further increased Java's power and appeal by improving the features provided in JDK 1.1 and adding new features—such as Swing, Java 2D, Drag and Drop, Collections, and CORBA support. The JDK 1.2 was renamed as the Java 2 Platform. A software platform for developing Enterprise applications, referred to as the Java 2 Platform, Enterprise Edition (J2EE), added support for servlets, Java Server Pages (JSP), Enterprise JavaBeans, naming and directory services, transactions, mail, and other features. The features provided by the J2EE have made the Java 2 Platform the platform of choice for developing Web-based applications and distributed Enterprise services.

Although the extensive capabilities provided by the Java 2 APIs are, by themselves, overwhelming reasons for choosing Java; Java is also an excellent language and execution environment for developing secure applications. Since Java's inception, security has been a major factor in the design of the Java programming language, runtime system, API, and toolset. The JDK 1.0 introduced the "sandbox" approach to securing mobile code. This was a major factor in its early success as a Web programming language. The JDK 1.1 added support for signed applets, which are trusted to step outside of the sandbox without compromising applet security. The JDK 1.1 also added the capabilities to work with message digests, digital signatures, and digital certificates.

The Security API of the Java 2 Platform made some modifications to the JDK 1.1 API and added capabilities for configurable application and applet security policies, X.509 version 3 digital certificates, and additional certificate-processing support. The Java 2 Security API also provides new tools for specifying security policies, code signing, and managing certificates.

The security capabilities of the Java 2 Platform have also been augmented by several security-oriented extensions:

- The Java Cryptography Extension (JCE) 1.2 provides a foundation for developing encryption, key generation, key agreement, and authentication algorithms. It also provides implementations of several popular cryptographic algorithms.

- The Java Secure Socket Extension (JSSE) provides a Java implementation of the Secure Sockets Layer (SSL) version 3 and Transport Layer Security (TLS) version 1 protocols. These protocols can be used to add security to existing Internet protocols, such as HTTP, telnet, and POP3.

- The Java Authentication and Authorization Service (JAAS) provides support for user authentication and access controls. It provides a Java implementation of the Pluggable Authentication Module (PAM) and classes and interfaces for controlling which users are able to run security-sensitive software.

When used together, the Java 2 Security API, the JCE 1.2, JSSE, and JAAS provide a comprehensive framework for developing secure, Web-based, distributed applications. When you combine the power and flexibility of the J2EE APIs, you have all you need to develop advanced applications for both the Web and the Enterprise intranet.

The Importance of Java Security

For many organizations, both public and commercial, the Internet has become a major forum for conducting business. It serves as a primary medium for advertising, marketing, sales, and customer support. It has helped new businesses grow at exponential rates and big businesses extend their market domination. Conversely, businesses that were slow to utilize the Internet have sometimes suffered the consequences.

With all the opportunities provided by the Internet come significant risks. Web servers can be taken over, and Web pages have sometimes been defaced. Private customer data can be publicly disclosed. Financial transactions might be falsified. Enterprise firewalls can be breached and Enterprise networks sabotaged. As important as it is for businesses to leverage the capabilities of the Internet, it is even more important that they can do so securely.

As the programming language of the Web, Java is central to developing secure Web-based applications. Java applets provide the capability to deliver executable content to Web browsers. JSP and servlets provide the capability to securely process browser requests. JDBC provides the capability for Web-based applications to securely access Enterprise databases. EJB provides the framework for securely deploying application business logic. Java RMI and CORBA provide a foundation for deploying distributed objects. The Java Security API and its security-related extensions enable fully distributed Web-based applications to be implemented and executed in a secure manner. If you want to develop secure Web-based applications, Java has a lot to offer.

Although I would like to tell you that Java is far ahead of its competition in the area of security, I can't. That's because it has no competition. Authenticode, Microsoft's approach to securing mobile code, relies solely on the good intentions of Web developers as the basis for its security. Authenticode doesn't stop the deployment of damaging code. It just requires that the code be properly signed. It is analogous to requiring a return address on a letter bomb.

If Java security is dominant in the area of client-side programming, it is even more so in the area of server-side programming. Java servlets and JSP are the only server-side programming technologies that are self-limiting. If you have a significant security flaw in a Perl, ASP, or ColdFusion script, a good hacker might be able to exploit it to take over the server. Servlets and Java server pages can be configured to implement *least privilege*. This means that users are given only those privileges that they need to perform their functions and nothing more. If a securely configured servlet contains a security flaw and is exploited, the hacker will only be able to obtain the privileges of the servlet (and nothing more).

The capability to contain damage is even more important than the capability to prevent it. The security design of the Java programming language, its object-oriented nature, and the security features of the Java runtime system all work together to encourage software developers to develop software that is simpler, more reliable, and less prone to security errors.

Java's security capabilities extend beyond the client and Web server to the databases, application logic, and Enterprise objects used by Web-based applications. JDBC and JSSE provide the capability for Web clients and servers to securely connect with back end databases. EJB provides a framework for securely deploying application components. RMI and CORBA can be combined with JSSE to support secure communication between distributed objects.

Java's extensive API and integrated security features make it a key technology to achieving both extranet and intranet security. Although it might be possible to apply non-Java technologies in a piecemeal fashion to secure a critical Web-based application, it will most likely result in a solution that is more costly, less portable, and less extensible. Compare an application that uses ActiveX on the client, Perl CGI scripts, Oracle database drivers, and a proprietary application server with one based on applets, JSP, JDBC, and EJB. Which do you think will be more secure, quicker and cheaper to field, more portable, and easier to maintain?

Attaining a high level of security is not easy to achieve in most Web applications. If it were, we wouldn't read about Web break-ins on a weekly basis. Good security requires careful planning, a sound architecture, a well-structured design, and near flawless implementation. It also requires a development and execution environment that is oriented toward security. The Java 2 Platform provides the development tools and execution environment. This book will show you how to use the Java 2 Platform to develop sound applications that are architected and designed with security as an integrated feature.

Who Should Read This Book

This book is for anyone who wants to design and build a secure Java application or applet. If you are an intermediate to experienced Java programmer and you want to learn how to secure your Java applications, this book will show you how. It will fill in any gaps in your knowledge of the Java runtime system and Security API. It will also introduce you to the JCE 1.2, JSSE, and JAAS. It will temper this knowledge with practical experience—gained by writing Java applications that take advantage of the security policy, code signing, encryption, authentication, authorization, and access control features of these APIs.

You'll learn how to apply Java's security features to develop signed applets, secure servlets, and connect securely to Enterprise databases. You'll learn how to add SSL to existing Java applications, strongly authenticate your users, and enforce individual and group access controls. You'll learn how to add security to e-commerce applications, securely access distributed objects using RMI and CORBA, and take advantage of the security features provided by Enterprise JavaBeans.

In addition to arming you with the knowledge and practical experience that you need to develop secure Java applications, this book will help you to develop the mindset of a security professional. By thoroughly understanding the rationale for Java's security features, you'll learn to use them to full advantage, avoid dangerous pitfalls, and build applications that are demonstrably secure.

How This Book is Organized

This book is organized into three parts, consisting of 15 chapters. Seven appendices provide supporting information and additional details related to the information covered in these chapters.

Part I, "The Foundations of Java Security," introduces the basic concepts that underlie Java security. It consists of the following chapters:

- Chapter 1—Security Basics: Discusses the basic concepts that underlie security and describes a basic model for building secure applications.
- Chapter 2—Java Security Overview: Provides a basic overview of Java security features and how these features are used to build secure Java applications and applets.
- Chapter 3—Java Application Security Access Control: Describes how Java 2 platform fine-grained and policy-based access control mechanisms can be employed in Java applications.
- Chapter 4—Applet Security: Covers the default applet security policy and ways of extending this policy, using signed applet code.

Part II, "Cryptographic Security," covers the cryptographic capabilities of the Java 2 API, the Java Cryptography Extension (JCE) 1.2, and the Java Secure Socket Extension (JSSE). It also covers cryptography packages that are available from providers other than Sun. The chapters of Part II are as follows:

- Chapter 5—Introduction to Cryptography: Provides a gentle introduction to the basic concepts of cryptography and describes how they are supported by Java 2/JCE 1.2.
- Chapter 6—Key Management and Digital Certificates: Introduces key management concepts and describes Java 2's support for key management.
- Chapter 7—Message Digests and Digital Signatures: Shows how to use Java 2's features for working with message digests, digital signatures, and digital certificates.
- Chapter 8—The Java Cryptography Extension: Provides an overview of the JCE 1.2, describes the capabilities it provides, and describes how to use the JCE and alternative security providers.
- Chapter 9—SSL and JSSE: Introduces SSL and JSSE and provides examples of how they are used to secure client-server communication.

Part III, "Distributed System Security," focuses on the security of distributed systems. It covers security issues related to network security, databases, the Java Authentication and Authorization Service (JAAS), CORBA, EJB, Java Server Pages (JSP), and Java servlets. Its chapters are as follows:

- Chapter 10—Distributed Enterprise Security Overview: Provides an overview of the basic distributed Java enterprise APIs and the means by which use of these APIs can be secured.
- Chapter 11—Databases and Database Security: Identifies database security concerns and ways to implement database security using JDBC.
- Chapter 12—The Java Authentication and Authorization Service: Introduces the JAAS and shows how to use it in Java applications.
- Chapter 13—CORBA Security: Discusses how to develop secure Java-based CORBA applications using standard CORBA Security services.
- Chapter 14—Enterprise JavaBeans Security: Discusses the security issues with EJB and describes how to develop secure EJB.
- Chapter 15—JSP and Java Servlet Security: Describes the security issues associated with the Common Gateway Interface (CGI) and provides approaches to securing Web applications developed with servlets and Java Server Pages.

A series of seven appendixes provide supporting information ranging from basic mathematics to information on installing the JCE. These appendices are as follows:

- Appendix A—Past Java Security Flaws: Summarizes all published Java security flaws.
- Appendix B—The Mathematics of RSA: Presents the mathematical foundations of the RSA cryptosystem.

- Appendix C—Downloading and Installing the JCE: Provides step-by-step instructions for downloading and installing the JCE.
- Appendix D—The Java 2 Security API: Summarizes the classes and interfaces to the Java 2 Security API.
- Appendix E—Downloading and Installing the Cryptix JCE 1.2: Provides step-by-step instructions for downloading and installing the Cryptix JCE 1.2 packages.
- Appendix F—Using the Keytool: Explains how to use the Java keytool.
- Appendix G—Using the `jarsigner` Tool: Explains how to use the Java `jarsigner` tool.

In addition to the chapters and appendices of this book, the book's Web site at `http://www.courseone.com/support/books/java/security` provides updates, corrections, and timely information related to Java security. Additional information resources specific to Java distributed enterprise security issues and solutions is accessible from `http://www.assuredtech.com/books/jsh`.

Getting Started

To use this book you'll need a computer and operating system that support the Java 2 Platform. There are a wide variety of operating systems that support the Java 2 Platform, including Windows 2000, NT, 98, and 95, Linux, and Solaris. Ports of the Java 2 Platform to many other operating systems are in the works. The examples used in this book were developed under Windows 98, Windows NT, and Linux. However, they are pure Java and will run under all Java 2 Platform implementations. Consult the book's Web site for updated code listings.

How to Use This Book

This book covers the breadth and depth of Java security. You can go directly to any chapter that addresses the topics that are of most interest to you. However, I recommend starting with the chapters of Part I, "The Foundations of Java Security," that cover Java security basics, the operation of the Java runtime system, Java security policies, and the security issues common to any Java application. By doing so, you'll establish a firm foundation for understanding the security mechanisms that apply to other areas of the Java API.

After learning the basics in Part I, I recommend that you read Part II, "Cryptographic Security,"—especially Chapter 5, "Introduction to Cryptography." Many of the advanced Java security features require a basic understanding of cryptography, message digests, digital signatures, and digital certificates. In addition, the appendices provide a great deal of background information related to the concepts and tools that are introduced in Part II.

After you get through Part II, you'll have the background you need to understand any of the chapters of Part III, "Distributed System Security." Much of the book's advanced security features for distributed enterprise system usage is covered in Part III and will be of interest to the enterprise developer with specific Java enterprise system development needs.

The Foundations of Java Security

PART

I

IN THIS PART

Security Basics

Security is, perhaps, the most important and necessary
assurance requirement to consider when deploying a system.
Because computing systems assume more and more widespread business and mission-critical functionality each day,
the cost associated with a breach of security is also increasing. Furthermore, because security problems are human-
induced problems, the range of possible problems is as
limitless as the human mind. Security, thus, becomes a cru-
cial problem to solve. This chapter prepares you with the
conceptual background to understand the notions and terminology used throughout the remainder of the book.

In this chapter, you will learn about the following:

- The basic model for providing security for computing
  applications
- The mechanisms available for encrypting and decrypting data
- The mechanisms for securely authenticating users and
  other systems and means for proving their involve-
  ment with security-critical actions
- The mechanisms for controlling user/system access to
  security-critical resources
- The mechanisms for providing domains of control in a
  security environment
- The auditing of security-sensitive events
- Security policy establishment and means for administering these policies and their associated domains

The Basic Security Model

Figure 1.1 depicts the basic security model that results from security problems and assurance-provisioning mechanisms. At the top of the diagram, a resource provider is shown offering some security-critical data or application resources. Such resources are security-critical because a malicious being, such as the hacker depicted at the bottom of the diagram, can corrupt, reference (that is, access), replace, delay access to, or deny access to such resources.

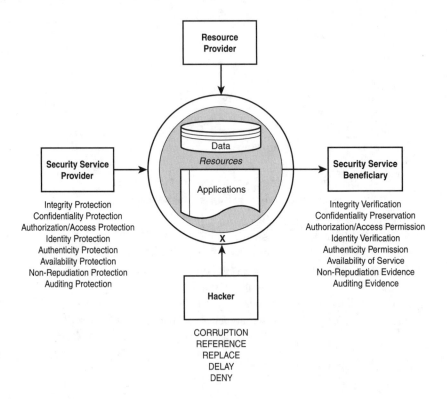

FIGURE 1.1

The basic security model.

A security service provider depicted on the left side of the diagram attempts to protect such resources from attack by providing protection services such as integrity, confidentiality, authorization and access, identity, authenticity, availability, nonrepudiation, and auditing-protection services. Such services attempt to thwart the hacker's best efforts.

The right side of the diagram shows the beneficiary of the security services. These services include the following:

- *Integrity Verification:* The beneficiary has some verification that the data or application is accurate.
- *Confidentiality Preservation:* The beneficiary has some assurance that confidentiality of the data or application has been preserved.
- *Authorization/Access Permission:* Properly authorized permission to access security-critical data, application, or other resource has been provided.
- *Identity Verification:* The beneficiary has some verification that the identity associated with the data or application source is who they say they are.
- *Authenticity Permission:* Properly authenticated permission to access some data, application, or other resource has been provided.
- *Availability of Service:* The beneficiary has access to the data, application, or other resource when it expects to have access.
- *Nonrepudiation Evidence*: The beneficiary has some evidence regarding from whom the data or application comes or has some evidence that an intended receiver actually received data sent to it.
- *Auditing Evidence*: The beneficiary has some evidence of security-critical operations that take place in the system.

Cryptography

Cryptography not only provides integrity and confidentiality protection, but it is also a key technology used by other security service components such as identity, authenticity, and nonrepudiation protection mechanisms. Because cryptography is such a fundamental component of a security solution, some folks mistakenly think that providing a secure solution means providing a solution using cryptography alone. This, as you have just seen in the preceding section, is not the case.

Classes of Cryptography

So what is cryptography, you ask? *Cryptography* is the basic science behind the process of taking some data or perhaps some code and running it through a cryptographic engine to generate some cryptographic material. Sometimes the process of generating cryptographic material is referred to, in general, as *cryptographic processing*. It takes a stream of input data and generates a stream of bits that represent some scrambled form (also called *cipher text*) of the original input data (also called *clear text*) or perhaps represent some token (also called a *message digest*) generated uniquely for a particular input sequence. Different classes of cryptographic engines exist, and different algorithms that implement these different engine classes have varying characteristics such as performance, security, licensing cost, and strength or quality of protection (QOP) .

As shown in Figure 1.2, if the output of the cryptographic engine represents some uniquely generated message digest, such a message digest can be used and sent to a receiver along with the data over which it was generated. The receiver can then run the received data through an identical cryptographic engine and generate its own message digest. If the received message digest compares with the newly generated message digest, the received data can be presumed to be accurate, and integrity is thus provided. The associated cryptographic engine is said to implement a *message digest algorithm*.

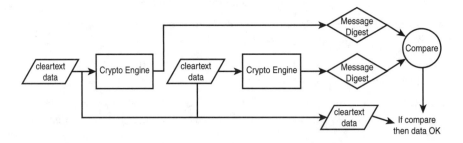

Message Digest Cryptography for Integrity

FIGURE 1.2

A message digest cryptography for integrity.

If the output of the cryptographic engine represents some cipher text data, you can send such information over a communications network or perhaps store it somewhere and be assured that confidentiality of the data is preserved. A reverse process can then run the data through another cryptographic engine and convert the cipher text data into its clear text original form. Only cryptographic engines that have some secret key and know the algorithm to run can perform the reverse cryptographic process. The cipher-text creation process in this context is referred to as *encryption*, and the cipher-text conversion to clear text is referred to as *decryption*. Very often, however, the entire process is simply referred to as *encryption*.

As you'll see, two types of keys can be used to perform the encryption process: *symmetric keys* and *asymmetric keys*. With symmetric key encryption, both encryption and decryption occur using the same secret key. As shown in Figure 1.3, secret symmetric keys can be used to maintain confidentiality only if no one else obtains access to the secret key. With asymmetric encryption, the two ends use keys with different values. One end uses a private key that must not be given to anyone else. The other end uses a public key that can be freely distributed.

If a private key is used to encrypt some data, as shown in Figure 1.4, a public key must be used to decrypt the data. In such a scenario, because the public key is freely distributed, no confidentiality is maintained. Rather, the data encrypted with the private key can be guaranteed to be signed by the holder of that key because no one else is supposed to have access to that key. Thus, in such a scenario, identity is provided. Furthermore, because a piece of data is encrypted with your private key, it is possible to implement certain nonrepudiation algorithms. That is, receivers may be able to prove that a particular data item was sent by you.

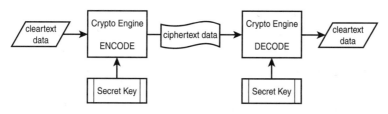

Symmetric Key Cryptography for Confidentiality

FIGURE 1.3

Symmetric key cryptography for confidentiality.

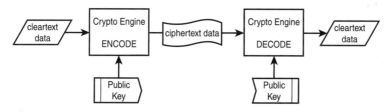

Asymmetric Key Cryptography for Identity and Non-Repudiation

FIGURE 1.4

Asymmetric key cryptography for identity and nonrepudiation.

Figure 1.5 illustrates that if a public key is used to encrypt some data, a private key must be used to decrypt the data. Thus, confidentiality is provided because only the holder of the private key can decrypt the data.

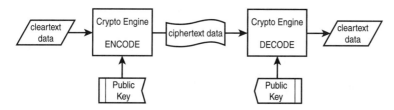

Asymmetric Key Cryptography for Confidentiality

FIGURE 1.5

Asymmetric key cryptography for confidentiality.

Message Digests

A message digest algorithm is a one-way function that generates a unique set of output bits based on a sequence of input bits. Different sequences of input bits generate a unique pattern of output bits within some probabilistic measure. Message digest algorithms come in various flavors:

- *Message Digest #2 (MD2):* A slow but very secure message digest algorithm producing 128-bit digest values.
- *Message Digest #4 (MD4):* Faster, but fairly insecure; also generates a 128-bit digest value.
- *Message Digest #5 (MD5):* A more secure version of MD4 but with speed advantages. It also produces a 128-bit digest value.
- *Secure Hash Algorithm (SHA):* Produces a 160-bit digest value.
- *Secure Hash Algorithm 1 (SHA-1):* A modification of SHA, overcoming a minor security flaw with SHA.
- *Message Authentication Code (MAC):* Uses a secret key along with a message digest algorithm to create message digests.

Symmetric Keys

Symmetric key (also called *secret key*) algorithms typically perform very well and can lead to very strong encryption possibilities. The main drawback of symmetric keys is that both sides of the encrypted stream need to have the same key. This presents a problem in terms of sharing keys and poses a greater risk that someone might obtain a handle to your secret key.

In practice, secret keys are usually first exchanged using an asymmetric key algorithm. Such key agreement or key exchange algorithms enable you to use a more powerful and secure asymmetric key algorithm to confidentially exchange a secret key. You then use the secret key throughout the remainder of an encrypted communications session. These are some of the most common symmetric key algorithms:

- *Data Encryption Standard (DES):* Uses a 56-bit secret key that is strong but possible to crack.
- *Triple-DES:* Strengthens DES by performing the DES algorithm three times with three different DES keys.
- *RC2 and RC4:* Can be used with up to 2,048-bit keys and provides for a very secure algorithm.
- *RC5:* Uses a configurable key size.

Asymmetric Keys

As shown in Figures 1.4 and 1.5, asymmetric keys can be used for providing identity, confidentiality, and (to a certain extent) nonrepudiation. Asymmetric key algorithms (also called *public key algorithms*) are generally more computationally intensive than symmetric and message digest algorithms. However, because asymmetric keys permit you to hold a private key that does not need to be distributed to other participants in an encryption session, the security of asymmetric keys is hard to compromise. Public keys can be freely distributed to those members of a community who want either to encrypt data using your public key and send you confidential messages or who want to verify the fact that an encrypted message was indeed sent by you.

When you encrypt data using your private key, the generated cipher text data is sometimes referred to as a *signature* because only the identity of the private key holder could have created such a pattern of bits. Following are some of the most common asymmetric key algorithms:

- *Digital Signature Algorithm (DSA):* Uses keys of any length, but is commonly restricted to keys between 512 bits and 1,024 bits via the Digital Signature Standard (DSS).
- *Rivest Shamir Adleman (RSA) algorithm:* Uses keys that can vary in length.
- *Diffie-Hellman algorithm:* Is used as a key exchange algorithm in which a secret key is generated and securely exchanged so that both parties can participate in a particular encrypted session.

Authentication and Nonrepudiation

In security systems, the term *principal* is used to mean an individual, an organization, or some other sender or receiver of messages. Identity protection in secure systems provides a way to uniquely identify a principal. Principal identification is a fundamental security operation utilized by many other security-protection mechanisms. For example, in determining whether access to a particular resource is allowed, the identity of the principal desiring access must be determined. Such principal identification must be performed in a secure manner. That is, someone can't just state his identity. If he falsely identifies himself as a principal with more system privileges than he actually possesses, he obtains access to certain parts of a system to which he should not have access. Thus, the assignment of principal identity in a system is, in itself, a security-critical operation.

Authentication represents the means by which principals securely identify themselves to a system. The system wants to make sure that you are who you say you are. To accomplish this task, principals must usually interact with some principal authenticator process or login module that takes certain secret information that only a particular principal would know or be able to generate. With such information in hand, the authenticator will determine whether the principal should be granted access to the system and (depending on the authentication technique) return a set of credentials defining the rights ascribed to that principal. Such credentials might be valid only for a particular session or perhaps for use within a certain security context. The security context in which valid credentials are defined might be a function of the thread or process from which the principal (or proxy for that principal) is acting.

Optionally, principals can allow other intermediate objects to delegate their credentials to calls on other objects. Thus, object A making a call on object B might authenticate itself with object B first, and then object B might call object C and delegate the credentials of object A to object C.

As a better example of how delegation can be useful, consider a distributed client that interfaces with a query server providing a common interface to many backend database-related constructs such as customer, order, and credit-card objects. Now suppose that the client makes a call on the query server and its credentials get passed to the server. (This assumes that the client already was authenticated and given credentials.) Now the server will make calls to the database-related constructs such as a credit-card object, and it needs certain credential information before it satisfies the query server's request. Delegation allows the query server to pass the credentials of the client onto the credit-card object so that the operation can be performed on behalf of the client. This might be important because certain client identities (for example, an administrator) might be allowed access to certain credit-card data to which other identities (for example, a customer) might not have access. Without delegation, the credit-card object would see all calls as being made by the identity of the query server. Thus, credit-card data access control will not be as fine-grained.

Authentication Types

Various techniques for securely allowing principals to identify themselves and authenticate themselves with a system have evolved over the years, including the following:

- Password-based identity and authentication
- Physical-token–based identity and authentication
- Biometrics-based identity and authentication
- Certificate-based identity and authentication

Password-Based Identity and Authentication

Perhaps the most common and familiar form of authentication is password-based authentication. With password-based authentication, a principal ID (for example, user ID) and password are entered into the system and passed to a principal authenticator, which determines whether the associated password matches its stored version of that particular principal's password.

Password-based identification is very easy to implement and is thus very common. However, a password is similar to a secret key in that both ends of a secure session must have a copy of the secret value (that is, key or password). The password must also be transmitted from the principal's location to the principal authenticator's location. If the path between principal and principal authenticator does not provide confidentiality protection, this transmission can expose the password to hacker theft.

Kerberos is a particular type of password-based authentication system in which a user password is known to a Kerberos-based server. Because both the Kerberos-based server and the principal know the password, they can encrypt and decrypt messages sent between them using the password as a secret symmetric key.

Physical-Token–Based Identity and Authentication

Physical-token–based authentication techniques offer a powerful but more costly and, thus, less common authentication solution. Physical-token–based authentication techniques typically involve using a physical item such as an automatic teller machine (ATM) card as principal identification. *Smart cards* are ATM-like cards with embedded miniprocessors that can be used to provide a more configurable means of physical-token identity.

Biometrics-Based Identity and Authentication

Biometrics-based authentication solutions are even less common than physical-token–based solutions, but they can provide a very powerful and difficult-to-crack identity and authenticity solution. Biometrics involves using some physical aspect of a person (for example, fingerprint or retinal characteristics of an eye) to identify that person. Needless to say, a hacker would be hard-pressed to mimic such identity unless, of course, the hacker could hijack someone's finger or eye. All such security is, however, predicated on the fact that the digital representation of this biometric information cannot be stolen. After such information is obtained, a hacker might be able to use it to bypass the security of a biometrics-based solution. This is problematic because new fingers and eyes are not easily adapted for users, whereas a new password or physical token can beeasily created.

Certificate-Based Identity and Authentication

Certificate-based authentication techniques are another authentication technique that has grown in popularity over recent years. A certificate is simply a block of data containing information used to identify a principal. Information in the certificate includes the principal's public key, information about the principal, dates in which the certificate is valid, information about the issuer of a certificate, and a signature generated by the certificate issuer.

As previously mentioned, a signature can be generated using a private key over some block of data to produce another block of data known as the signature. The generator of this signature using the private key is referred to as the signer. Then, this signature can only be decrypted using the public key of the signer, thus providing assurance in the identity of the signer.

Certificates come in handy when you're sending your public key to other entities. It enables them to identify information that was encrypted with your private key. Certificates also facilitate other entities being able to send information that only you can decrypt with your private key. Without a certificate, hackers might send some other entity a public key falsely identified as yours, and then sign messages to that entity (for example, an e-commerce Web site) with a private key corresponding to the misidentified public key.

Different certificate implementations have evolved with different formats, but the X.509 v3 certificate standard represents one of the more popular certificate types. The X.509 standard can be used to sign certificates using various signature algorithms. X.509 certificates contain version and serial-number information, information identifying the signature algorithm and its parameters, the Certificate Authority (CA) identity and signature, the dates of validity, and the principal identity and public key.

The Public Key Cryptography Standards (PKCS) define a binary format that can be used for storing certificates. PKCS itself is defined using formats identified by a number, such as PKCS #1 and PKCS #2. PKCS #7, for example, defines the cryptographic message syntax, and PKCS #8 defines the private key information syntax. Sometimes, certificates are also stored using the Privacy Enhanced Mail (PEM) ASCII format.

A certificate is signed by a third party CA so that if that CA says that the associated public key in the certificate is yours, the receiving entity can be assured that the public key is indeed yours and not one from some hacker. Of course, the same problem exists when initially providing a public key associated with the CA to a receiving entity. Such a problem can be solved, however, by using a common CA (such as Verisign) whose public key has been given to a community of users in a secure fashion. This one-time secure provision of a CA's public key used to verify certificates from multiple principals is certainly simpler than attempting to securely provide a public key for each principal in the community. Tools such as Web browsers often come preconfigured with the certificates of many common and trusted CAs.

Furthermore, certificates can be chained. Suppose your certificate was signed by CA-bar, and CA-bar's certificate was signed by CA-foo. Now, you send your certificate to some receiving entity. If the receiving entity trusts CA-bar's signature, it can trust your public key. Otherwise, it can consult the CA-bar certificate that was chained with yours and determine whether it trusts CA-foo's signature. If it trusts CA-foo, it can trust CA-bar's signature and, therefore, can trust your public key. The moral of this story, however, is that there always must be a trusted foo-like signer somewhere in the certificate chain for the receiving entity to trust your public key.

Certificates are typically requested from a certificate server at the site of a CA. You send a certificate signing request (CSR) to the CA's certificate server along with some other information to identify yourself as required by the CA. Very often the CA's certificate server will provide a

Web-based interface for submitting CSRs. The CA staff will then process your CSR and generate a public and private key pair for you if they grant your request. They will most likely send you a public key via email, but they should require that you retrieve your private key from them via some secure means such as through a secure Web connection download.

CAs also can maintain a Certificate Revocation List (CRL) that manages the list of certificates that have been revoked before their validity dates have expired. Entities can consult such CRLs periodically to be able to determine whether your certificate is still valid.

After you obtain your own private key and as you build up a collection of public keys and certificates from other principals, you'll need to store this information somewhere. Because your private key represents security-critical data, the storage mechanism should itself be secured. A key store represents a mechanism for storing private keys, public keys, and certificates. Web browsers and Web servers that support certificates come equipped with secured key stores. Furthermore, the Java 2 platform comes equipped with a proprietary secured key store, referred to as the Java Key Store (JKS).

Nonrepudiation

Nonrepudiation (NR) provides a way to prove that certain principals sent or received a particular message. NR tokens providing this evidence are generated and verified according to the following ways that NR is used:

- Generation and verification of an NR token for a message sent by a principal. Thus, the principal cannot deny sending a particular message.
- Generation and verification of an NR token for a message received by a principal. Thus, the principal cannot deny receiving a particular message.

When another principal obtains an NR token generated according to one of the preceding two scenarios, it essentially has evidence that the particular action occurred. In the event of a later dispute over whether such actions occurred, this evidence can be presented to some arbitrator or NR authority. NR involves the use of asymmetric keys to generate the NR tokens used as proof of principal identity.

Access Control

In this book, I use the terms *access control* and *authorization* interchangeably. Having access-control protection means providing a mechanism for limiting access by principals, based on their identity, to valued resources. Their identity might also be associated with security attributes such as a set of classification levels, privileges, permissions, or roles that can be used to provide more fine-grained, access-control decision making. Access control comes in many flavors including discretionary, role-based, mandatory, and firewall types of access control. I briefly present these various forms of access control here.

Discretionary Access Control

Although some principal Foo might have access to your file system, principal Bar might not. Such a Boolean decision-making process can be alleviated by using permissions. That is, giving specific permission to principal Bar for read-only access and full access to principal Foo might more closely model the access control protection you desire. Because principals can also identify a particular group, the permissions and privileges previously described can be used to establish access control for groups of individuals. Such access control based on principal (that is, individual or group) identity is sometimes referred to as *discretionary access control*. Discretionary access-control mechanisms typically maintain a list of principals and their associated permissions in an access control list (ACL). ACLs can be stored in a file or database and help make the administration of access control a fairly simple task.

Role-Based Access Control

A particular system-usage role can be associated with a collection of users. For example, an administrative role might be assigned to one or more system administrators responsible for maintaining your enterprise server. Roles are mapped to a particular principal or to a particular user group. When roles are mapped to a principal, the principal name involved with a particular role-sensitive operation is compared with the principal name extracted from the role to determine whether the operation is permitted to proceed. When roles are mapped to a group, a group associated with a principal involved with a particular role-sensitive operation is compared with the group extracted from the role to determine whether the operation is permitted to proceed. Such role-based access control requires that a list of roles be maintained and that mappings from role to user or user group be established.

Mandatory Access Control

Apart from using some explicit permission or privilege per individual or group, certain other access-control techniques are based on a classification level that a principal assumes. A classification level specifies the level of trust associated with that principal (for example, Top Secret, Confidential, Unclassified). Classification levels specified for principals have an implicit level of trust in which higher classification levels (for example, Top Secret) signify a higher level of trust than lower classification levels (for example, Unclassified). A classification level is also associated with a valued resource designating the minimum classification level needed by a principal to access that resource. If the principal's classification level is higher than or equal to the valued resource's classification level, the user can obtain access to the resource. This type of access control is sometimes referred to as *mandatory access control*. Mandatory access-control techniques alleviate the need for maintaining ACLs because the access decision logic is built into the classification scheme. Only a hierarchy of classification levels must be defined.

Firewall Access Control

A *firewall* is a mechanism by which access to particular TCP/IP ports on some network of computers is restricted based on the location of the incoming connection request. If the request is made from outside of the network, access may be restricted; if it is made from within the network, access may be granted. A firewall can also limit requests made from within its protected network to IP addresses outside of the network. Sometimes, however, such outgoing requests are routed around the firewall restrictions using a proxy server. Proxy servers used with firewall restrictions limit access to outgoing IP addresses in a more fine-grained fashion.

Domains

Access control can also be defined per some domain of protection. That is, various host machines or processes that all have the same access control policy can be grouped into a security domain (also called a *realm* or *security policy domain*). Thus, a set of permissions might be granted for one domain, and another set of permissions might be granted to another domain. A security domain can also refer to a location where mobile code comes from (that is, a codebase). Thus, by specifying a set of permissions for a particular domain, you might actually be specifying a set of permissions to be granted to mobile code coming from a particular URL. Such permissions dictate what access to valued resources is permitted for such mobile code running on your local machine.

Code in a domain can trust other code in the same domain to invoke certain operations that would not be permitted for code that sits outside of the domain. The domain is thus termed a *trusted domain*. Trusted domains are also sometimes referred to as *trusted computing bases*. For example, you might not require an encrypted session for database access from within a trusted domain, but you might require it for code that wants to access the database from outside the trusted domain.

Domains can also be partitioned into subdomains in which one or more subdomains are contained within an enclosing domain. The permissions applied to the outer domain can, thus, be inherited by the subdomains. Subdomains can further restrict which permissions apply to themselves, but they cannot generally specify permissions that are less restrictive than the enclosing domain.

Domains can also be federated. Federations of domains grant access to each other's resources at the domain level. For example, a domain named `sales.mysite.com` might grant one set of permissions to a domain named `accounting.mysite.com` and grant another set of more restrictive permissions to a domain named `partner.othersite.com`.

As a final note, when a particular security mechanism is used across multiple security domains, that security mechanism itself forms a domain of security. To distinguish this domain from security policy domains, the term *security technology domain* is used.

Auditing

Auditing involves logging security-critical operations that occur within a security domain. Auditing of such operations can be useful in trying to track down the sequence of events that led to a hack or, perhaps, in determining the identity of the hacker. Auditing is usually performed during authentication (logins), logouts, trusted resource access (for example, file access), and any modification of the security properties of a system.

This is the typical information logged during a security audit:

- Audit event type
- Timestamp of the event
- Identity of the principal initiating the event
- Identification of the target resource
- Permission being requested on the target resource
- Location from which the resource request is made

Because audit logs are used to provide evidence with respect to security-critical operations, the audit process and log itself tend to be security-critical. Therefore, they must be protected in some way from hackers corrupting, denying, or perhaps replacing log information. Audit logs are often maintained behind a trusted computing base and possibly encrypted for added confidentiality.

Policies and Administration

Whereas a security solution selects a set of security mechanisms to use in a security domain, the security policy represents the particular state in which these mechanisms are configured. If the particular security approach has provided security mechanisms that are not very configurable, the range of security policies you can define for such mechanisms will obviously be limited.

For example, suppose that a particular access-control protection solution has hard-coded method signatures on some access-control class for each type of permission being requested. Thus, for a particular permission request, you'll add a call from code to make such a request. Although this solution provides an access control solution, a solution that enables you to define such permission in a file would be more configurable and enable the creation of policies that are more manageable. This is a key difference between Java 1.1 security and Java 1.2/2.0 security.

Both security administration APIs and GUIs to manage such policies are sometimes provided to make the administration of security for a domain more manageable. Security administration tasks and associated policies that are commonly provided relate to the aforementioned security-protection mechanisms and include the following:

- Administration of the quality of protection (QOP) for cryptographic functions employed by a security domain
- Administration of which principals can be authenticated with a domain
- Administration of certificates, private keys, and public keys in a key store
- Administration of issuing certificates if you are a CA
- Administration of CRLs, if you are a CA
- Administration of which individuals belong to which groups
- Administration of permissions associated with particular principals
- Administration of classification levels associated with particular principals and resources
- Administration of other domain permissions and privileges
- Administration of which security-critical operations need to be audited
- Generation of audit log reports
- Generation of reports on the state of security in the system

Summary

Security protection in a computing system comes in the form of integrity verification, confidentiality preservation, authorization, identity verification, authenticity permission, availability of service, nonrepudiation evidence, and auditing evidence. Given the importance and complexity of security for a system, a wide range of techniques and models for security have been developed over the years to provide for such diverse protection requirements. This chapter has armed you with the conceptual background and terminology you'll need as a software architect or developer to understand such security provisioning techniques. In particular, this chapter lays much of the groundwork for you to best understand the Java security techniques described throughout the remainder of this book.

Java Security Overview

The Java 2 security model is, in general, a reliable way to build secure, distributed Java applications. The Java 2 security model implementation represents a bedrock of components and tools that any serious Java architect or developer must comprehend. We present an overview of Java security history in this chapter. Note that the early Java security features, which have been replaced by Java 2 security features, are largely ignored throughout the remainder of this book.

In this chapter, you will learn about

- The historical context for the evolving security model in Java.
- An overview of the Java security model as provided by the Java 2 platform.
- The role of the JVM's byte code verifier in providing security.
- The security aspects of the JVM's class loader.
- The security aspects of the JVM's security manager.
- The basic cryptographic infrastructure provided with the Java platform.

The History of Security in Java

Java was originally promoted for use by developers to create Java applets. Java applets enable code to be downloaded directly into a Web browser. This technology was one of the first to turn the Web browser into a framework that could support the execution of applications downloaded over the Web. Such a framework promised to provide a new paradigm for computing, in stark contrast to traditional desktop computing. With desktop computing, applications were loaded and executed by you on your machine. Whenever you needed updates to the application software, you had to obtain distributions from sources such as CDs and disks. You then loaded the updates yourself. Java applets promised a new paradigm in which mobile code is downloaded dynamically to the Web browser and automatically updated whenever you revisit the Web site from which the code was downloaded.

However, network performance has helped curb such grand visions by limiting the size of Java applets that users consider reasonable to download and, therefore, limiting the complexity of applications downloaded. Furthermore, the performance of JVM implementations equipped with Web browsers has also hampered the proliferation of Java applets on the Internet. Nevertheless, because Java applets brought mobile code into the limelight, Sun wisely considered security early in the development of the Java APIs. After all, if you are now downloading mobile Java code from some remote Web site onto your local machine, how much access to your local machine do you want to relinquish to such code? Many traditional desktop applications require access to your local file system. Do you really want a Java applet downloaded from some malicious Web site to have access to your file system?

Thus, security was a key consideration for Java from day one. Enterprise applications can also benefit from these security features. Although early models for Java security addressed Java applet issues, Java applications can now take advantage of the more sophisticated security model (available in the Java 2 platform) to enhance the security of distributed enterprise services.

The evolution of the Java security model introduced with each major Java version release is depicted in Figures 2.1 through 2.3. The Java version 1.0 platform provided a very limited security model known as the *sandbox* model, as shown in Figure 2.1. In the sandbox model, only local code had access to all the valuable resources (for example, files and new network connections) that are exposed and accessed by the Java Virtual Machine (JVM). Code downloaded from remote sources, such as applets, had access only to a limited number of resources. Thus, file-system access and the capability to create new connections were limited for remote code. This was a primary concern for JVM implementations equipped with Web browsers.

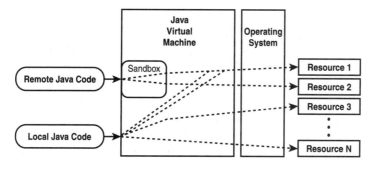

FIGURE 2.1
The Java 1.0 sandbox security model.

The Java 1.0 security model was somewhat too restrictive, however. The vision of providing downloadable applications over the Web was being stifled because such applications could not perform key operations such as file access or the creation of new network connections. If Web-browser vendors treated remote code like local code, the path was opened for malicious code to corrupt the local machine. Such an all-or-nothing model was replaced in Java 1.1 when a trusted security model was employed, as depicted in Figure 2.2.

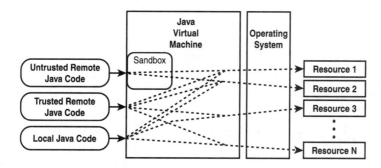

FIGURE 2.2
The Java 1.1 trusted code security model.

With the trusted code model, you can optionally designate whether code *signed* by certain providers would be allowed to have the full resource access it desired. Thus, you might actually trust that some Java code from Microsoft would be able to run inside your browser with full access to your system resources, much as you trust Microsoft when you install one of its many products on your system. Code or applet signing permits a company like Microsoft to sign its applet in such a way that you can verify that this code really came from this company. Thus, the signed applet is granted access to all your system resources, whereas untrusted code is confined to the sandbox.

The Java 2 platform (also called Java 1.2) really has paved the way for application security with a finer-grained security model, as depicted in Figure 2.3. Now local and remote code alike can be confined to utilize only particular domains of resources according to configurable policies. Thus, some Java code Foo might be limited to access resources confined by one domain, whereas some other Java code Bar might have access to a set of resources confined by some other domain. Domains of access and configurable security policies make the Java 2 platform much more flexible. Furthermore, relieving developers from making the distinction between remote and local code allows for more widely applicable solutions to application security problems instead of simply focusing on mobile code and Java applet security problems.

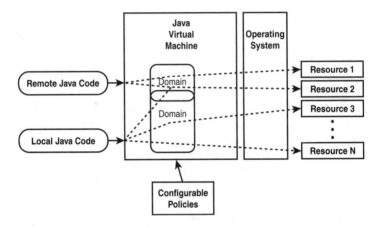

FIGURE 2.3

Java 1.2/2 configurable and fine-grained access security model.

Java Security Architecture

Figure 2.4 depicts the primary components of the standard set of APIs and mechanisms used to provide security for Java 2–based applications. In the lower half of the diagram are the core Java 2 security architecture and Java Cryptography Architecture (JCA), which together compose the Java 2 security platform that comes with the Java 2 platform. In the upper half of the diagram are the standard Java security extensions that ship separately from the Java 2 platform but are still dependent on different aspects of the Java 2 platform.

Although many commercial off-the-shelf (COTS) packages external to the components shown here are available, the components in Figure 2.4 represent what Sun designates as those that provide a standard interface. However, various COTS service-provider implementations that adhere to the interface standards defined by many of these Java security components are indeed available. Let's take a brief look at each of these components in more detail before we explore the details behind them in this chapter and throughout the book.

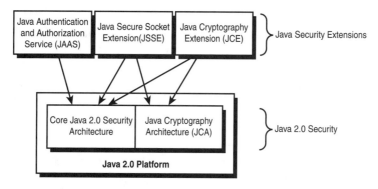

FIGURE 2.4
Java security architecture standard components.

Core Java 2 Security Architecture

Figure 2.5 shows the core Java 2 security architecture in the context of the rest of the Java 2 platform, operating system, resources, and Java code running atop the Java 2 platform. The pieces of this architecture that form the core of Java Security are the byte code verifier, class loader, security manager, access controller, permissions, policies, and protection domains.

The byte code verifier verifies that the byte codes being loaded from Java application code external to the Java platform adhere to the syntax of the Java language specification. The class loader is then responsible for actual translation of byte codes into Java class constructs that can be manipulated by the Java runtime environment. In the process of loading classes, different class loaders can employ different policies to determine whether certain classes should be loaded into the runtime environment. The class loader and the Java 2 platform classes themselves help limit access to valued resources by intercepting calls made to Java platform API and delegating decisions as to whether such calls can be made to the security manager. Java 1.0 and 1.1 made exclusive use of a security manager for such decision making, whereas Java 2 applications can use the access controller for more flexible and configurable access-control decision making. Finally, execution of code would not be possible without the beloved runtime execution engine.

Access control is the most significant addition to the Java 2 security platform, helping extend the security model to enable configurable and fine-grained access control. Java 2 permissions encapsulate configurable and extendable ways to designate access limitations and allowances that might be associated with valued resources. Java 2 policies provide the mechanisms needed to actually associate such permissions with valued resources in a configurable fashion. Finally, means for encapsulating domains of access control are also provided with the core Java 2 security model.

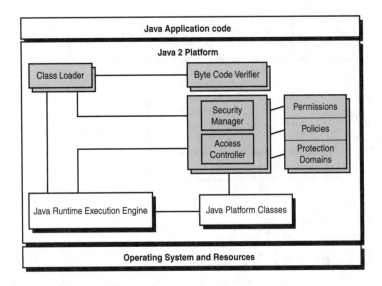

FIGURE 2.5

The core Java security architecture.

The java.security package contains the classes and interfaces that define the core Java security architecture. The java.security.acl package also contained access-control classes and interfaces that were core to the Java 1.1 security architecture, but have been superseded in Java 2 by newer access-control constructs. Finally, other security-related classes are embedded throughout the entire collection of Java platform packages. In this chapter and the next, I highlight which classes play a role in supporting the core Java security architecture.

Java Cryptography Architecture

The Java Cryptography Architecture (JCA) provides an infrastructure for performing basic cryptographic functionality with the Java platform. The scope of cryptographic functionality includes protecting data against corruption for the sake of data integrity using basic cryptographic functions and algorithms. Cryptographic signature-generation algorithms used for identifying sources of data and code are also built into the JCA. Because keys and certificates are a core part of identifying data and code sources, APIs for handling such features are also built into the JCA.

Although the JCA is part of the built-in Java security packages, as are the core Java 2 security architecture features, I distinguish the JCA from such core APIs largely due to the JCA's underlying service-provider interface. That is, different cryptographic implementations can be plugged into the JCA framework, whereas Java applications can still adhere to the same basic JCA interfaces. Sun does equip a default set of cryptographic functions with the JCA, however.

Java Cryptography Extension

The terms *encryption* and *cryptography* are sometimes used interchangeably. However, Sun adheres to the definition of *cryptography* that designates the provision of the basic data integrity and source identity functions supported by the JCA. *Encryption* is used to mean those functions used to encrypt blocks of data for the sake of added confidentiality until the data can be subsequently decrypted by the intended receiver. The Java Cryptography Extension (JCE) is provided as a Java security extension for these auxiliary encryption purposes.

Although most would logically argue that encryption is a core aspect of any secure system, Sun has purposely made JCE an extension to the Java platform. This is largely due to U.S. export restrictions on encryption technology. If Sun were to include the JCE as a core part of the Java platform, exportability of the Java platform itself would be hampered. Furthermore, although many commercial-grade encryption technologies have been developed by third par-ties, the JCE provides a standard service-provider and application-programmer interface model. Thus, even if different commercial-grade encryption implementations are used, the pro-grammer still uses the same API to the different underlying implementations.

Java Secure Socket Extension

Because Secure Sockets Layer (SSL) is one of the more commonly used encryption-based pro-tocols for integrity and confidentiality, Sun has developed the Java Secure Socket Extension (JSSE) as an extension to the Java security platform. The JSSE provides a standard interface along with an underlying reference implementation for building Java applications with SSL. Even if different commercial-grade underlying SSL implementations are used with the JSSE, the developer still uses the same interface to the applications. The JSSE is also more generi-cally defined to provide a standard interface to support other secure socket protocols such as the Transport Layer Security (TLS) and Wireless Transport Layer Security (WTLS) Wireless Transport Layer Security (WTLS) protocols.

Java Authentication and Authorization Service

The Java Authentication and Authorization Service (JAAS) extension to the Java security plat-form was developed to provide a standard way for limiting access to resources based on an authenticated user identity. Thus, standard APIs for login and logout are provided. In these, a standard interface for passing around secure user credentials and context makes it possible to swap in and out different underlying authentication model implementations. Thus, whether you use Kerberos or Smart Cards, the same API is provided.

Byte Code Verifier

Before the class loader bothers to register a class that it loads with the Java runtime environ-ment, it passes the loaded Java class byte codes to the byte code verifier (also called the class file verifier). The byte code verifier then analyzes the byte code stream for the Java class and verifies that this byte stream adheres to the Java language rules defined for classes. The byte code verifier accomplishes this task in two phases. In phase one of byte code verification, the internals of the Java class byte stream itself are analyzed. In phase two, the byte code verifier verifies references to other classes from this class.

Phase two verification occurs when the classes to which a class refers are actually referenced at runtime. Not only will the references be verified for correctness, but the relationship rules involving that reference also will be verified. For example, a referenced method on another class will be checked to see whether that method is visible (that is, public, package, protected, or private) to the current class.

The following verification checks are typically performed by the byte code verifier:

- Verify that class bytes begin with the 0xCAFEBABE byte stream.
- Verify that the byte stream is neither truncated nor padded with extra bytes.
- Verify that class bytes adhere to the correct format for the class itself, methods, fields, and other components of a Java class.
- Verify that there are no overflows of operands on the stack.
- Verify that there are no underflows of operands on the stack.
- Verify that proper visibility (public, package, protected, or private) of methods and field variables is defined and honored.
- Verify that final classes are not subclassed.
- Verify that final methods are not overridden.
- Verify that final variables are assigned an initial value and not modified.
- Verify that methods are invoked with the correct number and types of arguments.
- Verify that field variables of the class are assigned with values of the correct type.
- Verify that no local variable is accessed before it has an assigned value.
- Verify that the class has one superclass (except, of course, for java.lang.Object).

Although Java 1.1 did not verify classes that were loaded from the CLASSPATH and always verified classes that were loaded from outside the CLASSPATH, this behavior could be slightly modified with parameters passed to the java and jre commands. The -verify flag could induce verification of classes on the CLASSPATH as well. The -noverify flag could turn off verification of classes not on the CLASSPATH. The default verification of all classes not on the CLASSPATH could also be indicated with the -verifyremote flag.

Java 2 verifies all classes except the classes that are part of the core Java platform suite. Although the standard java executable command documentation for Java 2 does not explicitly list the -verify, -noverify, and -verifyremote options as valid command flags, some JVM implementations can indeed support use of the flags.

Class Loader

The class loader is one of the key components of a Java virtual machine responsible for managing the loading of Java class byte codes into the Java runtime environment. The class loader is responsible for

- Loading Java class byte codes from an input stream (for example, file or network).
- Inducing the byte code verifier to verify these byte codes.
- Inducing the security manager and access controller to verify access to resources.
- Handing the classes off to the Java runtime execution engine.

The class loader component is actually composed of one or more individual class loaders. A primordial class loader is baked into the Java virtual machine and is responsible for loading the core Java platform classes. Other class loaders can be implemented by adhering to a standard class loader interface. However, such class loaders are subject to more stringent security verifications than is the primordial class loader. Different class loader implementations are provided to offer different ways to load classes from different input streams using different policies.

Class Loader Architecture and Security

Figure 2.6 depicts the basic class loader architecture assumed by the Java security model. As a generic rule enforced by the standard class loader interface framework, when asked to load a class from an input stream, a class loader first checks its cached collection of classes to determine whether the class is already loaded. If it is loaded, the class loader can return the class without further processing. The security manager and access controller can then be consulted to determine whether access to the particular class is allowed. The primordial class loader is then consulted first to determine whether it can load the class. In Java 2, the primordial class loader loads core Java platform classes, whereas the Java 1.1 primordial class loader also loads classes from the CLASSPATH. In Java 2, auxiliary class loaders are consulted to load classes from the CLASSPATH as well as remote classes.

If the class was not loaded by the primordial class loader, the class is read from the input stream. The actual type of input stream used depends on the type of class loader. An input stream connected to a local file medium location or to a network medium location requires a class loader that can read classes from such mediums. The bytes read from the input stream are then fed through the byte code verification process. If successful byte code verification was performed, a java.lang.Class object is created that is used to describe the class for the virtual machine. Before the class is created, the security manager is consulted again to determine whether creation of such a class is permitted. Finally, if the class is loaded, the class is cached with its collection of other loaded classes.

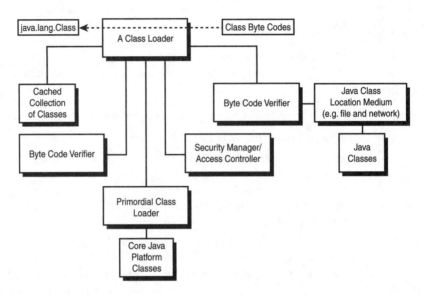

FIGURE 2.6

The class loader architecture.

When a class loaded by the class loader refers to another class, the same basic process for finding the referenced class is followed. Thus, you can see that a particular class loader will consult only the primordial class loader, its own cached collection of classes, and its associated input stream for a class to load. Different class loader instances within the same virtual machine do not consult one another to load classes. This separation of class loaders results in a separation of name spaces such that different implementations of classes with the same fully qualified name can live in different class loaders. This provides a security advantage in that a malicious class loader cannot corrupt the classes used by another class loader in the same virtual machine by purposely loading a malicious class into that class loader's name space.

Class-Loader Interfaces

In addition to the primordial class loader that is part of the Java platform, other common and predefined class loaders also exist. Perhaps one of the first common class-loader types to be implemented was the applet class loader. Applet class loaders were implemented by Web browser vendors to provide support for loading classes, which form the code of an applet, from the network via HTTP from within a Web browser. Applet class loaders typically determine from where to load these classes based on a CODEBASE tag that accompanies an applet tag in an HTML file.

Although no standard API for an applet class loader exists, Figure 2.7 shows the standard base class-loader class and three standard class-loader implementations that come equipped with the

Java platform via a UML class diagram. These standard class loader types are briefly described here:

- `java.lang.ClassLoader`: Represents the base class loader from which other class loaders should be extended. Core interfaces exist on the `ClassLoader` for loading classes, defining classes, finding classes, obtaining resource handles, and accessing class libraries. The `loadClass()` method is the single most important method on the `ClassLoader`. It is responsible for performing the actual load of a class.

- `java.security.SecureClassLoader`: The `SecureClassLoader` was introduced in Java 2 as a base class that offers the capability to associate classes with permissions and a code source. A code source identifies the URL and certificate associated with a class.

- `java.net.URLClassLoader`: This class loader was also introduced in Java 2 to load classes from a list of URLs. The URLs can be either JAR files or directories.

- `java.rmi.server.RMIClassLoader`: Left over from Java 1.1, the `RMIClassLoader` is used by RMI applications during marshaling and unmarshaling of classes passed as parameters or return values. The `RMIClassLoader` loads classes from the network using a list of URLs.

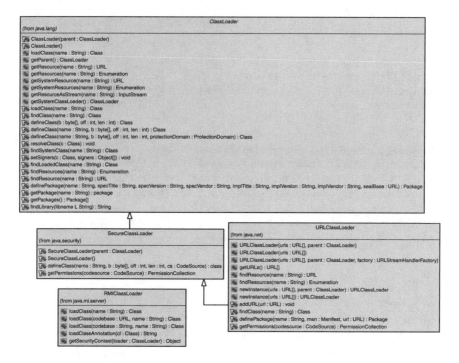

FIGURE 2.7

Standard class loader APIs.

The `URLClassLoader` class offers all you need in a class loader. It can load classes from the network via HTTP or from the file system. However, you might encounter a situation in which you need to implement your own class loader. For example, you might desire to load classes from a database or perhaps via some other protocol besides HTTP. In such a situation, you should still subclass `ClassLoader`, `SecureClassLoader`, or `URLClassLoader`. You'll then want to overload a few of the protected methods of the class you are extending.

Whereas Java 1.1–style class loader implementations often overrode the protected `ClassLoader.loadClass(String, boolean)` method, Java 2–style class-loader implementations are encouraged to override the protected `ClassLoader.findClass(String)` method. This is because most of the generic class loading logic can still be utilized by leaving the `loadClass()` method as is. The `loadClass()` method calls the `findClass()` method after preliminary calls are made, such as determining whether the class is already loaded and checking with the primordial class loader. The `findClass()` method can thus be specialized to look for the class on the specialized input stream that your class loader implementation desires to search for classes matching the fully qualified classname as an input parameter. If you have a block of data you've read from your input stream, you can run this class through the byte code verifier, as well as create an instance of a `Class` object by calling the `defineClass()` method. For example

```
public MyClassLoader extends ClassLoader
{
  protected Class findClass(String className){
    byte[] buffer = getMyData(className);
    Class returnClass = defineClass(className, buffer, 0, buffer.length);
    return returnClass;
  }

  private byte[] getMyData(String className){
    // This arbitrarily named method contains the logic
    // needed to retrieve the named class from the input stream
    // associated with your class loader implementation. Thus, this
    // method may read some data from a TCP/IP socket, for example,
    // given the name of a class and then return the bytes (byte codes)
    // associated with the read Java class.
  }
  ...
  // Implement other methods as needed
  ...
}
```

An explicit request to load a class using your custom class loader can be accomplished using the static `forName(String, boolean, ClassLoader)` method on `java.lang.Class`. The `String` parameter specifies the fully qualified classname to load, the `boolean` flag indicates whether the class should be initialized, and the `ClassLoader` parameter designates the class loader to use. Thus, you might explicitly load a class using your custom class loader and instantiate an instance of the class given the following call:

```
MyClassLoader myClassLoader = new MyClassLoader();
Class myQueryServerClass = Class.forName("com.beeshirts.QueryServer",
                                         true, myClassLoader);
QueryServer myQueryServer
            = (QueryServer) myQueryServerClass.newInstance();
```

Every reference to unloaded classes from the `myQueryServer` object can then use the class loader with which it was loaded. Of course, you can also call `loadClass()` on an instance of your custom class loader and use it to load the class initially, as shown here:

```
MyClassLoader myClassLoader = new MyClassLoader();
Class myQueryServerClass
            = myClassLoader.loadClass("com.beeshirts.QueryServer");
QueryServer myQueryServer
            = (QueryServer)  myQueryServerClass.newInstance();
```

Security Manager

The security manager component of the core Java security architecture is responsible for determining whether certain requests to access particular valued resources are to be allowed. To make this decision, the security manager considers the source (that is, Java class) making the request. Because access to many valued resources must first pass through the core Java classes from a Java class making the request, the core Java classes take the opportunity to first ask the security manager whether the request is allowed. If access is denied, a `java.lang.SecurityException` is thrown. If access is permitted, the call will proceed as normal.

Each Java virtual machine process instance allows only one security manager instance to exist (that is, a singleton). After the security manager is instantiated, the JVM can be configured so that the security manager cannot be replaced. It thus exists for the lifetime of the Java virtual machine process. Many Java virtual machines embedded in Web browsers will instantiate a security manager instance before the first Java applet is ever loaded and not permit the security manager to be replaced. Thus, the security manager in Web browsers cannot be replaced by a malicious Java applet. A malicious Java applet might, after all, replace the security manager with its own security manager instance that relaxes restrictions on which valued resources can be accessed.

Although Java applets run in a Java virtual machine process that has already instantiated a security manager, regular Java applications you create don't have this advantage. In Java 1.1, creating your own security manager was a tad tedious. Java 2 makes creating your own security manager for a Java application much simpler and makes it easily configurable. This is because a default and configurable security manager can be used with Java 2 applications; this manager is rich enough in flexible feature support for many applications. Thus, as you'll see, use of a security manager to protect access to valued resources can also be provided for Java applications.

Use of the default security manager can be specified from the command line during startup of your Java applications. The `java.security.manager` property can be passed to the Java virtual machine as a system property, specifying use of the default security manager in the following fashion:

```
java –Djava.security.manager MyApplication
java –Djava.security.manager=default MyApplication
```

Security Manager Interfaces

Figure 2.8 shows the `java.lang.SecurityManager` class encapsulating the key interface to the security manager currently instantiated in the Java machine process. The `java.lang.System.getSecurityManager()` method returns a handle to the currently instantiated `SecurityManager` object. If no security manager is instantiated, a null value is returned. The `java.lang.System.setSecurityManager()` call takes a `SecurityManager` input parameter and checks to see whether the existing security manager is allowed to be replaced by the calling class. If the security manager does not exist or if the class is allowed to replace the existing security manager, the operation proceeds and returns. Otherwise, a `SecurityException` is thrown.

The `SecurityManager` class is mainly populated with public `checkXXX()` style methods. Each `checkXXX()` method is defined to check whether access is allowed for a particular valued resource. If access is not allowed, the `checkXXX()` methods will throw `SecurityException` objects. Most of these methods are left over from the Java 1.0 and 1.1 versions of the `SecurityManager`. Java 2 has introduced the `checkPermission()` method, which is a more generic form of the other `checkXXX()` methods. In fact, each `checkXXX()` method now calls the generic `checkPermission()` method under the hood of Sun's Java 2 platform implementation. The `checkPermission()` method in turn calls the `java.security.AccessController` class.

The `AccessController` was added in Java 2 to provide the fine-grained and configurable access control functionality that is central to the new security model. Although the `SecurityManager` is still maintained for backward compatibility with existing applications and serves as a primary security management interface, the `AccessController` really subsumes the responsibility for algorithmic-access checking that was once the province of the `SecurityManager`. In the next chapter, I describe in more detail the `AccessController` and how the functionality of the Java 2 access control mechanisms replaces most of the `SecurityManager` API calls. Because I discuss the legacy `SecurityManager` calls in the next chapter in the context of Java 2 access control, I do not cover the `SecurityManager` API calls here. I will, however, briefly outline how a `SecurityManager` might be customized by your applications in a Java 1.1 fashion.

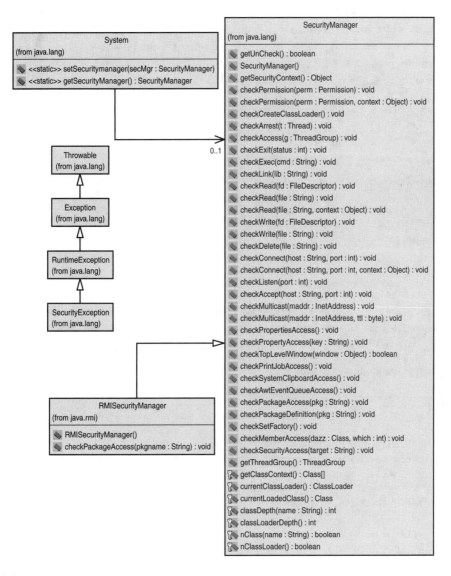

FIGURE 2.8

Security manager classes.

Custom Security Managers

Java 1.1 required that a `SecurityManager` be extended to provide your own custom application-specific access control policies. Implementing your own `SecurityManager` is no longer recommended for Java 2–based applications, however. Instead of writing code that overrides the methods of a `SecurityManager`, I demonstrate customization of access decision making in the next chapter via configuration of security permissions and policies. Because the Java 2 platform discourages `SecurityManager` subclassing, all the protected `SecurityManager` methods—with the exception of `getClassContext()`—have been deprecated in Java 2.

Classes, such as the `java.rmi.RMISecurityManager` class introduced in Java 1.1 and shown in Figure 2.8, simply override the methods that relate to modified behavior for specific valued resource access checking. Thus, an overridden `SecurityManager` in Java 1.1 that extends a few file-access–checking operations might look like this:

```java
public class CustomSecurityManager  extends SecurityManager
{
  public CustomSecurityManager()
  {
    super();
  }

  public void checkRead(String fileName)
  {
    if(fileName != null && fileName.endsWith(".java")){
    throw new SecurityException(" You are not allowed to read   "
        +" file names ending with .java");
    }
    super.checkRead(fileName);
  }

  public void checkWrite(String fileName)
  {
    if(fileName != null && fileName.endsWith(".java")){
      throw new SecurityException(" You are not allowed to write   "
        +" file names ending with .java");
    }
    super.checkWrite(fileName);
  }

  public void checkDelete(String fileName)
  {
    if(fileName != null && fileName.endsWith(".java")){
      throw new SecurityException(" You are not allowed to delete   "
        +" file names ending with .java");
    }
```

```
        super.checkDelete(fileName);
    }
}
```

To set this security manager as the security manager to use for your application's Java virtual machine process, you call `System.setSecurityManager()` with an instance of this `CustomSecurityManager` some time early in the process of starting your application (perhaps inside the `main()` method of your application) in this way:

```
System.setSecurityManager(new CustomSecurityManager());
```

At some point when your application attempts to access a file, the Java virtual machine will call the custom security manager for you under the hood. For example, the `java.io.FileInputStream` class calls `checkRead()` on the `SecurityManager`, which would actually use your registered `CustomSecurityManager` object. Your application code might also need to make such calls explicitly as shown here:

```
public void myFileAccessMethod(String fileName){
    SecurityManager secMgr = System.getSecurityManager();
    if(secMgr != null){
        secMgr.checkRead(fileName);
    }
    // If got this far, then can proceed on with method...
}
```

If the preceding explicit `checkRead()` call throws a `SecurityException`, the `myFileAccessMethod()` call will be terminated before the rest of the method can proceed and will return with the `SecurityException` thrown. Because the `SecurityException` class extends the `java.lang.RuntimeException` class, the fact that the `myFileAccessMethod()` can throw such an exception does not need to be explicitly declared in the method signature.

Java Cryptography Architecture

The Java Cryptography Architecture (JCA) equipped with the Java platform was first introduced with Java 1.1. The JCA provides basic cryptographic functions used for the following primary purposes:

- To protect data communicated or stored for integrity
- To identify a principal associated with data that has been communicated or retrieved from storage
- To provide support for generating keys and certificates used to identify data sources
- To provide a framework for plugging in different cryptographic algorithms from different service providers

You should not assume too much from the word *cryptography* in JCA. The JCA is not really useful for encrypting data communicated or stored for decryption by an intended receiver. Such cryptographic functionality used to provide confidentiality is possible with the JCE. Because of U.S. export restrictions, the JCE is shipped separate from the Java platform, whereas the JCA does not have such limitations. Furthermore, although SSL represents one of the more popular crypto-related protocols in the Internet era, it is not packaged with the JCA. Rather, SSL interface support is provided separately from the Java platform in the JSSE package.

This section provides an overview of the architecture of JCA. A more detailed explanation and sample uses of different components of the JCA are presented later in the book.

The Architecture of JCA

The JCA is composed of a number of classes and interfaces that implement basic cryptographic functionality. These are the Java 2 platform packages, which contain classes and interfaces that make up the JCA:

- `java.security`: The set of core classes and interfaces for the JCA plug-and-play service provider framework and cryptographic operation APIs. Note that this package also contains core Java security architecture classes and interfaces.
- `java.security.cert`: A set of certificate management classes and interfaces.
- `java.security.interfaces`: A set of interfaces used to encapsulate and manage DSA and RSA public and private keys.
- `java.security.spec`: A set of classes and interfaces used to describe public and private key algorithm and parameter specifications.

Figure 2.9 depicts the top-level architecture of the JCA with a mixture of actual Java classes and conceptual classes (that is, not real code-based classes, but simply representative of concepts). At the top of the diagram is the `java.security.Security` class that is mainly responsible for managing a collection of Cryptographic Service Providers (CSPs). A CSP represents a service provider that implements one or more cryptographic functions that adhere to the cryptographic interfaces defined in the JCA. Information about each CSP is encapsulated by the `java.security.Provider` abstract class. CSPs (shown as `SomeCSPImpl` in Figure 2.9) extend the `Provider` abstract class with specific implementations of methods on the `Provider` class.

Each CSP will implement one or more cryptographic engines. A cryptographic engine represents a particular cryptographic algorithm and set of parameters to that algorithm that perform some cryptographic functionality. For example, the MD5 message digest algorithm is a particular algorithm and set of parameters used to generate an encrypted stream of data based on another stream of data. MD5 belongs to a general class of cryptographic engines referred to as a message digest cryptographic engine.

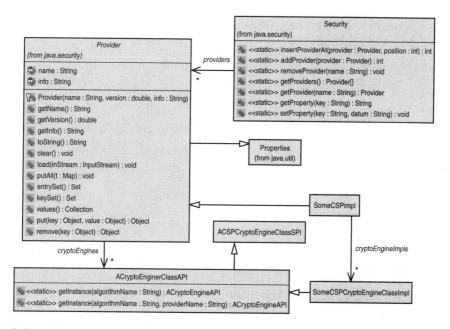

FIGURE 2.9
The top-level architecture of JCA.

The various cryptographic engines (for example, `SomeCSPCryptoEngineImpl`) supplied by a CSP implement some standard cryptographic service-provider interface (for example, `ACryptoEngineClassSPI`) provided by the JCA. Each service provider interface is extended by a cryptographic engine API (for example, `ACryptoEngineClassAPI`) used by the applications programmer. Each cryptographic engine API provides a static `getInstance(String)` method that takes the name of a particular algorithm name related to that engine class and returns a concrete instance of the requested cryptographic engine using that algorithm if it exists. Otherwise, a `java.security.NoSuchAlgorithmException` exception is thrown. A static `getInstance(String, String)` method on each cryptographic engine API specifies a particular CSP to use.

Cryptographic Engines

The `java.security.MessageDigest` abstract class is an example of a cryptographic engine API, whereas the `java.security.MessageDigestSpi` abstract class represents the cryptographic service-provider interface that must be implemented. The protected methods of `MessageDigestSpi` will be visible and relevant only to the CSP's implementation.

Figure 2.10 shows the various standard cryptographic engine types defined by the JCA. These cryptographic-engine APIs and their helper classes rest at the core of how the JCA is used by application developers. The primary functionality provided by each cryptographic engine type in Figure 2.10 is described here:

- `MessageDigest`: Creates and verifies message digests
- `Signature`: Creates and verifies digital signatures
- `KeyPairGenerator`: Generates public and private key pairs
- `KeyFactory`: Converts between secure keys and key specifications
- `KeyStore`: Modifies information in a secure key storage repository
- `CertificateFactory`: Generates certificates and certificate revocation lists
- `AlgorithmParameters`: Encodes crypto algorithm parameters
- `AlgorithmParameterGenerator`: Creates crypto algorithm parameters
- `SecureRandom`: Creates random numbers

Cryptographic Service Providers

The JCA shipped with the Java platform comes equipped with a default CSP implemented by Sun. The `String` name used with the JCA APIs to designate this default provider is `SUN`. The default Sun CSP implementation provides support for the following cryptographic engine and algorithm combinations:

- MD5 message digest algorithm
- SHA-1 message digest algorithm
- DSA for signatures
- DSA key pair generator
- DSA algorithm parameters
- DSA algorithm parameter generator
- DSA key factory
- JKS key store (JKS involves a proprietary algorithm)
- X.509 certificate factory
- SHA1PRNG pseudo-random number generator algorithm (an IEEE standard)

You can install a CSP for use with your Java runtime environment by simply placing a JAR or ZIP file with the classes that implement the JCA CSP interfaces somewhere on your `CLASSPATH`. You must configure the `java.security` file under the root directory of your Java installation in the `<JavaRootInstall>\lib\security\` directory. In that file, add the fully qualified classnames of your CSPs that extend the `Provider` class. The order of preference specifies which CSP to use in the event that an algorithm selected for use is implemented by another CSP. For example, the following `java.security` file entries specify that Sun's default

CSP is preferred before Sun's RSA JCA CSP implementation:

```
# List of providers in order from most to least preferred CSP
security.provider.1=sun.security.provider.Sun
security.provider.2=com.sun.rsajca.Provider
```

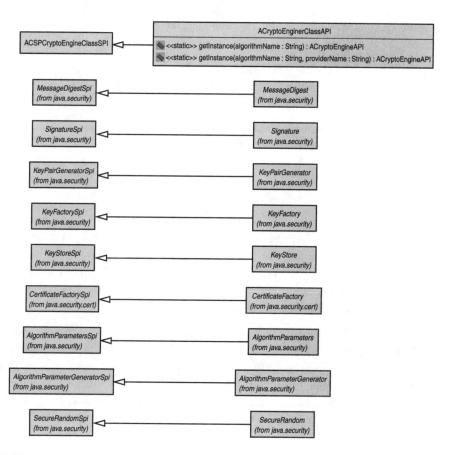

FIGURE 2.10

JCA cryptographic engine classes.

CSPs can also be added and removed programmatically from within your JVM process. Only trusted applications can perform such operations, however. A *trusted application* here refers to an application running without a security manager installed or an application that has been granted permission to add and remove CSPs. We discuss how to configure such permissions in the next chapter. However, suffice it to say here that adding and removing CSPs with the

Security class is rather straightforward, assuming that your application has the proper permissions:

```
// Install SunJCE CSP by first creating a Provider instance
Provider providerSunJce = new com.sun.crypto.provider.SunJCE();
// Then add provider using Security class and obtain preference number
int providerPreferenceJCE = Security.addProvider(providerSunJce);

// Or set the preference number yourself increasing preference numbers
// of any providers already installed at that preference level
Provider providerATI = new com.assuredtech.security.JCAProvider();
int providerPreferenceATI = Security.insertProviderAt(providerATI, 1);

// A provider can be removed dynamically using Security class
// For example, to remove default Sun CSP
Security.removeProvider("SUN");
```

Summary

The Java security architecture provides a standards-based interface for Java developers to create secure Java applications. The core Java security architecture is composed of a byte code verifier, one or more class loaders, and a security manager/access control framework. The byte code verifier provides support for low-level object corruption checking. The class loader provides further protection in terms of authenticity of trusted code. The security manager and access control, of course, provide authorization protection.

Also part of the Java 2 platform, the JCA provides plug-and-play service-provider–based protection of data and programs for integrity and identity. Extensions to the Java platform such as the JCE and JSSE provide protection for confidentiality, whereas the JAAS provides enhanced authenticity and authorization protection. In terms of major security architecture components currently not supported by Java, any standard interfaces for nonrepudiation and security auditing are currently lacking. The next chapter describes practical usage of access control.

Java Application Security Access Control

Java security provides a collection of APIs and tools for infusing security into your Java applications. Infrastructure for providing fine-grained and configurable access control is built into the core Java security architecture via use of Java 2 permissions, policy files, and access controller functionality. This chapter describes the core Java 2 security architecture in more detail and explains how to use such an infrastructure in your Java applications.

In this chapter, you will learn about

- The permission APIs available to the Java security programmer.
- The security policy APIs available to the Java security programmer.
- The security domains and the access-control mechanisms available in the Java security framework.

Permissions

As part of the new Java 2 security model for providing fine-grained and configurable access control, a hierarchy of extendable-permissions APIs has been added to the Java platform. Permission objects encapsulate the concept of a permission to access some valued resource. Permissions have names referring to a target resource for which a permission is to be granted or denied. Permissions also have a series of actions that scope the set of operations that can be performed on the target resource.

Permissions are classified according to types using subclasses from base permission types in the Java API. For example, a file permission extends the concept of an abstract permission so that the target name represents one or more filenames or directories and the action list represents actions that can be performed on targets, such as read or write. These new Java 2 permission objects replace the permission-related constructs in the java.security.acl package.

Permissions Architecture

Figure 3.1 shows the basic architecture of Java 2 permissions. At the root of the permissions architecture is the java.security.Permission abstract class, which conceptualizes a permission to access some valued resource. A Permission object has a target name of a valued resource (for example, a filename) that is retrieved via the getName() method. A Permission object can also return a String defining the set of actions to be performed on the target resource. The actions String is, typically, a comma-separated list of actions related to a target. For example, actions such as read, write might be the set of actions related to a particular target filename. The implies(Permission) method of the Permission class is used to indicate whether the Permission object, passed in as a parameter, is granted if the current Permission object is granted. The checkGuard() method on the Permission object is implemented by virtue of the fact that the Permission object implements the java.security.Guard interface (described later in this chapter).

Subclasses of Permission can also implement the newPermissionCollection() method to return an object that extends the java.security.PermissionCollection abstract class. The PermissionCollection object is used to encapsulate a collection of one or more Permission objects and includes methods to add permissions and return the list of permissions it contains.

Adding permissions to a PermissionCollection object is allowed only if it is not read-only. Read-only access can be set with the setReadOnly() method and tested with the isReadOnly() method. It might be necessary to store certain subclasses of Permission as a homogeneous collection of permissions so that a call to implies() on the PermissionCollection object can make sense for that particular permission type. Whereas the PermissionCollection represents a collection of Permission objects of the same type, the java.security.Permissions class encapsulates a collection of heterogeneous permissions. The Permissions class accomplishes this by storing permissions of the same type in their own separate PermissionCollection objects.

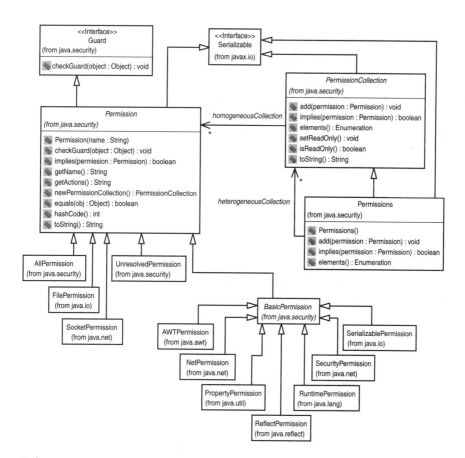

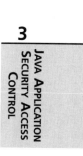

FIGURE 3.1
The Java 2 permissions architecture.

Permission Types

The `Permission` class contains several subclasses, as shown in Figure 3.1. In the interest of conserving space, I've left the operation signatures of such classes out of the diagram. However, all the classes simply overload methods defined on the base `Permission` class. Although each class does define its own constructors, most classes have two constructors either of the form `Constructor(String name)`, taking a permission name parameter, or of the form `Constructor(String name, String actions)`, taking a permission name and action `String`. A description of how to use each permission subclass, including sample constructor usage, is presented in Table 3.1.

TABLE 3.1   Java Security Permission Types

Permission Type (and Package)	Permission Usage	Description
AllPermission (java.security)	`AllPermission ap = new AllPermission();`	Grants permission to every resource.
FilePermission (java.io)	`FilePermission fp = new FilePermission("C:\\temp\\sampleFile.txt", "read");`	Gives permission to read a file.
	`FilePermission fp = new FilePermission("C:\\temp", "read");`	Gives permission to read directory information (not every file in the directory).
	`FilePermission fp = new FilePermission("C:\\temp\\*", "read");`	Gives permission to read every file in the directory.
	`FilePermission fp = new FilePermission("C:\\temp\\-", "read");`	Gives permission to read every file in and under the directory.
	`FilePermission fp = new FilePermission("<<ALL FILES>>", "read");`	Gives permission to read every file on the file system.
	`FilePermission fp = new FilePermission("C:\\temp\\test.exe ", "read, write, delete, execute");`	Gives permission to read, write, delete, and execute a file.
Socket Permission java.net)	`SocketPermission sp = new SocketPermission("www.assuredtech.com", "accept");`	Gives permission to accept connection from a single domain name.
	`SocketPermission sp = new`	Gives permission

TABLE 3.1 Continued

Permission Type (and Package)	Permission Usage	Description
	`SocketPermission("205.277.44.44",` `                "accept, connect");`	to accept connection from and connect to a particular IP address.

	`SocketPermission sp = new`
	`  SocketPermission("*.com",`
	`                "accept, connect");`
		Gives permission to accept/connect for any domain name that ends with .com.

	`SocketPermission sp = new`
	`  SocketPermission( "*.assuredtech.com:80",`
	`                "accept, connect");`
		Gives permission to accept/connect on port 80 under assuredtech.com domain.

	`SocketPermission sp = new`
	`  SocketPermission("*.assuredtech.com:1024-",`
	`                "accept, connect");`
		Accepts/connects on the unreserved ports.

	`SocketPermission sp = new`
	`  SocketPermission("*.assuredtech.com:-1023",`
	`                "accept, connect");`
		Accepts/connects on the reserved ports.

	`SocketPermission sp = new`
	`  SocketPermission(`
	`    "www.assuredtech.com:4000:4020",`
	`    "accept, connect");`
		Accepts/connects on ports 4000 to 4020.

	`SocketPermission sp = new` `  SocketPermission( "*", "accept, connect");`	Accepts/connects every machine on every port.

	`SocketPermission sp = new`
	`  SocketPermission( "",`
	`                "accept, listen, connect");`
		Accepts/connects/ listens only on localhost.

	`SocketPermission sp = new`
	`  SocketPermission("localhost",`
	`                "accept, listen, connect");`	

Unresolved	`String type = // class name of permission`	When a permission

3

JAVA APPLICATION SECURITY ACCESS CONTROL

TABLE 3.1   Continued

Permission Type (and Package)	Permission Usage	Description
Permission (java.security)	```String name = // permission name``` ```String actions = // permission action list``` ```java.security.cert.Certificate[] certs=``` ``` // certificates of signed permission class``` ```UnresolvedPermission up = new``` ``` UnresolvedPermission(type, name,``` ``` actions, certs);```	object is to be created for permissions that have yet to be associated with a particular Permission subclass, the Unresolved Permission object is used as a placeholder until the actual permission type is created.
BasicPermission (java.security)	```// BasicPermission is abstract base``` ```// class for subclasses such as...``` ```BasePermissionSubClass bp = new``` ```BasePermissionSubClass("com.ati.*");```	An abstract base class that does not have actions simply designates whether you have access to an associated resource. The main utility is the way way that permissions are named using dot-separated hierarchy and wildcards.
AWTPermission (java.awt)	```AWTPermission awtp = new``` ``` AWTPermission("accessClipboard");```	Gives permission to access the system clipboard.
	```AWTPermission awtp = new``` ``` AWTPermission("accessEventQueue");```	Gives permission to access the system event queue.

TABLE 3.1 Continued

Permission Type (and Package)	Permission Usage	Description
	`AWTPermission awtp = new` `AWTPermission("listenToAllAWTEvents");`	Gives permission to listen to all AWT events.
	`AWTPermission awtp = new AWTPermission(` `"showWindowWithoutWarningBanner");`	Gives permission to show the windows without any warning banner (Trusted/Untrusted Applet).
NetPermission (java.net)	`NetPermission np = new NetPermission(` `"requestPasswordAuthentication");`	Gives permission to get a password from a registered system authenticator.
	`NetPermission np = new NetPermission(` `"setDefaultAuthenticator");`	Gives permission to register the authenticator used to get authentication information.
	`NetPermission np = new NetPermission(` `"specifyStreamHandler");`	Gives permission to designate a stream handler when creating a URL.
Property Permission (java.util)	`PropertyPermission pp = new` `PropertyPermission( "java.*",` `"read, write");`	Gives permission to get and set properties that start with java..
	`PropertyPermission pp = new` `PropertyPermission("*", "read");`	Gives permission to get every property.

TABLE 3.1 Continued

Permission Type (and Package)	Permission Usage	Description
reflect Permission (java.lang. reflect)	`ReflectPermission rp = new` `    ReflectPermission("suppressAccessChecks");`	Gives permission for access methods and fields in a class for public, default package, protected, and private elements on reflected objects.
Runtime Permission (java.lang)	`RuntimePermission rp = new` `    RuntimePermission("createClassLoader");`	Gives permission to create a new class loader.
	`RuntimePermission rp = new` `    RuntimePermission("getClassLoader");`	Gives permission to get the current class loader.
	`RuntimePermission rp = new` `    RuntimePermission("setSecurityManager");`	Gives permission to change the current security manager.
	`RuntimePermission rp = new` `    RuntimePermission("createSecurityManager");`	Gives permission to create a new security manager.
	`RuntimePermission rp = new` `    RuntimePermission("exitVM");`	Gives permission to exit from a JVM.
	`RuntimePermission rp = new` `    RuntimePermission("setFactory");`	Gives permission to set a different socket factory.
	`RuntimePermission rp = new` `    RuntimePermission("setIO");`	Gives permission to change standard I/O streams.

TABLE 3.1 Continued

Permission Type (and Package)	Permission Usage	Description
	`RuntimePermission rp = new` `  RuntimePermission("modifyThread");`	Gives permission to change the state of a thread.
	`RuntimePermission rp = new` `  RuntimePermission("stopThread");`	Gives permission to stop a thread.
	`RuntimePermission rp =new` `  RuntimePermission("modifyThreadGroup");`	Gives permission to modify the thread group.
	`RuntimePermission rp = new` `  RuntimePermission("readFileDescriptor");`	Gives permission to read from a file descriptor.
	`RuntimePermission rp = new` `  RuntimePermission("writeFileDescriptor");`	Gives permission to write to a file descriptor.
	`RuntimePermission rp = new` `  RuntimePermission("loadLibrary.myLibrary");`	Gives permission to load a new dynamic shared library.
	`RuntimePermission rp = new` `  RuntimePermission("queuePrintJob");`	Gives permission to start a print job.
	`RuntimePermission rp = new` `  RuntimePermission("accessDeclaredMembers");`	Gives permission to access declared members.

	`RuntimePermission rp = new`
	`  RuntimePermission(`
	`    "defineClassInPackage.myPackage");`
		Gives permission to define classes in a package.

	`RuntimePermission rp = new`
	`  RuntimePermission(`
	`    "accessClassInPackage.myPackage");`
		Gives permission to access classes in a package.

TABLE 3.1 Continued

Permission Type (and Package)	Permission Usage	Description
Security Permission (java.security)	`SecurityPermission sp =new` `  SecurityPermission("getPolicy");`	Gives permission to get security policy information.
	`SecurityPermission sp = new` `  SecurityPermission("setPolicy");`	Gives permission to set a security policy.
	`SecurityPermission sp = new` `  SecurityPermission("setSignerKeyPair");`	Gives permission to set a new signed key pair.
	`SecurityPermission sp = new` `  SecurityPermission("getSignerPrivateKey");`	Gives permission to get a private key.

	`SecurityPermission sp = new`
	`  SecurityPermission(`
	`    "addIdentityCertificate");`
		Gives permission to add a new certificate.

	`SecurityPermission sp = new`
	`  SecurityPermission(`
	`    "removeIdentityCertificate");`
		Gives permission to remove security identity.

	`SecurityPermission sp = new` `  SecurityPermission("printIdentity");`	Gives permission to get the security identity.
	`SecurityPermission sp = new` `  SecurityPermission("setIdentityInfo");`	Gives permission to set security identity information.
	`SecurityPermission sp = new` `  SecurityPermission("getProperty.myKey");`	Gives permission to get the security property using a given key.
	`SecurityPermission sp = new` `  SecurityPermission("setProperty.myKey");`	Gives permission to set a security property using a given key.

TABLE 3.1 Continued

Permission Type (and Package)	Permission Usage	Description
	`SecurityPermission sp = new` `  SecurityPermission("setSystemScope");`	Gives permission to change the system scope.

	`SecurityPermission sp = new`
	`  SecurityPermission(`
	`    "removeProviderProperty.myProviderName");`
		Gives permission to remove a provider property.

	`SecurityPermission sp = new`
	`  SecurityPermission(`
	`    "putProviderProperty.myProviderName");`
		Gives permission to add a new property to the provider.

	`SecurityPermission sp = new`
	`  SecurityPermission(`
	`    "clearProviderProperties.myProviderName");`
		Gives permission to clear all the provider properties.

	`SecurityPermission sp = new`
	`  SecurityPermission(`
	`    "removeProvider.myProviderName");`
		Gives permission to remove a provider.

	`SecurityPermission sp =new`
	`  SecurityPermission(`
	`    "insertProvider.myProviderName");`
		Gives permission to insert a new provider.

Serializable Permission (java.io)	`SerializablePermission sp = new`
	`  SerializablePermission(`
	`    "enableSubclassImplementation");`
		Gives permission to implement subclasses of object input and output streams for serialization.

	`SerializablePermission sp = new`
	`  SerializablePermission(`
	`    "enableSubstitution");`
		Gives permission to substitute objects during serialization.

Custom Permission Types

Although the standard permission types already encapsulate permissions for most of the prede-fined valued resources with which a Java Virtual Machine (JVM) can interact, the creation of application-specific permissions might be necessary from time to time. Customization is accomplished simply by extending one of the permission types.

Typically, you will extend either the `Permission` class or the `BasicPermission` class. If you are extending the `Permission` class, implementing the `implies()`, `equals()`, `getActions()`, and `hashCode()` methods is your primary concern, as well as implementing any permission-specific constructors. If you are extending the `BasicPermission` class, you can rely on the default implementation of methods that `BasicPermission` provides or provide implementation for such methods yourself. You can implement both constructor forms defined in the `BasicPermission` class, however, for taking a name and name/actions pair as parameters even if you do not make use of actions. For example

```
public class AssuredtechPermission extends BasicPermission
{

  public AssuredtechPermission(String name){...}

  public AssuredtechPermission(String name, String actions){...}

  // Will rely on BasicPermission default method implementations
}
```

Security Policies

Although permissions to access valued resources from a JVM are encapsulated by the Java API hierarchy for permissions, the management of such permissions in a configurable fashion is encapsulated by the new Java 2 security policy infrastructure. Security policies provide a pro-grammer-friendly way to configure which permissions are granted to which resources. Although a minimalist API exists to encapsulate security policy configuration, a default policy management framework is provided with the Java 2 platform to enable the configuration of security policies for a Java application without any additional tools. Such a default security policy management framework provides a mechanism for you to define security policies using a simple ASCII policy file format. Furthermore, a GUI-based policy tool utility can also be used to manipulate the security policy file.

As you'll see shortly, a policy file can be used to define which permissions are granted to cer-tain domains of protection. A domain of protection is defined by a URL indicating where the code to be subject to a particular set of security policies comes from. A domain of protection can also be defined by one or more identities that define whom the code comes from.

Security Policy File Format

In the default implementation of security policy management with the Java 2 platform, a security policy is defined in an ASCII text file. A security policy file defines an optional key-store entry, and one or more permissions grant entries of the following general form

```
[keystore "keystore_URL", "keystore_type";]

grant [SignedBy "list of names"] [, CodeBase "URL"]
{
    permission permission_class_name [ "name" ] [, "actions"]
                                    [, SignedBy "list of names"];
    permission ...
};

grant ...
```

Keywords used in the policy file, designated by boldface words in the preceding lines, are case insensitive. Each policy file entry specified for a security domain begins with the grant keyword and contains one or more permission definitions for the particular domain of protection. Each permission entry begins with the permission keyword and is followed by the fully qualified permission classname. Permission target names and a comma-separated list of actions also follow a permission designation. The SignedBy field following the permission is optionally provided with a comma-separated list of alias names that indicate who signed the Java code for the permissions class. As you'll see in a later section, Java code can be signed so that you can securely verify that such code is from the intended supplier. The keystore entry designates which URL and type of storage mechanism to consult for signed classes.

Each grant entry delimiting a domain of protection can also contain a SignedBy field designating the fact that code being executed in the JVM associated with the grant entry is signed by the named signers. A CodeBase field can also be associated with a grant entry to relate a set of permissions to a resource location where the code is loaded. A code base URL that ends with / indicates all Java class files in a particular directory. A code base URL that ends with /* indicates all Java class files and JAR files in a particular directory. A code base URL that ends with / - indicates all Java class files and JAR files in a particular directory and its subdirectories.

Custom permission types and each of the standard Java permission types listed in Table 3.1 can be defined in a security policy file in the previously mentioned format. I discuss code signing in a later section. For example (excluding concern for permissions code security), the following security policy file entries represent valid grant permission entries using a few of the same standard Java permission usage examples shown in Table 3.1:

```
grant
{
```

```
permission java.io.FilePermission "C:\\temp\\sampleFile.txt", "read";
permission java.io.FilePermission "C:\\temp", "read";
permission java.io.FilePermission "C:\\temp\\*", "read";
permission java.io.FilePermission "<<ALL_FILES>>", "read";
permission java.io.FilePermission "C:\\temp\\test.exe ",
                                    "read, write, delete, execute";
};

grant CodeBase http://code.assuredtech.com/-"
{
 permission java.net.SocketPermission "www.assuredtech.com", "accept";
 permission java.util.PropertyPermission "java.*", "read, write";
 permission java.lang.RuntimePermission "setSecurityManager";
};
```

Referencing Properties in Policy Files

You'll notice that in the preceding policy file example, a system-dependent file separator (\\) was used in the policy file definitions. Use of such constructs makes your policy file system dependent. You might consider using the standard Java `file.separator` system property instead of referring to a construct in order to keep your security policy file system independent. You can refer to such properties and others defined for your current running JVM process using a simple convention in your security policy file. The convention simply requires that you encapsulate properties between two curly braces preceded by a dollar sign as shown here:

`${aProperty}`

The JVM will expand such a property when it reads the security policy file. For example, the standard `user.home` and `file.separator` Java system properties can be referenced in your security policy file to grant file-read permissions to all files from a user's home directory as shown here:

```
grant
{
 permission java.io.FilePermission "${user.home}${file.separator}* ",
                                          "read";
}
```

Using Security Policy Files

Now that you know how to define policies in a security policy file, you will learn where to create such files and how to make your Java applications use the policies defined in such files.

A default system security file is defined relative to the root directory of your Java install and is contained in [JAVA_HOME]\lib\security\java.security. That file contains two entries (created during the installation of your Java environment) that indicate where a default Java-system security policy file and user-specific security policy file are installed:

```
policy.url.1=file:${java.home}/lib/security/java.policy
policy.url.2=file:${user.home}/.java.policy
```

The system security policy file is referenced first. If it is not present, the user security policy file is referenced. If neither file is present, a most-restrictive security policy is assumed akin to the Java 1.0 sandbox model. Additional policies can be referenced in the java.security file using incremental policy.url.X indices (that is, policy.url.3 and so on). These index numbers specify the search order in which the JVM should attempt to load security policy files. As soon as a file is located, the search stops and that policy file is used.

If you want to define a policy file to be read from your own application-specific location, you can pass in the -Djava.security.policy system property to the command line when starting your Java application. This property is used to define the location of your own security policy file as exemplified here:

```
java –Djava.security.policy=assuredtech/assuredtech.policy
➥ –Djava.security.manager com.assuredtech.MySecureServer
```

Note that the -Djava.security.manager property designates that the default system security manager will be used as opposed to having an application install its own security manager. As a final note, if you desire to disable the capability for applications to define their own policy files, a policy.allowSystemProperty property in the java.security file can override the default value of true if you set the property to false.

Security Policy Tool

The Java 2 environment also comes equipped with a GUI-based tool for editing security policy files if you prefer not to hand-edit ASCII files. The policytool program is located under the root directory of your Java installation in [JAVA_HOME]\bin\policytool. Figure 3.2 shows what the policytool looks like after you have selected an entry of a particular policy file for editing. You can also create and save new policy files. When the policy file is open, you can add, remove, and edit individual permissions with an easy-to-understand GUI. Adding permissions is particularly simple, as shown in Figure 3.3. Here you see that drop-down lists of permission types, candidate names, and candidate actions can simplify adding permissions to an entry.

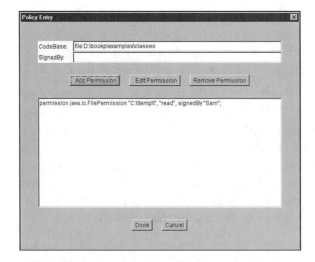

FIGURE 3.2
Viewing an entry with the Java security policy tool.

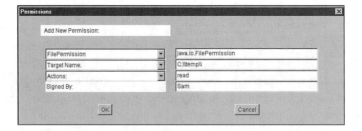

FIGURE 3.3
Adding permissions with the Java security policy tool.

Security Policy APIs

A minimalist API exists for encapsulating security policies. The `java.security.Policy` abstract class implements a static `getPolicy()` method returning a handle to the currently installed policy, and the static `setPolicy()` method enables you to set a new system-wide security policy. The `getPolicy()` method can be invoked if the `SecurityPermission` getPolicy allows it to be, and the `setPolicy()` method can be invoked if the `SecurityPermission` setPolicy allows it to be.

When you're setting a new security policy, the new policy must extend the `Policy` class and implement the `getPermissions()` and `refresh()` methods. The `getPermissions()` method takes a `java.security.CodeSource` object defining the code-base URL and signed by certificates (discussed later) and returns the defined permissions allowed for such a code source as a `PermissionCollection` object. The `refresh()` method must refresh the policy information from the underlying policy storage mechanism associated with the newly defined `Policy` implementation.

Alternatively, the default policy implementation to use with your JVM instance can be specified with a `policy.provider` property in the `java.security` file:

```
policy.provider=com.assuredtech.security.GenericPolicy
```

As a final note, if a new policy object is not set using `Policy.setPolicy()` or if the `policy.provider` property is set, the default security policy provided by Sun is used. Sun's implementation of the default security policy that extends the `Policy` class and reads policy information from the previously mentioned policy files is contained in the class `sun.security.provider.PolicyFile`.

Java Access Control

Access control in Java 2 is managed by a new access controller construct. As mentioned in Chapter 2, "Java Security Overview," the `SecurityManager` interfaces of Java 1.1 are still maintained for backward compatibility, but all `checkXXX()` methods defined on the `SecurityManager` can now delegate to the new `java.security.AccessController` class. The `SecurityManager` can implement such delegation by calling the generic `checkPermission(Permission)` methods now defined on the `SecurityManager` for every `checkXXX()` previously defined. The `SecurityManager.checkPermission()` method can then delegate calls to the `AccessController.checkPermission()` method. For example, for an implementation of the `SecurityManager.checkRead(String fileName)` method, you might use this:

```
checkPermission( new FilePermission(fileName, "read") );
```

And the corresponding `SecurityManager.checkPermission(Permission permission)` method might look like this:

```
java.security.AccessController.checkPermission( permission );
```

Thus, whereas permissions and policies help encapsulate and configure access levels to valued resources, the access control mechanisms in Java provide the infrastructure between Java code making calls to valued resources and the actual implemented access control for such resources. That is, Java access control provides the mechanisms in the Java security architecture that use permissions and policies to actually allow or disallow access to valued resources.

Access Control Architecture

Figure 3.4 presents the architecture of access control in Java 2. At the top of this architecture is the SecurityManager class, which reveals only the two checkPermission() methods new in Java 2; these methods simply delegate calls to AccessController and the AccessControlContext classes. The AccessController represents a decision maker for determining access allowance or denial (checkPermission()), a manager for designating which code should run as privileged (doPrivileged()), and a way to obtain a handle to the current access control context for use in other contexts (getContext()). The AccessControlContext class encapsulates the context pertinent to access control such as a particular stack state of execution. Thus, contexts can obtain handles to AccessControlContext objects from other contexts to determine whether access is permitted in that context.

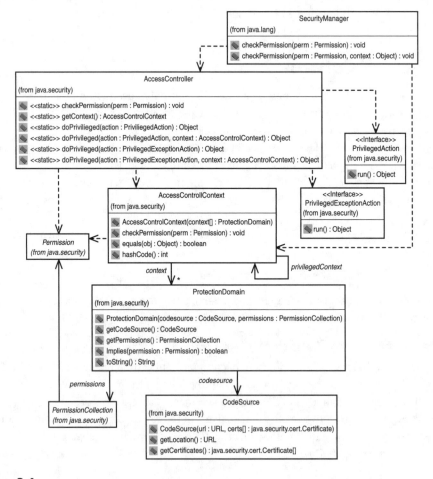

FIGURE 3.4

The Java 2 access control architecture.

An `AccessControlContext` can have one or more `ProtectionDomain` objects. Each `ProtectionDomain` object encapsulates the permissions granted to a particular code base. A `ProtectionDomain` can thus be viewed as one grant entry in a policy file in which the entry has one or more permissions, a potential code base, and a potential set of code-signing alias names. A `ProtectionDomain` object stores such permissions in a `PermissionCollection` object and the code base in a `CodeSource` object. The `CodeSource` object encapsulates the `CodeBase` location in a URL and the `SignedBy` entries in an array of `Certificate` objects. Thus, code from the same code source that is signed by the same signers belongs to the same protection domain. Thus, when `checkPermission()` is called on an `AccessControlContext` object, it checks the permissions associated with the collection of `ProtectionDomain` objects associated with its context.

The `doPrivileged()` methods on the `AccessContoller` can be used to perform certain actions as a privileged caller. Access control decisions will short-circuit permission checking if the calling code action was called from a `doPrivileged()` call assuming that the calling domain was allowed to execute such operations. Normally, the `doPrivileged()` operation uses the `PrivilegedAction` interface to mark privileged operations that do not throw exceptions:

```
AccessController.doPrivileged( new PrivilegedAction()
  {
    public Object run()
    {
      // some privileged action
      // perhaps return some value or return null
    }
  }
);
```

If your privileged operation throws an exception, you will use the `PrivilegedExceptionAction` interface as shown here:

```
AccessController.doPrivileged( new PrivilegedExceptionAction()
  {
    public Object run() throws SomeException
    {
      // some privileged action that throws some exception
      // perhaps return some value or return null
    }
  }
);
```

Both forms of the `doPrivileged()` method also take an `AccessControlContext` object as a second argument to designate a particular context to use for restricting privileges.

Because the getContext() method exists on AccessController, a current
AccessControlContext can be retrieved and used later to check the permissions associated
with one context from another context by calling checkPermission() on that
AccessControlContext. The SecurityManager also has a checkPermission(Permission,
Object) method that takes an AccessControlContext object as an argument and performs the
same exact check. For example

```
// Store AccessControlContext for use in another context
AccessControlContext acc = AccessController.getContext();
 ...
 // Change context
 ...
FilePermission myPermission = new FilePermission("MyFile.txt", "read");
// Call check permission on context directly...
acc.checkPermission(myPermission);
// ...or call check permission on security manager which does
//     same thing as above method call...
(System.getSecurityManager()).checkPermission(myPermission, acc);
```

Guarded Objects

When resource access needs to be provided to an object in a different thread, a
java.security.GuardedObject can be used to protect access to that resource as depicted
in Figure 3.5. The sender in this case creates a GuardedObject with the Object encapsulating
an interface to that resource and another object that implements the java.security.Guard
interface. An object that implements the Guard interface is responsible for taking the resource
object as a parameter to a checkGuard() call, and it throws a SecurityException if access is
not allowed. After a GuardedObject is constructed, a receiver in another thread will have to
first call getObject() on the GuardedObject to obtain access to the resource object. The
GuardedObject then calls checkGuard() on the Guard implementation. Because the
java.lang.Permission class implements the Guard interface, it can be used as shown here:

```
// Create the guarded object in one thread
Socket sock = new Socket("myHost.com", 8000);
SocketPermission perm = new SocketPermission "myHost.com:8000",
"connect,accept");
GuardedObject gObject  = new GuardedObject(sock, perm);
    . . .
// Now need to use gObject from another thread
// This will throw exception if this thread is not allowed access
Socket mySock = (Socket) gObhect.getObject();
```

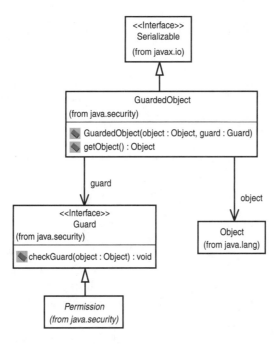

FIGURE 3.5
Guarded objects.

SecurityManager-to-Access Control Mapping

Now that you have an understanding of the basic role assumed by the `AccessController` and `AccessControlContext` classes, it should be apparent to you not only how such access control constructs can provide every function call provided by the `SecurityManager`, but also how it extends such calls to be more generic. Such generality is provided by virtue of the `checkPermission()` methods implemented on both the `AccessController` and the `AccessControlContext` classes. Table 3.2 shows how the `SecurityManager` calls map to calls on the new access control constructs.

TABLE 3.2   SecurityManager-to-Access Control Mapping

SecurityManager *Call*	AccessController *or* AccessControlContext *Call(s)*
`checkPermission(Permission perm)`	`AccessController.checkPermission(perm)`
`checkPermission(Permission perm, Object ctx)`	`((AccessControlContext) ctx).check Permission(perm)`
`checkAccess(Thread t)`	`AccessController.checkPermission(new RuntimePermission("modify Thread"))`
`checkAccess(ThreadGroup g)`	`AccessController.checkPermission(new RuntimePermission("modifyThread Group"))`
`checkExit(int status)`	`AccessController.checkPermission(new RuntimePermission("exitVM"))`
`checkExec(String cmd)`	`AccessController.checkPermission(new FilePermission(cmd, "execute"))`
`checkLink(String lib)`	`AccessController.checkPermission(new RuntimePermission ("loadLibrary."+lib))`
`checkRead(FileDescriptor fd)`	`AccessController.checkPermission(new RuntimePermission("readFile Descriptor"))`
`checkRead(String file)`	`AccessController.checkPermission(new FilePermission(file, "read"))`
`checkRead(String file, Object ctx)`	`((AccessControlContext) ctx).checkPermission(new FilePermission(file, "read"))`
`checkWrite(FileDescriptor fd)`	`AccessController.checkPermission(new RuntimePermission("writeFile Descriptor"))`

`checkWrite(String file)`	```AccessController.
checkPermission(new
FilePermission(file, "write"))```
`checkDelete(String file)`	```AccessController.
checkPermission(new
FilePermission(file, "delete"))```
`checkConnect(String host, int port)`	```if (port == -1) {
((AccessControlContext)
ctx).checkPermission(new
SocketPermission
(host,"resolve"));
}else {
((AccessControlContext)
ctx).checkPermission(new
SocketPermission(host+":"
+port,"connect"));
}```
`checkConnect(String host, int port, Object ctx)`	```if (port == -1) {
AccessController.
checkPermission(new
SocketPermission
(host,"resolve"));
}else {
AccessController.check
Permission(new
SocketPermission
(host+":"
➥ +port,"connect"));
}```
`checkListen(int port)`	```if (port == 0) {
AccessController.
checkPermission(new
SocketPermission
("localhost:1024-",
"listen"));
}else{
AccessController.
checkPermission(new
SocketPermission
("localhost:"```

TABLE 3.2 Continued

SecurityManager *Call*	AccessController *or* AccessControlContext *Call(s)*
	+port,"listen")); }
checkAccept(String host, int port)	AccessController. checkPermission(new SocketPermission (host+":"+port,"accept"))
checkMulticast(InetAddress maddr)	AccessController. checkPermission(new SocketPermission (maddr.getHostAddress(), "accept,connect"))
checkMulticast(InetAddress maddr, byte ttl)	AccessController. checkPermission(new SocketPermission(maddr. getHostAddress(), ➥ "accept,connect"))
checkPropertiesAccess()	AccessController. checkPermission(new PropertyPermission("*", "read,write"))
checkPropertyAccess(String key)	AccessController. checkPermission(new PropertyPermission (key,"read"))
checkTopLevelWindow(Object window)	AccessController. checkPermission(new AWTPermission("showWindowWithout WarningBanner"))
checkPrintJobAccess()	AccessController. checkPermission(new RuntimePermission ("queuePrintJob"))
checkSystemClipboardAccess()	AccessController. checkPermission(new AWTPermission ("accessClipboard"))

TABLE 3.2 Continued

SecurityManager *Call*	AccessController *or* AccessControlContext *Call(s)*

checkAwtEventQueueAccess()	AccessController.
	checkPermission(new
	  AWTPermission
	  ("accessEventQueue"))

checkPackageAccess(String pkg)	AccessController.
	checkPermission(new
	  RuntimePermission(
	  "accessClassInPackage." + pkg))

checkPackageDefinition(String pkg)	AccessController.
	checkPermission(new
	  RuntimePermission(
	  "defineClassInPackage." +
	  pkg));

checkSetFactory()	AccessController.
	checkPermission(new
	  RuntimePermission
	  ("setFactory"))

checkMemberAccess(Class clazz, ➥ int which)	AccessController. checkPermission(new RuntimePermission("accessDeclare dMembers"))
checkSecurityAccess(String target)	AccessController. checkPermission(new SecurityPermission (target))

By examining Table 3.2, you can also deduce how permission entries set in a security policy file will affect calls to the SecurityManager.check*XXX*() methods. For example, if the entry

`permission java.io.FilePermission "C:\\temp\\sampleFile.txt", "read";`

appears in your security policy file, the following SecurityManager call associated with the same code base will return without throwing an exception:

`(System.getSecurityManager()).checkRead("C:\\temp\\sampleFile.txt");`

Also, the following SecurityManager call associated with the same code base will throw a security access control exception:

`(System.getSecurityManager()).checkWrite("C:\\temp\\sampleFile.txt");`

Fine-Grained and Configurable Access Control Example

Given the fine-grained and flexible configuration of permissions via a security policy file and your understanding of how the access controller can provide security for your applications, the following example can be run in various modes to illustrate how simple it is to make a Java application utilizing such features:

```java
package ejava.jsecuritych3;
import java.io.FileInputStream;
import java.io.IOException;
import java.io.FileNotFoundException;
import java.security.AccessControlException;

public class CheckPermissions
{
  public static void main(String[] args)
  {
    // check whether the application has permission to read
    // properties.

    String operatingSystem = (String)System.getProperty("os.name");
    String javaVersion = (String)System.getProperty("java.version");
    try{
      String javaDirectory = (String)System.getProperty("java.home");
      String userHomeDir = (String)System.getProperty("user.home");
      String myFile = (String)System.getProperty("myFile");
      FileInputStream fin = new FileInputStream(myFile);
    }
    catch(FileNotFoundException fne){
      System.out.println("File not found Exception "+fne);
      System.exit(0);
    }
    catch(AccessControlException ace){
      System.out.println("Security Access Control Exception "+ace);
      System.exit(0);
    }
  }
}
```

The CheckPermissions.main() method first attempts to read a number of system properties and subsequently creates a file input stream associated with a file read in from the myFile system property. Files and the java.home and os.home system properties all represent valued resources that can be protected by default Java security permissions. When you run this example with no security manager (the default), it runs successfully because no security checks are performed. You simply specify an arbitrary file for which read permissions are checked using the myFile system property. To run the example without a security manager, type this:

```
java -DmyFile=D:\bookp\testfile.txt ejava.jsecuritych3.CheckPermissions
```

> **NOTE**
>
> You'll need to create or identify your own file to use with this example. This file must be specified using the `myFile` system property as shown earlier.

If you then run the program by loading a security manager, the program will throw a runtime `AccessControlException` when it attempts to read the system property `java.home`. `AccessControlException` objects are also thrown for attempted access to `os.home` and when an attempt is made to read the file. The default security manager and security policies that come equipped with a JDK distribution restrict access to such system properties. Thus, an exception is thrown when you run this:

```
java -Djava.security.manager -DmyFile=D:\bookp\testfile.txt
➥ ejava.jsecuritych3.CheckPermissions
```

Now suppose that you have defined a `checkPermissionsPolicy` file as shown here:

```
grant{
 permission java.util.PropertyPermission  "java.home" , "read";
 permission java.util.PropertyPermission  "user.home" , "read";
 permission java.util.PropertyPermission  "myFile", "read";
 permission java.io.FilePermission "${myFile}", "read";
};
```

If you now use this `checkPermissionsPolicy` file, all desired permissions will be granted, and the program can be run successfully. With `EJAVA_HOME` defined to be the root directory for your sample code, your command to test this example might look like this:

```
java -Djava.security.manager -Djava.security.policy=
➥%EJAVA_HOME%\examples\src\ejava\jsecuritych3\checkPermissionsPolicy
➥ -DmyFile=D:\bookp\testfile.txt
➥ ejava. jsecuritych3.CheckPermissions
```

Summary

Because security is an involved problem and many facets of protection must be provided, the Java application security architecture is proportionately involved. Given the security protection built into the platform, Java provides a relatively simple API to these protection mechanisms. Java-based access control is greatly simplified in Java 2 (compared to Java 1.1) by the provision of a new fine-grained and configurable policy-file–based permissions architecture.

Applet Security

Applet security is a major concern among Web users and applet developers. From a user's perspective, an exploitable applet security flaw can result in sensitive data being modified or disclosed or a computer being rendered inoperable. From a developer's perspective, strong applet security is necessary to make Web users comfortable with applets. However, too high a level of security limits an applet's capabilities.

The Java 2 security model meets both user and developer needs. It enables users to maintain high levels of security, by default, and also to relax these security controls to take advantage of additional applet capabilities that are provided by trusted developers.

In this chapter, you'll learn how to use the Java 2 security model to develop applets that extend the bounds of the applet sandbox and use previously restricted capabilities. You'll cover the issues involved with specifying an applet security policy and the use of signed applets in a more flexible security policy. You'll then investigate the use of the `jar` and `jarsigner` tools in the packaging and signing of applets in terms of JAR files. Next, you will study issues involved with signing certificates and learn how to sign applets for use with both Internet Explorer and Netscape Navigator.

Extending the Sandbox

One of the most appealing features of Java in its debut as a Web programming language was the comprehensive security built into the Java runtime environment. The Java sandbox provided a mechanism for untrusted code to be downloaded from the Web and executed in a secure manner. The sandboxes of JDK 1.0 and 1.1 had some holes, but Sun encouraged the Internet community to find those holes and then quickly fixed them. The security model implemented by the Java sandbox has been strengthened and, at the same time, made more flexible from JDK 1.0 to JDK 1.2. In addition, JDK 1.2 provides a number of security mechanisms that can be used within the sandbox. One of the most powerful security features introduced in JDK 1.2 is the capability to specify a security policy for applets and applications. This feature gives software developers a great deal of flexibility in functionality that they can incorporate into their applets and applications. At the same time, it provides users with total control over the access they allow to these programs. The configurable security policy of JDK 1.2 enables Java software developers to provide the capabilities their users want, and it enables users to limit those capabilities based on their degree of trust in the source of the Java software they execute.

The JDK 1.0 Sandbox

To understand how the configurable security policy works and why it is useful, it is helpful to trace the evolution of Java security. JDK 1.0 introduced the *sandbox* approach to applet security. In this approach, all standalone Java applications are trusted by default and are allowed unrestricted access to your system resources (file system, network, and other programs). Applets that are loaded over the network are, by default, untrusted and prevented from accessing your local file system and other programs. In addition, applets are only allowed to make network connections to the host from which they are loaded.

The objective of the JDK 1.0 sandbox was to protect users from malicious applets downloaded from the Web. As I mentioned earlier, with the exception of a few security holes (which were subsequently corrected) the JDK 1.0 sandbox met this objective. However, in blocking potentially hostile applet accesses, the 1.0 sandbox also removed useful applet capabilities.

For an example of the security provided by the JDK 1.0 sandbox, consider the applet shown in Listing 4.1 and referenced in Listing 4.2. This applet reads the file specified in an applet's fileName parameter and displays the file's contents in a TextArea object. (If a security exception occurs, it is displayed in the TextArea object instead.) When you view the applet using Microsoft Internet Explorer 5.0, you receive the security exception shown in Figure 4.1.

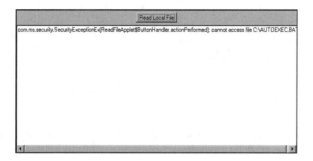

FIGURE 4.1

A security exception is thrown when an applet tries to go outside of the sandbox.

LISTING 4.1   The `ReadFileApplet`

```java
import java.applet.*;
import java.awt.*;
import java.awt.event.*;
import java.io.*;

public class ReadFileApplet extends Applet {
 TextArea text = new TextArea();
 Button goButton = new Button("Read Local File");
 Panel panel = new Panel();
 String fileName = "";
 public void init() {
  fileName = getParameter("fileName");
  setLayout(new BorderLayout());
  goButton.addActionListener(new ButtonHandler());
  panel.add(goButton);
  add("North",panel);
  add("Center",text);
 }
 class ButtonHandler implements ActionListener {
  public void actionPerformed(ActionEvent e){
   String s = e.getActionCommand();
   if("Read Local File".equals(s)){
    try {
     FileInputStream inStream = new FileInputStream(fileName);
     int inBytes = inStream.available();
     byte inBuf[] = new byte[inBytes];
     int bytesRead = inStream.read(inBuf,0,inBytes);
     text.setText(new String(inBuf));
```

LISTING 4.1   Continued

```
  }catch(Exception ex){
    text.setText (ex.toString());
  }
 }
 }
}
}
```

LISTING 4.2   The `ReadFileApplet.htm` File

```
<HTML>
<HEAD>
<TITLE>An Applet that reads local files</TITLE>
</HEAD>
<BODY>
<H1>An Applet that reads local files.</H1>
<APPLET CODE="ReadFileApplet.class" HEIGHT=300 WIDTH=600>
<PARAM NAME="fileName" VALUE="C:\AUTOEXEC.BAT">
Text displayed by browsers that are not Java-enabled.
</APPLET>
</BODY>
</HTML>
```

The JDK 1.1 Sandbox

The JDK 1.1 sandbox was designed to maintain the security of the JDK 1.0 approach while allowing certain applets to be designated as *trusted*. Trusted applets are allowed to perform accesses that exceed the bounds of the sandbox. The Security API of JDK 1.1 provides the capability to digitally sign an applet and then verify that signature before an applet is loaded and executed. This capability enables browsers to authenticate that an applet is signed by a trusted party and that it has not been modified since the time of its signature. Given this additional level of security assurance, signed applets are considered to be as trustworthy as (or even more trustworthy than) standalone application programs.

When I configure Internet Explorer 5.0 to trust my Web site (www.jaworski.com) and to allow applets from trusted hosts to access local files, I can execute the `ReadFileApplet` in Listing 4.1, and have it read and display the contents of my `AUTOEXEC.BAT` file, as shown in Figure 4.2.

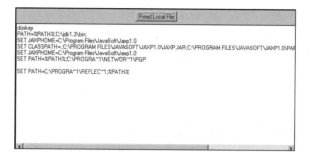

FIGURE 4.2
JDK 1.1 security allows trusted applets to go outside of the sandbox.

The JDK 1.1 security approach is a significant improvement on the JDK 1.0 approach because it enables applet designers to add useful capabilities such as reading from and writing to the local file system, launching programs, and advanced networking. The shortcomings of the JDK 1.1 sandbox stem from its bipolar approach to security—an applet is either untrusted and confined to the sandbox, or it is trusted and given unrestricted access outside the sandbox. Applications are always trusted and given unrestricted access.

The problem with the JDK 1.1 approach is that it violates the security principle of *least privilege*. This principle states that an application should be given only those privileges that it needs to carry out its function and no more. According to least privilege, trusted applets and applications should be limited in the privileges they are allowed. For example, now that Internet Explorer 5.0 is reconfigured to run the `ReadFileApplet`, it will allow all applets from `www.jaworski.com` full access to my local file system. If Internet Explorer 5.0 implemented least privilege, I would be able to select the applets from `www.jaworski.com` that would have the privilege of accessing my local files.

JDK 1.2 Least Privilege

JDK 1.2 introduces a security architecture for implementing least privilege. This architecture is based on the capability to specify a security policy that determines what accesses an applet or application is allowed based on its source and on the identities of those who have signed the applet on application code.

The security policy feature of JDK 1.2 enables you to specify the following types of policies easily and without programming:

- Grant all applets from `http://www.trusted.com/` permission to read files in the `C:\tmp` directory.

- Grant all applets (from any host) permission to listen on TCP ports greater than 1023.

4

- Grant all applets signed by Mary and Ted (hypothetical Java programmers) that are from `http://www.trusted.com` permission to read and write to files in the `C:\tmp` directory.

- Grant all applications loaded from the `C:\trusted` directory permission to set security properties.

The next section shows how to specify the details of a particular security policy.

Specifying an Applet Security Policy

Specifying a custom security policy is easy to do. All you have to do is edit the appropriate policy configuration file. JDK 1.2 provides you with a number of ways to do this:

- You can create or edit the default system policy file located at `<java.home>\lib\ security\java.policy`, where `<java.home>` identifies the location of your JDK 1.2 installation. It is specified by the value of the `java.home` system property. By default, `java.home` is `C:\jdk1.2.2\jre`. If you edit `java.policy`, the new policy will apply to all users of your JDK 1.2 installation.

- You can set the value of the `policy.java` system property to the name of an alternative security policy file.

- You can create or edit the user policy file located at `<user.home>\.java.policy`, where `<user.home>` identifies the current user's home directory. It is specified by the value of the `user.home` system property.

- You can set the value of the `java.policy` property to a different user security policy file using the `-D` command-line option. For example, suppose that you want to run the `Test` class using the `test.policy` user security policy file. You could use the `-D` option as follows:

```
java -Djava.policy="test.policy" Test
```

- You can change the class used to implement the security policy from `java.security.PolicyFile` to another class by editing the `java.security` file located at `<java.home>\lib\security\java.security`. Change the line

```
policy.provider=java.security.PolicyFile
```

to

```
policy.provider=OtherClass
```

where `OtherClass` is the fully qualified name of the class to be used.

When the Java byte code interpreter is run, it loads in the system policy followed by the user policy. If neither of these policies is available, the original sandbox policy is used.

The Contents of the Security Policy File

The policy file (system or user) consists of a series of statements, referred to as *grant entries*, that identify the permissions granted to code (applet or application) based on both the location from which it is loaded and on any signers of the code.

> **NOTE**
>
> In JDK 1.2, all code, whether it is an applet that is loaded from a remote host or an application from the local file system, is associated with a *code source*. This code source is defined by the URL from which the code is loaded and a list of signers of the code. These signers are identified by the names associated with the signers' public keys. These names are referred to as *aliases*. The aliases and keys are stored in a user's keystore, as described in Chapter 6, "Key Management and Digital Certificates."

The grant entries of the security policy identify a code source (URL and list of signers), followed by the permissions granted to that code source. The permissions (also referred to as *permission entries*) specify the actions that a code source can take with respect to a protected resource. If all this seems too abstract, hang in there. After I cover the syntax of grant entries and provide a few examples, the process of setting up a security policy will appear quite simple.

The Syntax of Grant Entries

Grant entries begin with the keyword `grant`, followed by optional `SignedBy` or `CodeBase` clauses, followed by an opening bracket (`{`), followed by a list of permission entries, followed by a closing bracket (`}`) and a semicolon. The syntax of a grant entry follows:

```
grant [SignedBy "signer_names"] [, CodeBase "URL"] {
  permission entries
};
```

The `SignedBy` clause contains a comma-separated list of the aliases of the signers of the code to which the grant entry applies. If the code has not been signed or the signers don't factor into the policy, the `SignedBy` clause can be omitted. Examples of `SignedBy` clauses follow:

```
SignedBy "Bill"
SignedBy "Bill,Ted"
SignedBy "Bill,Ted,Alice"
```

The aliases are not case sensitive. For example, `"Bill"` and `"bill"` are equivalent.

The `CodeBase` clause identifies the URL of the location from which the code is loaded.

Examples follow:

```
CodeBase "http://www.trusted.com"
CodeBase "http://www.trusted.com/omega/version5/"
CodeBase "file:/local/applets/"
```

The first example specifies that the grant entry applies to all code that is loaded from www.trusted.com. The second example specifies that the grant entry applies to all code that is loaded from /omega/version5/ (and all subdirectories) of www.trusted.com. The third example specifies that the grant entry applies to all code that is loaded from the \local\applets directory (and all subdirectories) of the local file system.

If the CodeBase clause is omitted, the grant entry applies to all code locations. Note that syntactically the CodeBase clause might appear before the SignedBy clause. If both clauses are present, they are separated by a comma.

Using Signed Applets

By signing an applet, an organization (or individual) can indicate that the organization has reviewed the applet for security and believes that the signed applet is free from security defects. The signature also implies that the organization takes responsibility for the applet in cases where there is a security malfunction. Signing also provides the user with a mechanism for verifying that a signed applet originates from a particular organization and has been delivered to the user without modification. For these reasons, a user can determine that he or she is able to extend a certain level of trust to an applet that is signed by a reputable organization.

An applet is signed in two steps. In the first step, the applet's class files are archived in a JAR file using the jar tool. In the second step, the jarsigner tool is used to sign the JAR file. The result is a signed JAR file that can be used to distribute the signed applet.

Appendix G, "Using the jarsigner Tool," covers the use of the jar and jarsigner tools. However, I'll provide you with a quick example of their operation in the following sections. I'll archive and sign the ReadFileApplet of Listing 4.1.

Creating the JAR file

To create a JAR file named rf.jar that contains the ReadFileApplet.class and ReadFileApplet$ButtonHandler.class files, go to the directory where these files reside and execute the following command:

```
jar -cf rf.jar *.class
```

This adds both of the .class files to the rf.jar archive. You can then verify the archive file by listing its contents:

```
jar -tf rf.jar
META-INF/
META-INF/MANIFEST.MF
ReadFileApplet$ButtonHandler.class
ReadFileApplet.class
```

The META-INF directory and MANIFEST.MF file are created by the jar tool.

To use rf.jar, you must modify ReadFileApplet.htm to include the ARCHIVE="rf.jar" attribute in the APPLET tag as shown in Listing 4.3.

LISTING 4.3   Using the ARCHIVE Attribute of the APPLET Tag

```
<HTML>
<HEAD>
<TITLE>An Applet that reads local files</TITLE>
</HEAD>
<BODY>
<H1>An Applet that reads local files.</H1>
<APPLET CODE="ReadFileApplet.class" ARCHIVE="rf.jar" HEIGHT=300 WIDTH=600>
<PARAM NAME="fileName" VALUE="C:\AUTOEXEC.BAT">
Text displayed by browsers that are not Java-enabled.
</APPLET>
</BODY>
</HTML>
```

Signing the JAR File

The rf.jar file won't be useful unless I sign it. This is easily accomplished using jarsigner. However, it requires me to generate a keystore as described in Chapter 6.

Suppose that I have a keystore named MyStore, with password MyPassword, and alias Me. I can sign rf.jar using the private key of Me as follows:

```
jarsigner -keystore MyStore -storepass MyPassword -keypass MyPassword rf.jar Me
```

The rf.jar file is updated as follows:

- A signature (.SF) file is added to the META-INF directory. The name of this signature file is the first eight characters of the alias used to sign the file. This name can be changed using the -sigFile option.

- A signature block (.DSA) file is added to the META-INF directory. The name of the signature block file is generated in the same way as the signature file.

The signature file identifies each file in the JAR file, the digest algorithm used in the signing process, and a digest value. The digest value is the digest computed from the file's entry in the manifest file.

The signature block file contains the signature of the signature file and a certificate that authenticates the public key corresponding to the private key used in the signature generation. The signature block file is a binary file.

> **NOTE**
>
> A JAR file may have multiple signers. Each signer signs the JAR file in succession.

Specifying a Signed Applet Policy

Now that you've signed `rf.jar`, update your policy to give the signed applet additional privileges. I edited my `jre/lib/security/java.policy` file to give files signed by me the following permission:

```
permission java.io.FilePermission "C:\\AUTOEXEC.BAT", "read";
```

When I ran `ReadFileApplet.htm` using `appletviewer` it was able to read my `AUTOEXEC.BAT` file as shown in Figure 4.3.

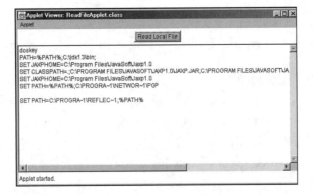

FIGURE 4.3
Reading AUTOEXEC.BAT *from an applet.*

Obtaining a Signing Certificate

In order to sign JAR files for use with Internet Explorer and Navigator, you'll have to obtain a signing certificate from a certificate authority (CA). Because of incompatibilities between Internet Explorer and Navigator, you'll need a separate certificate for each browser. If you get your certificate from a big name CA, such as Verisign (`www.verisign.com`), you can expect to pay a steep price (approximately $1000). You can save quite a bit of money by getting your certificates from lesser-known CAs, such as Thawte (`www.thawte.com`; approximately $250). Because both Internet Explorer and Navigator support Thawte certificates, a Thawte certificate is just as good as a Verisign certificate.

Working with Different Browsers

After you obtain your browser-specific signing certificates, you'll want to obtain the latest documentation on Navigator's and Internet Explorer's signing APIs. Because versions 4 and 5 of these browsers do not directly support the Java 2 API, you'll have to deal with browser-specific extensions to the JDK 1.1 API in order to make your signed applets work with these browsers. Another alternative is to use the Java plug-in, which supports Java 2 and will reduce the problems of having to deal with browser-specific APIs.

Summary

In this chapter, you looked at the security mechanisms used by the JRE from the point of view of the applet developer and learned how applet security policies can be tailored by users to allow more trusted applets to have additional privileges when they are executed in the user's browser.

Cryptographic Security

PART

II

IN THIS PART

Introduction to Cryptography

In Part 1, you learned about the foundations for Java security: the sandbox, runtime system, and security policies. In this part, you'll focus on cryptography and its applications. You'll cover secret- and public-key cryptography, message digests, digital signatures, key management, the Java Cryptography Extension (JCE), and the Secure Sockets Layer (SSL) protocol.

This chapter provides you with the background information that you need to understand Java's support for cryptographic security. It provides an introduction to cryptography and covers secret- and public-key algorithms. It also explains the basics of message digests, digital signatures, and digital certificates. When you finish this chapter, you'll have all the background information you need to understand the remaining chapters of Part 2.

A Short History of Secret Writing

The word *cryptography* is derived from the Greek words *krỳptus* (hidden) and *gráphein* (to write). Cryptography, or secret writing, has been used to protect the secrets of humankind from the time people began to write. David Kahn, in his epic book on cryptanalysis, *The Codebreakers*, identifies the use of cryptography in Egypt in 1900 BC, in Mesopotamia in 1500 BC, and in the writing of the Bible in 500 BC.

One of the most famous of the ancient practitioners of cryptography was Julius Caesar, who developed a cipher, known as the *Caesar cipher*, that is based on a fixed rotation of the letters of the alphabet. Figure 5.1 illustrates the operation of the Caesar cipher. It maps each letter of the alphabet to another letter that is a fixed number of letters (the rotation amount) away. For example, with a rotation of 1, A is mapped to B, B to C, ..., Y to Z, and Z to A. (Letters at the end of the alphabet are mapped in a circular fashion to letters at the beginning of the alphabet.) With a rotation of 13, A is mapped to N, B is mapped to O, ..., Y to L, and Z to M. We'll come back to the Caesar cipher later in this chapter and present a Java applet that shows how it works.

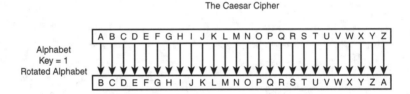

The Caesar Cipher

Alphabet
Key = 1
Rotated Alphabet

The phrase "Java Security" is enciphered as "KBWB TFDVSJUZ."

FIGURE 5.1
The Caesar cipher.

NOTE

Cipher

A *cipher* is a cryptographic algorithm that is used to convert readable text (referred to as *plaintext*) into an encoded form (referred to as *ciphertext*). For a cipher to be useful, there must be a way to convert backwards from ciphertext to the original plaintext.

NOTE

rot13

The Caesar cipher with a rotation of 13 is referred to as *rot13*.

Cryptography continued to be used in Europe, the Middle East, and North Africa through the Middle Ages. Many of the ciphers were substitution ciphers. Refer to Figure 5.2. A *substitution cipher* is a cipher in which ciphertext characters are substituted for plaintext characters. In a simple substitution cipher, a single ciphertext character is substituted for a single plaintext character. In a *polyalphabetic substitution cipher*, multiple ciphertext characters are substituted for groups of plaintext characters.

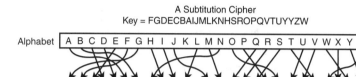

A Subtitution Cipher
Key = FGDECBAIJMLKNHSROPQVTUYYZW

The phrase "Java Security" is enciphered as "MFUF QCDTPJVZ."

FIGURE 5.2
Substitution Ciphers.

Polyalphabetic substitution ciphers were invented in the 15th century by Leon Battista Alberti. They remained popular until the 1800s, when they began to be broken. You'll see a Java program that uses a simple substitution cipher later in this chapter in the section, "A Simple Substitution Cipher."

NOTE

Cryptography and the Kama Sutra

Cryptography is the 44th and 45th of 64 yogas in the Kama Sutra of Vatsayana.

Cryptography was used by both the North and South during the Civil War and in every major war since then. The North had discovered the three main keys (Manchester Bluff, Complete Victory, and Come Retribution) and sometimes deciphered messages more quickly than the Confederate recipients.

During World War I, British cryptographers intercepted and decoded a message from the German Foreign Minister Arthur Zimmermann to the German Minister to Mexico that offered Mexico United States' land in exchange for support to Germany. The impact of the deciphered message on American public opinion resulted in the U.S. joining the war shortly thereafter.

Cryptography and cryptanalysis were essential to achieving military victories over the Japanese and Germans in World War II. The breaking of Japanese ciphers provided American commanders with detailed information on Japanese war plans that led to several important victories, such as the Battle of Midway. Polish and British cryptanalysts broke German ciphers, such as the Enigma machine. Their work resulted in the destruction of a large number of German U-boats, the sinking of the Bismark, and significant German losses in military operations, such as the invasion of Crete.

The National Security Agency (NSA) was established in 1952 as the focal point for U.S. cryptographic and cryptanalytic efforts. NSA achieved many successes during the Cold War with the Soviet Union. Some of these successes are documented at the National Cryptologic Museum Web site at `http://www.nsa.gov:8080/museum/tour.html`.

During the last 25 years, many important events have occurred in the development of cryptography:

- 1977: The U.S. Data Encryption Standard (DES) was adopted. Public key cryptography was introduced by Whitfield Diffie and Martin Hellman. (We'll cover public key encryption later in this chapter.)
- 1977: Ronald Rivest, Adi Shamir, and Len Adleman invented the RSA public key system.
- 1984: The ElGamal public key algorithm was developed by Taher ElGamal.
- 1990: The International Data Encryption Algorithm (IDEA) was proposed by Xuejia Lai and James Massey.
- 1991: The immensely popular Pretty Good Privacy (PGP) program was released to the public.
- 1993: The Secure Hash Algorithm (SHA) was adopted by the National Institute of Standards and Technology (NIST) .
- 1993: The X.509 recommendation (digital certificates) was approved by the International Telecommunication Union (ITU).
- 1994: The Digital Signature Standard (DSS) was adopted by the National Institute of Standards and Technology (NIST).
- 1995: The Secure Sockets Layer (SSL) was developed by Netscape.

Because of the enormous popularity of the Web and its use in electronic commerce, encryption technology in the form of SSL and its associated encryption algorithms has reached the average consumer. Online businesses now rely on SSL, X.509 certificates, and both public and secret key technologies to ensure the security of financial transactions, online services, and customer information.

Cryptography, Cryptanalysis, and Cryptology

Historically, cryptography has been the study of algorithms and protocols for securing messages during transmission and storage. However, there is no need to limit its application to messages. Cryptography can be used with files, serialized objects, or any sequence of bytes.

Cryptography is not limited to preserving the secrecy of encrypted data. It can also be used to support integrity, authentication, and nonrepudiation. Data integrity is a level of assurance that information has not been deliberately or inadvertently modified or replaced in transit or storage. For example, if an encrypted message is modified, it will almost always fail to be decrypted. Integrity controls, such as message digests and digital signatures, enable a person to verify that a message or file has not been modified or that a false one has not been substituted for a legitimate one.

Authentication is the process of proving one's identity. Cryptographic controls also help in this regard. For example, a person can prove his/her identity through the use of an encryption key that is uniquely associated with the identity. Closely related to authentication is nonrepudiation. *Nonrepudiation* is the capability to demonstrate that an action, such as the sending of a message, was performed by a person with a particular identity. This is usually accomplished by showing that the action involved the use of a cryptographic key that is unique to the identity.

Cryptanalysis is the study of breaking cryptographic algorithms and protocols.

NOTE

Cryptography Terms

If terms like *cryptographic key* and *digital signature* are new to you, hang in there. These terms will be explained later in this chapter.

Both cryptography and cryptanalysis are part of the larger field called *cryptology*, which is the general study of ciphers and their vulnerabilities. Refer to Figure 5.3. In this book, I focus on cryptography, but I'll identify the vulnerabilities that are exploited by cryptanalysts when it is appropriate.

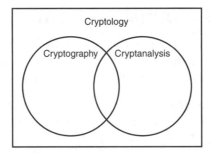

FIGURE 5.3
Cryptology = Cryptography + Crytanalysis.

Ciphers

Plaintext is converted to ciphertext using cryptographic algorithms, called *ciphers*. Although modern cryptologists rely heavily on mathematics in developing, analyzing, and breaking ciphers, you don't have to be a mathematical whiz to use them. In this section, you'll learn some simple ciphers to get a feel for how they work and how they're implemented in Java. In later sections, you'll cover more advanced algorithms and cryptographic concepts.

The Caesar Cipher

Earlier in this chapter, you were introduced to the Caesar cipher. (Figure 5.1 provides a summary of its operation.) Although this cipher is very simple (and very easy to break), it illustrates features that are common to a large class of ciphers.

NOTE

Help in Compiling and Running Programs

To be able to compile and run the sample programs in this book, you need to be able to set up the proper PATH and CLASSPATH environment variables, be able to set up the correct directory structure for a package, and be able to execute a class that is defined in a particular package. Appendix F, "Using the Keytool," shows you how to do these things.

Listing 5.1 contains the code for a CaesarCipher class, which provides static methods for encrypting and decrypting char values and String objects according to a key value. *Encryption* is the process of transforming plaintext into ciphertext, and *decryption* is the process of transforming ciphertext back to the plaintext from which it originated. Encryption and decryption are often controlled by *keys*, which are values that add variety to how plaintext is transformed into ciphertext (and vice versa). Refer to Figure 5.4.

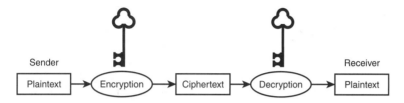

FIGURE 5.4
Encryption and decryption using keys.

LISTING 5.1   The `CaesarCipher` Class

```
package com.jaworski.security.handbook;

// Provide a static implementation of the Caesar cipher.
public class CaesarCipher {
 // Encrypt a String
 public static String encrypt(String s, int key) {
  String returnValue = "";
  for(int i=0;i<s.length();++i) {
   char c = s.charAt(i);
   c = encrypt(c,key);
   returnValue += String.valueOf(c);
  }
  return returnValue;
 }
 // Decrypt a String
 public static String decrypt(String s, int key) {
  return encrypt(s,-key);
 }
 // Encrypt a single character
 public static char encrypt(char c, int key) {
  if(c >= 'a' && c <= 'z') c=Character.toUpperCase(c);
  if(c >= 'A' && c <= 'Z') c=rotate(c,key);
  return c;
 }
 // Decrypt a single character
 public static char decrypt(char c, int key) {
  if(c<'A' || c>'Z') return c;
  else return rotate(c,-key);
 }
```

5

INTRODUCTION TO CRYPTOGRAPHY

LISTING 5.1   Continued

```
// Perform the alphabetic rotation
private static char rotate(char c, int key) {
  key = key % 26;
  int n = (c - 'A' + key) % 26;
  if(n < 0) n += 26;
  return (char) (n + 'A');
 }
}
```

In key-based cryptography, the encryption and decryption algorithms might be well known. However, the decryption key and (sometimes) the encryption key are well guarded. After plaintext is encrypted using a particular encryption key, the ciphertext that is produced can only be decrypted using the decryption key that is associated with the encryption key.

In the Caesar cipher, the key is the number of characters to rotate the alphabet. Encryption consists of selecting a letter key places to the right of the letter being sent. Decryption consists of selecting a letter that is key places to the left of the letter being decrypted.

NOTE

Caesar Cipher

The Caesar cipher organizes the alphabet in a circular fashion with the letter A following the letter Z.

The CaesarCipher class provides the static encrypt() and decrypt() methods for encrypting and decrypting char values and String objects. The private rotate() method performs the actual alphabetical rotation. Note that lowercase letters are converted to uppercase and that nonletter characters are ignored.

Listing 5.2 provides the CaesarCipherApplet class that can be used to test the CaesarCipher class. The CaesarCipherApplet class allows you to type plaintext in one text area and select an encryption key. When you click the Encrypt button, the corresponding ciphertext appears in the second text area. Refer to Figure 5.5.

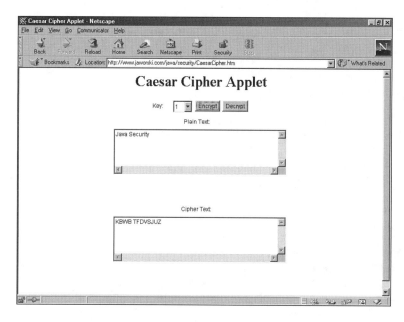

FIGURE 5.5

The CaesarCipherApplet *illustrates the use of the Caesar cipher.*

LISTING 5.2   The CaesarCipherApplet Class

```
package com.jaworski.security.handbook;

import java.awt.*;
import java.awt.event.*;
import java.applet.*;

public class CaesarCipherApplet extends Applet {
 // Declare GUI elements
 private TextArea plainText = new TextArea(5,50);
 private TextArea cipherText = new TextArea(5,50);
 private Choice keyChoice = new Choice();
 private Button encrypt = new Button("Encrypt");
 private Button decrypt = new Button("Decrypt");

 // Define key
 private int key = 0;

 public CaesarCipherApplet() {
  // Setup key choices
```

LISTING 5.2   Continued

```
for(int i=0;i<26;++i)
 keyChoice.add(""+i);
// Layout applet
layoutApplet();
// Add event handlers
keyChoice.addItemListener(new ChoiceHandler());
encrypt.addActionListener(new ButtonHandler());
decrypt.addActionListener(new ButtonHandler());
// Display applet
resize(400,400);
}
private void layoutApplet() {
 // All these panels are used so that the applet displays
 // well under Navigator and Internet Explorer.
 Panel keyPanel = new Panel();
 keyPanel.add(new Label("Key: "));
 keyPanel.add(keyChoice);
 keyPanel.add(encrypt);
 keyPanel.add(decrypt);
 Panel textPanel = new Panel();
 Panel textPanel1 = new Panel();
 Panel textPanel2 = new Panel();
 textPanel1.add(new Label("     Plain Text:     "));
 textPanel1.add(plainText);
 textPanel2.add(new Label("     Cipher Text:     "));
 textPanel2.add(cipherText);
 textPanel.setLayout(new GridLayout(2,1));
 textPanel.add(textPanel1);
 textPanel.add(textPanel2);
 setLayout(new BorderLayout());
 add("North",keyPanel);
 add("Center",textPanel);
}
 class ChoiceHandler implements ItemListener {
  // Set the key based on the selected choice.
  public void itemStateChanged(ItemEvent e) {
   key = new Integer(keyChoice.getSelectedItem()).intValue();
  }
 }
 class ButtonHandler implements ActionListener {
  // Handle the Encrypt and Decrypt buttons
  public void actionPerformed(ActionEvent e) {
   if(e.getActionCommand().equals(encrypt.getLabel()))
    cipherText.setText(CaesarCipher.encrypt(plainText.getText(),key));
```

LISTING 5.2   Continued

```
    else if(e.getActionCommand().equals(decrypt.getLabel()))
      plainText.setText(CaesarCipher.decrypt (cipherText.getText(),key));
  }
 }
}
```

The applet also supports decryption. When you enter ciphertext in the second text area, select a key and click the Decrypt button, the corresponding plaintext appears in the first text area.

You can access the `CaesarCipherApplet` on the Web at `www.samspublishing.com`. When you reach that page, click the Product Support link. On the next page, enter this book's ISBN number (0672316021) to access the page containing the code. Listing 5.3 shows the CaesarCipher.htm file that is used to run the applet.

LISTING 5.3   The CaesarCipher.htm File

```
<HTML>
<HEAD><TITLE>Caesar Cipher Applet</TITLE></HEAD>
<BODY>
<H1 ALIGN="CENTER">Caesar Cipher Applet</H1>
<P ALIGN="CENTER">
<APPLET CODE="com.jaworski.security.handbook.CaesarCipherApplet.class"
 WIDTH="400" HEIGHT="400">
[Caesar Cipher Applet]
</APPLET>
</P>
</BODY>
</HTML>
```

Cryptanalysis of the Caesar Cipher

It doesn't take a trained cryptanalyst to realize that the Caesar cipher is pretty weak. There are only 26 possible keys, one of which causes the plaintext to be mapped to itself. This brings up an important point about the size of the key space: In order for a key-based cipher to be effective, its key space must be large.

NOTE

Key Space

A cipher's *key space* is the set of all possible keys that work with that cipher.

Your next question should be, "How large is large?" The size of a key space is typically measured in terms of the number of bits in the key. An n-bit key space has 2^n different keys. For a 32-bit key this amounts to 4,294,967,296 different keys. Although this might seem like a large number, it is rather small. A fast computer can search through four billion keys within a day.

The U.S. Government considers 40-bit algorithms safe to export. *Safe to export* means that it can be cracked without any difficulty. A 40-bit key space has 1,099,511,627,776 possible keys. Checking a trillion possible key values is fairly easy for a small network of fast computers.

The U.S. Data Encryption Standard (DES) uses a 56-bit key. This results in a key space of 72,057,594,037,927,936 keys. This key space is still rather small. The DES has been successfully broken and is being replaced by the Advanced Encryption Standard (AES). The AES home page is at http://csrc.nist.gov/encryption/aes/aes_home.htm.

Many other cryptographic algorithms operate with greater key sizes or even variable size keys. For example, the IDEA algorithm uses 128-bit keys; and the RC5 cipher of RSA Data Security, Inc. uses key sizes up to 2048 bits. A key size of 128 bits yields a key space greater than 3 followed by 34 zeros, which is trillions of trillions of billions. A key space of this size is effective against brute force key searches.

Cracking the Caesar Cipher

Test your skill at cryptanalysis. The following ciphertext was created using the Caesar cipher. See if you can determine what the original plaintext is

    P JHTL. P ZHD. P JVUXBLYLK.

Hint: Use the CaesarCipherApplet and try different key values until you find one that works.

A Simple Substitution Cipher

Substitution ciphers were one of the more popular types of ciphers from the Middle Ages through the 19th century. You still see them today as cryptograms in puzzle magazines. Simple substitution ciphers replace one letter of the alphabet with another. Decryption is accomplished by reversing the process. More complex substitution ciphers work with groups of letters. One group of letters is replaced by another group of letters. These types of ciphers are referred to as polyalphabetic substitution ciphers.

Even simple substitution ciphers are more complex than the Caesar cipher. If you are able to decipher one letter of ciphertext under the Caesar cipher, you can decipher any letter of the cipher text. This is not the case with the simple substitution cipher.

The key to the simple substitution cipher is the mapping of plaintext letters to the cipher text letters. This key can be expressed as a 26-letter string. For example, the key "ZXVTRPNLJHFDBACEGIKMOQSUWY" means that A is mapped to Z, B is mapped to X, C is mapped to V,…, Y is mapped to W, and Z is mapped to Y. The number of usable keys for the simple substitution cipher is 26!, which is a mathematical term meaning 26 x 25 x 24 x 23 x … 3 x 2 x 1. The value of 26! is greater than four followed by 26 zeros, which is trillions of trillions.

Listing 5.4 contains the `LetterSubstitution` class. This class encapsulates the notion of a letter mapping (shuffled alphabet) as described in the previous paragraph. The `LetterSubstitution()` constructor creates a mapping in which each character is mapped to itself. The public methods of this class are as follows:

- `getLetter()`—This method returns the plaintext letter that corresponds to a particular ciphertext letter.

- `getSubstitute()`—This method returns the ciphertext letter that corresponds to a particular plaintext letter.

- `isUpperCaseLetter()`—This method tests a character to see if it is an uppercase letter between *A* and *Z*.

- `mapTo()`—This method is used to map a particular plaintext character to a ciphertext character.

- `randomize()`—This method creates a pseudo-random mapping between plaintext and ciphertext characters. *Pseudo-random* means that it appears to be random, but is not truly random. Truly random numbers are unpredictable. The random numbers generated by the `Math.random()` method are very predictable—after you know how `Math.random()` works.

- `toString()`—This method returns a `String` representation of a `LetterSubstitution` object.

To use the `LetterSubstitution` class, create a `LetterSubstitution` object and use the `mapTo()` method to adjust the mapping of plaintext letters to ciphertext letters. To encrypt a letter, use the `getSubstitute()` method. To decrypt a letter, use the `getLetter()` method.

LISTING 5.4   The `LetterSubstitution` Class

```
package com.jaworski.security.handbook;

// Encapsulate the concept of a shuffled alphabet.
public class LetterSubstitution {
 public static final int NUM_LETTERS = 26;
 // Maps (0 - 26) to the indices of the substituted letters.
```

LISTING 5.4 Continued

```
// E.g., substitution[3] = 10 means that d (3) maps to k (10).
protected int[] substitution = new int[NUM_LETTERS];

public LetterSubstitution() {
 // Set the default (no change) substitution.
 for(int i=0;i<NUM_LETTERS;++i) {
  substitution[i] = i;
 }
}


// Retrieve the letter which is mapped to c.
public char getLetter(char c) {
 c = Character.toUpperCase(c);
 if(isUpperCaseLetter(c)) {
  for(int i=0;i<NUM_LETTERS;++i) {
   if(substitution[i] == (c - 'A'))
    return (char) (i+'A');
  }
 }
 return c;
}


// Find the letter that is substituted for c.
public char getSubstitute(char c) {
 c = Character.toUpperCase(c);
 if(isUpperCaseLetter(c)) {
  c = (char) (substitution[c-'A'] + 'A');
 }
 return c;
}


// Is the character A-Z?
public static boolean isUpperCaseLetter(char c) {
 if(c >= 'A' && c <= 'Z') return true;
 return false;
}


// Substitute c2 for c1.
public void mapTo(char c1, char c2) {
 c1=Character.toUpperCase(c1);
 c2=Character.toUpperCase(c2);
 if(isUpperCaseLetter(c1) && isUpperCaseLetter(c2)) {
  substitution[c1-'A'] = c2 - 'A';
 }
```

LISTING 5.4   Continued

```
    }

    // Come up with a pseudo-random substitution.
    public void randomize() {
     boolean[] used = new boolean[NUM_LETTERS];
     for(int i=0;i<NUM_LETTERS;++i) {
      int n = ((int) (NUM_LETTERS*1000*Math.random())) % NUM_LETTERS;
      while (used[n]) {
       n = (n + 1) % NUM_LETTERS;
      };
      substitution[i] = n;
      used[i] = true;
     }
    }

    // Allow the substitution to be displayed.
    public String toString() {
     String s = "(";
     for(int i=0;i<NUM_LETTERS;++i) {
      s += substitution[i];
      if(i!=NUM_LETTERS-1) s+=",";
     }
     s += ")";
     return s;
    }
}
```

Listing 5.5 shows the LetterCipher class, which is a simple substitution cipher that uses a
LetterSubstitution object as a key. It provides static encrypt() and decrypt() methods
that encrypt char values and String objects. You should note the similarity between this class
and the CaesarCipher class of Listing 5.1.

LISTING 5.5   The LetterCipher Class

```
package com.jaworski.security.handbook;

// Support encryption using a LetterSubstitution object.
public class LetterCipher {
 // Encrypt a String object.
 public static String encrypt(String s, LetterSubstitution k) {
  String returnValue = "";
  for(int i=0;i<s.length();++i) {
   char c = s.charAt(i);
```

LISTING 5.5 Continued

```
   c = encrypt(c,k);
   returnValue += String.valueOf(c);
  }
  return returnValue;
 }
 // Decrypt a String object.
 public static String decrypt(String s, LetterSubstitution k) {
  String returnValue = "";
  for(int i=0;i<s.length();++i) {
   char c = s.charAt(i);
   c = decrypt(c,k);
   returnValue += String.valueOf(c);
  }
  return returnValue;
 }
 // Encrypt a single character.
 public static char encrypt(char c, LetterSubstitution k) {
  return k.getSubstitute(c);
 }
 // Decrypt a single character.
 public static char decrypt(char c, LetterSubstitution k) {
  return k.getLetter(c);
 }
}
```

Listing 5.6 presents the LetterCipherApplet class, which is used to test out the LetterCipher class. It presents a GUI that is similar to the CaesarCipherApplet. You can access the applet online at www.samspublishing.com or by using the LetterCipher.htm file that is shown in Listing 5.7.

LISTING 5.6   The LetterCipherApplet Class

```
package com.jaworski.security.handbook;

import java.awt.*;
import java.awt.event.*;
import java.applet.*;

public class LetterCipherApplet extends Applet {
 // Define key
 private LetterSubstitution key = new LetterSubstitution();

 // Declare GUI elements
```

LISTING 5.6 Continued

```java
private TextArea plainText = new TextArea(5,50);
private TextArea cipherText = new TextArea(5,50);
private Button keyButton = new Button("Select Key");
private Button encrypt = new Button("Encrypt");
private Button decrypt = new Button("Decrypt");
private KeyDialog keyDialog = new KeyDialog();

public LetterCipherApplet() {
 // Layout applet
 layoutApplet();
 // Add event handlers
 keyButton.addActionListener(new ButtonHandler());
 encrypt.addActionListener(new ButtonHandler());
 decrypt.addActionListener(new ButtonHandler());
 // Display applet
 resize(400,400);
}
private void layoutApplet() {
 // All these panels are used so that the applet displays
 // well under Navigator and Internet Explorer.
 Panel keyPanel = new Panel();
 keyPanel.add(keyButton);
 keyPanel.add(encrypt);
 keyPanel.add(decrypt);
 Panel textPanel = new Panel();
 Panel textPanel1 = new Panel();
 Panel textPanel2 = new Panel();
 textPanel1.add(new Label("     Plain Text:     "));
 textPanel1.add(plainText);
 textPanel2.add(new Label("     Cipher Text:     "));
 textPanel2.add(cipherText);
 textPanel.setLayout(new GridLayout(2,1));
 textPanel.add(textPanel1);
 textPanel.add(textPanel2);
 setLayout(new BorderLayout());
 add("North",keyPanel);
 add("Center",textPanel);
}
 class ButtonHandler implements ActionListener {
 // Handle the Encrypt and Decrypt buttons
 public void actionPerformed(ActionEvent e) {
  if(e.getActionCommand().equals(encrypt.getLabel()))
   cipherText.setText(LetterCipher.encrypt(plainText.getText(),key));
  else if(e.getActionCommand().equals(decrypt.getLabel()))
```

LISTING 5.6   Continued

```
    plainText.setText(LetterCipher.decrypt(cipherText.getText(),key));
   else if(e.getActionCommand().equals(keyButton.getLabel()))
    keyDialog.setVisible(true);
  }
}
class KeyDialog extends Frame {
 // GUI controls
 private Button ok = new Button("OK");
 private Button cancel = new Button("Cancel");
 private Label[] labels = new Label[NUM_LETTERS];
 private Choice[] choices = new Choice[NUM_LETTERS];

 // Defined for convenience
 private static final int NUM_LETTERS = 26;
 private final String[] alphabet =
  {"A","B","C","D","E","F","G","H","I","J","K","L","M",
   "N","O","P","Q","R","S","T","U","V","W","X","Y","Z"};

 KeyDialog() {
  setTitle("Key Dialog");
  setup();
  pack();
  setBounds(50,50,400,400);
 }
 private void setup() {
  // Create and initialize labels
  for(int i=0;i<labels.length;++i)
   labels[i] = new Label(alphabet[i]+": ");
  // Create and initialize choices
  for(int i=0;i<choices.length;++i) {
   choices[i] = new Choice();
   for(int j=0;j<alphabet.length;++j)
    choices[i].add(alphabet[j]);
   choices[i].select(i);
  }
  // Layout GUI
  Panel northPanel = new Panel();
  northPanel.add(ok);
  northPanel.add(cancel);
  Panel centerPanel = new Panel();
  centerPanel.setLayout(new GridLayout(13,7));
  for(int i=0;i<13;++i) {
   centerPanel.add(labels[i]);
   centerPanel.add(choices[i]);
```

LISTING 5.6 Continued

```
    centerPanel.add(new Label("      "));
    centerPanel.add(new Label("      "));
    centerPanel.add(new Label("      "));
    centerPanel.add(labels[i+13]);
    centerPanel.add(choices[i+13]);
   }
   add("North",northPanel);
   add("Center",centerPanel);
   // Add event handlers
   ok.addActionListener(new ActionListener() {
    public void actionPerformed(ActionEvent e) {
     for(int i=0;i<alphabet.length;++i)
      key.mapTo(alphabet[i].charAt(0),
       choices[i].getSelectedItem().charAt(0));
     keyDialog.setVisible(false);
    }
   });
   cancel.addActionListener(new ActionListener() {
    public void actionPerformed(ActionEvent e) {
     keyDialog. setVisible(false);
    }
   });
  }
 }
}
```

LISTING 5.7 The LetterCipher.htm File

```
<HTML>
<HEAD><TITLE>Letter Substitution Cipher Applet</TITLE></HEAD>
<BODY>
<H1 ALIGN="CENTER">Letter Substitution Cipher Applet</H1>
<P ALIGN="CENTER">
<APPLET CODE="com.jaworski.security.handbook.LetterCipherApplet.class"
 WIDTH="400" HEIGHT="400">
[Letter Cipher Applet]
</APPLET>
</P>
</BODY>
</HTML>
```

Figure 5.6 shows the applet's display. If you click on the Select Key button, the window shown in Figure 5.7 is displayed. You can use this window to set up a letter subsitution mapping.

Make sure that you don't map two or more plaintext letters to the same ciphertext letter. If you do, the decryption operation won't work correctly. After you've set up your substitution mapping, click the OK button to return to the applet.

Type in a plaintext message in the text area and click the Encrypt button. The corresponding ciphertext is displayed in the second text area. You can use the Decrypt button to reverse the process. Note that lowercase letters are converted to uppercase and that nonletter characters are ignored.

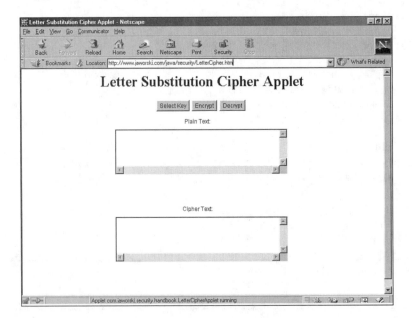

FIGURE 5.6
The LetterCipherApplet *illustrates the use of a simple substitution cipher.*

Cryptanalysis of the Simple Substitution Cipher

At first glance, you might think that the simple substitution cipher is pretty strong—especially, because its key space is greater than 4×10^{26}. However, it is vulnerable to another kind of cryptanalytic attack—one which uses the letter patterns in a particular language and the frequency with which letters occur. We'll focus on English, but the same type of analysis can be applied to other languages.

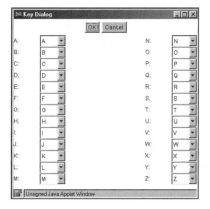

Figure 5.7

Selecting a letter substitution mapping.

In English, the letters *e* and *t* occur more frequently than other letters, such as *q* and *z*. Table 5.1 shows the relative frequency of the letters *A–Z* that can be expected in a sample of 100 letters. This table does not mean that the letter *e* will always occur 13 times. However, on average in typical English text, it will occur 13 times out of every 100 characters.

Table 5.1 Single Letter Frequencies in English

Letter	Frequency
A	8.0
B	1.5
C	3.0
D	4.0
E	13.0
F	2.0
G	1.5
H	6.0
I	6.5
J	.5
K	.5
L	3.5
M	3.0
N	7.0
O	8.0

TABLE 5.1 Continued

Letter	Frequency
P	2. 0
Q	.2
R	6.5
S	6.0
T	9.0
U	3.0
V	1.0
W	1.5
X	.5
Y	2.0
Z	.2

Similar frequency distributions can be created for digraphs (2-letter combinations), trigraphs (3-letter combinations), and n-graphs (n-letter combinations). These frequency distributions can provide a cryptanalyst with a great deal of information that can break a simple substitution cipher (and other ciphers, as well). In addition, to letter frequency distributions, the cryptanalyst can use a dictionary of words of the English language to automatically check a particular letter substitution mapping. For example, the single-letter words of English are *a*, and *I*. The two-letter words are shown here.

an	he	no
as	id	of
at	if	on
ax	in	or
be	is	so
by	it	to
do	me	up
go	my	we

In addition to Table 5.1 and the previous list, the cryptanalyst has other information at his disposal—such as word frequencies and the basic rules of English grammar. These are usually enough to crack simple substitution ciphers.

To illustrate this point, let's apply this knowledge to the following ciphertext:

```
QEEY NBGRAGA PJRAG ARTDUI RF KWNG GWPI TNSP, NFY
OEFAPCMPFGUI NBP DPBXPOGUI MFRFGPBPAGRFQ RF KWNG GWPI NBP.
N BPNUUI QBPNG DEPG RA GWP TEAG MFDEPGRONU EX NUU OBPNGMBPA.
ZMG RFXPBREB DEPGA NBP NZAEUMGPUI XNAORFNGRFQ. GWP KEBAP
GWPRB BWITPA NBP, GWP TEBP DROGMBPACMP GWPI UEES. GWP
TPBP XNOG EX WNLRFQ DMZURAWPY N ZEES EX APOEFY-BNGP
AEFFPGA TNSPA N TNF CMRGP RBBPARAGRZUP. WP URLPA GWP
DEPGBI WP ONFFEG KBRGP. GWP EGWPBA
KBRGP GWP DEPGBI GWNG GWPI YNBP FEG BPNURHP.
```

Let's start by calculating the letter frequencies. The 378 letters contained in the ciphertext appeared with the frequencies shown in Table 5.2.

TABLE 5.2   Letter Frequencies of the Ciphertext

Letter	Frequency
A	6.35
B	7.67
C	0.79
D	2.38
E	6.61
F	5.29
G	11.90
H	0.26
I	3.17
J	0.26
K	1.32
L	0.53
M	2.65
N	7.67
O	2.38
P	15.61
Q	1.32
R	6.61
S	1.06
T	2.12
U	3.97
V	0.00
W	5.56
X	1.85
Y	1.32
Z	1. 32

Table 5.2 shows that *P* is the most frequent letter followed by *G*. Based on Table 5.1, these letters are likely to be *E* and *T*. Because the word *the* is a common word (and also words like *their*, *they*, *these*, *those*, and *them*), you might expect words that begin with the letters *P_G* or *G_P* to begin with *the*. Sure enough, 12 words begin with *GWP*. It's a safe guess that *T* maps to *G*, *H* to *W*, and *E* to *P*.

Now let's work on the one-letter words. There are three one-letter *N* words. Either *A* maps to *N* or *I* maps to *N*. Because the article *a* is more common than the pronoun *I*, let's map *A* to *N*.

Based on the results so far, the plaintext is as follows:

```
____  A_T_ _T_ E___T _____ __ _HAT THE_ _A_E, A__
___E_ _E_T_ A_E _E_E_T_ ____TE_E_T___ __ _HAT THE_ A_E.
A _EA___ _EAT __ET __ THE ___T ____ET_A__ A__ __EAT__E_ .
__T ___E____ __ET_ A_E A____TE__ _A___AT___ . THE ____E
THE__ _H_E_ A_E, THE ___E ___T_E__E THE_ ____. THE
_E_E _A_T __ HA____ _____HE_ A ____ __ _E_____-_ATE
____ET_ _A_E_ A _A_ ___TE ___E__T__E. HE ___E_ THE
__ET__ HE _A___T ___TE. THE _THE__
___TE THE __ET__ THAT THE_ _A_E __T _EA___E.
```

Now we're down to playing hangman. There are four words of the form *A_E* where the middle letter is the high-frequency ciphertext letter *B*. Although there are several words that are of the form *A_E*, the word *are* is of the highest frequency and also has the high-frequency letter *R*. Substituting the 29 *R*'s we get

```
____  ART_T_ E___T _____ __ _HAT THE_ _A_E, A__
___E_ _E_T__ ARE _ER_E_T__ ____TERE_T___ __ _HAT THE_ ARE.
A REA___ _REAT __ET __ THE ___T ____ET_A__ A__ _REAT_RE_ .
__T ___ER__R __ET_ ARE A_____TE__ _A___AT___ . THE __R_E
THE_R RH__E_ ARE, THE __RE ___T_RE___E THE_ ____. THE
_ERE _A_T __ HA____ _____HE_ A ____ __ _E_____-RATE
____ET_ _A_E_ A _A_ ___TE _RRE___T___E. HE ___E_ THE
__ETR_ HE _A___T _R_TE. THE _THER_
_R_TE THE __ETR_ THAT THE_ _ARE __T REA___E.
```

Now let's fill out our collection of vowels by identifying the ciphertext words that do not have a ciphertext *N* or *P* (that is, plaintext *A* or *E*) in them. These words are as follows:

```
QEEY ARTDUI RF RA TEAG EX ZMG UEES ZEES FEG
```

The ciphertext letter *E* is in six of these words, three times in the combination *EE*. Because the overall frequency of *E* is high, it is a good bet that *E* is the letter *O* (*I*, *U*, and *Y* do not appear as *II*, *UU*, and *YY*). This leaves the words *RF*, *RA*, and *ZMG*.

Eliminating the two-letter words with *E*, *T*, *H*, *E*, *A*, *R* and *O*, we have:

```
by id if in is my up
```

The high frequency of the ciphertext *R* would indicate that it is mapped from the letter *I*. Substituting *O* for *E* and *I* for *R* we get

```
_OO_ ARTI_T_ E_I_T _I____ I_ _HAT THE_ _A_E, A__
_O__E__E_T__ ARE _ER_E_T__ __I_TERE_TI__ I_ _HAT THE_ ARE.
A REA___ _REAT _OET I_ THE _O_T ___OETI_A_ O_ A__ _REAT_RE_.
__T I__ERIOR _OET_ ARE A__O_TE__ _A__I_ATI__. THE _OR_E
THEIR RH__E_ ARE, THE _ORE _I_T_RE___E THE_ _OO_. THE
_ERE _A_T O_ HA_I__ ____I_HE_ A _OO_ O_ _E_O__-RATE
_O__ET_ _A_E_ A _A_ __ITE IRRE_I_TI__E. HE _I_E_ THE
_OETR_ HE _A__OT _RITE. THE OTHER_
_RITE THE _OETR_ THAT THE_ _ARE _OT REA_I_E.
```

Now for some more hangman. The words *_RITE* and *_HAT* both begin with the same cipher-text letter *K*. You can safely guess that *W* maps to *K* because no other letter will work. You should also notice the word *_OET* and guess that *P* maps to *D*. The plaintext now looks like this:

```
_OO_ ARTI_T_ E_I_T _I_P__ I_ WHAT THE_ _A_E, A__
_O__E__E_T__ ARE PER_E_T__ __I_TERE_TI__ I_ WHAT THE_ ARE.
A REA___ _REAT POET I_ THE _O_T __POETI_A_ O_ A__ _REAT_RE_.
__T I__ERIOR POET_ ARE A__O_TE__ _A__I_ATI__. THE WOR_E
THEIR RH__E_ ARE, THE _ORE PI_T_RE___E THE_ _OO_. THE
_ERE _A_T O_ HA_I__ P___I_HE_ A _OO_ O_ _E_O__-RATE
_O__ET_ _A_E_ A _A_ __ITE IRRE_I_TI__E. HE _I_E_ THE
POETR_ HE _A__OT WRITE. THE OTHER_
WRITE THE POETR_ THAT THE_ _ARE _OT REA_I_E.
```

At this point, you have a lot of information with which to work. Using dictionary mapping, you can now find the following mappings:

- *Y* maps to *I* (from *POETR_*).

- *S* maps to *A*, *B* maps to *Z*, and *L* maps to *U*. (from *IRRE_I_TI__E*).

This leaves us with the following:

```
_OO_ ARTISTS E_IST SI_PLY I_ WHAT THEY _A_E, A__
_O_SE__E_TLY ARE PER_E_TLY __I_TERESTI__ I_ WHAT THEY ARE.
A REALLY _REAT POET IS THE _OST __POETI_AL O_ ALL _REAT_RES.
B_T I__ERIOR POETS ARE ABSOL_TELY _AS_I_ATI__. THE WORSE
THEIR RHY_ES ARE, THE _ORE PI_T_RES__E THEY LOO_. THE
_ERE _A_T O_ HA_I__ P_BLISHE_ A BOO_ O_ SE_O__-RATE
SO__ETS _A_ES A _A_ __ITE IRRESISTIBLE. HE LI_ES THE
POETRY HE _A__OT WRITE. THE OTHERS
WRITE THE POETRY THAT THEY _ARE _OT REALI_E.
```

A few more insights and we're almost done:

- *X* maps to *J* (from *E_IST*).
- *M* maps to *T* (from *SI_PLY*).
- *F* maps to *X* and *C* maps to *O* (from *PER_E_TLY*)
- *U* maps to *M* (from *B_T*).
- *Z* maps to *H* (from *REALI_E*).

This results in the following nearly completed cryptanalysis:

```
_OO_ ARTISTS EXIST SIMPLY I_ WHAT THEY MA_E, A__
CO_SE_UE_TLY ARE PERFECTLY U_I_TERESTI__ I_ WHAT THEY ARE.
A REALLY _REAT POET IS THE MOST U_POETICAL OF ALL CREATURES.
BUT I_FERIOR POETS ARE ABSOLUTELY FASCI_ATI__. THE WORSE
THEIR RHYMES ARE, THE MORE PICTURES_UE THEY LOO_. THE
MERE FACT OF HA_I__ PUBLISHE_ A BOO_ OF SECO__-RATE
SO__ETS MA_ES A MA_ _UITE IRRESISTIBLE. HE LI_ES THE
POETRY HE CA__OT WRITE. THE OTHERS
WRITE THE POETRY THAT THEY _ARE _OT REALIZE.
```

Now, we can make the following observations:

- *N* maps to *F* and *G* maps to *Q* (from *FASCI_ATI__*)
- *Q* maps to *C* (from *PICTURES_UE*)
- *D* maps to *Y* (from *SECO__-RATE*)
- *K* maps to *S* (from *LOO_*)
- *V* maps to *L* (from *LI_ES*)

The cryptanalysis yields the following quote from Oscar Wilde:

```
Good artists exist simply in what they make, and
consequently are perfectly uninteresting in what they are.
A really great poet is the most unpoetical of all creatures.
But inferior poets are absolutely fascinating. The worse
their rhymes are, the more picturesque they look. The
mere fact of having published a book of second-rate
sonnets makes a man quite irresistible. He lives the
poetry he cannot write. The others
write the poetry that they dare not realize.
```

The key used in the cipher is as follows:

```
NZOYPXQWRVSUTFEDCBAGMLKJIH
```

The key is read: *A* maps to *N*, *B* maps to *Z*, *C* maps to *O*, …, *Y* maps to *I*, and *Z* maps to *H*.

The purpose of this example is to show you how information about letter frequencies and word patterns can be used to defeat a simple substitution cipher. However, not all cryptanalysis is as easy as in this example. Cryptanalysis of more complex ciphers requires a more thorough background in mathematics and communication theory.

Secret-Key Cryptography

In some encryption algorithms, the encryption and decryption keys are the same, or the decryption key can be calculated from the encryption key within a useful time frame. These algorithms are known as *secret-key* algorithms, *private-key* algorithms, or *symmetric* algorithms. These algorithms require that the encryption key be kept secret. They also require that the sender and receiver coordinate the use of their secret keys. The Data Encryption Standard (DES) is an example of a secret-key algorithm.

The Data Encryption Standard (DES)

In 1977, the DES was adopted by the NIST as the standard encryption algorithm for protecting unclassified information within the United States. The DES held up pretty well to public cryptanalytic attacks until the mid-1990s when attacks based on differential cryptanalysis and linear cryptanalysis were identified. In 1997, the first of several successful DES attacks was announced. The Electronic Frontier Foundation (http://www.eff.org/descracker/) organized several successful DES-cracking efforts. By January 1999, the EFF was breaking DES within 24 hours.

Despite its vulnerability, DES is still in use in many applications and provides reasonable security in cases where the cost of carrying out a DES attack outweighs the value of the information being protected. For example, it would cost much more money to decrypt my DES-encrypted credit card information than could be gained (if any could be) by using that information. In addition, DES is being used in more sophisticated ways, such as in the TripleDES algorithm. These protect DES from being broken using publicly-available computing resources and cryptanalysis techniques.

NOTE

The DES Algorithm

The DES algorithm is defined in Federal Information Processing Standard (FIPS) 46-2 and is available online at http://www.itl.nist.gov/fipspubs/fip46-2.htm. Other supporting FIPS are also available from NIST, such as guidelines for using DES (http://www.itl.nist.gov/fipspubs/fip74.htm) and DES modes of operation (http://www.itl.nist.gov/fipspubs/fip81.htm).

5

INTRODUCTION TO
CRYPTOGRAPHY

DES uses a 64-bit key, 8 bits of which are used for error-correction (parity). This results in an effective key size of 56 bits. The same key is used for both encryption and decryption. DES encrypts and decrypts 64 bits (8 bytes) at a time and produces 64 bits of cipher text. The algorithm consists of a key-independent permutation on the input data, followed by a key-dependent cipher, followed by the inverse of the original permutation. A *permutation* is a mathematical operation that causes the input data to be shuffled. Figure 5.8 provides an overview of the operation of DES encryption and decryption. Consult FIPS 46-1 for the details of the actual cipher functions and FIPS 74 for guidelines on using DES.

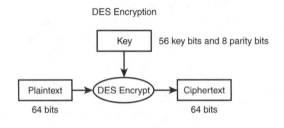

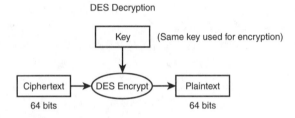

FIGURE 5.8

How DES is used for encryption and decryption.

DES Modes

The DES algorithm may be used in several modes of operation depending on its application. Four of these modes are described in FIPS 81:

- Electronic Codebook (ECB) mode—Encryption is performed in 8-byte blocks with subsequent ciphertext being independent of previous plaintext or ciphertext.

- Cipher Block Chaining (CBC) mode—Encryption is performed in 8-byte blocks with the ciphertext output of encrypting block n being combined (XORed) with the plaintext input of block $n+1$.

- Cipher Feedback (CFB) mode—Encryption is performed on a number of bits fewer than 64 bits with the ciphertext output of previous bits being combined (XORed) with the plaintext of new bits.

- Output Feedback (OFB) mode—DES is used to create a pseudo-random bit stream that is combined with plaintext via an XOR (exclusive OR) operation to produce a ciphertext stream.

In addition to the above four modes, an additional mode, known as Propagating Cipher Block Chaining (PCBC), is in popular use. PCBC differs from CBC in that both the ciphertext output of encrypting block *n* and the plaintext input of block *n* are combined with the plaintext input of block *n+1*.

The following subsections describe each of these modes and discuss their advantages and disadvantages for particular types of applications.

NOTE

DES Operating Modes

The DES operation modes are generic in nature and can be used with other ciphers, such as DESede and Blowfish.

ECB Mode and Padding

ECB mode is the most basic DES mode. Each 8-byte block of ciphertext that is produced is independent of any other ciphertext and only depends on 8 bytes of plaintext.

When less than 8 bytes of plaintext are to be encrypted (such as the last bytes of a file or message), additional bytes are added to create a 64-bit input buffer. This is known as *padding*. The problem with padding is that when a message (or other object) is decrypted, there needs to be a way to tell the original message from the padding.

To solve this problem, RSA Data Security, Inc. developed a standard, known as Public Key Cryptography Standard #5 (PKCS#5) padding. PKCS#5 padding works as follows:

- If *n* is the number of bytes that need to be added, the value of each of the added bytes is *n*.
- If no additional bytes need to be added, 8 bytes of padding are added with 8 as the value of each additional byte.

PKCS#5 padding always results in additional bytes being added as padding. When received ciphertext is decrypted, the last byte of the recovered plaintext identifies the number of padding bytes that should be removed. Figure 5.9 covers PKCS#5 padding.

PACK#5 Padding

Bytes In Last Block	Pad With
1	7 7 7 7 7 7 7
2	6 6 6 6 6 6
3	5 5 5 5 5
4	4 4 4 4
5	3 3
6	2 2
7	1
8	8 8 8 8 8 8 8 8

FIGURE 5.9
How PKCS#5 padding works.

Figure 5.10 shows how ECB mode works. The advantage of ECB is that each 8-byte block of ciphertext is independent of all others. If an error occurs in transmitted ciphertext, only 8 bytes are affected by the error. This also means that different sections of ciphertext can be decrypted independently of others. For example, if the fields of a database record are aligned on 8-byte boundaries, one field of the record can be decrypted, even if the others are still encrypted.

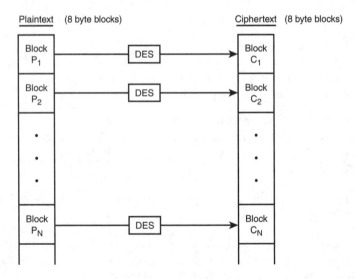

FIGURE 5.10
How ECB mode works.

ECB also has some disadvantages, most of which have to do with security. If plaintext is usually formatted (such as in a message format), the ciphertext will be dependent on the format. This might allow someone to infer information about ciphertext. For example, suppose that messages that begin with "To Mr. X" encrypt to ciphertext that begins with "XsQr+/93." An adversary may monitor your outgoing messages and be able to identify all messages to Mr. X by the ciphertext pattern "XsQr+/93." Another disadvantage of ECB is that an adversary is free to take pot shots at your ciphertext. Suppose electronic commerce transactions (such as funds transfers) are encrypted using ECB. An adversary can modify one bit of ciphertext of selected transactions hoping to change a deposit of $1 to a deposit of a larger amount.

More sophisticated attacks are also possible. For example, an adversary might simply copy the ciphertext of his $1 deposit and retransmit it a million times. This is known as a *replay attack*. He might also combine blocks from different messages to create new messages (providing that each message is encrypted with the same key).

CBC Mode

Figure 5.11 illustrates the operation of CBC mode during encryption. It works as follows:

- The first block (8 bytes) of plaintext (P_1) is XORed with an initialization vector (pseudo-random data) and then encrypted to produce the first block of ciphertext (C_1).
- Each block of ciphertext (C_n) that is produced is XORed with the next block of plaintext (P_n+1) and then encrypted to produce the next block of ciphertext (C_n+1).

When encrypting the final block, PKCS#5 padding can be performed in the same manner as in ECB mode. Other techniques can be used to produce ciphertext that is the same length as the plaintext.

Figure 5.12 shows how decryption works in CBC mode. The first block of ciphertext (C_1) is decrypted and then XORed with the initialization vector (IV) to produce the first block of plaintext (P_1). After each subsequent block of ciphertext (C_{n+1}) is decrypted, the result is XORed with the previous block of ciphertext (C_n) to produce the next block of plaintext (P_n).

NOTE

CBC Initialization Vector

The IV used in encryption must be the same IV used in decryption. This might require coordination between the sender and receiver.

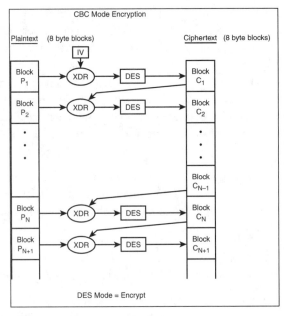

FIGURE 5.11

How CBC mode encryption works.

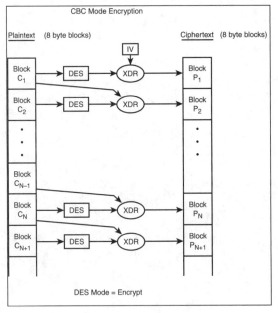

FIGURE 5.12

How CBC mode decryption works.

The advantage of CBC is that it is less vulnerable to attacks launched against ECB. By changing the IV, messages with the same plaintext format will not exhibit an analogous ciphertext format. In addition, changes to one block of ciphertext will affect subsequent blocks of ciphertext, making it more difficult for an attacker to induce smaller plaintext modifications. However, this comes at the expense of being able to independently decrypt blocks of ciphertext.

The disadvantage of CBC is that an adversary can make changes that are localized to two blocks of ciphertext (16 bytes). This is sufficient granularity for some attacks.

PCBC Mode

PCBC mode is similar to CBC mode except that after the first block of ciphertext is computed, both the plaintext (P_n) and ciphertext (C_n) of the previous block are XORed with the plaintext of the next block (P_{n+1}) before being encrypted. Decryption occurs by decrypting a ciphertext block (C_{n+1}) and then XORing the result with the ciphertext of the plaintext (P_n) and ciphertext (C_{n+1}) of the previous blocks to produce the original plaintext (P_{n+1}). Refer to Figure 5.13. Padding may be used in the same manner as it is for ECB and CBC.

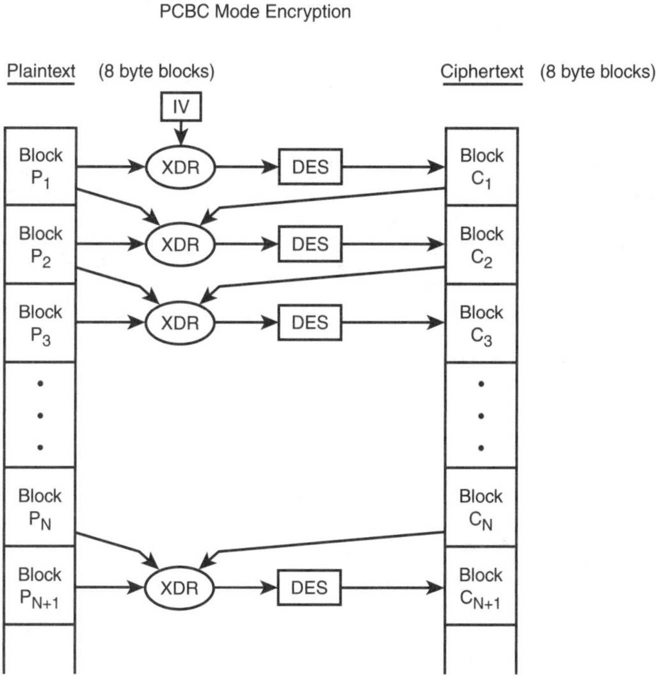

FIGURE 5.13
How PCBC mode works.

The advantage of PCBC is that an error in the ciphertext of a message causes all remaining ciphertext to be decrypted incorrectly. This prevents an adversary from making local ciphertext modifications that result in local plaintext changes.

The disadvantage of PCBC is that ciphertext cannot be decrypted in independent blocks. In order to recover the plaintext of a certain block, you must decrypt all ciphertext up to that block. Another disadvantage of PCBC is that under certain circumstances two ciphertext blocks can be swapped with the resulting plaintext errors being localized to a portion of the decrypted plaintext.

CFB Mode

CFB mode is used with applications which do not lend themselves to working with 8-byte blocks of data. Take a character terminal application, such as telnet, for example. When a user presses a keyboard key, that byte is immediately sent from the client's terminal emulation software to a remote server. The application being run on the server might not be designed to wait for 7 more bytes of terminal data to be buffered and sent.

Figure 5.14 shows the operation of CFB mode. It can be designed to work with any number of bits up to 64 bits. The most common form of CFB works with 8 bits (one byte) at a time and is known as CFB8. It works as follows:

1. An 8-byte IV is initialized to a value that is different for every plaintext stream.
2. The IV is encrypted to produce an 8-byte shift register.
3. The first 8 bits of plaintext are XORed with the leftmost 8 bits in the shift register to produce the first 8 bits of ciphertext.
4. The shift register is shifted 8 bits to the left, and the last 8 bits of ciphertext are shifted in to the rightmost 8 bits of the shift register.
5. The shift register is encrypted.
6. The next 8 bits of plaintext are XORed with the leftmost 8 bits in the shift register to produce the next 8 bits of ciphertext.
7. Steps 4 through 6 are repeated until all plaintext has been encrypted.

The previous steps allow 8 bits of plaintext to be encrypted at a time.

Decryption is accomplished as shown in Figure 5.15. I'll describe it in terms of CFB8—you can generalize the description by substituting n bits for 8 bits.

1. An 8-byte IV is initialized to the same value used for encryption and then encrypted to produce an 8-byte shift register.
2. The first 8 bits of ciphertext are XORed with the leftmost 8 bits in the shift register to produce the first 8 bits of plaintext.

3. The shift register is shifted 8 bits to the left, and the last 8 bits of ciphertext are shifted in to the rightmost 8 bits of the shift register.

4. The shift register is encrypted.

5. The next 8 bits of ciphertext are XORed with the leftmost 8 bits in the shift register to produce the next 8 bits of plaintext.

6. Steps 3 through 5 are repeated until all ciphertext has been decrypted.

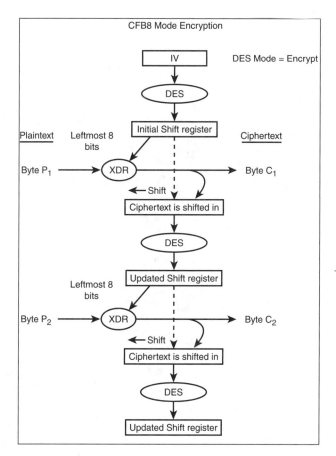

FIGURE 5.14

How CFB8 mode encryption works.

The main advantage of CFB is that it allows data to be encrypted and transmitted in units of fewer than 64 bits. In CFB8, a single bit ciphertext error results in an error to 9 bytes of the resulting plaintext. This prevents an adversary from making local changes to the ciphertext that result in local changes to the resulting plaintext. This is an advantage only if the adversary doesn't know the plaintext in advance. If the adversary knows the plaintext, he can make multiple bit changes to the ciphertext that allow the resulting plaintext to be predictably modified.

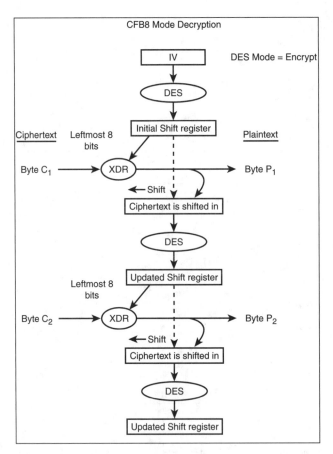

FIGURE 5.15
How CFB mode decryption works.

CFB is slower than ECB and CBC. Because an encryption operation is required every *n* bits instead of every 64 bits, more encryption operations take place. In CFB8, eight times as many encryptions are required than in ECB or CBC.

OFB Mode

OFB is similar to CFB except that the ciphertext is not fed back into the shift register. Instead, the output of the shift register is fed back into itself. (The number of bits that are fed back after each encryption is known as the *feedback size*.) This means that neither the plaintext nor the ciphertext is ever encrypted. The ciphertext is produced by simply XORing the plaintext with the output of the shift register, as shown in Figure 5.16. Because the output of the shift register does not depend on the plaintext, it can be computed in advance.

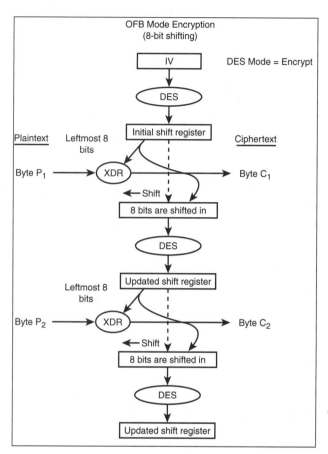

FIGURE 5.16

How OFB mode works.

The four modes discussed in the previous sections (ECB, CBC, PCBC, and CFB) are examples of *block ciphers*—that is they are designed to encrypt blocks of text. OFB is an example of a *stream cipher*—it is used to encrypt a stream of bits. Any number of bits can be encrypted at one time by XORing the plaintext bits with the shift register output.

NOTE

Keystream

A *keystream* is a bit stream that is generated from a keyed cipher and XORed with plaintext to produce ciphertext.

5

INTRODUCTION TO
CRYPTOGRAPHY

The other advantages of OFB are mixed. A single error in the ciphertext only results in a single bit error in the recovered plaintext. This is an advantage in streaming audio and video where errors have a minimal impact on the decrypted media stream. However, it is a disadvantage in text message transmission where an adversary can make local ciphertext changes that result in local changes to the recovered plaintext.

OFB has problems with key reuse. If the same key is used more than once, an adversary can recover the output of the shift register and use that to determine the plaintext that is transmitted. The solution to this vulnerability is to never use the same key more than once. OFB is also vulnerable to periodicity in the output produced from the shift register. For a 64-bit shift register, this can vary from 2^{32} bits to $2^{64}-1$, depending on the feedback size. The solution to this vulnerability is to use the same feedback size as the shift register size (64 bits) and to change the key as often as is practical.

Which Mode Should I Use?

Having covered ECB, CBC, PCBC, CFB, and OFB, you might wonder which encryption mode is the appropriate one for each type of application. Figure 5.17 provides a decision tree that you can use to select an encryption mode.

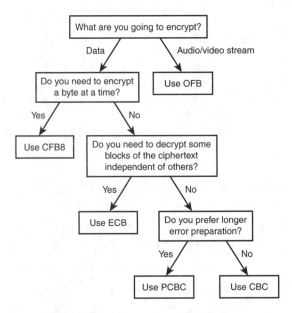

FIGURE 5.17

Selecting an encryption mode.

If your application uses encryption to protect streaming audio or video transmissions, OFB is probably the best choice. It will prevent the stream from disclosure and, at the same time, minimize the impact of any transmission errors that occur in the ciphertext.

If you need to encrypt blocks of data that contain fewer than 64 bits, such as those in remote terminal applications, CFB is a good choice. CFB8 provides support for byte-level encryption, but it also provides more protection against adversary modification than does OFB.

If you need to be able to decrypt independent blocks of the ciphertext, such as fields within a database record, ECB is your best bet. However, this convenience is offset by the fact that an adversary might modify the ciphertext of each block to create errors in specific parts of the plaintext.

For all other cases, you can use CBC or PCBC. In PCBC, an error in the ciphertext causes all remaining ciphertext to be decrypted incorrectly. In CBC, error propagation is limited to 16 bytes. Depending on your application, one of these results might be more advantageous than the other. CBC is used much more than CBC because it is covered by FIPS 81, and PCBC is not.

A DES Example

You've covered quite a bit of information about DES and its operating modes. It's time to break things up a bit with a Java example. Listings 5.8 and 5.9 provide a simple example of a Java program that uses DES. To compile and run the program, you'll need to download and install the Java Cryptography Extension (JCE). JCE is a standard extension API that supports DES and other cryptographic algorithms. It is available from Sun for download to users in the United States and Canada. You can get it at `http://java.sun.com/products/jce/`. Appendix E, "Downloading and Installing the Cryptix JCE 1.2," provides instructions on installing the JCE.

If you are not capable of downloading the JCE in the United States or Canada, you can obtain a free clean room copy of the JCE from Cryptix at `http://www.cryptix.org`.

The `DESEncryptConsoleApp` program of Listing 5.8 encrypts a plaintext file and creates a new file that holds the ciphertext. When you run the program, it looks for a file named DESKey.ser in the directory from which the program is run. The DESKey.ser file contains the secret DES key that is used in the file encryption. If the program doesn't find the file, it will generate a new secret DES key, create a new file named DESKey.ser, and store the key in the file.

For example, you can use the program to encrypt the DESEncryptConsoleApp.java file and store it in the file temp.bin as follows:

```
java com.jaworski.security.handbook.DESEncryptConsoleApp ➡
DESEncryptConsoleApp.java temp.bin
```

The file temp.bin contains binary data that is the ciphertext for DESEncryptConsoleApp.java. To decrypt it, use the `DESDecryptConsoleApp` program of Listing 5.8. This program uses the DESKey.ser file that was generated by `DESEncryptConsoleApp` to perform the decryption. You use it as follows:

```
java com.jaworski.security.handbook.DESDecryptConsoleApp temp.bin temp.txt
```

The plaintext corresponding to the ciphertext of temp.bin is stored in the file temp.txt. Open temp.txt with a text editor to verify that the decryption process worked correctly.

There are a few items about the coding of DESEncryptConsoleApp that you should be aware of:

- The javax.crypto package is imported.
- The SecretKey interface is used to encapsulate a DES key.
- A SecretKey object is generated by the KeyGenerator class by passing the algorithm name (DES) to the static getInstance() method.
- A Cipher object is created by passing the cipher parameters (DES/ECB/PKCS5Padding) to the static getInstance() method of the Cipher class.
- The Cipher object is initialized by invoking its init() method and specifying the encryption mode (ENCRYPT_MODE or DECRYPT_MODE) and the SecretKey object.
- A CipherOutputStream object is used to perform the encryption and write the ciphertext to an output stream. The CipherOutputStream() constructor takes the name of the output stream and the Cipher object as its arguments.

The DESDecryptConsoleApp program is similar to the DESEncryptConsoleApp program. However, it has the following important differences:

- It does not generate any keys. The SecretKey object is read from the DESKey.ser file.
- The Cipher object is initialized to DECRYPT_MODE.
- A CipherInputStream object is used to read and decrypt the input file.

You'll learn the details of how these classes and interfaces work in Chapter 8, "The Java Cryptography Extension."

LISTING 5.8 The DESEncryptConsoleApp Program

```
package com.jaworski.security.handbook;

import java.io.*;
import java.security.*;
import javax.crypto.*;

public class DESEncryptConsoleApp {
 public static void main(String[] args) {
  String help = "Usage: java com.jaworski.security.handbook.";
  help += "DESEncryptConsoleApp plaintextfile ciphertextfile";
  if(args.length != 2) System.out.println(help);
  else desEncrypt(args[0],args[1]);
 }
 public static void desEncrypt(String f1, String f2) {
```

LISTING 5.8 Continued

```java
// Generate a key
SecretKey key = null;
try {
 // Does a DESKey.ser file exist?
 ObjectInputStream keyFile = new ObjectInputStream(
  new FileInputStream("DESKey.ser"));
 key = (SecretKey) keyFile.readObject();
 keyFile.close();
}catch(FileNotFoundException e) {
 // If not, generate and save a new key.
 try {
  KeyGenerator keygen = KeyGenerator.getInstance("DES");
  key = keygen.generateKey();
  ObjectOutputStream keyFile = new ObjectOutputStream(
   new FileOutputStream("DESKey.ser"));
  keyFile.writeObject(key);
  keyFile.close();
 }catch(NoSuchAlgorithmException ex) {
  System.out.println("DES key generator not found.");
  System.exit(0);
 }catch(IOException ex) {
  System.out.println("Error saving key.");
  System.exit(0);
 }
}catch(Exception e) {
  System.out.println("Error reading key.");
  System.exit(0);
}
// Create a cipher
Cipher cipher = null;
try {
 cipher = Cipher.getInstance("DES/ECB/PKCS5Padding");
 cipher.init(Cipher.ENCRYPT_MODE,key);
}catch(InvalidKeyException e) {
 System.out.println("Key is invalid.");
 System.exit(0);
}catch(Exception e) {
 System.out.println("Error creating cipher.");
 System.exit(0);
}
// Read and encrypt file.
try {
 BufferedInputStream in = new BufferedInputStream(
  new FileInputStream(f1));
```

LISTING 5.8   Continued

```java
CipherOutputStream out = new CipherOutputStream(
 new BufferedOutputStream(new FileOutputStream(f2)),
 cipher);
// Read the file and encrypt
int i;
do {
 i = in.read();
 if(i != -1) out.write(i);
} while(i != -1);
 in.close();
 out.close();
}catch(IOException e) {
 System.out.println("Error reading/encrypting.");
 }
 }
}
```

LISTING 5.9   The DESDecryptConsoleApp Program

```java
package com.jaworski.security.handbook;

import java.io.*;
import java.security.*;
import javax.crypto.*;

public class DESDecryptConsoleApp {
 public static void main(String[] args) {
  String help = "Usage: java com.jaworski.security.handbook.";
  help += "DESDecryptConsoleApp ciphertextfile plaintextfile";
  if(args.length != 2) System.out.println(help);
  else desEncrypt(args[0],args[1]);
 }
 public static void desEncrypt(String f1,String f2) {
  // Open the key file -- It must be in the current directory.
  SecretKey key = null;
  try {
   // Does a DESKey.ser file exist?
   ObjectInputStream keyFile = new ObjectInputStream(
    new FileInputStream("DESKey.ser"));
   key = (SecretKey) keyFile.readObject();
   keyFile.close();
  }catch(FileNotFoundException e) {
   // If not, report error and exit.
```

LISTING 5.9   Continued

```
  System.out.println("Key file not found.");
  System.exit(0);
 }catch(Exception e) {
  System.out.println("Error reading key.");
  System.exit(0);
 }
 // Create a cipher
 Cipher cipher = null;
 try {
  cipher = Cipher.getInstance("DES/ECB/PKCS5Padding");
  cipher.init(Cipher.DECRYPT_MODE,key);
 }catch(InvalidKeyException e) {
  System.out.println("Key is invalid.");
  System.exit(0);
 }catch(Exception e) {
  System.out.println("Error creating cipher.");
  System.exit(0);
 }
 // Read and decrypt file.
 try {
  CipherInputStream in = new CipherInputStream(
   new BufferedInputStream(new FileInputStream(f1)),
   cipher);
  BufferedOutputStream out = new BufferedOutputStream(
   new FileOutputStream(f2));
  int i;
  do {
   i = in.read();
   if(i != -1) out.write(i);
  } while(i>0);
  in.close();
  out.close();
 }catch(Exception e) {
  System.out.println(e);
  System.out.println("Error reading/decrypting.");
 }
 }
}
```

DESede

Because of the popularity of DES and its limitations that were exposed in the mid to late 1990s, cryptographers have looked for ways to improve the security of DES while still retaining the basic cipher. Variations of DES, known as DESede or Triple DES, use three itera-tions of DES as follows:

1. Plaintext is encrypted via DES using key 1 to produce ciphertext.
2. The ciphertext resulting from step 1 is DES decrypted using key 2 to produce new ciphertext. (If key 1 does not equal key 2, the decryption acts as a second encryption.)
3. The ciphertext from step 2 is DES encrypted with key 3 to produce the final ciphertext.

If the three keys are different, the effective keysize of DESede is 168 bits, which is an enor-mously larger keyspace than 56-bit DES. One variation of DESede sets key 3 equal to key 1. This results in an effective keysize of 112 bits, which is still a significant improvement over ordinary DES. Figure 5.18 summarizes how DESede uses DES.

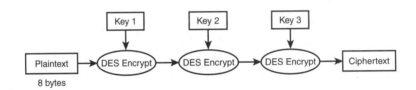

FIGURE 5.18
How DESede uses DES.

The advantage of DESede is that it provides an easy way to bolster the strength of DES, although still retaining the same basic algorithm. In addition, DESede supports the five DES modes covered in the previous sections. DESede is documented in FIPS 46-3 and is supported by the JCE 1.2.

NOTE

Advanced Encryption Standard (AES)

NIST is currently developing a long term replacement for DES, known as AES. At the time of this writing, NIST was still selecting AES from among 15 competing algo-rithms. For more information on AES, check out its Web site at
`http://csrc.nist.gov/encryption/aes/aes_home.htm`.

Blowfish

Blowfish is a secret-key cipher designed by Bruce Schneier, a leader in the field of cryptography and the author of the best-selling book *Applied Cryptography*. The algorithm is not patented, it's royalty-free, and it does not require a license.

Blowfish is a 64-bit block cipher that is intended as a plug-in replacement for DES. It outperforms DES in encryption speed and is a much stronger cipher. Its key length varies between 32 bits and 448 bits.

Because Blowfish, like DES, is a 64-bit block cipher, it can be easily used to replace DES and is compatible with the DES modes that you studied earlier in this chapter. Blowfish is supported by the JCE 1.2. Listings 5.10 and 5.11 show how easy it is to replace DES with Blowfish. These listings are equivalent to Listings 5.8 and 5.9, except that references to DES are changed to Blowfish references.

> **NOTE**
>
> **Blowfish Code**
>
> The source code to Blowfish is available for download from Bruce Schneier's Web site at http://www.counterpane.com/labs.html.

> **NOTE**
>
> **Twofish**
>
> Bruce Schneier's company, Counterpane Systems, developed Twofish, which is a candidate for the AES. Twofish is a 128-bit block, secret-key algorithm that supports key sizes of 128, 192, or 256 bits. Like Blowfish, Twofish is not patented, royalty-free, and requires no licensing.

LISTING 5.10   The BlowfishEncryptConsoleApp Program

```
package com.jaworski. security.handbook;

import java.io.*;
import java. security.*;
import javax.crypto.*;

public class BlowfishEncryptConsoleApp {
```

LISTING 5.10   Continued

```java
public static void main(String[] args) {
 String help = "Usage: java com.jaworski.security.handbook.";
 help += "BlowfishEncryptConsoleApp plaintextfile ciphertextfile";
 if(args.length != 2) System.out.println(help);
 else blowfishEncrypt(args[0],args[1]);
}
public static void blowfishEncrypt(String f1, String f2) {
 // Generate a key
 SecretKey key = null;
 try {
  // Does a BlowfishKey.ser file exist?
  ObjectInputStream keyFile = new ObjectInputStream(
   new FileInputStream("BlowfishKey.ser"));
  key = (SecretKey) keyFile.readObject();
  keyFile.close();
 }catch(FileNotFoundException e) {
  // If not, generate and save a new key.
  try {
   KeyGenerator keygen = KeyGenerator.getInstance("Blowfish");
   key = keygen.generateKey();
   ObjectOutputStream keyFile = new ObjectOutputStream(
    new FileOutputStream("BlowfishKey.ser"));
   keyFile.writeObject(key);
   keyFile.close();
  }catch(NoSuchAlgorithmException ex) {
   System.out.println("Blowfish key generator not found.");
   System.exit(0);
  }catch(IOException ex) {
   System.out.println("Error saving key.");
   System.exit(0);
  }
 }catch(Exception e) {
   System.out.println("Error reading key.");
   System.exit(0);
 }
 // Create a cipher
 Cipher cipher = null;
 try {
  cipher = Cipher.getInstance("Blowfish/ECB/PKCS5Padding");
  cipher.init(Cipher.ENCRYPT_MODE,key);
 }catch(InvalidKeyException e) {
  System.out.println("Key is invalid.");
  System.exit(0);
 }catch(Exception e) {
```

LISTING 5.10   Continued

```java
    System.out.println("Error creating cipher.");
    System.exit(0);
  }
  // Read and encrypt file.
  try {
    BufferedInputStream in = new BufferedInputStream(
     new FileInputStream(f1));
    CipherOutputStream out = new CipherOutputStream(
     new BufferedOutputStream(new FileOutputStream(f2)),
     cipher);
    // Read the file and encrypt
    int i;
    do {
     i = in.read();
     if(i != -1) out.write(i);
    } while(i != -1);
    in.close();
    out.close();
   }catch(IOException e) {
    System.out.println("Error reading/encrypting.");
   }
  }
}
```

LISTING 5.11   The `BlowfishDecryptConsoleApp` Program

```java
package com.jaworski. security.handbook;

import java.io.*;
import java.security.*;
import javax.crypto.*;

public class BlowfishDecryptConsoleApp {
 public static void main(String[] args) {
  String help = "Usage: java com.jaworski.security.handbook.";
  help += "BlowfishDecryptConsoleApp ciphertextfile plaintextfile";
  if(args.length != 2) System.out.println(help);
  else blowfishEncrypt(args[0],args[1]);
 }
 public static void blowfishEncrypt(String f1,String f2) {
  // Open the key file — It must be in the current directory.
  SecretKey key = null;
  try {
```

LISTING 5.11   Continued

```
  // Does a BlowfishKey.ser file exist?
  ObjectInputStream keyFile = new ObjectInputStream(
   new FileInputStream("BlowfishKey.ser"));
  key = (SecretKey)  keyFile.readObject();
  keyFile.close();
 }catch(FileNotFoundException e) {
  // If not, report error and exit.
  System.out.println("Key file not found.");
  System.exit(0);
 }catch(Exception e) {
  System.out.println("Error reading key.");
  System.exit(0);
 }
 // Create a cipher
 Cipher cipher = null;
 try {
  cipher = Cipher.getInstance("Blowfish/ECB/PKCS5Padding");
  cipher.init(Cipher.DECRYPT_MODE,key);
 }catch(InvalidKeyException e) {
  System.out.println("Key is invalid.");
  System.exit(0);
 }catch(Exception e) {
  System.out.println("Error creating cipher.");
  System.exit(0);
 }
 // Read and decrypt file.
 try {
  CipherInputStream in = new CipherInputStream(
   new BufferedInputStream(new FileInputStream(f1)),
   cipher);
  BufferedOutputStream out = new BufferedOutputStream(
   new FileOutputStream(f2));
  int i;
  do {
   i = in.read();
   if(i != -1) out.write(i);
  } while(i>0);
  in.close();
  out.close();
 }catch(Exception e) {
  System.out.println(e);
  System.out.println("Error reading/decrypting.");
  }
 }
}
```

Rivest Ciphers

Ronald Rivest is one of the key figures in modern cryptography. He is a co-inventor of the RSA public-key encryption algorithm, a professor at the Massachusetts Institute of Technology, and a founder of RSA Data Security, Inc. He is also the inventor of a list of ciphers that bear his name. They are RC2, RC4, RC5, and RC6. The *RC* stands for Ron's code. (RC1 and RC3 never amounted to much.) The Rivest ciphers are summarized as follows:

- RC2—A proprietary secret-key algorithm of RSA Data Security, Inc. that is a 64-bit block cipher with a variable-length key. It is significantly faster than DES. When restricted to a 40-bit key, RC2 is exportable from the U.S.

- RC4—A once-proprietary, secret-key algorithm of RSA Data Security, Inc., RC4 was posted to the Usenet in 1994. Like RC2, it uses a variable-length key. It operates in an OFB-like mode where a keystream is produced from the cipher and XORed with the plaintext to produce ciphertext. Like RC2, it is faster than DES and when confined to a 40-bit key is exportable from the U.S.

- RC5—A patented, secret-key block encryption algorithm of RSA Data Security, Inc. It can be used with a number of key sizes and block sizes.

- RC6—RSA Data Security's candidate for the AES. It is a secret-key block encryption algorithm that is based on RC5. Like RC5, it can be used with a number of key sizes and block sizes. It is intended to support 128-bit input and output blocks, as required by the AES requirements.

The JCE 1.2 does not support any of the Rivest ciphers. However, RC2 and RC4 are supported by the Cryptix package. You'll learn more about the Cryptix package in Chapter 8.

Public Key Cryptography

In the previous sections of this chapter, we delved into secret-key encryption. However, secret-key encryption is not the only way in which data can be encrypted. One of the most important cryptographic breakthroughs of the 20th century was the development of public-key encryption.

Public-key algorithms, or *asymmetric* algorithms, are based on the use of separate encryption (public) and decryption (private) keys. Public-key algorithms require that it be computationally infeasible to calculate the private key from the public key. Because of this requirement, the encryption key can be made public without affecting the security of the encryption algorithm. Figure 5.19 shows how public-key cryptography works.

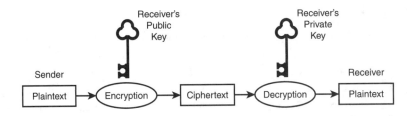

FIGURE 5.19

How public-key encryption works.

Whitfield Diffie and Martin Hellman were the first to go public with the idea of public-key cryptography in 1976. However, in 1997, the Communications–Electronics Security Group (CESG) of the United Kingdom released previously secret information that public-key cryptography was invented by James Ellis of the CESG in 1970.

The Rivest, Shamir, Adleman (RSA) Algorithm

Although public-key cryptography was introduced by Diffie and Hellman, the most famous public-key algorithm was developed by Ronald Rivest, Adi Shamir, and Len Adleman in 1977. This algorithm is known as the RSA algorithm and takes the initials of its inventors. RSA is significant because it can be used for both encryption and digital signatures. Refer to the section, "Digital Signatures," later in this chapter.

RSA's security depends on the difficulty of factoring large numbers. (A nonfactoring cryptanalysis of RSA might be possible, but nobody has found one yet.)

The following is a summary of how RSA works. A detailed explanation of the mathematics of RSA is provided in Appendix D, "The Java 2 Security API." Appendix D also contains algorithms for setting up an RSA system, encryption, decryption, and signature computation/verification.

1. Two large (100 digits or more) prime numbers p and q are generated with $n = pq$.
2. A public key e is selected as an integer such that e is relatively prime to $(p-1)(q-1)$. Two integers are relatively prime if they have no common factors.
3. The private key d is computed such that $ed \bmod ((p-1)(q-1))$ is *1*.
4. Encryption is performed on plaintext numbers m that are smaller than n by calculating $m^e \bmod n$.
5. Decryption is performed on ciphertext c by calculating $c^d \bmod n$.

Figure 5.20 provides a summary of RSA's operation. The prime numbers p and q are critical to security and should be destroyed or kept secret.

- p and q are secret prime numbers
- n = pq
- e is relatively prime to (p–1) (q–1)
- d is secret and is e⁻¹ mod ((p–1) (q–1))
- m is plaintext
- c is ciphertext

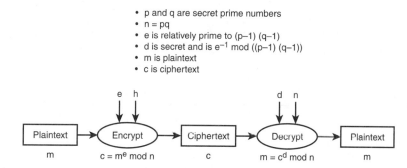

FIGURE 5.20

How RSA works.

An RSA Example

To give you a taste of how RSA works, let's use the primes 11 and 13 to yield $n = 143$. (In a real RSA application, you would choose primes that are hundreds of digits long.). We must select e such that e is relatively prime to $(p-1)(q-1) = 120$. Because the only factors of 120 are 2, 3 and 5, we can set $e = 7$. Next, we must calculate d so that $7d$ mod 120 is 1. You can do this by multiplying 7 times the digits 2, 3, 4, ... until you find a value for which $7n$ mod 120 is 1. In this case, d is 103.

We should only encrypt numbers that are less than n. We'll limit ourselves to one ASCII character (7 bits) at a time. In a real application, you would want to encrypt at least 64-bit values.

Let's take the number 74, which is the ASCII code for the letter *J*. To encrypt 74, we calculate 74^7 mod 143, which is 35. (You can do this on a scientific calculator.)

The ciphertext for the letter J is the number 35. Let's decrypt 35 by taking 35^{103} mod 143. This is too much for a typical scientific calculator, so I wrote the BigCalculation program, shown in Listing 5.12. BigCalculation uses the BigInteger class of java.Math to perform the calculations. The value of 35^{103} mod 143 is calculated to be 74, which is the original plaintext value.

LISTING 5.12   The BigCalculation Program

```
package com.jaworski.security.handbook;

import java.math.*;

public class BigCalculation {
 public static void main(String[] args) {
  BigInteger b1 = new BigInteger("35");
  BigInteger b2 = b1.pow(103);
```

LISTING 5.12 Continued

```
 BigInteger b3 = new BigInteger("143");
 BigInteger b4 = b2.mod(b3);
 System.out. println(b4);
 }
}
```

Using RSA

When using RSA, a person or organization (X) publishes his or her public key (e and n) to the world. When another person (Y) wishes to send an encrypted message to X, they break the message into blocks (m_1, m_2, ...) that are smaller than n and encrypt each block using e by calculating $m_1{}^e$ mod n, $m_2{}^e$ mod n, ..., for each message. Typical message block sizes are multiples of 64 bits. Padding is used with partial blocks. Refer to Figure 5.21.

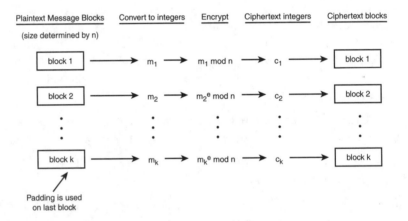

FIGURE 5.21

How RSA is used to encrypt messages.

When X receives the encrypted message blocks (c_1, c_2, ...), he decrypts the message blocks by calculating $c_1{}^d$ mod n, $c_2{}^d$ mod n, and so on. Because only X knows the value of d, no other person is able to decrypt the message sent from Y. When X wants to send a message to Y, he must obtain Y's public key and encrypt messages to Y using that key.

The advantage of public key encryption over secret key encryption is that X and Y do not need to share a key. They can publish their public keys to the world and keep their private keys only to themselves.

> **NOTE**
>
> ## RSA and JCE 1.2
>
> RSA is not supported by the JCE 1.2. However, it is supported by the Cryptix package. You can find more information about RSA in Appendix B, "The Mathematics of RSA."

RSA Performance and Security

The main disadvantage of RSA and other public-key algorithms is that they are very slow compared to secret-key algorithms. RSA is, typically, 100 to 1000 times slower than comparable implementations of DES. Because of their slowness, public-key algorithms are typically used to securely exchange secret keys for use with secret-key algorithms. Chapter 6, "Key Management and Digital Certificates," covers key-exchange protocols.

Although RSA has not been broken, an advance in mathematics can make it obsolete. Given an efficient way to factor large numbers, RSA could be easily broken. In addition, RSA and other public-key encryption algorithms are vulnerable to a number of attacks that depend on the way the algorithm is put to use. You'll learn more about these vulnerabilities in Chapter 7, "Message Digests and Digital Signatures."

The ElGamal Algorithm

Although RSA is one of the more popular public-key algorithms, there are several others, one of which is the ElGamal algorithm that was developed by Taher ElGamal in 1984. It is not patented and may be freely used.

The security of the ElGamal algorithm is based on the difficulty of calculating a discrete logarithm in a finite field. If you don't know what this means, check with Appendix B, which explains the underlying mathematics. If you don't care, read on.

Figure 5.22 summarizes the ElGamal algorithm. It works as follows:

1. Select a prime number p and two random numbers g and x that are less than p.
2. The public key consists of g, p and y, where $y = g^x \bmod p$. The private key is x. For large g, x, and p, it is difficult to calculate x knowing y, g, and p.
3. To encrypt a message block m, choose a random number k that is relatively prime to $(p-1)$ and calculate $a = g^k \bmod p$ and $b = my^k \bmod p$. The ciphertext of m is both a and b.
4. To decrypt a and b, calculate $m = (b/a^x) \bmod p$.

To see how ElGamal operates, we'll work a short example using small numbers. In a real implementation, you would want to choose p to be at least 512 bits. For our example, we'll choose $p = 131$, $g = 10$, $x = 7$, and $y = 10^7 \bmod 131 = 115$.

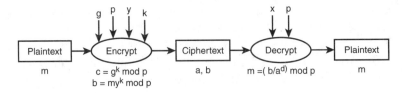

The ELGamal Algorithm
- p is prime
- g and x are random and less than p
- $y = g^x \bmod p$
- k is a random number that is uniquely generated for each encryption and relatively prime to p_{-1}
- m is plaintext
- a and b are ciphertext

FIGURE 5.22

How ElGamal works.

We'll encrypt the letter *J* (ASCII value 74) by selecting $k = 3$ (which is relatively prime to 130) and computing $a = 10^3 \bmod 131 = 83$ and $b = (74 * 115^3) \bmod 131 = 30$.

The values of *a* and *b* (83 and 30) are the ciphertext associated with 74 (J). To decrypt *a* and *b*, we calculate $m = (30/83^7) \bmod 131 = (30 * ((83^7 \bmod 131)^{-1} \bmod 131) \bmod 131) = (30 * 96^{-1} \bmod 131) \bmod 131 = (30 * 116) \bmod 131 = 74$.

NOTE

Calculating Multiplicative Inverses Modulo p

If *p* is prime, then $n^{-1} \bmod p$ is an integer *m* such that $(n*m) \bmod p = 1$. Also, $i^j \bmod p = (i^j \bmod p)^{-1} \bmod p$.

Message Digests

Cryptographic techniques are not limited to preserving the secrecy of messages, files, and other objects. They are also used to support the following:

- Integrity—To detect whether a message or object was modified or replaced

- Authentication—To verify that a message or other object actually originated from a person or organization with a particular identity

- Nonrepudiation—To prevent someone from denying that he or she sent a message or performed an operation on an object

The previous tasks are accomplished through the use of message digests and digital signatures. Message digests are covered in this section, and digital signatures are covered later in this chapter in the section, "Digital Signatures."

A message digest is a special kind of function, referred to as a *one-way* (hash) function. A one-way function is easy to calculate, but difficult to reverse. Figure 5.23 illustrates this concept. A good analogy is a paper shredder. It's easy to put a paper document in a shredder to create shredded paper. But, it is very difficult to shredded paper and recreate the original document.

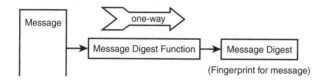

FIGURE 5.23
One-way functions are computationally difficult to reverse.

NOTE

Math Basics

If you are unfamiliar with the mathematical concept of a function, check out Appendix B.

Message digests are a special kind of one-way function. They compute values, referred to as *message digests* or *hash values*, that are used as fingerprints for messages. Good message digest functions have the following properties:

- Given a particular message digest value, it is computationally infeasible to compute a message that will produce that value under the message digest function.

- It is computationally infeasible to find two messages that yield the same message digest value under the message digest function.

Note that there is nothing secret about a message digest function—it is publicly available and uses no keys. The Message Digest 5 (MD5) and Secure Hash Algorithm 1 (SHA-1) algorithms are examples of message digest algorithms. Both of these algorithms are supported by the Java 2 Platform SDK.

MD5

MD5 is a message digest function developed by Ron Rivest. There are prior (MD1 through MD4) message digests, but MD5 is currently the most popular. (MD5 is actually an extension to MD4.) It is in the public domain and is documented in RFC 1321. MD5 operates on messages of arbitrary length and produces a 128-bit (16-byte) message digest.

Listing 5.13 provides a console program that can be used to calculate message digest values on files. It takes a filename pattern (filename with or without wild card characters) and calculates and displays the MD5 message digest for those files. For example, if you run MD5 on `MessageDigestConsoleApp.java`, you will get the following results:

```
java com.jaworski.security.handbook.MessageDigestConsoleApp
➥MessageDigestConsoleApp.java
MessageDigestConsoleApp.java: bd9ed7ba76f9f6f4dcb2e7c53b77ecce
```

If you come up with a different message digest value, your file is different from mine. Perhaps you have an extra line at the end of the file or maybe an extra space somewhere in the file. When I run `MessageDigestConsoleApp` on its .class file I get the following message digest value:

```
java com.jaworski.security.handbook.MessageDigestConsoleApp
➥MessageDigestConsoleApp.class
MessageDigestConsoleApp.class: 70102bf74c46371e2a878f82f6f8325a
```

Try running `MessageDigestConsoleApp` on some text files and then slightly modifying the files to see how the message digest changes. Also make a copy of a file and rename it to see if the message digest stays the same.

You should note the following about the coding of `MessageDigestConsoleApp`:

- It is not necessary to import `javax.crypto` or use JCE. All the classes and interfaces needed to calculate message digests are provided by the Java 2 Platform SDK (in the `java.security` classes).

- The `getInstance()` method of the `MessageDigest` class is used to create a `MessageDigest` object. The name of the message digest algorithm (MD5) is passed as an argument to `getInstance()`.

- A `DigestInputStream` object is created to read an input stream and calculate a message digest on that stream. The input stream and the `MessageDigest` object are passed as arguments to the `DigestInputStream()` constructor.

- After the stream has been read, the `getMessageDigest()` method of `DigestInputStream` is invoked to calculate the final value of the message digest.

LISTING 5.13 The `MessageDigestConsoleApp` Program

```java
package com.jaworski.security.handbook;

import java.io.*;
import java.security.*;

public class MessageDigestConsoleApp {
 private static int BUFFER_SIZE = 32*1024;
 public static void main(String[] args) {
  String help = "Usage: java com.jaworski.security.handbook.";
  help += "MessageDigestConsoleApp files";
  if(args.length == 0) {
   System.out.println(help);
   return;
  }
  for(int i=0;i<args.length;++i) {
   // Computer message digest for files identified
   // by each command line argument.
   System.out.println(args[i]+": "+md(args[i]));
  }
 }
 public static String md(String f) {
  // Compute message digest for file named by f.
  BufferedInputStream file;
  // Create an MD5 message digest
  MessageDigest md;
  DigestInputStream in;
  String digestString = "";
  try {
   // Open the file
   file = new BufferedInputStream(new FileInputStream(f));
   // Create an MD5 message digest
   md = MessageDigest.getInstance("MD5");
   // Filter the file as a DigestInputStream object
   in = new DigestInputStream(file,md);
   int i;
   byte[] buffer = new byte[BUFFER_SIZE];
   // Read the file and compute the digest
   do {
    i = in.read(buffer,0,BUFFER_SIZE);
   } while(i == BUFFER_SIZE);
   // Get the final digest and convert it to a String.
   md = in.getMessageDigest();
   in.close();
   byte[] digest = md.digest();
```

LISTING 5.13   Continued

```
    digestString = Conversion.byteArrayToHexString(digest);
  }catch (FileNotFoundException e) {
   return f+" not found.";
  }catch (NoSuchAlgorithmException e) {
    return "MD5 not supported.";
  }catch (IOException e) {
   return "Error reading from "+f+".";
  }
  // Return the final digest as a String.
  return digestString;
 }
}
```

NOTE

Conversion Class

`MessageDigestConsoleApp` makes use of the `Conversion` class that is shown in Listing 5.15.

SHA-1

SHA-1 is a message digest function that was developed by NIST. It operates on messages up to 2^{64} bits (a huge message size) and produces a 160-bit digest value. Like MD5, SHA-1 is based on MD4 and was designed to overcome some of the potential vulnerabilities in MD4. The Java 2 Platform SDK makes it easy to switch from MD5 to SHA-1. Listing 5.14 presents a SHA-1 version of the `MessageDigestConsoleApp` program. Note that it was only necessary to change references from *MD5* to *SHA-1*.

NOTE

SHA-1

SHA-1 is documented in FIPS 180-1 (`http://www.itl.nist.gov/fipspubs/fip180-1.htm`).

LISTING 5.14   The SHA1ConsoleApp Program

```java
package com.jaworski.security.handbook;

import java.io.*;
import java.security.*;

public class SHA1ConsoleApp {
 private static int BUFFER_SIZE = 32*1024;
 public static void main(String[] args) {
  String help = "Usage: java com.jaworski.security.handbook.";
  help += "SHA1ConsoleApp files";
  if(args.length == 0) {
   System.out.println(help);
   return;
  }
  for(int i=0;i<args.length;++i) {
   // Computer message digest for files identified
   // by each command line argument.
   System.out.println(args[i]+": "+md(args[i]));
  }
 }
 public static String md(String f) {
  // Compute message digest for file named by f.
  BufferedInputStream file;
  // Create an SHA-1 message digest
  MessageDigest md;
  DigestInputStream in;
  String digestString = "";
  try {
   // Open the file
   file = new BufferedInputStream(new FileInputStream(f));
   // Create an SHA-1 message digest
   md = MessageDigest.getInstance("SHA-1");
   // Filter the file as a DigestInputStream object
   in = new DigestInputStream(file,md);
   int i;
   byte[] buffer = new byte[BUFFER_SIZE];
   // Read the file and compute the digest
   do {
    i = in.read(buffer,0,BUFFER_SIZE);
   } while(i == BUFFER_SIZE);
   // Get the final digest and convert it to a String.
   md = in.getMessageDigest();
   in.close();
   byte[] digest = md.digest();
```

LISTING 5.14   Continued

```
  digestString = Conversion.byteArrayToHexString(digest);
}catch (FileNotFoundException e) {
  return f+" not found.";
}catch (NoSuchAlgorithmException e) {
   return "SHA-1 not supported.";
}catch (IOException e) {
  return "Error reading from "+f+".";
}
// Return the final digest as a String.
return digestString;
}
}
```

Base 64 Encoding

The message digest programs from the previous section make use of the Conversion class shown in Listing 5.15. This class provides methods for converting arrays of bytes to String objects that display the bytes in hexadecimal and base 64 format. Base 64 format provides an easy way to convert a binary file to printable text so that it can be displayed or included in the text of a message. It is documented in RFC 1421.

When using base 64, three binary bytes are converted to four printable characters, as follows:

- The bytes are laid out one after another to form a 24-bit sequence.
- The 24-bit sequence is organized into four 6-bit units.
- Each of the 6-bit units represents an integer value between 0 and 63.
- Four characters are selected from Table 5.4 using these four integer values.

In some cases, such as at the end of a message or file, you might only have one or two bytes to convert. In these cases, padding is used to perform the conversion. This is accomplished as follows:

- When encoding two bytes, the bytes form a 16-bit sequence. Two zero bits are added to form a 18-bit sequence. The 18-bit sequence is organized into three 6-bit values, which are used to select three characters from Table 5.4. A fourth padding character (=) is appended to these three characters.
- When encoding a single byte, the byte forms a 8-bit sequence. Four zero bits are added to form a 12-bit sequence. The 12-bit sequence is organized into two 6-bit values which are used to select two characters from Table 5.4. Two padding characters, each of which are =, are appended to the two characters from Table 5.4.

In addition to the above encoding scheme, RFC 1421 also specifies that the encoded data should be organized into lines of 64 characters with the last line of an encoding permitted to contain fewer than 64 characters.

TABLE 5.4 Base 64 Encoding

Value	Code	Value	Code	Value	Code	Value	Code
0	A	16	Q	32	g	48	w
1	B	17	R	33	h	49	x
2	C	18	S	34	i	50	y
3	D	19	T	35	j	51	z
4	E	20	U	36	k	52	0
5	F	21	V	37	l	53	1
6	G	22	W	38	m	54	2
7	H	23	X	39	n	55	3
8	I	24	Y	40	o	56	4
9	J	25	Z	41	p	57	5
10	K	26	a	42	q	58	6
11	L	27	b	43	r	59	7
12	M	28	c	44	s	60	8
13	N	29	d	45	t	61	9
14	O	30	e	46	u	62	+
15	P	31	f	47	v	63	/

Listings 5.16 and 5.17 contain the Base64EncodeConsoleApp and Base64DecodeConsoleApp programs. Base64EncodeConsoleApp takes two arguments: the name of the file to be encoded and the name of the file to which the encoded output should be written. Base64DecodeConsoleApp takes similar arguments—the name of the file to be decoded and the name of the file to which the decoded output should be written.

LISTING 5.15 The Conversion Class

```
package com.jaworski.security.handbook;

import java.util.*;

// Provides static type/format conversion methods.
public class Conversion {
```

LISTING 5.15   Continued

```java
private static String[] hexDigits = {"0","1","2","3","4","5","6","7",
  "8","9","a","b","c","d","e","f"};
// Convert a byte to a hexadecimal String
public static String byteToHexString(byte b) {
 int n = b;
 if(n < 0) n = 256 + n;
 int d1 = n / 16;
 int d2 = n % 16;
 return hexDigits[d1]+hexDigits[d2];
}
// Convert a byte array to a hexadecimal String
public static String byteArrayToHexString(byte[] b) {
 String result = "";
 for(int i=0;i<b.length;++i)
  result += byteToHexString(b[i]);
 return result;
}
// Convert a byte array to a base 64 string (see RFC 1421)
public static String byteArrayToBase64String(byte[] b, int len) {
 String s = "";
 // Organize into three byte groups and convert
 int n = len / 3;
 int m = len % 3;
 for(int i=0; i<n; ++i) {
  int j = i*3;
  s += toBase64(b[j],b[j+1],b[j+2]);
 }
 if(m == 1) s += toBase64(b[len-1]);
 else if(m==2) s += toBase64(b[len-2],b[len-1]);
 // Insert a new line every 64 characters
 String result = "";
 len = s.length();
 n = len / 64;
 m = len % 64;
 for(int i=0; i<n; ++i) {
  result += s.substring(i*64,(i+1)*64) + "\n";
 }
 if(m > 0) result += s.substring(n*64,len) + "\n";
 return result;
}
// Convert a byte array to a base 64 string (see RFC 1421)
public static String byteArrayToBase64String(byte[] b) {
 return byteArrayToBase64String(b,b.length);
}
```

LISTING 5.15   Continued

```
// Perform the base64 transformation
private static String toBase64(byte b1,  byte b2, byte b3) {
 int[] digit = new int[4];
 digit[0] = (b1 & 0xFC) >>> 2;
 digit[1] = (b1 & 0x03) << 4;
 digit[1] |= (b2 & 0xF0) >> 4;
 digit[2] = (b2 & 0x0F) << 2;
 digit[2] |= (b3 & 0xC0) >> 6;
 digit[3] = (b3 & 0x3F);
 String result = "";
 for(int i=0;i<digit.length;++i)
  result += base64Digit(digit[i]);
 return result;
}
// Perform a padded base64 transformation
private static String toBase64(byte b1, byte b2) {
 int[] digit = new int[3];
 digit[0] = (b1 & 0xFC) >>> 2;
 digit[1] = (b1 & 0x03) << 4;
 digit[1] |= (b2 & 0xF0) >> 4;
 digit[2] = (b2 & 0x0F) << 2;
 String result = "";
 for(int i=0;i<digit.length;++i)
  result += base64Digit(digit[i]);
 result += "=";
 return result;
}
// Perform a padded base64 transformation
private static String toBase64(byte b1) {
 int[] digit = new int[2];
 digit[0] = (b1 & 0xFC) >>> 2;
 digit[1] = (b1 & 0x03) << 4;
 String result = "";
 for(int i=0;i<digit.length;++i)
  result += base64Digit(digit[i]);
 result += "==";
 return result;
}
private static char base64Digit(int i) {
 if(i<26) return (char) ('A' + i);
 if(i<52) return (char) ('a' + (i - 26));
 if(i<62) return (char) ('0' + (i - 52));
 if(i == 62) return '+';
 else return '/';
```

5

INTRODUCTION TO
CRYPTOGRAPHY

LISTING 5.15   Continued

```java
}
// Convert a base 64 string to a byte array (see RFC 1421)
public static byte[] base64StringToByteArray(String s)
  throws NumberFormatException {
 String t = "";
 for(int i=0;i<s.length();++i) {
  char c = s.charAt(i);
  if(c == '\n') continue;
  else if((c>='A' && c<='Z') || (c>='a' && c<='z') ||
    (c>='0' && c<='9') || c=='+' || c=='/') t += c;
  else if(c=='=') break;
  else throw new NumberFormatException();
 }
 int len = t.length();
 int n = 3*(len/4);
 switch(len % 4) {
 case 1:
  throw new NumberFormatException();
 case 2:
  len += 2;
  n += 1;
  t += "==";
  break;
 case 3:
  ++len;
  n += 2;
  t += "=";
  break;
 }
 byte[] b = new byte[n];
 for(int i=0; i < len/4; ++i) {
  byte[] temp = base64ToBytes(t.substring(4*i,4*(i+1)));
  for(int j=0;j<temp.length;++j) {
   b[3*i+j] = temp[j];
  }
 }
 return b;
}
private static byte[] base64ToBytes(String s) {
 int len = 0;
 for(int i=0;i<s.length();++i)
  if(s.charAt(i) != '=') ++len;
 int[] digit = new int[len];
 for(int i=0;i<len;++i) {
```

LISTING 5.15 Continued

```java
  char c = s.charAt(i);
  if(c>='A' && c<='Z') digit[i] = c - 'A';
  else if(c>='a' && c<='z') digit[i] = c - 'a' + 26;
  else if(c>='0' && c<='9') digit[i] = c - '0' + 52;
  else if(c=='+') digit[i] = 62;
  else if(c=='/') digit[i] = 63;
  }
  byte[] b = new byte[len-1];
  switch(len) {
  case 4:
   b[2] = (byte) ((((digit[2]) & 0x03) << 6) | digit[3]);
  case 3:
   b[1] = (byte) ((((digit[1]) & 0x0F) << 4) | ((digit[2] & 0x3C) >>> 2));
  case 2:
   b[0] = (byte) ((digit[0] << 2) | ((digit[1] & 0x30) >>> 4));
  }
  return b;
 }
}
```

LISTING 5.16 The Base64EncodeConsoleApp Program

```java
package com.jaworski. security.handbook;

import java.io.*;
import java.security.*;

public class Base64EncodeConsoleApp {
 private static final int BUFFER_SIZE = 48;
 public static void main(String[] args) {
  String help = "Usage: java com.jaworski.security.handbook.";
  help += "Base64EncodeConsoleApp infile outfile";
  if(args.length != 2) {
   System.out.println(help);
   return;
  }
  base64Encode(args[0],args[1]);
 }
 public static void base64Encode(String f1,String f2) {
  try {
   BufferedInputStream in = new BufferedInputStream(
    new FileInputStream(f1));
   PrintWriter out = new PrintWriter(new BufferedWriter(
```

LISTING 5.16 Continued

```
  new FileWriter(f2)));
 byte[] buffer = new byte[BUFFER_SIZE];
 int i;
 do {
  i = in.read(buffer,0,BUFFER_SIZE);
  if (i == BUFFER_SIZE)
   out.print(Conversion.byteArrayToBase64String(buffer,i));
  else if(i > 0)
   out.println(Conversion.byteArrayToBase64String(buffer,i));
 } while(i == BUFFER_SIZE);
 in.close();
 out.close();
 } catch(IOException e) {
 System.out.println("I/O error.");
 }
 }
}
```

LISTING 5.17   The `Base64DecodeConsoleApp` Program

```
package com.jaworski.security. handbook;

import java.io.*;
import java.security.*;

public class Base64DecodeConsoleApp {
 public static void main(String[] args) {
  String help = "Usage: java com.jaworski.security.handbook.";
  help += "Base64DecodeConsoleApp infile outfile";
  if(args.length != 2) {
   System.out.println(help);
   return;
  }
  base64Decode(args[0],args[1]);
 }
 public static void base64Decode(String f1,String f2) {
  try {
   BufferedReader in = new BufferedReader(
    new FileReader(f1));
   BufferedOutputStream out = new BufferedOutputStream(
    new FileOutputStream(f2));
   String line;
   while((line = in.readLine()) != null) {
```

LISTING 5.17   Continued

```
    byte[] b = Conversion.base64StringToByteArray(line);
    out.write(b,0,b.length);
    }
    in.close();
    out.close();
  } catch(IOException e) {
    System.out.println("I/O error.");
  }
 }
}
```

To see how they work, use `Base64EncodeConsoleApp` to encode
`Base64EncodeConsoleApp.class` and put the output in a file named temp.txt:

```
java com.jaworski.security.handbook.Base64EncodeConsoleApp
➥Base64EncodeConsoleApp.class temp.txt
```

Listing 5.18 shows the contents of temp.txt. Now decode temp.txt to produce
`Base64EncodeConsoleApp.class` again as follows:

```
java com.jaworski.security.handbook.Base64DecodeConsoleApp temp.txt
➥Base64EncodeConsoleApp.class
```

You can verify that the decoding worked by trying to run `Base64EncodeConsoleApp` again.

LISTING 5.18   The Contents of temp.txt

```
yv66vgADAC0AYgMAAAAwCABACABFCABJBwBOBwBPBwBQBwBRBwBSBwBTBwBUBwBV
BwBWBwBXBwBYBwBZBwBaCgAOACUKAAcAJgoACAAnCgANACcKAAkAKAoACgAoCgAQ
ACgKABAAKQoABQAqCgAGACsKAAcALAoADQAsCQARAC0KAA0ALgoADAAvCgANAC8K
AAcAMAoAEAAxCgAPADIMAD4ANAwAPgA1DAA+ADYMAD4AOQwASgA4DABLADoMAEwA
OwwATQA0DABcAEcMAF0AOQwAXgA5DABfADwMAGAAMwwAYQA3AQAUKClMamF2YS9s
YW5nL1N0cmluZzsBAAMoKVYBABgoTGphdmEvaW8vSW5wdXRTdHJlYW07KVVBABMo
TGphdmEvaW8vV3JpdGVyOylWAQAmKExqYXZhL2xhbmcvT2JqZWN0OylMamF2YS9s
YW5nL1N0cmluZzsBACwoTGphdmEvbGFuZy9TdHJpbmc7KUxxqYXZhL2xhbmcvU3Ry
aW5nQnVmZmVyOwEAFShMamF2YS9sYW5nL1N0cmluZzspVgEAJyhMamF2YS9sYW5n
L1N0cmluZzttMamF2YS9sYW5nL1N0cmluZzspVgEAFyhbQkkpTGphdmEvbGFuZy9T
dHJpbmc7AQAHKFtCSUkpSQEAFihbTGphdmEvbGFuZy9TdHJpbmc7KVVBAAY8aW5p
dD4BAAtCVUZGRVJfU01aRQEAJUUhc2U2NEVuY29kZUNvbnNvbGVBcAgaW5maWx1
IG91dGZpbGUBABtCYXNlNjRFbmNvZGVDb25zb2x1QXBwLmphdmEBAARDb2R1AQAN
Q29uc3RhbnRWYWx1ZQEAAUkBAApJL08gZXJyb3IuAQAPTGluZU51bWJlclRhYmx1
AQAVTGphdmEvaW8vUHJpbnRTdHJlYW07AQAKU291cmNlRmlsZQEAK1VzYWdlOiBq
YXZhIGNvbS5qYXdvcnNraS5zZWN1cml0eS5oYW5kYm9vay4BAAZhcHBlbmQBAAxi
YXN1NjRFbmNvZGUBABdieXR1QXJyYXl1b0Jhc2U2NFN0cmluZwEABWNsb3N1AQA1
Y29tL2phd29yc2tpL3N1Y3VyaXR5L2hhbmRib29rL0Jhc2U2NEVuY29kZUNvbnNv
```

LISTING 5.18   Continued

```
bGVBcHABACljb20vamF3b3Jza2kvc2VjdXJpdHkvaGFuZGJvb2svQ29udmVyc2lv
bgEAG2phdmEvaW8vQnVmZmVyZWRJbnB1dFN0cmVhbQEAFmphdmEvaW8vQnVmZmVy
ZWRXcml0ZXIBABdqYXZhL2lvL0ZpbGVJbnB1dFN0cmVhbQEAEmphdmEvaW8vRmls
ZVdyaXRlcgEAE2phdmEvaW8vSU9FeGNlcHRpb24BABNqYXZhL2lvL1ByaW50U3Ry
ZWFtAQATamF2YS9pby9QcmludFdyaXRlcgEAEGphdmEvbGFuZy9PYmplY3QBABBq
YXZhL2xhbmcvU3RyaW5nAQAWamF2YS9sYW5nL1N0cmluZ0J1ZmZlcgEAEGphdmEv
bGFuZy9TeXN0ZW0BAARtYWluAQADb3V0AQAFcHJpbnQBAAdwcmludGxuAQAEcmVh
ZAEACHRvU3RyaW5nAQAHdmFsdWVPZgAhAAUADgAAAAEAAAAgA/AEQAAQBDAAAAAgAB
AAMAAQA+ADQAAQBCAAAAHQABAAEAAAAFKrcAErEAAAABAEYAAAAGAAEAAAAGAAkA
SwA6AAEAQgAAAOkABwAGAAAAebsAB1m7AAlZKrcAFrcAE027AA1ZuwAIWbsAClkr
twAXtwAUtwAVThAwvAg6BCwZBAMQMLYAIjYFFQUUQMKAAES0ZBBUFuAAbtgAfpwAT
FQWeAA4tGQQVBbgqAG7YAIRUFEDCf/8wstgAcLbYAHacADFeyAB4SA7YAILEAAQAA
AGwAbwALAAEARgAAAFYAFQAAABIAAAATAAQAFAAMABMAEAAVABgAFgAgABUAJwAX
AC0AGgA4ABsAPwAcAEoAGwBNAB0AUgAeAF0AHwBkACAAaAAhAGwAEgBvACIAcAAj
AHgAEQAJAFsAPQABAAEIAAABfAAMAAgAAAC8SBEy7ABBZK7gAJLcAGBICtgAZtgAj
TCq+BZ8AC7IAHiu2ACCxKgMyKgQyuAAasQAAAEARgAAAB4ABwAAAAkAAwAKABcA
CwAdAAwAJAANACUADwAuAAgAAgBIAAAAgBB
```

Digital Signatures

Message digests provide a great way to tell if a message or other object has been accidentally or deliberately altered. However, they cannot tell you whether a message or object was actually created by a particular individual or organization. That's where digital signatures come in.

A digital signature is a value that is computed from a sequence of bytes using a secret key. It indicates that the person who holds the secret key has verified that the contents of the message are correct and authentic. Digital signatures often use public-key encryption algorithms with a slight twist—a private key is used for encryption, and a public key is used for decryption. This approach is often implemented as follows.

Signature generation follows these steps:

1. A message digest is computed.
2. The message digest is encrypted using the private key of a public/private key pair, producing the message's digital signature.

Signature verification follows these steps:

1. The signature is decrypted using the public key of a public/private key pair, producing a message digest value.
2. The message digest value is compared with the message digest calculated from the original message.

3. If both digest values match, the signature is authentic. Otherwise, either the signature or the message has been tampered with.

NOTE

Message Authentication Codes

Digital signatures that are computed via secret-key cryptography are referred to as *message authentication codes* and are covered in Chapter 7.

The preceding approach to signature generation/verification has the following features of real-world signatures, as well as other features that provide additional benefits:

- Unforgeability—Because the signer uses his private key and the private key is secret, only he can sign messages with that key.

- Verifiability—Because the signer's public key is openly available, anyone with access to the message and signature can verify that the message was signed by the signer and that neither the message nor signature have been altered.

- Single use—A signature is unique to a particular message. It is computationally infeasible to use a signature with another message.

- Non-repudiation—After a signer has signed a message and the message and signature have been sent to others, the signer cannot claim that he didn't sign the message (unless the signer can prove that his private key was stolen).

- Sealing—A signed message is digitally sealed. It cannot be altered without invalidating the signature.

Figure 5.24 summarizes the mechanics of using digital signatures.

The Digital Signature Algorithm

An example of a digital signature algorithm is the National Institute of Standards and Technology's (NIST) Digital Signature Algorithm (DSA). DSA, like the ElGamal public-key algorithm, depends on the difficulty of computing discrete logarithms for its security. It makes use of the following:

- p = a prime number that is between 512 and 1024 bits in length and whose length is a multiple of 64 bits.

- q = a prime number that is a divisor of $p\text{-}1$ and is 160 bits in length.

- $g = h^{(p\text{-}1)/q} \bmod p$ where $1 < h < p\text{-}1$ and g is greater than 1.

- x = a random integer greater than 0 and less than q.
- $y = g^x \bmod p$
- k = a random integer greater than 0 and less than q. A new random value of k is generated for each signature.

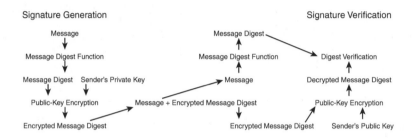

FIGURE 5.24

How digital signatures work.

The values of p, q, and g are public. The value of k is private and must be kept secret. The public key is y and the private key is x.

A signature is calculated as follows:

- A message digest value (m) of the object to be signed is calculated using SHA-1.
- The value $r = (g^k \bmod p) \bmod q$ is calculated.
- The value $s = (k^{-1}(m+xr)) \bmod q$ is calculated.

The values of r and s are the signature. (If either r or s are zero, a new value of k is generated, and a new signature is calculated.)

Signature verification is performed as follows. The values r', and s' represent the values of r, and s that are received by the verifier:

- The values of r' and s' are verified to be greater than 0 and less than q.
- The message digest m' of the received object is calculated. (The value of m' should equal m if the object has not been modified.)
- The value $w = (s')^{-1} \bmod q$.
- The value $u1 = (m'w) \bmod q$.
- The value $u2 = (r'w) \bmod q$.
- The value $v = ((g^{u1} y^{u2}) \bmod p) \bmod q$.

The signature is verified in $v = r'$. DSA is documented in FIPS 186-1 (`http://csrc.nist.gov/fips/fips1861.pdf`). FIPS 186-1 contains a mathematical proof that $v = r'$ if $m' = m$, $r' = r$, and $s' = s$. You'll see an example of using the DSA in Chapter 7.

Digital Certificates

Digital signatures provide a great way to authenticate that a message or object was created or reviewed by a particular person or organization. However, there is one catch—you need a way to determine whether the public key used by the signer is, in fact, the signer's key. That's where certificates come in.

Digital certificates are messages signed by a certification authority (CA) that certify the value of an entity's public key. A certification authority is an entity that is trusted to verify that other entities are who they claim to be and that they use a particular public key with a particular public-key encryption algorithm. To obtain a certificate from a CA, you usually have to submit documentation that proves your identity or that of your organization. For example, the certification process helps prevent unauthorized individuals from setting up business on the Web using the identity of Microsoft or Bank of America. Figure 5.25 illustrates the use of digital certificates.

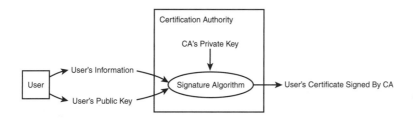

FIGURE 5.25
How digital certificates are used.

In a large networking environment, such as the Internet, multiple levels of CAs might be required. In this case a high-level CA, such as Verisign, Inc., the U.S. Post Office, or the National Security Agency, might provide certificates for second-level CAs. These second-level CAs can then provide certificates for other organizations. Individual companies can themselves act as a certification authority for their employees. A hierarchical certification structure, such that shown in Figure 5.26, is the result. Certification of an entity at the leaves and branches of this hierarchy depends on the certification of entities at higher levels within the hierarchy. These hierarchical certification relationships are referred to as certification chains.

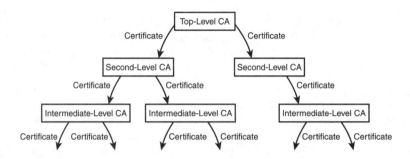

FIGURE 5.26

Multiple levels of certification authorities.

The X.509 certificates of the International Standards Organization are a popular digital certificate format. X.509 identifies a particular format and content for digital certificates. This format has been popularized by Netscape's Secure Sockets Layer (SSL), the Java Archive (JAR) file format, and Privacy Enhanced Mail (PEM), as well as other emerging Internet security standards. X.509 certificates contain the following information:

- The version of X.509 being used with the certificate (1, 2, or 3)
- The entity's name and public key
- A range of dates for which the certificate is valid
- A serial number assigned by the CA
- The name of the CA
- A digital signature created by the CA

The current version of X.509 is 3, although version 1 certificates are still in use. Version 3 provides the capability to add custom extensions to certificates, such as email and IP addresses.

With respect to Java, the primary use for digital certificates is to support code authentication, as shown in Figure 5.27. Developers of Java code can digitally sign their code using their private keys. Users of the code verify the developers' signatures using the developers' public keys. Developers use digital certificates as a secure way to inform users of their public keys. Chapter 7 covers the details of Java's support of digital certificates.

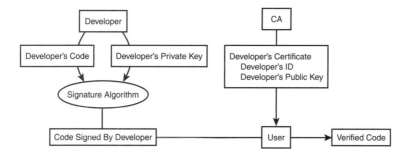

FIGURE 5.27

Using certificates to sign Java code.

Summary

This chapter covered the background information that you need to understand Java's support for cryptographic security. It provided an introduction to cryptography and covered secret- and public-key algorithms. It also explained the basics of message digests, digital signatures, and digital certificates. In the next chapter, you'll study the Java Security API's support of key management.

Key Management and Digital Certificates

In Chapter 5, "Introduction to Cryptography," you learned the basics of cryptography. You saw how cryptographic algorithms use keys to convert plaintext into ciphertext. You also learned about secret- and public-key cryptography.

In this chapter, you'll cover key management, which is the heart of any cryptographic system. You'll learn how keys are securely generated, stored, and distributed. You'll also learn how the key management of the Java Security API changed from JDK 1.1 to JDK 1.2. When you finish this chapter, you'll have a solid understanding of the key management classes and interfaces of the Java Security API.

Importance of Key Management

Key management is one of the most challenging aspects of setting up a cryptographic security system. In order for a cryptosystem to work and be secure, each of its users must have a set of secret keys (in a secret-key system) and or a public-private key pair (in a public-key system). This involves generating the keys and securely distributing them to the users or providing the users with a way of generating the keys. It also involves providing the users with the capability to securely store and manage secret and private keys. In public-key systems, key management includes the capability to verify and manage the public keys of other users who are signed in the form of digital certificates. Figure 6.1 provides an overview of these key management activities.

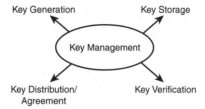

FIGURE 6.1

Key management is an essential part of any cryptographic security system.

Although the key management activities shown in Figure 6.1 seem to be fairly simple and straightforward, a number of security issues are involved with these activities:

- If secret or private keys are not securely generated, it might be possible for an adversary to guess a key by attacking the key generation algorithm. For example, if a key generation algorithm is used with the same seed to generate two or more keys, it might be possible to use the value of one key to guess the values of the other keys.

- There is a significant tradeoff when determining whether to allow users to generate their own keys. If a user is able to securely generate his own key, he does not need to trust the organizations and individuals that generated and distributed the key. If the organization to which the user belongs is not able to decrypt the user's data or communications, the organization must trust that the user is using his key(s) in an appropriate manner. If a user is not able to securely generate his own key, the security of the user and the organization as a whole is jeopardized.

- If a user is not able to securely store his keys, the user's keys might be compromised. Another party might be able to decrypt the user's data and communications or falsely sign objects as originating from the user. This is especially significant if the user's keys are insecurely stored on a computer that is accessible via the Internet.

- If the key management system employed by the user (and organization) causes the user to easily lose track of his keys and does not support key recovery, important information that is encrypted might be rendered inaccessible. In many cases, this is equivalent to having the data destroyed as the result of flaws in the key management system.

- If the key management system does not allow a user to verify the public keys of other users, it might be possible for one user to masquerade as another. For example, user A might substitute his public key for that of user B in order to read secret information that is being sent to user B. Digital certificates provide a countermeasure to this vulnerability.

The above issues, as a minimum, must be considered when selecting and implementing a key management system.

Key Management and Digital Certificates

CHAPTER 6

165

6

KEY MANAGEMENT
AND DIGITAL
CERTIFICATES

Key Representation

The Key interface of the java.security package is used to represent a key. It extends the
java.io.Serializable interface to enable keys to be serialized and stored in files or transmitted via streams. The Key interface defines the following three methods:

- getAlgorithm()—Returns the name of the algorithm with which the key is used. Every
  Key object is associated with a unique algorithm, such as DES, DSA, and RSA.

- getEncoded()—Returns the key as a byte array in the key's primary encoding format,
  such as RAW or PKCS#8. If the key does not support encoding, the null value is
  returned.

- getFormat()—Returns the format in which the key is encoded. For example, RAW or
  PKCS#8.

You'll see an example of how these methods are used in the KeyGeneratorApp program of the
next section.

> **NOTE**
>
> ## PKCS
>
> *PKCS* stands for Public Key Cryptography Standard. These standards are developed
> by RSA Data Security, Inc. and are available from http://www.rsasecurity.com/
> rsalabs/pkcs or http://www.rsa.com.

The Key interface is extended by the PrivateKey and PublicKey interfaces of java.security
and the SecretKey interface of the javax.crypto package. PrivateKey and PublicKey are
used to identify the private and public keys of a public-key algorithm. SecretKey is used to
reference a symmetric (secret) key, such as a DES key. None of the three interfaces defines
any methods or constants. Their purpose is simply to type keys as private, public, or secret.

The PrivateKey interface is extended by the DSAPrivateKey and RSAPrivateKey interfaces of
java.security.interfaces and the DHPrivateKey interface of javax.crypto.interfaces.
They are used to represent private keys that are used in the DSA and RSA algorithms and the
Diffie-Hellman key agreement algorithm. You'll learn more about the Diffie-Hellman algorithm later in this chapter in the section, "Key Agreement."

The DSAPrivateKey, RSAPrivateKey, and DHPrivateKey interfaces provide methods for
accessing the private key and other values. For example, RSAPrivateKey provides the
getModulus() method, even though the modulus is not private. RSAPrivateKey is further

extended by `RSAPrivateCrtKey`, which provides access to the Chinese Remainder Theorem (CRT) coefficient, the values p and q, and other values used to set up an RSA system. The Chinese Remainder Theorem and its application to RSA is described in PKCS#1.

The `PublicKey` interface is extended by the `DSAPublicKey` and `RSAPublicKey` interfaces of `java.security.interfaces` and the `DHPublicKey` interface of `javax.crypto.interfaces`. These interfaces provide methods for accessing public-key values and are analogous to `DSAPrivateKey`, `RSAPrivateKey`, and `DHPrivateKey`. Note that there is no public-key analog to `RSAPrivateCrtKey`.

Both `DSAPrivateKey` and `DSAPublicKey` extend the `DSAKey` interface of `java.security.interfaces`. `DSAKey` defines the `getParams()` method, which returns a `DSAParams` object. `DSAParams` provides methods for accessing the g, p, and q values of a DSA key pair. Refer to Chapter 5 for more information about these values.

In a similar fashion, `DHPrivateKey` and `DHPublicKey` extend the `DHKey` interface of `javax.crypto.interfaces`. `DHKey` defines the `getParams()` method, which returns a `DHParameterSpec` object. `DHParameterSpec` is part of the `javax.crypto.spec` package and provides methods for accessing the l, p, and g values of a Diffie-Hellman key pair. These values are discussed later in this chapter in the section, "Key Agreement."

Figure 6.2 summarizes the relationships between the key interfaces described in this section. In addition to these interfaces, the `KeyPair` class of `java.security` is used to encapsulate a public-private key pair. It implements `java.io.Serializable` and provides the `getPublic()` and `getPrivate()` methods for accessing the individual keys of the key pair.

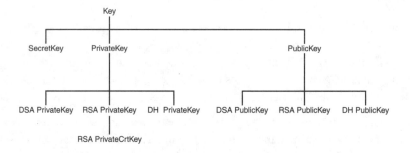

FIGURE 6.2
Key interfaces of the Java Security API.

Key Generation

The first step in secure key management is to generate keys securely. If the output of a key generation algorithm can be easily predicted, it is possible for an adversary to guess the keys

Key Management and Digital Certificates

CHAPTER 6

167

6

KEY MANAGEMENT
AND DIGITAL
CERTIFICATES

that you are using. The Security API provides the capability to securely generate both public-private key pairs and secret keys. Keys are generated using key generator classes. The KeyPairGenerator class of java.security is used to generate KeyPair objects that can be used in public-key algorithms. The KeyGenerator class of java.security is used to generate secret keys for use in algorithms, such as DES or DESede.

The KeyPairGenerator Class

The KeyPairGenerator class is an abstract class. Instances of KeyPairGenerator are created using the static getInstance() method. This method takes a String object that identifies the algorithm name as a parameter. A second version of this method also allows the provider to be identified. A provider is a collection of packages that supply a set of cryptographic algorithms. The Security API provides a default provider, referred to as Sun. The JCE and the Cryptix packages are also providers and are referred to as SunJCE and Cryptix.

For example, if you have the Cryptix provider installed, you can create a KeyPairGenerator object for RSA using:

```
KeyPairGenerator kpg = KeyPairGenerator.getInstance("RSA","Cryptix");
```

The getInstance() method throws a NoSuchAlgorithmException exception if the algorithm cannot be found for the specified provider.

> **NOTE**
>
> ### Factories
>
> In your study of Java, you'll often come across classes whose instances are not created by a constructor. Instead, the class typically provides static methods for creating object instances. These types of classes are referred to as factory classes or factories. The methods, such as getInstance(), that are used to create instances of the class are referred to as *factory methods*.

After you create a KeyPairGenerator object using getInstance(), you need to initialize it using the initialize() method. The initialize() method has a void return type and takes on the following forms:

- initialize(int keysize)—This is the simplest form. You only need to specify the size of the key (in bits) that will be generated by the KeyPairGenerator. Make sure that you pick a size that is appropriate for the type of algorithm you are using. For example, DSA keys must be between 512 and 1024 bits and a multiple of 64. A SecureRandom object is automatically generated for use in initializing the KeyPairGenerator object.

The SecureRandom object is used to randomize the KeyPairGenerator so that it does not generate in a predictable fashion. The SecureRandom class is covered in the section, "Secure Random Numbers and Key Generation," later in this chapter.

- initialize(int keysize, SecureRandom random)—In this form, you supply your own SecureRandom object. If you use this form, you do not have to depend on Sun's SecureRandom object to generate your keys.

- initialize(AlgorithmParameterSpec params)—This form supplies an AlgorithmParameterSpec object that enables the KeyPairGenerator to be initialized in an algorithm-specific fashion. The AlgorithmParameterSpec interface does not define any methods or constants. It simply identifies an object that is used as a parameter to a cryptographic algorithm. To use this form of initialize(), you need to know more detail about the way in which the algorithm is implemented by the cryptographic provider. This form of initialize() automatically generates a SecureRandom object for randomizing the KeyPairGenerator object.

- initialize(AlgorithmParameterSpec params, SecureRandom random)—This form is similar to the last, but it enables the user to supply his own SecureRandom object. It provides you with the most control over how a KeyPairGenerator is initialized.

After you've initialized a KeyPairGenerator object, you can create KeyPair objects using the genKeyPair() method. For example, the following code shows how a pair of 512-bit key objects are created for use with the DSA algorithm:

```
KeyPairGenerator kpg = KeyPairGenerator.getInstance("DSA");
kpg.initialize(512);
KeyPair keys = kpg.genKeyPair();
```

A complete example of key pair generation is provided by the KeyGeneratorApp program of Listing 6.1.

NOTE

Time Requirements for Key Generation

Key generation is a computationally intensive process. Depending on the size of the key that you are generating and your computer's performance, key generation can take up to a minute (or longer).

Key Management and Digital Certificates

CHAPTER 6

169

6

KEY MANAGEMENT
AND DIGITAL
CERTIFICATES

> **NOTE**
>
> ### Service Provider Interface Classes
>
> The KeyPairGenerator class is a subclass of KeyPairGeneratorSpi. The "Spi" is used to indicate that it is a service provider interface class. The service provider interface class defines abstract methods that must be implemented by a service provider in order to provide an implementation of a key pair generator.

The KeyGenerator Class

The KeyGenerator class of java.security is similar to the KeyPairGenerator class of java.security in the way that it is used to generate keys. However, KeyGenerator generates a single SecretKey object instead of a KeyPair object. SecretKey objects are used in symmetric encryption algorithms, such as DES, DESede, and IDEA.

A KeyGenerator object is created using a getInstance() method in the same way as KeyPairGenerator. For example, the following creates a DES KeyGenerator object:

```
KeyGenerator kg = KeyGenerator.getInstance("DES");
```

KeyGenerator objects are initialized via their init() method, which corresponds to the initialize() method of KeyPairGenerator. The init() method has the following five forms:

- init(int keysize)—Initializes the KeyGenerator object for a key of a specified bit-size (for example, 56 bits for DES) using the default SecureRandom object.
- init(int keysize, SecureRandom random)—Initializes the KeyGenerator object for a key of a specified bit-size using a user-supplied SecureRandom object.
- init(SecureRandom random)—Initializes the KeyGenerator object using a user-supplied SecureRandom object. A bit size that is appropriate for the algorithm is used.
- init(AlgorithmParameterSpec params)—Initializes the KeyGenerator using implementation-specific algorithm parameters.
- init(AlgorithmParameterSpec params, SecureRandom random)—Initializes the KeyGenerator using implementation-specific algorithm parameters and a user-supplied SecureRandom object.

After you've initialized the KeyGenerator, you use its generateKey() method to generate a SecretKey object. For example, the following generates a 168-bit SecretKey object for DESede:

```
KeyGenerator kg = KeyGenerator.getInstance("DESede");
kg.init(168);
SecretKey skey = kg.generateKey();
```

Note that DESede also can be used with an 112-bit key.

The `KeyGeneratorApp` Program

The `KeyGeneratorApp` program shown in Listing 6.1 illustrates the use of the `KeyPairGenerator` and `KeyGenerator` classes. It takes an algorithm name and a key size as arguments and generates a key or key pair that is appropriate for the algorithm and key size. For example, the following generates a 56-bit DES key.

```
java com.jaworski.security.handbook.KeyGeneratorApp DES 56
Algorithm: DES
Key size: 56
Secret key in RAW format:
C0nZkh9iJrY=
```

The key is displayed in Base64 notation. Refer to Chapter 5 if you are unfamiliar with Base64. You'll need to use the `com.jaworski.security.handbook` package that was introduced in Chapter 5 in order to compile `KeyGeneratorApp`.

You can also use `KeyGeneratorApp` to generate public key pairs. The following generates a pair of 512-bit DSA keys:

```
java com.jaworski.security.handbook.KeyGeneratorApp DSA 512
Algorithm: DSA
Key size: 512
Private key in PKCS#8 format:
MIHGAgEAMIGoBgcqhkjOOAQBMIGcAkEA/KaCzo4Syrom78z3EQ5SbbB4sF7ey80e
tKII864WF64B81uRpH5t9jQTxeEu0ImbzRMqzVDZkVG9xD7nN1kuFwIVAJYu3cw2
nLqOuyYO5rahJtk0bjjFAkBnhHGyepz0TukaScUUfbGpqvJE8FpDTWSGkx0tFCcb
njUDC3H9c9oXkGmzLik1Yw4cIGI1TQ2iCmxBblC+eUykBBYCFD69FUYsLXc8WkW8
mUSfx1aYuUI9

Public key in X.509 format:
MIHwMIGoBgcqhkjOOAQBMIGcAkEA/KaCzo4Syrom78z3EQ5SbbB4sF7ey80etKII
864WF64B81uRpH5t9jQTxeEu0ImbzRMqzVDZkVG9xD7nN1kuFwIVAJYu3cw2nLqO
uyYO5rahJtk0bjjFAkBnhHGyepz0TukaScUUfbGpqvJE8FpDTWSGkx0tFCcbnjUD
C3H9c9oXkGmzLik1Yw4cIGI1TQ2iCmxBblC+eUykA0MAAkAx/giYWj84hB87YaIe
O44cZfUVY8gFJZhpF1PV/enrRu8xThK2YemTQOC7htnJaPnS3lGQ3QdFz7OJiOPo
afnE
```

LISTING 6.1   The `KeyGeneratorApp` Program

```
package com.jaworski. security.handbook;

import java.security.*;
import javax.crypto.*;
```

LISTING 6.1   Continued

```java
public class KeyGeneratorApp {
 // The algorithm's name
 private String algorithm = "";
 // The size of the key (in bits) to generate
 private int keySize = 0;
 // Placeholder for secret keys
 private SecretKey skey = null;
 // Placeholder for public key pairs
 private KeyPair keys = null;

 public static void main(String[] args) {
  if(args.length != 2) {
   String err = "Usage: com.jaworski.security.handbook";
   err += ".KeyGeneratorApp algorithmName keySize";
   System.out.println(err);
   System.exit(0);
  }
  // Convert the key size to an int value
  int size = (new Integer(args[1])).intValue();
  // Create a KeyGeneratorApp object
  KeyGeneratorApp app = new KeyGeneratorApp(args[0],size);
  // Generate the key or key pair
  app.generate();
  // Display the key or key pair
  app.display();
 }
 public KeyGeneratorApp(String algorithm, int keySize) {
  this.algorithm = algorithm;
  this.keySize = keySize;
 }
 private void generate() {
  try {
   // Try to generate a public key pair
   KeyPairGenerator kpg = KeyPairGenerator.getInstance(algorithm);
   kpg.initialize(keySize);
   keys = kpg.genKeyPair();
  }catch(NoSuchAlgorithmException ex1) {
   // Try to generate a secret key
   try {
    KeyGenerator kg = KeyGenerator. getInstance(algorithm);
    kg.init(keySize);
    skey = kg.generateKey();
   }catch(NoSuchAlgorithmException ex2) {
    System.out.println("Algorithm not supported: "+algorithm);
    System.exit(0);
```

LISTING 6.1 Continued

```
    }
   }
  }
  private void display() {
   if(skey != null) {
    // Display the secret key
    System.out.println("Algorithm: "+algorithm);
    System.out.println("Key size: "+keySize);
    System.out.println("Secret key in "+skey.getFormat()+" format:");
    // Use Base64 encoding
    String skeyString =
     Conversion.byteArrayToBase64String(skey.getEncoded());
    System.out.println(skeyString);
   }else if(keys != null) {
    // Display the public key pair
    System.out.println("Algorithm: "+algorithm);
    System.out.println("Key size: "+keySize);
    PrivateKey priKey = keys.getPrivate();
    PublicKey pubKey = keys.getPublic();
    System.out.println("Private key in "+priKey.getFormat()+" format:");
    // Use Base64 encoding
    String priKeyString =
     Conversion.byteArrayToBase64String(priKey.getEncoded());
    System.out.println(priKeyString);
    System.out.println("Public key in "+pubKey.getFormat()+" format:");
    String pubKeyString =
     Conversion.byteArrayToBase64String(pubKey.getEncoded());
    System.out.println (pubKeyString);
   }
  }
 }
```

Secure Random Numbers and Key Generation

Random numbers are important in cryptography. They are typically used to make the results of operations, such as key generation, difficult to predict. Unfortunately, computers do not generally produce truly random numbers. Instead, random-number–generation algorithms are used produce streams of pseudorandom numbers. Some pseudorandom number generators (PRNG) are more random (and therefore, less predictable) than others. A higher degree of randomness is achieved by seeding the PRNG with a randomly-selected value and using a cryptographically strong algorithm. A cryptographically strong algorithm is one that has the property that it is computationally difficult to determine any values produced by the algorithm without knowledge of the seed.

> **NOTE**
>
> ## Seeds
>
> A *seed* is a value that is used to initialize a pseudorandom number generation algorithm.

> **NOTE**
>
> ## `java.util.Random` is Not Random
>
> The `java.util.Random` class is a PRNG, but it is not secure. Random produces a predictable sequence of numbers that can be guessed without the seed value. In addition, the default seed is generated from the current time, which is also predictable.

The `SecureRandom` class of `java.security` can be used to access the secure PRNG algorithms of different package providers. It provides the following constructors:

- `SecureRandom()`—Creates a `SecureRandom` object that is initialized with a seed value that is randomly generated by a thread-timing algorithm. This seed might not be secure —that is, it might be predictable.

- `SecureRandom(byte[] seed)`—Creates a `SecureRandom` object that is seeded using the supplied byte array.

In general, if you want a higher degree of security, you should seed the `SecureRandom` object yourself. If the security of your random number generation isn't of paramount importance, you can trust Sun's seed generation algorithm. You can also reseed a `SecureRandom` object using the `setSeed(long seed)` or `setSeed(byte[] seed)` methods.

The `SecureRandom` class also provides two static (factory) methods for creating `SecureRandom` objects:

- `getInstance(String algorithm)`—Returns a `SecureRandom` object that implements the specified algorithm.

- `getInstance(String algorithm, String provider)`—Returns a `SecureRandom` object from the identified provider that implements the specified algorithm.

The above methods do not seed the `SecureRandom` objects that they create. However, if a `SecureRandom` object is used before it is seeded, the object seeds itself using an internal seed-generation algorithm.

Sun provides a default `SecureRandom` algorithm that is named SHA1PRNG. This algorithm follows Appendix G.7 of IEEE standard 1363. It generates a random number sequence that is 64-bits of the SHA-1 hash value of the seed value and a 64-bit counter. The counter is incremented by one to produce subsequent values in a random stream. It is implemented by the `sun.security.provider.SecureRandom` class. You can create an instance of this algorithm using

```
SecureRandom srnd = SecureRandom.getInstance("SHA1PRNG");
```

After you've created and seeded a `SecureRandom` object, you can use it to generate random values using the `next()` and `nextBytes()` methods:

- `next(int numBits)`—Overrides the `next()` method of `java.util.Random`, allowing the inherited methods of `Random`, such as `nextInt()`, to be used securely. The value of numBits is between 0 and 32 inclusive and identifies the number of bits in the result that are to be randomly generated.

- `nextBytes(byte[] randomBytes)`—Generates random bytes and puts them in the randomBytes array.

The `SecureRandomApp` program of Listing 6.2 shows how the `SecureRandom` class is used. It takes the number of random bytes to generate, followed by an optional seed value, as arguments. It displays the random bytes using Base64 notation. For example, the following generates 100 random bytes using the seed value of 8975247094543084:

```
java com.jaworski.security.handbook.SecureRandomApp 100 8975247094543084
1jR9VZdQQN5OaeB939/seLCtC6MhUEvsg7eXLh+5Ye+uPzh5/k08IM0Vaj+Mz/PB
1/VTwBem3GRs2lR4a8cyEkbCs9STwa7ppbHdQBnlXBQLf67AiMgQnzpwS2lkhrHA
dXNAyw==
```

Try using this program with and without seed values. You'll notice that when the program is forced to seed itself, it runs much more slowly. That's because the seed generation algorithm is very computationally intensive.

LISTING 6.2   The SecureRandomApp Program

```
package com.jaworski.security.handbook;
import java.security.*;
import javax.crypto.*;

public class SecureRandomApp {
 public static void main(String[] args)
   throws NoSuchAlgorithmException {
  if(args.length == 0) {
   String err = "Usage: com.jaworski.security.handbook";
   err += ".SecureRandomApp numBytes [seed]";
```

Key Management and Digital Certificates

CHAPTER 6

175

6

KEY MANAGEMENT
AND DIGITAL
CERTIFICATES

LISTING 6.2 Continued

```
  System.out.println(err);
  System.exit(0);
}
// Converts args[0] to an int value
int numBytes = (new Integer(args[0])).intValue();
// Converts args[1] to a long value
long seed = 01;
if(args.length > 1) seed = (new Long(args[1])).longValue();
// Create a SecureRandom object
SecureRandom srand = SecureRandom.getInstance("SHA1PRNG");
// Seed it
if(seed != 01) srand.setSeed(seed);
// Generate numBytes random bytes
byte[] bytes = new byte[numBytes];
srand.nextBytes(bytes);
// Display the bytes
String s = Conversion.byteArrayToBase64String(bytes);
System.out.println(s);
 }
}
```

Key Translation

The Key interface and its subinterfaces provide a way to encapsulate keys while they are stored in a Java program. Because Key implements the java.io.Serializable interface, Key objects can be written to streams. This allows keys to be stored in files or sent out over network connections. However, storing or transmitting keys as Key objects poses some problems if they are to be used in applications that are not written in Java. For example, you can create a DES or DSA key that is used in a Java application that might need to be made available to an encryption algorithm that is written in another language or that is implemented in hardware or firmware.

Key translators provide the capability to translate keys from Java objects to a Java-independent array of bytes. There are three primary key translator classes: java.security.KeyFactory, javax.crypto.SecretKeyFactory, and javax.crypto.spec.SecretKeySpec. These classes may be used to translate Key objects into java.security.spec.KeySpec objects. The KeySpec interface does not define any classes or methods. It is used to identify a class as providing an external representation of a Key object. The KeySpec interface is implemented by the following classes of java.security.spec and javax.crypto.spec:

- java.security.spec.DSAPrivateKeySpec —Provides access to the values (g, p, q, and x) of a DSA private key.

- `java.security.spec.DSAPublicKeySpec`—Provides access to the values (g, p, q, and y) of a DSA public key.

- `java.security.spec.EncodedKeySpec`—Provides access to the values (as a byte array) of an encoded public or private key.

- `java.security.spec.RSAPublicKeySpec`—Provides access to the values (modulus and exponent) of an RSA public key.

- `java.security.spec.RSAPrivateKeySpec`—Provides access to the values (modulus and exponent) of an RSA private key.

- `java.security.spec.RSAPrivateCrtKeySpec`—Provides access to the values (p, q, private and public exponents, and Chinese Remainder Theorem coefficients) of an RSA private key.

- `javax.crypto.spec.DESedeKeySpec`—Provides access to the values (as a byte array) of a DESede (Triple DES) secret key.

- `javax.crypto.spec.DESKeySpec`—Provides access to the values (as a byte array) of a DES secret key.

- `javax.crypto.spec.DHPrivateKeySpec`—Provides access to the values (g, p, and x) of a Diffie-Hellman private key.

- `javax.crypto.spec.DHPublicKeySpec`—Provides access to the values (g, p, and y) of a Diffie-Hellman public key.

- `javax.crypto.spec.PBEKeySpec`—Provides access to the password (as a char array) of a password-based encryption key.

- `javax.crypto.spec.SecretKeySpec`—Provides access to a secret key in a provider-independent manner.

In some cases, the values returned by a `KeySpec` object can also be obtained by the `Key` object that implements the algorithm-specific key.

The `KeyFactory` Class

The `KeyFactory` class provides the capability to translate between `KeySpec` objects and `PublicKey` and `PrivateKey` objects. Translation is supported in a bidirectional manner. Instances of `KeyFactory` are created using the `getInstance()` factory method. This method takes an algorithm name and an optional provider name and produces a `KeyFactory` object that supports the specified algorithm and provider. After you've created a `KeyFactory` object, you can translate between `KeySpec`, `PublicKey`, and `PrivateKey` objects using the following methods:

- `getKeySpec(Key key, Class keySpec)`—Returns a `KeySpec` object corresponding to the specified `Key` and `KeySpec` class.

Key Management and Digital Certificates

CHAPTER 6

177

6

KEY MANAGEMENT
AND DIGITAL
CERTIFICATES

- generatePrivate(KeySpec keySpec)—Returns the PrivateKey object corresponding to the supplied KeySpec object.

- generatePublic(KeySpec keySpec)—Returns the PrivateKey object corresponding to the supplied KeySpec object.

- translateKey(Key key)—Translates a Key object from one provider into a Key object that is used with the KeyFactory.

In addition, the getAlgorithm() and getProvider() methods return the algorithm and Provider object associated with the KeyFactory class.

The DSAKeyTranslatorApp program of Listing 6.3 shows how the KeyFactory class can be used to translate DSA PrivateKey and PublicKey objects into DSAPrivateKeySpec and DSAPublicKeySpec objects. It then displays the values associated with these KeySpec objects:

```
C:\jdk1.2.2\com\jaworski\security\handbook>java
➥com.jaworski.security.handbook.DSAKeyTranslatorApp

DSA Private Key

x = 397480743646798716881501857599780760012942323174

DSA Public Key

g = 5421644057436475141609648488325705128047428394380474376
➥834667300766108262613900542681289080713724597310673074119355136085795982097390
➥670890367185141189796

p = 1323237689519861240754793071826743575772852702962340
➥887224515603975771302903636871914645218604120423735052178524033704875207146279
➥8273003935646236777459223

q = 857393771208094202104259627990318636601332086981

y = 1035330373894177285405842560959848832825611548643000
➥976296872480125362277083073724612877886879121275235854365316117646399506807057
➥0812429772438851594321128
```

LISTING 6.3   The DSAKeyTranslatorApp Program

```
package com.jaworski.security.handbook;

import java.security.*;
import java.security.spec.*;

public class DSAKeyTranslatorApp {
 public static void main(String[] args)
```

LISTING 6.3   Continued

```
   throws NoSuchAlgorithmException, InvalidKeySpecException {
   // Generate a 512-bit DSA key pair
   KeyPairGenerator kpg = KeyPairGenerator.getInstance("DSA");
   kpg.initialize(512);
   KeyPair keys = kpg.genKeyPair();
   // Obtain the private and public keys
   PrivateKey priKey = keys.getPrivate();
   PublicKey pubKey = keys.getPublic();
   // Convert the PrivateKey into a DSAPrivateKeySpec object
   KeyFactory kf = KeyFactory.getInstance("DSA");
   DSAPrivateKeySpec dsaPriKeySpec = (DSAPrivateKeySpec)
    kf.getKeySpec(priKey,DSAPrivateKeySpec.class);
   // Convert the PublicKey into a DSAPublicKeySpec object
   DSAPublicKeySpec dsaPubKeySpec = (DSAPublicKeySpec)
    kf.getKeySpec(pubKey,DSAPublicKeySpec.class);
   // Print the keys
   System.out.println("\nDSA Private Key");
   System.out.println("\nx = "+dsaPriKeySpec.getX());
   System.out.println("\nDSA Public Key");
   System.out.println("\ng = "+dsaPubKeySpec.getG());
   System.out.println("\np = "+dsaPubKeySpec.getP());
   System.out.println("\nq = "+dsaPubKeySpec.getQ());
   System.out.println("\ny = "+dsaPubKeySpec.getY());
  }
}
```

The SecretKeyFactory Class

The SecretKeyFactory class of javax.crypto is similar to the KeyFactory class of java.security except that it supports key translation for SecretKey objects. Its getInstance(), getAlgorithm(), and getProvider() methods work in the same manner as those of KeyFactory. In addition to these methods, it supports the following:

- generateSecret(java.security.spec.KeySpec keySpec)—Returns a SecretKey object that corresponds to the supplied KeySpec.

- getKeySpec(SecretKey key, java.lang.Class keySpec)—Returns a KeySpec object corresponding to the supplied SecretKey object and the KeySpec class.

- translateKey(SecretKey key)—Returns a SecretKey object that corresponds to the SecretKeyFactory. This method may be used to translate keys between provider formats.

The JCE 1.2 SecretKeyFactory implementation provides support for both DES and DESede.

Key Agreement

Key agreement, key exchange, or key distribution is the process by which multiple communicating parties can come to agreement about which keys to use to carry out encrypted (or signed) communication.

In public key systems, key agreement is greatly simplified. The communicating parties publish their public keys or send them to the other parties. The public keys are typically distributed using digital certificates. The certificates are used by the recipients to authenticate that the public key they've received actually belongs to the party that sent or published the key. After a party's public key is received, all communication with that party is encrypted using the public key.

Key agreement in secret-key systems is much more complicated. Typically, a unique secret-key is used between pairs of communicating parties, and that key is limited to a single session or a fixed period of time (day, week, month, and so on). In an organization with 1000 users, whose users, on average, communicate with a subset of 20 other users, about 1020 different keys will be needed to support secret communication. In addition, these keys must be changed at the end of the key's useful period (session, day, week, month, and so on). That's a lot of keys to be distributed!

The key distribution problem can be ameliorated by having groups of users share the same key and by extending the key lifetime to a longer period. However, both of these measures weaken the security of the overall system. In addition, neither solves the fundamental problem of how to physically distribute the keys. In some organizations, keys are physically distributed by courier and are loaded into cryptographic devices manually or via electronic keying devices. However, in most cases, the best approach to secret key distribution is to use a key agreement protocol.

A key agreement protocol uses a public-key algorithm to enable two or more communicating parties to arrive at the same secret key. Typically, The secret key is used to enable secret communication for a single session (or fixed part of a session). This key is referred to as a session key.

For example, in a simple key agreement protocol, one party might simply encrypt a session key using the public key of another party and then send the encrypted key to that party. Secret communication takes place when the other party receives and decrypts the session key. Although this approach works and is in practice today, an even more efficient approach to key agreement was developed by Whitfield Diffie and Martin Hellman. It is known as the Diffie-Hellman key agreement protocol. This protocol has the advantage that none of the communicating parties needs to have any knowledge (including the public key of the other parties) in advance. I'll summarize how the protocol works for two communicating parties, which is its typical use. However, it is easily generalized to three or more parties.

Figure 6.3 summarizes the operation of the Diffie-Hellman key agreement protocol. Parties A and B use a common modulus p and base g, so that g is primitive modulus p. This means that for any integer k between 1 and p-1, there exists an integer n such that k = gn mod p. The values of p and g can be published or simply exchanged between A and B. For security reasons, the value of p should be chosen so that it is fairly large (512 bits or more).

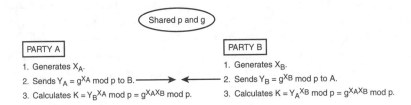

FIGURE 6.3

How Diffie-Hellman key agreement works.

Given that both sides agree on p and g, each party picks a random integer x and calculates g^x. That is, party A picks x_A and calculates $y_A = g^{x_A}$ mod p, and party B picks x_B and calculates $y_B = g^{x_B}$ mod p. Then, A and B send the calculated values (y_A and y_B) to each other. Due to the difficulty of calculating discrete logarithms over a large finite field, it is computationally infeasible for someone to calculate x_A from y_A or x_B from y_B.

After party A receives y_B from B, he calculates $y_B{}^{x_A}$ mod p, which equals $g^{(x_A\, x_B)}$ mod p. Party B calculates $y_A{}^{x_B}$ mod p, which equals $g^{(x_A\, x_B)}$ mod p. In this manner, both parties arrive at the same session value, which can then be used to calculate the session key value using a standard convention.

NOTE

Diffie-Hellman Terminology

The values x_A and x_B are referred to as the private keys of A and B. The values y_A and Y_B are referred to as their public keys. However, none of these values are used to perform encryption.

NOTE

N-Party Diffie-Hellman Key Agreement

A key agreement between three or more parties can be reached using the Diffie-Hellman approach if each of the parties sends its public key value (directly or indirectly) to each of the other parties. The final key value is $g^{(x_1\, x_2\, \ldots\, x_n)}$ mod p where x_1, x_2, ..., x_n are the private key values selected by each of the n parties involved in the key exchange.

Simple Key Management for Internet Protocols (SKIP)

The modulus p and base SKIP (Simple Key Management for Internet Protocols) g of the Diffie-Hellman key agreement protocol have been standardized in SKIP. SKIP (http://www.skip.org) is an Internet standard that allows hosts to agree on a session key for the encryption of Internet Protocol (IP) datagrams. It is typically used to support Virtual Private Networks (VPNs). SKIP uses the following (1224 bit) modulus:

```
F488FD584E49DBCD20B49DE49107366B336C380D451D0F7C88B31C7C5B2D8EF6F3C923C043F0A55
➥B188D8EBB558CB85D38D3
34FD7C175743A31D186CDE33212CB52AFF3CE1B1294018118D7C84A70A72D686C40319C807297AC
A950CD9969FABD00A509B
➥0246D3083D66A45D419F9C7CBD894B221926BAABA25EC355E92F78C7
```

The value 2 is used as the base value g. This simplifies the calculation of the values that are exchanged between parties. However, the selection of 2 as the base in no way weakens the security of the key agreement protocol, which is entirely dependent upon the modulus and the randomness in which the values XA and XB are generated.

The KeyAgreementApp program of Listing 6.4 provides an example of using the SKIP modulus and base values.

JCE Support for Key Agreement

The JCE supports key agreement via the KeyAgreement class of javax.crypto. This class is a factory class and supports protocol- and algorithm-independent key agreements. Its getInstance() method allows a key agreement algorithm and an optional provider to be specified. The JCE provides support for the Diffie-Hellman key agreement protocol. A Diffie-Hellman KeyAgreement object is created as follows:

```
KeyAgreement ka = KeyAgreement.getInstance("DH");
```

In order for two or more parties to come to a key agreement, each party must create and initialize a KeyAgreement object. A KeyAgreement object is initialized by invoking the object's init() method with the party's private key (that is, x value in Diffie-Hellman). The init() method has four forms that allow a combination of SecureRandom and AlgorithmParameterSpec objects to be specified in the KeyAgreement. The SecureRandom object is used to select a specific source of randomness. The AlgorithmParameterSpec object is used to specify additional algorithm-specific parameters to be used in the key agreement protocol.

Having created and initialized a KeyAgreement object, each of the parties involved in the key agreement execute the different phases of the key agreement. These phases will vary with the specific key agreement protocol that is being used. In a Diffie-Hellman key agreement between two parties there is only one phase. In this phase, the public key (y value) of the other party is used to update the KeyAgreement object. The doPhase() method takes a public key value that is received from another communicating party and a boolean value as its arguments. The boolean value indicates whether or not the phase being completed is the last phase of the agreement.

After a party completes the last phase of the key agreement protocol (using doPhase()), it can generate the secret that was communicated during the key agreement. This is accomplished using the generateSecret() method. Three forms of this method are provided:

- byte[] generateSecret()—Returns the secret as a byte array.
- int generateSecret(byte[] sharedSecret, int offset)—Puts the secret in a byte array at the specified offset. Returns an int value that identifies the number of bytes that were copied into the array.
- SecretKey generateSecret(String algorithm)—Returns the secret as a SecretKey object of the specified algorithm.

The first two forms return the secret as a byte array. You have to then create a SecretKey using the byte array. The third form is more convenient, allowing you to directly return the SecretKey object that is to be used as the session key. The KeyAgreementApp program of Listing 6.4 illustrates the former approach. The DESKeyAgreementApp program of Listing 6.5 modifies KeyAgreementApp to generate a DES session key.

In addition to the other methods described in this section, the KeyAgreement class provides the getAlgorithm() and getProvider() methods, which return the algorithm name and provider of the key agreement protocol.

Examples of Implementing Key Agreements

The KeyAgreementApp program of Listing 6.4 shows how the KeyAgreement class can be used to carry out a Diffie-Hellman key agreement.

When you run the program, it generates results of the following form. The specific keys that are generated vary with each program invocation. These results identify the public key (y values) used by parties 1 and 2 and the shared (secret) key values that each party generated. As you can see from the output, both parties came to an agreement:

```
java com.jaworski.security.handbook.KeyAgreementApp
1 is generating a key pair
1 is creating a key agreement object
1 is using
33634790967268890469070837468857019256932941871618713286768464112178
16969808909899556062850271107910498245245696204122939096966686476950884770736557
55776748551435566862547886071883549944659809884215619441521684400690198460511914
41903923724617365981439015248896544194450483990656024177431416707699544588898192
for its public key
```

Key Management and Digital Certificates

CHAPTER 6

183

6

KEY MANAGEMENT
AND DIGITAL
CERTIFICATES

```
2 is generating a key pair
2 is creating a key agreement object
2 is using 52391995999987231331771181473622426428391629058577494833970214812165
5
05028839986611598332478322502025273634994211413767373455213083289045507717383026
33382867884541461287178750384382950818933648377962018038766577522049763488257862
74640916388594974114709729107804122140600158456441081172010749417337123469809309
30
for its public key
1 is using 1626748810372091123181193179290934567379088805465451010843057535868
87
80413969210484870490440170617184583400181301385191257361884845873927654370470276
26745380182951511116823478696377857810032344187807259998536046471082450690169864
1
11247011659584063460819404791677311718597534510070618064903232080536322088318749
 for its shared key
2 is using 1626748810372091123181193179290934567379088805465451010843057535868
87
80413969210484870490440170617184583400181301385191257361884845873927654370470276
26745380182951511116823478696377857810032344187807259998536046471082450690169864
1
11247011659584063460819404791677311718597534510070618064903232080536322088318749
 for its sharedkey
```

LISTING 6.4   The KeyAgreementApp Program

```java
package com.jaworski. security.handbook;
import java.math.*;
import java.security.*;
import java.security.spec.*;
import javax.crypto.*;
import javax.crypto.spec.*;
import javax.crypto.interfaces.*;

public class KeyAgreementApp {
 // SKIP base and modulus values are represented by a
 // DHParameterSpec object
 static DHParameterSpec skipParameterSpec;
 public static void main(String[] args) throws Exception {
  // Create common base and modulus used with SKIP
  createBaseAndModulus();
  // Generate key pair for 1
  System.out.println("1 is generating a key pair");
  KeyPairGenerator kpg1 = KeyPairGenerator.getInstance("DH");
  kpg1.initialize(skipParameterSpec);
  KeyPair kp1 = kpg1.generateKeyPair();
  // Create a KeyAgreement object using the private key
  System.out.println("1 is creating a key agreement object");
  KeyAgreement ka1 = KeyAgreement.getInstance("DH");
  DHPrivateKey privateKey1 = (DHPrivateKey) kp1.getPrivate();
  DHPublicKey publicKey1 = (DHPublicKey) kp1.getPublic();
  ka1.init(privateKey1);
  System.out.println("1 is using "+publicKey1.getY()+
   " for its public key");
```

LISTING 6.4   Continued

```java
// Generate key pair for 2
System.out.println("2 is generating a key pair");
KeyPairGenerator kpg2 = KeyPairGenerator.getInstance("DH");
kpg2.initialize(skipParameterSpec);
KeyPair kp2 = kpg2.generateKeyPair();
// Create a KeyAgreement object using the private key
System.out.println("2 is creating a key agreement object");
KeyAgreement ka2 = KeyAgreement.getInstance("DH");
DHPrivateKey privateKey2 = (DHPrivateKey) kp2.getPrivate();
DHPublicKey publicKey2 = (DHPublicKey) kp2.getPublic();
ka2.init(privateKey2);
System.out.println("2 is using "+publicKey2.getY()+
  " for its public key");
// Use the KeyAgreement object of 1 to generate its shared key
ka1.doPhase(publicKey2,true);
byte[] sharedKey1 = ka1.generateSecret();
System.out.println("1 is using "+new BigInteger(1,sharedKey1)+
  " for its shared key");
// Use the KeyAgreement object of 2 to generate its shared key
ka2.doPhase(publicKey1,true);
byte[] sharedKey2 = ka2.generateSecret();
System.out.println("2 is using "+new BigInteger(1,sharedKey2)+
  " for its shared key");
}
static void createBaseAndModulus() {
  // The SKIP modulus value
  String s = "F488FD584E49DBCD20B49DE49107366B336C380D451D0F7C88" +
    "B31C7C5B2D8EF6F3C923C043F0A55B188D8EBB558CB85D38D3" +
    "34FD7C175743A31D186CDE33212CB52AFF3CE1B1294018118D" +
    "7C84A70A72D686C40319C807297ACA950CD9969FABD00A509B" +
    "0246D3083D66A45D419F9C7CBD894B221926BAABA25EC355E9" +
    "2F78C7";
  BigInteger base = BigInteger.valueOf(2);
  BigInteger modulus = new BigInteger(s,16);
  skipParameterSpec = new DHParameterSpec (modulus,base);
}
}
```

Key Management and Digital Certificates

CHAPTER 6

185

6

KEY MANAGEMENT
AND DIGITAL
CERTIFICATES

The DESKeyAgreementApp program of Listing 6.5 has a slight modification to the KeyAgreementApp program of Listing 6.4. It uses a different form of the generateSecret() method to generate a DES key as the shared session key. This program's output is as follows:

```
java com.jaworski.security.handbook.DESKeyAgreementApp
1 is generating a key pair
1 is creating a key agreement object
1 is using 15177879253301326947315953762481089625421483689071080525066649764558
1915676613641976326903880344277495906833414673264483038879362356759653572010854
5801642968362377933831356003220939239008981400965122625185915368035571674577831
10684825513252913055338348923468204255204654964687110235232317977288416701977147
 for its public key
2 is generating a key pair
2 is creating a key agreement object
2 is using 1102273029528402762423420592220415540898350326124250817205228591743
881185928392293108138750709969455027811008272342981314608376159452009305375628
543422654367436707289457131319229122998309390341901322448842734532220946996739
56347137395429424848849909685210638675428212663284630031689573476744053300277447
 for its public key
1 is using e48095e2ad7e22c2 as its DES session key
2 is using e48095e2ad7e22c2 as its DES session key
```

LISTING 6.5   The DESKeyAgreementApp Program

```
 package com.jaworski.security. handbook;
import java.math.*;
import java.security.*;
import java.security.spec.*;
import javax.crypto.*;
import javax.crypto.spec.*;
import javax.crypto.interfaces.*;

public class DESKeyAgreementApp {
 // SKIP base and modulus values are represented by a
 // DHParameterSpec object
 static DHParameterSpec skipParameterSpec;
 public static void main(String[] args) throws Exception {
  // Create common base and modulus used with SKIP
  createBaseAndModulus();
  // Generate key pair for 1
  System.out.println("1 is generating a key pair");
  KeyPairGenerator kpg1 = KeyPairGenerator.getInstance("DH");
  kpg1.initialize(skipParameterSpec);
  KeyPair kp1 = kpg1.generateKeyPair();
  // Create a KeyAgreement object using the private key
```

LISTING 6.5   Continued

```
System.out.println("1 is creating a key agreement object");
KeyAgreement ka1 = KeyAgreement.getInstance("DH");
DHPrivateKey privateKey1 = (DHPrivateKey) kp1.getPrivate();
DHPublicKey publicKey1 = (DHPublicKey) kp1.getPublic();
ka1.init(privateKey1);
System.out.println("1 is using "+publicKey1.getY()+
  " for its public key");
// Generate key pair for 2
System.out.println("2 is generating a key pair");
KeyPairGenerator kpg2 = KeyPairGenerator.getInstance("DH");
kpg2.initialize(skipParameterSpec);
KeyPair kp2 = kpg2.generateKeyPair();
// Create a KeyAgreement object using the private key
System.out.println("2 is creating a key agreement object");
KeyAgreement ka2 = KeyAgreement.getInstance("DH");
DHPrivateKey privateKey2 = (DHPrivateKey) kp2.getPrivate();
DHPublicKey publicKey2 = (DHPublicKey) kp2.getPublic();
ka2.init(privateKey2);
System.out.println("2 is using "+publicKey2.getY()+
  " for its public key");
// Use the KeyAgreement object of 1 to generate its shared key
ka1.doPhase(publicKey2,true);
SecretKey sharedKey1 = ka1.generateSecret("DES");
System.out.println("1 is using "+
  Conversion.byteArrayToHexString(sharedKey1.getEncoded())+
  " as its DES session key");
// Use the KeyAgreement object of 2 to generate its shared key
ka2.doPhase(publicKey1,true);
SecretKey sharedKey2 = ka2.generateSecret("DES");
System.out.println("2 is using "+
  Conversion.byteArrayToHexString(sharedKey2.getEncoded())+
  " as its DES session key");
}
static void createBaseAndModulus() {
  // The SKIP modulous value
  String s = "F488FD584E49DBCD20B49DE49107366B336C380D451D0F7C88" +
    "B31C7C5B2D8EF6F3C923C043F0A55B188D8EBB558CB85D38D3" +
    "34FD7C175743A31D186CDE33212CB52AFF3CE1B1294018118D" +
    "7C84A70A72D686C40319C807297ACA950CD9969FABD00A509B" +
    "0246D3083D66A45D419F9C7CBD894B221926BAABA25EC355E9" +
    "2F78C7";
  BigInteger base = BigInteger.valueOf(2);
  BigInteger modulous = new BigInteger(s,16);
  skipParameterSpec = new DHParameterSpec(modulous,base);
}
}
```

Key Storage and Password-Based Encryption

Key storage is another critical aspect of key management. After you generate a secret key (or a private key of a public-private key pair), you must either commit the key to memory or store it in some fashion. Because most of us don't have the capability to memorize a single key (never mind a whole set of keys), we tend to store the keys.

Keys can be stored in a number of ways: You can write them down or print them, you can store them in a file, you can store them in a smart card, or you can store them in a tamperproof electronic keying device. Although most of you currently don't use smart cards or electronic keying devices to store your keys, it is likely that you'll encounter them in the not-too-distant future. Right now, your choices are to store them in hardcopy form or store them on your hard disk.

Hardcopy key storage is cumbersome and insecure. Although you might be able to print a key, you generally have to type it back in. For sizeable keys, that's usually a major inconvenience. You can use a scanner to scan in a previously printed key. However, you won't always have a scanner available when you need it. In any case, you don't want to carry around a wad of key printouts with you. Finally, hardcopy keys can be easily copied or stolen.

In most cases, keys are stored on disk. This makes them vulnerable to being disclosed to anyone who can obtain access to the disk or, in the case of a hard disk, to the computer in which the disk is used. If the computer is connected to the Internet, there's the potential for hackers to obtain access to your computer and then to keys.

The obvious countermeasure to storing your keys on disk is to encrypt them. But this solution tends to be a circular one. What do you do with the key that you used to encrypt the keys that are stored on your computer? The answer to this dilemma is to use password-based encryption (PBE) as shown in Figure 6.4.

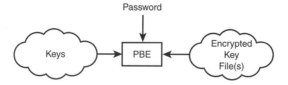

FIGURE 6.4
Using password-based encryption to protect your keys.

PBE uses a password or passphrase to generate an encryption key. In many applications, PBE also uses a random value, referred to as a salt, to increase the effort required to decrypt a password-encrypted file. The salt is combined with the password to encrypt the file as shown in Figure 6.5.

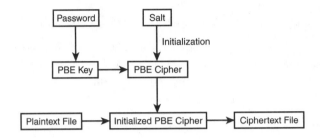

FIGURE 6.5

A salt value is used to increase the strength of password-based encryption.

The JCE supports PBE by providing an implementation of the RSA, Inc. PKCS #5: Password-Based Encryption Standard. Its algorithm name is PBEWithMD5AndDES when specified with the Cipher class. The algorithm operates in CBC mode and supports PKCS5Padding (covered in Chapter 5).

PBE is supported via the PBEKeySpec and PBEParameterSpec classes of javax.crypto.spec. A PBEKeySpec object is passed as an argument to the generateSecret() method of SecretKeyFactory to create a SecretKey object. The PBEKeySpec() constructor takes a char array as an argument. The getPassword() method returns the password that is used to create the PBEKeySpec object.

CAUTION

Storing Passwords as String Objects

String objects are immutable and cannot be overwritten once they are created. For this reason, it is not a good idea to store passwords as String objects.

The PBEParameterSpec class is used to specify the salt and iteration count values that are used to initialize a PBEWithMD5AndDES Cipher object. The salt is passed as a byte array, and the iteration count is passed as an int value to the PBEParameterSpec() constructor. The getSalt() and getIterationCount() methods return these values.

Going from password to a SecretKey object involves the following steps:

1. Store the password in a char array.

2. Pass the char array as an argument to the PBEKeySpec constructor to create a PBEKeySpec object.

3. Create a `SecretKeyFactory` object by passing `"PBEWithMD5AndDES"` as an argument to the `SecretKeyFactory getInstance()` method.

4. Generate a `SecretKey` object by invoking the `generateSecret()` method of the `SecretKeyFactory` object, passing the `PBEKeySpec` object as an argument.

The `PBEApp` program of Listing 6.6 illustrates each of the preceding steps. When you run the program, it displays the window shown in Figure 6.6. Type in a password phrase in the text field and click the Generate Key button. A `SecretKey` object is created and displayed in the text area (using Base64 notation), as in Figure 6.7.

After you've used PBE to create a `SecretKey` object, you need to go through a few more steps before you can create a `PBEWithMD5AndDES` Cipher object and begin encrypting. These steps are summarized as follows:

1. Generate a salt value.

2. Pass the salt value and an iteration count as arguments to the `PBEParameterSpec` constructor to create a `PBEParameterSpec` object. An interation count of 20 is generally sufficient.

3. Create a Cipher object by passing `"PBEWithMD5AndDES"` as an argument to the Cipher `getInstance()` method.

4. Initialize the Cipher object by passing the encryption mode, `PBEKeySpec` object, and `PBEParameterSpec` object as arguments to the Cipher object's `init()` method.

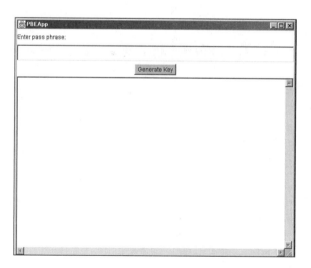

FIGURE 6.6

The opening window of the PBEApp *program.*

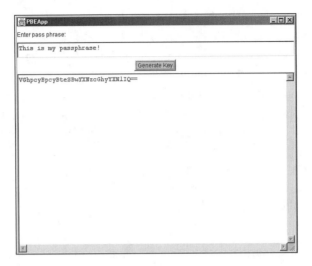

FIGURE 6.7

The SecretKey *object corresponding to the pass phrase is displayed in the text area.*

The PBEFileEncryptApp program of Listing 6.7 shows how the preceding steps are accomplished. When you run the program, it displays the window shown in Figure 6.8. Type in a password phrase in the text field (its contents are replaced by asterisks) and then select Encrypt from the File pulldown menu. A Select File to Encrypt dialog box appears, as shown in Figure 6.9. Use it to select a file to be encrypted.

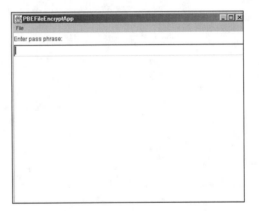

FIGURE 6.8

The opening window of the PBEFileEncryptApp *program.*

Key Management and Digital Certificates

CHAPTER 6

191

6

KEY MANAGEMENT
AND DIGITAL
CERTIFICATES

FIGURE 6.9

The Select File to Encrypt dialog box.

After you've selected a file to encrypt, a Save Encrypted File as dialog box appears, as shown in Figure 6.10. Use it to identify the name and location of the ciphertext file. After closing the dialog box, the selected file is encrypted and stored as ciphertext in the specified location. You can open the ciphertext file to verify that it is indeed ciphertext.

FIGURE 6.10

The Save Encrypted File As dialog box.

To decrypt the ciphertext file, select Decrypt from the File menu. (Make sure that the same password used to encrypt the file is entered into the text field.) A Select File to Decrypt dialog box appears. Use it to open the ciphertext file. A Save Decypted File As dialog box follows. Use it to identify the name and location of the decrypted plaintext file. You can then check the decrypted file to verify that it matches the file that was initially encrypted.

LISTING 6.6   The PBEApp Program

```
package com.jaworski.security.handbook;
import java.awt.*;
import java.awt.event.*;
import java.security.*;
import javax.crypto.*;
import javax.crypto.spec.*;

public class PBEApp extends Frame {
 private int WIDTH = 600;
 private int HEIGHT = 500;
 private TextField inputTF;
 private TextArea outputTA;
 public static void main(String[] args) {
  new PBEApp();
 }
 public PBEApp() {
  super("PBEApp");
  setup();
  pack();
  setSize(WIDTH,HEIGHT);
  addWindowListener(new WindowHandler());
  setVisible(true);
 }
 void setup() {
  // Create panels for the input and output text fields
  Panel inputPanel = new Panel();
  Panel outputPanel = new Panel();
  Panel buttonPanel = new Panel();
  inputPanel.setLayout(new GridLayout(3,1));
  outputPanel.setLayout(new GridLayout(1,1));
  Label inputLabel = new Label("Enter pass phrase:");
  Button generateButton = new Button("Generate Key");
  generateButton.addActionListener(new ButtonHandler());
  inputTF = new TextField(70);
  outputTA = new TextArea(10,70);
  inputTF.setFont(new Font("Monospaced",Font.PLAIN,14));
  outputTA.setFont(new Font("Monospaced",Font.PLAIN,14));
  // Add the components to the panels
  inputPanel.add(inputLabel);
  inputPanel.add(inputTF);
  buttonPanel.add(generateButton);
  inputPanel.add(buttonPanel);
```

Key Management and Digital Certificates

CHAPTER 6

193

6

KEY MANAGEMENT
AND DIGITAL
CERTIFICATES

LISTING 6.6   Continued

```java
 outputPanel.add(outputTA);
 // Add to the frame
 add("North",inputPanel);
 add("Center",outputPanel);
}
private String generatePBEKey(char[] charArray) {
 String s = "";
 try {
  // Use the char array to create a PBEKeySpec
  PBEKeySpec keySpec = new PBEKeySpec(charArray);
  // Create a SecretKeyFactory for the PBE key
  SecretKeyFactory keyFactory =
   SecretKeyFactory.getInstance("PBEWithMD5AndDES");
  // Generate the key from the key spec
  SecretKey key = keyFactory.generateSecret(keySpec);
  // Convert the key to a byte buffer
  byte[] keyBuffer = key.getEncoded();
  // Convert the byte buffer to a Base64 string
  s = Conversion.byteArrayToBase64String(keyBuffer);
 }catch(Exception e) {
  s = e.toString();
 }
 // Return the key as a string or
 // any exception that was generated.
 return s;
}
class ButtonHandler implements ActionListener {
 public void actionPerformed(ActionEvent e) {
  // Generate the PBE key and put it in the text area
  outputTA.setText(generatePBEKey(inputTF.getText().toCharArray()));
 }
}
class WindowHandler extends WindowAdapter {
 public void windowClosing(WindowEvent e) {
  setVisible(false);
  dispose();
  System. exit(0);
 }
}
}
```

LISTING 6.7   The `PBEFileEncryptApp` Program

```
package com.jaworski. security.handbook;

import java.io.*;
import java.awt.*;
import java.awt.event.*;
import java.security.*;
import javax.crypto.*;
import javax.crypto.spec.*;

public class PBEFileEncryptApp extends Frame {
 private int WIDTH = 500;
 private int HEIGHT = 400;
 private int BUFFER_SIZE = 8;
 private TextField inputTF;
 public static void main(String[] args) {
  new PBEFileEncryptApp();
 }
 public PBEFileEncryptApp() {
  super("PBEFileEncryptApp");
  setup();
  pack();
  setSize(WIDTH,HEIGHT);
  addWindowListener(new WindowHandler());
  setVisible(true);
 }
 void setup() {
  // Create panel for password input
  Panel inputPanel = new Panel();
  inputPanel.setLayout(new GridLayout(2,1));
  Label inputLabel = new Label("Enter pass phrase:");
  inputTF = new TextField(70);
  inputTF.setFont(new Font("Monospaced",Font.PLAIN,14));
  inputTF.setEchoChar('*');
  inputPanel.add(inputLabel);
  inputPanel.add(inputTF);
  add("North",inputPanel);
   // Setup menu bar
  MenuBar menuBar = new MenuBar();
  Menu fileMenu = new Menu("File");
  MenuItem fileEncrypt = new MenuItem("Encrypt");
  MenuItem fileDecrypt = new MenuItem("Decrypt");
  MenuItem fileExit = new MenuItem("Exit");
  fileMenu.add(fileEncrypt);
  fileMenu.add(fileDecrypt);
```

LISTING 6.7   Continued

```
 fileMenu.add(fileExit);
 fileEncrypt.addActionListener(new MenuItemHandler());
 fileDecrypt.addActionListener(new MenuItemHandler());
 fileExit.addActionListener(new MenuItemHandler());
 menuBar.add(fileMenu);
 setMenuBar(menuBar);
}
Cipher createCipher(int mode) throws Exception {
 // Get the pass phrase out of the text field
 char[] charArray = inputTF.getText().toCharArray();
 // Create a PBEKeySpec from the pass phrase
 PBEKeySpec keySpec = new PBEKeySpec(charArray);
 // Create a SecretKeyFactory
 SecretKeyFactory keyFactory =
  SecretKeyFactory.getInstance("PBEWithMD5AndDES");
 // Generate a secret key using the keyspec
 SecretKey key = keyFactory.generateSecret(keySpec);
 // Create the salt using the MD5 digest of the pass phrase
 MessageDigest md = MessageDigest.getInstance("MD5");
 md.update(inputTF.getText().getBytes());
 byte[] digest = md.digest();
 byte[] salt = new byte[8];
 for(int i=0;i<8;++i) salt[i] = digest[i];
 // Create a PBEParameterSpec using the salt
 PBEParameterSpec paramSpec = new PBEParameterSpec(salt,20);
 // Create an instance of the cipher
 Cipher cipher = Cipher.getInstance("PBEWithMD5AndDES");
 // Initialize it for encryption/decryption with the key and salt
 cipher.init(mode,key,paramSpec);
 return cipher;
}
void encryptFile() {
 try {
  // Create and initialize a cipher
  Cipher cipher = createCipher(Cipher.ENCRYPT_MODE);
  // Select input file
  String inPathString =
   getPath("Select file to encrypt",FileDialog.LOAD);
  if(inPathString == null) return;
  // Select output file
  String outPathString =
   getPath("Save encrypted file as",FileDialog.SAVE);
  if(outPathString == null) return;
  // Open files and encrypt/decrypt
```

LISTING 6.7 Continued

```java
  applyCipher(inPathString,outPathString, cipher,"Encrypting ...");
 }catch(Exception ex) {
  ex.printStackTrace();
 }
}
void decryptFile() {
 try {
  // Create and initialize a cipher
  Cipher cipher = createCipher(Cipher.DECRYPT_MODE);
  // Select input file
  String inPathString =
   getPath("Select file to decrypt",FileDialog.LOAD);
  if(inPathString == null) return;
  // Select output file
  String outPathString =
   getPath("Save decrypted file as",FileDialog.SAVE);
  if(outPathString == null) return;
  // Open files and encrypt/decrypt
  applyCipher(inPathString,outPathString, cipher,"Decrypting ...");
 }catch(Exception ex) {
  ex.printStackTrace();
 }
}
void applyCipher(String inFile,String outFile,Cipher cipher,
  String message) throws Exception {
 // Open input file using a CiperInputStream
 CipherInputStream in = new CipherInputStream(
  new BufferedInputStream(new FileInputStream(inFile)),cipher);
 // Open output file
 BufferedOutputStream out = new BufferedOutputStream(
  new FileOutputStream(outFile));
 // Notify user that encryption/decryption is in progress
 WaitDialog dialog = new WaitDialog(message);
 dialog.pack();
 dialog.setBounds(100,100,150,100);
 dialog.show();
 // Encrypt/decrypt file
 byte[] buffer = new byte[BUFFER_SIZE];
 int numRead = 0;
 do {
  numRead = in.read(buffer);
  if(numRead > 0) out.write(buffer,0,numRead);
 } while(numRead == 8);
 in.close();
```

Key Management and Digital Certificates

CHAPTER 6

197

6

KEY MANAGEMENT
AND DIGITAL
CERTIFICATES

LISTING 6.7   Continued

```
   out.close();
   // Remove dialog box after a second
   Thread.sleep(1000);
   dialog.hide();
   dialog.dispose();
  }
  String getPath(String title,int mode) {
   FileDialog fd = new FileDialog(this,title,mode);
   fd.show();
   // If file a file has not been selected then return null
   String inDirectoryString = fd.getDirectory();
   String inFileString = fd.getFile();
   if(inDirectoryString == null || inFileString == null)
    return null;
   return inDirectoryString + inFileString;
  }
  class MenuItemHandler implements ActionListener {
   public void actionPerformed(ActionEvent e) {
    String s = e.getActionCommand();
    if(s.equals("Encrypt")) encryptFile();
    else if(s.equals("Decrypt")) decryptFile();
    else{
     setVisible(false);
     dispose();
     System.exit(0);
    }
   }
  }
  class WindowHandler extends WindowAdapter {
   public void windowClosing(WindowEvent e) {
    setVisible(false);
    dispose();
    System.exit(0);
   }
  }
  class WaitDialog extends Dialog {
   public WaitDialog(String s) {
    super(PBEFileEncryptApp.this,"Please wait");
    setLayout(new BorderLayout());
    add("Center",new Label(s,Label.CENTER));
   }
  }
}
```

Key Management Differences Between JDK 1.1 and the Java 2 Platform (version JDK 1.2)

The key management approach used in the Java Security API has focused on user-oriented key generation and management. The Java security API and the JCE provide the user with the capability to securely generate public-private key pairs and secret keys. Keys can be securely stored by encrypting them using password-based encryption. Public keys are distributed and validated using digital certificates.

Although, numerous capabilities (such as support for X.509 version 3 certificates) have been added in JDK 1.2, the basic approaches to these key management activities have remained the same between JDK 1.1 and the Java 2 platform (version JDK 1.2). The major difference between JDK 1.1 to JDK 1.2 is the way in which the public keys of other users are managed. I'll cover these differences in the following sections.

JDK 1.1 Key Management

JDK 1.1 uses an approach, referred to as identity-based key management, that associates public keys with identities. Identities are entities, such as individuals, organizations, or software programs, that are capable of possessing and using a public key. Identities are implemented by the java.security.Identity class and are organized in a hierarchical fashion into identity scopes. An identity scope is a collection of identities and is implemented by the java.security.IdentityScope class. Because IdentityScope is a subclass of Identity, an IdentityScope can contain both Identity and IdentityScope objects. Another subclass of Identity, java.security.Signer, represents an identity that possesses a private key that is used for signing. Figure 6.11 illustrates the relationships between the Identity, IdentityScope, and Signer classes.

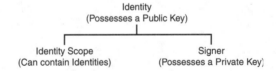

FIGURE 6.11

The JDK 1.1 approach to public key management classes.

I'll cover the Identity, IdentityScope, and Signer classes in more detail in the following subsections. But, before doing so, I must warn you that these classes are deprecated in JDK 1.2 and have been replaced by a new public-key management mechanism. If you are only interested in JDK 1.2 key management, you can safely skip the following subsections. However, if you are interested in how key management changed from JDK 1.1 to JDK 1.2 then read on.

The `Identity` Class

The `Identity` class implements the `java.security.Principal` interface, which provides the capability to access the name of an `Identity` and obtain a String representation of an `Identity`. The `Principal` interface is used by the interfaces of the `java.security.acl` package to define access control policies. You can think of an `Identity` object as a `Principal` object that has a public key and is organized into a hierarchy of `IdentityScope` objects. The constructors of the `Identity` class allow the `Principal` to be named and (optionally) the `IdentityScope` to be specified. The `getPublicKey()` and `setPublicKey()` methods enable the `Identity`'s `PublicKey` object to be accessed. The `addCertificate()`, `getCertificates()`, and `removeCertificate()` methods support the management of certificates that authenticate the `Identity`'s public key.

> **NOTE**
>
> ## JDK 1.1 Certificates
>
> The `java.security.Certificate` interface defines methods that encapsulate the notion of a JDK 1.1 certificate. This interface has been deprecated in JDK 1.2 and replaced by the `Certificate` class of the `java.security.cert` package.

The `IdentityScope` Class

The `IdentityScope` class extends `Identity` to provide a context for organizing identities. One of the `Identity` class's constructors allows an `Identity`'s scope to be specified. A similar constructor is provided in the `IdentityScope` class, allowing an `IdentityScope` object to be created within the scope of another `IdentityScope` object. If an `Identity` is created without an `IdentityScope`, it is created in the default no scope scope.

Names and public keys are unique within an `IdentityScope`. No two identities within the same scope can have the same name or public key. The JDK 1.1 javakey tool is used to manage an `IdentityScope` object, referred to as the system identity scope. This identity scope is specified by the system.scope property of the \lib\security\java.security file of the base JDK 1.1 installation directory. This `IdentityScope` object is stored in serialized form by the javakey tool.

> **NOTE**
>
> ## Javakey is No Longer Supported
>
> The JDK 1.1 javakey tool has been replaced by the JDK 1.2 keytool and jarsigner tools and is no longer supported.

The `Signer` Class

The `Signer` subclass of `Identity` enables an Identity to possess a private key. The `getPrivateKey()` and `setKeyPair()` methods support the management of this key. Note that a `Signer` may be created within an `IdentityScope` in the same manner as an `Identity` or `IdentityScope` object.

JDK 1.2 Key Management

The identity-based key management scheme of JDK 1.1 has been replaced by a keystore-based approach in JDK 1.2. A keystore is a container for secret keys, public-private key pairs, and certificates that attest to the validity of a public key. Figure 6.12 illustrates this concept.

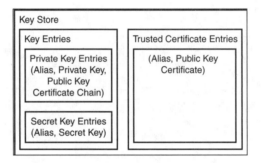

FIGURE 6.12
What's inside a keystore?

A keystore may contain two types of entries:

- Key Entry—Holds either a secret key or a public-private key pair (and a chain of certificates that authenticates the public key). A key entry can be used to sign objects and to provide a certificate that authenticates your signature.

- Trusted Certificate Entry—Holds a public key certificate of another party. By having the certificate in the keystore, you trust that the certificate belongs to the subject/owner identified in the certificate. You can use a trusted certificate entry to authenticate information received from a third party.

A keystore can have multiple key entries and multiple trusted certificate entries. For example, you can have multiple public-private key pairs (in the form of key entries) that you use for work, personal correspondence, shopping, and banking. You can have trusted certificate entries for co-workers, friends, family, and acquaintances.

Each of the entries in a keystore is associated with a unique alias. This alias is a String that identifies the use of a key entry (for example, "Personal email" or "Code signing") or the name

Key Management and Digital Certificates

CHAPTER 6

201

6

KEY MANAGEMENT
AND DIGITAL
CERTIFICATES

of the entity with which a trusted certificate is associated ("Jason" or "Emily"). Figure 6.13 shows how aliases are used within a keystore.

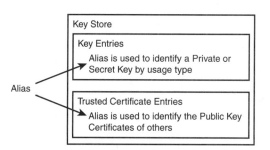

FIGURE 6.13

Aliases are used to identify keystore entries associated with aliases.

The KeyStore Class

The java.security.KeyStore class encapsulates the notion of a KeyStore. It is an abstract class that is implemented by provider-specific implementations. The getInstance() method is a factory method that is used to create KeyStore objects by name, and optionally, by provider. The keystore type supported by the JDK 1.2 is JKS for Java keystore. The PKCS12 type is also defined (but not implemented) in JDK 1.2. This type is defined in PKCS#12.

The KeyStore class provides a number of methods that are used to manage a keystore and its entries.:

Keystore management methods are as follows:

- getInstance(String type)—A static factory method that creates a KeyStore object of the specified type.

- getInstance(String type, String provider)—A static factory method that creates a KeyStore object of the specified type from the specified provider.

- getDefaultType()—Returns the default keystore type as specified in the Java security properties file or JKS if the property does not exist.

- getType()—Returns the keystore type as a String object.

- getProvider()—Returns the Provider object that created this KeyStore object.

- load(InputStream stream, char[] password)—Loads the KeyStore object from the specified input stream. The password is used to verify the integrity of the keystore's data.

- store(OutputStream stream, char[] password)—Writes the keystore to the specified output stream, protecting its integrity with the specified password.

- `size()`—Returns the number of entries in the keystore.
- `deleteEntry(String alias)`—Deletes the entry identified by the alias.

Alias and certificate management methods are as follows:

- `aliases()`—Returns an Enumeration of all the alias names in the keystore.
- `containsAlias(String alias)`—Returns a boolean value indicating whether the specified alias is in the keystore.
- `getCertificate(String alias)`—Returns the Certificate (`java.security.cert.Certificate`) associated with the specified alias or null if the alias does not exist or does not have a certificate.
- `getCertificateAlias(Certificate cert)`—Returns the alias of the first keystore entry whose certificate matches the specified certificate or null if no match occurs.
- `getCertificateChain(String alias)`—Returns the certificate chain associated with the specified alias.
- `getCreationDate(String alias)`—Returns the date of creation of the entry with the given alias or null if the alias does not exist.
- `getKey(String alias, char[] password)`—Returns the Key object associated with the specified alias via the supplied key decryption password. Returns null if the alias does not reference a key entry.

Key entry management methods are as follows:

- `isKeyEntry(String alias)`—Returns a boolean value indicating whether the alias references a key entry.
- `setKeyEntry(String alias, byte[] key, Certificate[] chain)`—If the alias does not exist, creates a key entry for the alias. If the alias exists and is a key entry, the entry's key is replaced. Otherwise, a KeyStoreException is thrown. A certificate chain is only needed for a private key (that is, the certificate chain of the associated public key).
- `setKeyEntry(String alias, Key key, char[] password, Certificate[] chain)`—If the alias does not exist, creates a key entry for the alias. If the alias exists and is a key entry, the entry's key is replaced. Otherwise, a KeyStoreException is thrown. A certificate chain is only needed for a private key (that is, the certificate chain of the associated public key). The password is used to protect the key.

Trusted certificate management methods are as follows:

- `isCertificateEntry(String alias)`—Returns a boolean value indicating whether the alias references a trusted certificate entry.

Key Management and Digital Certificates

CHAPTER 6

203

6

KEY MANAGEMENT
AND DIGITAL
CERTIFICATES

- `setCertificateEntry(String alias, Certificate cert)`—If the alias does not exist, creates a trusted certificate entry for the alias. If the alias exists and is a trusted certificate entry, the entry's certificate is replaced. Otherwise, a `KeyStoreException` is thrown.

A keystore might or might not be persistent. If the keystore is persistent, it is loaded from a stream using the `load()` method. If the keystore is not persistent, it is still loaded via the `load()` method, but a null value is used as the input stream. In either case, the keystore is loaded before it is used. A password can be supplied to the `load()` method to check the integrity of the data that is loaded. The implementation of the password is provider-specific. However, it is typically combined with the keystore data to calculate a message digest when the keystore data is stored via the `store()` method. When the keystore is loaded (via `load()`) the supplied password is used to recalculate the digest as shown in Figure 6.14.

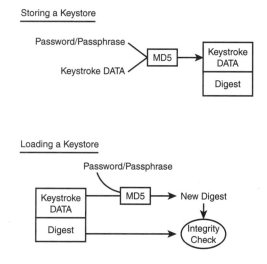

FIGURE 6.14

Using a password to check the integrity of a keystore.

In most cases, you won't need need to access a `KeyStore` object directly in your programs. The JDK 1.2 keytool program enables you to manage the system `KeyStore` object directly from the command line.

The Keytool

The keytool was introduced with the Java 2 SDK. It is used to management keys and certificates and provides an implementation of the `java.security.KeyStore` class. It supports the following capabilities:

- Key pair generation—Generates a public and private key pair (that is, a key entry) and creates an X.509 v1 self-signed certificate for the public key. The certificate is stored as a single-element certificate chain.

- Management of key entries—Allows key entries to be created, imported, exported, listed, and deleted.

- Management of trusted certificate entries—Allows the certificates and certificate chains of others to be imported, exported, listed, and deleted.

- JDK 1.1 identity database importing—Allows the identity database used by the JDK 1.1 to be imported.

- Certificate Signing Request (CSR) generation—CSRs can be generated for submission to a certification authority.

- Password management—Passwords can be used to protect private keys or the entire keystore. Passwords can be changed through keytool commands.

- Help—Provides help to the user in terms of command summaries.

The keystore managed by the keytool contains two types of entries: key entries and trusted certificate entries. *Key entries* contain a secret or private key that is protected (weakly encrypted) using a password. A *private key* entry is accompanied by a certificate chain that corresponds to its associated public key.

A *trusted certificate entry* is a public key certificate of someone other than the owner of the keystore. The keystore owner *trusts* that the public key in the certificate is really that of the identify specified in the certificate. These certificates are typically self-signed by the identity referred to in the certificate.

NOTE

The Java Keystore

The Java Keystore (JKS) is the default keystore implementation provided by the Java 2 SDK. It is U.S. exportable and does not provide strong encryption for the private keys that it protects. You can use other keystore implementations provided by other package providers. To do so, replace the default keystore with another keystore by specifying the keystore in the keytool command line or by setting the keystore.type property in the java.security configuration file.

Key Management and Digital Certificates

CHAPTER 6

205

6

KEY MANAGEMENT
AND DIGITAL
CERTIFICATES

The Keytool and the Jarsigner Tool

The jarsigner tool uses the keystore that is managed by keytool to verify the signa-tures of signed applets. You'll learn about the jarsigner tool in Chapter 4, "Applet Security." The keytool and the jarsigner tool replace the javakey tool of JDK 1.1.

Each keystore entry is associated with a unique alias. The alias is a short name for the identity to which the keystore entry applies. For example, I use the alias jamie for myself. I also have the aliases lisa, emily, and jason. Aliases are not case sensitive—for example, jamie, Jamie, and JAMIE are all equivalent.

Figure 6.15 provides an overview of the keytool's operation. The keytool command set and an extended example of the keytool's operation is provided in Appendix F, "Using the Keytool."

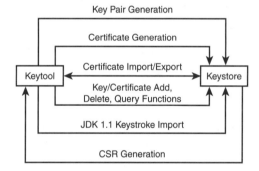

FIGURE 6.15
Using the keytool.

Summary

In this chapter, you've covered the details of the Java Security API's support of key manage-ment. You learned how keys are securely generated, stored, and distributed. You also learned how the key management of the Java Security API changed from JDK 1.1 to JDK 1.2. In the next chapter, you'll learn the details of the Java Security API's support for message digests, digital signatures, and digital certificates.

Message Digests and Digital Signatures

In Chapter 5, "An Introduction to Cryptography," and Chapter 6, "Key Management and Digital Certificates," you were introduced to message digests and digital signatures. These are important elements of Java security because they provide the basic mechanism for trusted code distribution. In this chapter, you'll take a closer look at message digests and digital signatures, study their classes and interfaces, and gain practical experience in creating digests and signatures. You'll also cover message authentication codes (MACs) and learn how they can be used to protect the integrity of messages that are sent over insecure communication channels.

Message Digest Classes and Interfaces

Support for message digests is provided by the following five classes of the `java.security` package:

- `MessageDigestSpi`—The `MessageDigestSpi` class is an abstract class that offers a service provider interface for the development of `MessageDigest` classes. It defines abstract methods that must be implemented by a cryptographic service provider to supply the implementation of a particular message digest algorithm.

- MessageDigest—The MessageDigest class is a subclass of MessageDigestSpi that provides a basic implementation of a message digest. It supports the MD5 and SHA message digest algorithms.

- DigestInputStream—The DigestInputStream class, a subclass of java.io.FilterInputStream, is used to compute a message digest from the data that is read from a stream.

- DigestOutputStream—The DigestOutputStream class, a subclass of java.io.FilterOutputStream, is used to compute a message digest from the data that is written to a stream.

- DigestException—The DigestException class, a subclass of GeneralSecurityException, is thrown as the result of errors in message digest calculation.

These classes are described in the following sections.

MessageDigestSpi

MessageDigestSpi is a service provider interface (SPI) class that defines abstract methods that are to be supplied by MessageDigest implementations. These methods include engineDigest(), engineGetDigestLength(), engineReset(), and engineUpdate(). You don't need to learn these methods unless you're going to build your own custom MessageDigest implementation. However, I'll summarize them here:

- protected abstract void engineUpdate(byte input)—Updates the digest with the value of a byte.

- protected abstract void engineUpdate(byte[] input, int *offset*, int *len*) —Updates the digest with the array of bytes, beginning at *offset* and continuing for *len* bytes.

- protected abstract byte[] engineDigest()—Completes the message digest computation and returns the message digest value as a byte array.

- protected int engineDigest(byte[] *buf*, int *offset*, int *len*)—Completes the message digest computation and returns the number of bytes in the digest. The digest is stored in *buf* as specified by *offset* and *len*.

- protected int engineGetDigestLength()—Returns the message digest length in bytes.

- protected abstract void engineReset()—Resets the digest to its initial starting point.

- `Object clone()`—Provides support for implementing the `Cloneable` interface. Returns a clone if the `MessageDigest` implementation implements `Cloneable`.

If you are interested in creating your own `MessageDigest` implementation, check the Java 2 API documentation of these functions.

MessageDigest

The `MessageDigest` class provides a concrete (nonabstract) subclass of `MessageDigestSpi` that serves as the foundation for message digest computation. It supports the MD5 and SHA message digest algorithms.

The `MessageDigest` constructor is protected. `MessageDigest` objects are created via the static `getInstance()` method. A `String` identifying the type of message digest algorithm to be used is supplied as an argument:

```
MessageDigest md = MessageDigest.getInstance("MD5");
```

The methods of `MessageDigest` are as follows:

- `static MessageDigest getInstance(String algorithm)`—Creates a `MessageDigest` object that implements the specified digest algorithm.
- `static MessageDigest getInstance(String algorithm, String provider)`— Creates a `MessageDigest` object that implements the specified algorithm from the specified provider (if available).
- `String getAlgorithm()`—Returns a `String` that identifies the algorithm used by the `MessageDigest` object.
- `void update(byte input)`—Updates the digest computation using the specified byte.
- `void update(byte[] input)`—Updates the digest computation using the specified array of bytes.
- `void update(byte[] input, int offset, int len)`—Updates the digest computation using the specified portion of an array of bytes.
- `byte[] digest(`—Finishes the hash computation and returns the message digest as a byte array.
- `byte[] digest(byte[] input)`—Updates the digest computation using the specified array of bytes, finishes the digest computation, and returns the digest as a `byte` array.
- `int digest(byte[] buf, int offset, int len)`—Finishes the digest computation and returns the number of bytes in the message digest. The message digest is written to the specified location in `buf`.
- `int getDigestLength()`—Returns the length of the digest in bytes.

- `void reset()`—Resets the digest to its initial state.
- `Provider getProvider()`—Returns the provider of the `MessageDigest` object.
- `String toString()`—Returns a `String` representation of the `MessageDigest` object.
- `Object clone()`—Returns a clone of the `MessageDigest` if the implementation starts the `Cloneable` interface.
- `static boolean isEqual(byte[] `*`digesta`*`, byte[] `*`digestb`*`)`—Compares two `MessageDigest` objects for equality and returns a boolean value indicating the result of the comparison.

The basic approach to message digest computation uses `getInstance()` to create a `MessageDigest` object, `update()` to update the digest value with a sequence of bytes, and `digest()` to complete the calculation and retrieve the final digest value. The following section illustrates how this is done.

Computing Message Digests

The `MessageDigestTestApp` program (Listing 7.1) shows how to use the `MessageDigest` class to calculate message digests. It performs each of the seven message digest test cases that are documented at the end of RFC 1321. When you run the program, it produces the following output:

```
Test case:
Expected result:    d41d8cd98f00b204e9800998ecf8427e
Calculated result:  d41d8cd98f00b204e9800998ecf8427e

Test case:          a
Expected result:    0cc175b9c0f1b6a831c399e269772661
Calculated result:  0cc175b9c0f1b6a831c399e269772661

Test case:          abc
Expected result:    900150983cd24fb0d6963f7d28e17f72
Calculated result:  900150983cd24fb0d6963f7d28e17f72

Test case:          message digest
Expected result:    f96b697d7cb7938d525a2f31aaf161d0
Calculated result:  f96b697d7cb7938d525a2f31aaf161d0

Test case:          abcdefghijklmnopqrstuvwxyz
Expected result:    c3fcd3d76192e4007dfb496cca67e13b
Calculated result:  c3fcd3d76192e4007dfb496cca67e13b

Test case:          ABCDEFGHIJKLMNOPQRSTUVWXYZabcdefghijklmnopqrstuvwxyz
                    ➥0123456789
```

```
Expected result:    d174ab98d277d9f5a5611c2c9f419d9f
Calculated result: d174ab98d277d9f5a5611c2c9f419d9f

Test case:          12345678901234567890123456789012345678901234567890
                    ➡012345678901
2345678901234567890
Expected result:    57edf4a22be3c955ac49da2e2107b67a
Calculated result: 57edf4a22be3c955ac49da2e2107b67a
```

As you can see, the program passes all the test cases. The `testCase` array contains the seven values to be tested, and the `expectedResult` array contains the expected MD5 digests for these values.

The `performMD5Test()` method performs the MD5 test for each value. It creates a `MessageDigest` object using `getInstance()` and invokes the `update()` method to process the bytes corresponding to the test case. The `digest()` method is then invoked to retrieve the digest value. The `Conversion` class (covered in Chapter 5) is used to convert the digest from a `byte` array to a `String` object. The results of the test are then displayed.

LISTING 7.1   The `MessageDigestTestApp` Program

```
package com.jaworski.security.handbook;

import java.security.*;

public class MessageDigestTestApp {
// MD5 test suite from RFC 1321
static String[] testCase = {"", "a", "abc", "message digest",
 "abcdefghijklmnopqrstuvwxyz",
 "ABCDEFGHIJKLMNOPQRSTUVWXYZabcdefghijklmnopqrstuvwxyz0123456789",

 "12345678901234567890123456789012345678901234567890123456789012345678
➡90"};
static String[] expectedResult = {"d41d8cd98f00b204e9800998ecf8427e",
 "0cc175b9c0f1b6a831c399e269772661",
 "900150983cd24fb0d6963f7d28e17f72",
 "f96b697d7cb7938d525a2f31aaf161d0",
 "c3fcd3d76192e4007dfb496cca67e13b",
 "d174ab98d277d9f5a5611c2c9f419d9f",
 "57edf4a22be3c955ac49da2e2107b67a"};

 public static void main(String[] args) {
  for(int i=0; i<testCase.length; ++i)
   performMD5Test(i);
 }
```

LISTING 7.1   Continued

```
static void performMD5Test(int i) {
 try {
  MessageDigest md = MessageDigest.getInstance("MD5");
  md.update(testCase[i].getBytes());
  String s = Conversion.byteArrayToHexString(md.digest());
  System.out.println("\nTest case:         "+testCase[i]);
  System.out.println("Expected result:   "+expectedResult[i]);
  System.out.println("Calculated result: "+s);
 }catch(NoSuchAlgorithmException e) {
  System.out.println("MD5 is not supported.");
  System.exit(0);
 }
 }
}
```

DigestInputStream and DigestOutputStream

The DigestInputStream and DigestOutputStream classes simplify the computation of message digests for sequences of bytes that are read from or written to streams.
DigestInputStream is used to compute a message digest on a sequence of bytes that is read
from a stream. DigestOutputStream is used to calculate a message digest on bytes that are
written to a stream. These classes extend java.io.FilterInputStream and
java.io.FilterOutputStream, making them digest-calculating input and output filters.

The DigestInputStream constructor takes the InputStream to be filtered and a
MessageDigest object as arguments:

```
DigestInputStream(InputStream stream, MessageDigest digest)
```

The InputStream is the stream for which the message digest is to be calculated. The
MessageDigest object is created using the static getInstance() method of MessageDigest.

The methods of DigestInputStream are as follows:

- void setMessageDigest(MessageDigest *digest*)—Sets the MessageDigest object to
  be used with the stream. Because the MessageDigest object is supplied with the
  DigestInputStream constructor, this method is needed only when you want to substitute
  a new MessageDigest object.

- void on(boolean on)—Turns the digest calculation on or off. By default, the digest calculation is on, and the digest is updated for all bytes read from the stream. You can turn
  it off for selected input and then turn it on again.

- int read()—Reads a byte from the input stream and returns it as an int value. The
  message digest is updated if the digest function is on.

- `int read(byte[] b, int off, int len)`—Reads bytes from the input stream into a byte array and returns the number of bytes read. The message digest is updated if the digest function is on.
- `MessageDigest getMessageDigest()`—Returns the message digest associated with the stream.
- `String toString()`—Returns a `String` representation of the digest input stream and its associated `MessageDigest` object.

`DigestOutputStream` is the output analog of `DigestInputStream`. The `DigestOutputStream` constructor takes the `OutputStream` to be filtered and a `MessageDigest` object as its arguments:

`DigestOutputStream(OutputStream stream, MessageDigest digest)`

The `OutputStream` is the stream for which the message digest is to be calculated. The `MessageDigest` object is created using the `static getInstance()` method of `MessageDigest`.

The methods of `DigestOutputStream` are as follows:

- `void setMessageDigest(MessageDigest digest)`—Sets the `MessageDigest` object to be used with the stream. Because the `MessageDigest` object is supplied with the `DigestInputStream` constructor, this method is needed only when you want to substitute a new `MessageDigest` object.
- `void on(boolean on)`—Turns the digest calculation on or off. By default, the digest calculation is on and the digest is updated for all bytes read from the stream. You can turn it off for selected input and then turn it on again.
- `void write(byte[] b, int off, int len)`—Writes the specified portion of the `byte` array to the output stream. The message digest is updated using the bytes that are written if the digest calculation is on.
- `void write(int b)`—Writes the byte to the output stream and updates the message digest (if the digest function is on).
- `MessageDigest getMessageDigest()`—Returns the message digest associated with the stream.
- `String toString()`—Returns a `String` representation of the digest input stream and its associated `MessageDigest` object.

The basic approach to working with `DigestInputStream` and `DigestOutputStream` is to create a `MessageDigest` object and then provide it to the `DigestInputStream` or `DigestOutputStream` constructors to create an appropriate digest stream object. Use the stream to perform input or output and then retrieve the updated `MessageDigest` object. Finally, invoke the `digest()` method of the `MessageDigest` object to retrieve the final digest value.

Working with Digest Streams

The `DigestStreamTestApp` program (see Listing 7.2) illustrates the use of the `DigestOutputStream` and `DigestInputStream` classes. It verifies one of the SHA-1 test cases described in FIPS 180-1. It performs the verification using `DigestOutputStream` and then using `DigestInputStream`. The program produces the following results:

```
Output test case: abcdbcdecdefdefgefghfghighijhijkijkljklmklmnlmnomnopnopq
Expected result:   84983e441c3bd26ebaae4aa1f95129e5e54670f1
Calculated result: 84983e441c3bd26ebaae4aa1f95129e5e54670f1

Input test case: abcdbcdecdefdefgefghfghighijhijkijkljklmklmnlmnomnopnopq
Expected result:   84983e441c3bd26ebaae4aa1f95129e5e54670f1
Calculated result: 84983e441c3bd26ebaae4aa1f95129e5e54670f1
```

The `performOutputTest()` method creates a `MessageDigest` object that implements the SHA algorithm and a `FileOutputStream` object that writes to the file `sha-results.txt`. A `DigestOutputStream` object is then created using the `MessageDigest` and `FileOutputStream` objects.

The `write()` method of `DigestOutputStream` is used to write the test string to the output stream. The updated `MessageDigest` object is then retrieved from the `DigestOutputStream`, and its digest is retrieved via the `digest()` method. The results of the test are then displayed.

The `performInputTest()` method is very similar to the `performOutputTest()` method except that `performInputTest()` reads the data that was written to `sha-results.txt` and performs the digest calculation on the values that are read.

LISTING 7.2   The `DigestStreamTestApp` Program

```
package com.jaworski.security.handbook;

import java.security.*;
import java.io.*;

public class DigestStreamTestApp {
// SHA test suite from FIPS 180-1
static String testCase =
 "abcdbcdecdefdefgefghfghighijhijkijkljklmklmnlmnomnopnopq";
static String expectedResult =
 "84983e441c3bd26ebaae4aa1f95129e5e54670f1";

 public static void main(String[] args) {
  performOutputTest();
  performInputTest();
 }
 static void performOutputTest() {
```

LISTING 7.2   Continued

```
 try {
  MessageDigest md = MessageDigest.getInstance("SHA");
  FileOutputStream fout = new FileOutputStream("sha-results.txt");
  DigestOutputStream out = new DigestOutputStream(fout,md);
  byte[] b = testCase.getBytes();
  out.write(b,0,b.length);
  md = out.getMessageDigest();
  String s = Conversion.byteArrayToHexString(md.digest());
  System.out.println("\nOutput test case: "+testCase);
  System.out.println("Expected result:    "+expectedResult);
  System.out.println("Calculated result:  "+s);
 }catch(Exception e) {
  System.out.println(e);
  System.exit(0);
 }
}
static void performInputTest() {
 try {
  MessageDigest md = MessageDigest.getInstance("SHA");
  FileInputStream fin = new FileInputStream("sha-results.txt");
  DigestInputStream in = new DigestInputStream(fin,md);
  byte[] b = new byte[testCase.length()];
  in.read(b,0,testCase.length());
  md = in.getMessageDigest();
  String s = Conversion.byteArrayToHexString(md.digest());
  System.out.println("\nInput test case: "+(new String(b)));
  System.out.println("Expected result:    "+expectedResult);
  System.out.println("Calculated result:  "+s);
 }catch(Exception e) {
  System.out.println(e);
  System. exit(0);
 }
 }
}
```

DigestException

DigestException, a subclass of java.security.GeneralSecurityException, is used to indicate that an exception has occurred during the calculation of a message digest. It is thrown by
the engineDigest() method of MessageDigestSpi and the digest() method of
MessageDigest.

Message Authentication Codes

Message authentication codes (MACs) are message digests that are computed using secret key cryptography. The key is used to detect modifications to a message that is sent over an insecure communication channel. For example, consider Figure 7.1. A wants to send message m to B. A calculates md, the message digest of m, and sends both m and md over an unprotected network to B. However, C intercepts m and md, modifies m (creating m'), and creates md' (the message digest of m'). C then sends m' and md' to B. When B verifies md', he finds that it is the correct message digest for m'.

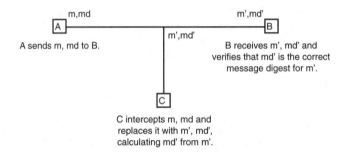

FIGURE 7.1

A security issue involving the use of message digests for message authentication.

Because message authentication codes use a key in the calculation of the message digest, messages that are sent out with a MAC cannot be intercepted, modified, and retransmitted without detection. For example, in Figure 7.2, if C modifies A's message, C must have A's key in order to calculate the MAC of the modified message.

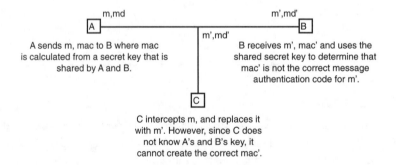

FIGURE 7.2

Using MACs for message authentication.

In the preceding example, a secure key distribution/agreement protocol is needed to distribute the key that is shared between A and B. Chapter 6 covers key distribution/agreement.

A MAC that uses a message digest or hash function is referred to as an HMAC. For example, HMACs can be created for use with MD5 or SHA-1. An HMAC uses a secret key with the message digest algorithm. RFC 2104 describes the use of HMACs.

Support for message authentication codes is provided with the `MacSpi` and `Mac` classes of `javax.crypto` (part of the Java Cryptography Extension). These classes are covered in the following sections.

MacSpi

The `MacSpi` class is an abstract class that offers a service provider interface for developing a provider-specific implementation of the `Mac` class. Its methods are as follows:

- `protected abstract void engineInit(java.security.Key key, java.security.spec.AlgorithmParameterSpec params)` —Initializes the MAC with the specified secret key and algorithm parameters.

- `protected abstract void engineUpdate(byte input)` —Updates the MAC with the given byte.

- `protected abstract void engineUpdate(byte[] input, int offset, int len)` —Updates the MAC with the specified portion of the `input` array.

- `protected abstract int engineGetMacLength()` —Returns the length of the MAC in bytes.

- `protected abstract void engineReset()` —Resets the MAC, but retains the secret key that initialized the MAC.

- `protected abstract byte[] engineDoFinal()` —Finishes the MAC computation and returns the MAC as a `byte` array. The MAC is reset but still retains the secret key with which it was initialized.

- `java.lang.Object clone()` —Provides the basis for implementing the `Cloneable` interface.

You don't need the preceding methods unless you want to develop your own MAC implementation. Most of us will use the default `Mac` class that is provided with `javax.crypto`.

Mac

The `Mac` class is the main class that is used in MAC calculation. The `Mac` class provides support for two MAC algorithms: HMAC-MD5 and HMAC-SHA1, both of which are described in RFC 2104, "HMAC: Keyed-Hashing for Message Authentication." The strings "`HmacMD5`" and "`HmacSHA1`" are used to identify these algorithms.

The `Mac` class, like `MessageDigest`, is a factory class. `Mac` objects are created using the static `getInstance()` method:

```
Mac mac = Mac.getInstance("HmacSHA1");
```

Another form of `getInstance()` enables a specific service provider to be identified.

The methods of `Mac` are as follows:

- `static Mac getInstance(java.lang.String algorithm)` —Creates a `Mac` object that implements the specified algorithm.
- `static Mac getInstance(java.lang.String algorithm, java.lang.String provider)` —Creates a `Mac` object that implements the specified algorithm and is from the specified provider.
- `void init(java.security.Key key)` —Initializes the `Mac` object with the given key.
- `void init(java.security.Key key, java.security.spec.AlgorithmParameterSpec params)` —Initializes the `Mac` object with the specified key and algorithm parameters.
- `void update(byte input)` —Updates the MAC with the specified byte.
- `void update(byte[] input)` —Updates the MAC with the specified `byte` array.
- `void update(byte[] input, int offset, int len)` —Updates the MAC with the identified portion of the `byte` array.
- `byte[] doFinal()` —Finishes the MAC operation and returns the MAC as a `byte` array.
- `byte[] doFinal(byte[] input)` —Processes the `byte` array, finishes the MAC operation, and returns the MAC as a `byte` array.
- `void doFinal(byte[] output, int outOffset)` —Processes the specified portion of the `byte` array, finishes the MAC operation, and returns the MAC as a `byte` array.
- `java.lang.String getAlgorithm()` —Returns the name of the algorithm used with the `Mac` object.
- `int getMacLength()` —Returns the length of the MAC in bytes.
- `java.security.Provider getProvider()` —Returns the provider of the `Mac` object.
- `void reset()` —Resets the `Mac` object.
- `java.lang.Object clone()` —Provides support for implementing the `Cloneable` interface.

You'll learn how to use these methods to calculate MACs in the next section, "MACs in Action."

MACs in Action

The `MACApp` program (shown in Listing 7.3) illustrates how MACs are created. It takes a text string (enclosed in quotes) as an argument

```
java com.jaworski.security.handbook.MACApp "This is a test."
```

and produces the following output:

```
Message: This is a test.
MAC:     ac2d81f3e5019f707fdc45ea05e842a9
```

The `performMACTest()` method uses the `getInstance()` method of `Mac` to create a `Mac` object that implements the `HmacMD5` algorithm. It creates a `KeyGenerator` object that works with `HmacMD5` and then generates a `SecretKey` object for use in initializing the `Mac` object. The initialization is performed using the `init()` method. The `update()` method is then used to update the `Mac` object with the text string that was typed at the command line. The `doFinal()` method completes the MAC calculation and returns the MAC as a `byte` array. The results of the calculation are then displayed.

LISTING 7.3   The `MACApp` Program

```
package com.jaworski.security.handbook;

import java.security.*;
import javax.crypto.*;

public class MACApp {
 static String errorMessage =
  "Usage: com.jaworski.security.handbook.MACApp testString";
 public static void main(String[] args) {
  if(args.length < 1)
   System.out.println(errorMessage);
  else performMACTest(args[0]);
 }
 static void performMACTest(String s) {
  try {
   String alg = "HmacMD5";
   Mac mac = Mac.getInstance(alg);
   KeyGenerator kg = KeyGenerator.getInstance(alg);
   SecretKey key = kg.generateKey();
   mac.init(key);
   mac.update(s.getBytes());
   byte[] b = mac.doFinal();
   System.out.println("\nMessage: "+s);
   System.out.println("MAC:     "+
    Conversion.byteArrayToHexString((b)));
```

LISTING 7.3 The MACApp Program

```
 }catch(Exception e) {
  System.out.println(e);
  System.exit (0);
 }
 }
}
```

Signature Classes and Interfaces

Digital signatures and the NIST digital signature algorithm were introduced in Chapter 5. In this section, you'll cover the signature classes of java.security in detail and learn how to use them to create signed objects.

SignatureSpi

The SignatureSpi class provides a service provider interface for the Signature class. SignatureSpi is implemented by developers who want to provide their own custom implementations of the Signature class. It defines the following methods:

- protected abstract void engineInitSign(PrivateKey *privateKey*)—Initializes the Signature object with the specified private key for use in signing operations.

- protected void engineInitSign(PrivateKey *privateKey*, SecureRandom *random*)— Initializes the Signature object with the specified private key and source of randomness for use in signing operations.

- protected abstract void engineInitVerify(PublicKey *publicKey*)—Initializes the Signature object with the specified public key for use in signature verification operations.

- protected void engineSetParameter(AlgorithmParameterSpec *params*)—Initializes the signature engine with the specified parameter set.

- protected abstract void engineSetParameter(String *param*, Object *value*)— This method has been deprecated in JDK 1.2 and is replaced by the previous engineSetParameter() method.

- protected abstract Object engineGetParameter(String *param*)—This method has been deprecated in JDK 1.2.

- protected abstract void engineUpdate(byte *b*)—Updates the data to be signed or verified using the specified byte.

- protected abstract void engineUpdate(byte[] *b*, int *off*, int *len*)—Updates the data to be signed or verified using the specified portion of the byte array.

- `protected abstract byte[] engineSign()`—Finishes the signature operation and returns the signature as a `byte` array.

- `protected int engineSign(byte[] outbuf, int offset, int len)`—Finishes the signature operation and returns the signature via `outbuf`.

- `protected abstract boolean engineVerify(byte[] sigBytes)`— Verifies the signature specified by `sigBytes`.

- `Object clone()`—Provides support for implementing the `Cloneable` interface.

The preceding abstract methods must be implemented by a service provider that implements a signature algorithm.

Signature

The `Signature` class provides a default implementation of the `SignatureSpi` abstract methods and supports both signature generation and verification. It supports an algorithm referred to as `SHA1withDSA`. This algorithm calculates an SHA-1 digest of a sequence of bytes and uses DSA to create and verify DSA digital signatures. DSA is described in FIPS PUB 186. The `Signature` class is a factory class, and `Signature` objects are created with the static `getInstance()` method:

```
Signature sign = Signature.getInstance("DSA");
```

A second form of the method allows a particular service provider to be specified.

The methods of `Signature` are as follows:

- `static Signature getInstance(String algorithm)`—Creates a `Signature` object that implements the specified signature algorithm.

- `static Signature getInstance(String algorithm, String provider)`—Creates a `Signature` object that implements the specified signature algorithm and is supplied from the specified provider (if available).

- `void setParameter(AlgorithmParameterSpec params)`—Initializes the signature engine with the specified parameter set.

- `void setParameter(String param, Object value)`—This method has been deprecated in JDK 1.2. Use the previous form of `setParameter()`.

- `Object getParameter(String param)`—This method has been deprecated in JDK 1.2.

- `Provider getProvider()`—Returns the provider of the `Signature` object.

- `String getAlgorithm()`—Returns the name of the algorithm used with the `Signature` object.

- `void initSign(PrivateKey privateKey)`—Initializes the `Signature` object for signing with the specified private key.

- `void initSign(PrivateKey *privateKey*, SecureRandom *random*)`—Initialize the `Signature` object for signing with the specified private key and source of randomness.

- `void initVerify(PublicKey *publicKey*)`—Initializes the `Signature` object for verification with the specified public key.

- `void update(byte *b*)`—Updates the data to be signed or verified by a byte.

- `void update(byte[] *data*)`—Updates the data to be signed or verified using the specified byte array.

- `void update(byte[] *data*, int *off*, int *len*)`—Updates the data to be signed or verified using the specified portion of the `byte` array.

- `byte[] sign()` —Returns the signature that has been calculated as a `byte` array.

- `int sign(byte[] *outbuf*, int *offset*, int *len*)` —Stores the calculated signature in `outbuf` and returns the length of the signature in bytes.

- `boolean verify(byte[] *signature*)`—Verifies the specified signature and returns a boolean value indicating the success or failure of the verification.

- `String toString()`—Returns a representation of the `Signature` object.

- `Object clone()`—Provides support for implementing the `Cloneable` interface.

The `Signature` class also defines the `protected state` variable, which can be in one of the three states, `UNINITIALIZED`, `SIGN`, and `VERIFY`.

Creating and Verifying Digital Signatures

The `SignApp` program of Listing 7.4 shows how signatures are created and verified. It takes a text string as an argument

```
java com.jaworski.security.handbook.SignApp "This is a test."
```

and produces the following output:

```
Generating key pair ...
Generating signature ...

Message: This is a test.
Private key:
MIIBTAIBADCCASwGByqGSM44BAEwggEfAoGBAOcC6xh0xr7EX6GtF7KwkrwutkQ1
uz8Y7yn2i+v1/X1gmsSKLqBBpIuJCKvPiZkepWUNmQlqCfX3YKUu9a4ULOEXzDDj
Gn7tAeZF8fJqybtj1jQy2G77ymXievqQ1SXTC8ksYl1Og0iAK29hQ2zvCCMx+eGu
8CEUjuYwsDV//ybXAhUA6BMUoT4DcaUi40c9nYZ6mqn0HncCgYEAg4IN8kl0qLaE
LZ20GZnvngOY4MxozByPMrzsmXIFRIPUZsZbosCXfHp8xso3pz5DJfMtX10sUnxK
uUYCiQ4j6GxqHvr3qt9QT03eP/bXx5DG0LmZ6s1wdIzJI6bibMYZtvTyP4VPsgVj
yGiFX/uAZDELX3PYcmjZ94rBhjV9j+0EFwIVAI5j5RYwxYQEBbBtFFGlyOd4XE2V
```

Public key:
MIIBtzCCASwGByqGSM44BAEwggEfAoGBAOcC6xh0xr7EX6GtF7KwkrwutkQ1uz8Y
7yn2i+v1/X1gmsSKLqBBpIuJCKvPiZkepWUNmQlqCfX3YKUu9a4ULOEXzDDjGn7t
AeZF8fJqybtjljQy2G77ymXievqQ1SXTC8ksYl1Og0iAK29hQ2zvCCMx+eGu8CEU
juYwsDV//ybXAhUA6BMUoT4DcaUi40c9nYZ6mqn0HncCgYEAg4IN8kl0qLaELZ20
GZnvngOY4MxozByPMrzsmXIFRIPUZsZbosCXfHp8xso3pz5DJfMtX10sUnxKuUYC
iQ4j6GxqHvr3qt9QT03eP/bXx5DG0LmZ6s1wdIzJI6bibMYZtvTyP4VPsgVjyGiF
X/uAZDELX3PYcmjZ94rBhjV9j+0DgYQAAoGAX1ZnfHw1ixOqxnF4uZ9qSo4mfAbD
saPS1Ts+AOXq77tOL3NWDjSZJOGQVkfua5+K0F76FI6tm/zpOlo2u1HurLELL+t4
g6OwMzkVztbWfW5JagHZwdnbs87jtyu2TwjuOLCGJrp82uCXXW+zU+Jdy0/64871
ZSfTdGK+EQ7eocM=

Signature:
MC4CFQDa3LzcBGuxW+HnSYcQ2nGY4Z+vPwIVAMLI+KF/DknI7tJ55D8K7DnN45tf

```
Verifying signature ...
Signature verified!
```

The program uses the NIST Digital Signature Algorithm for signing and is organized according to the generateKeyPair(), performSigning(), and performVerification() methods. The generateKeyPair() method returns a KeyPair object that is used in both performSigning() and performVerification(). The performSigning() method returns a byte array representation of a Signature object. The performVerification() method verifies this signature.

The generateKeyPair() method creates a KeyPairGenerator object for DSA and generates a KeyPair. This process can take a few minutes on a slow computer.

The performSigning() method creates a Signature object and then initializes it, via initSign(), for signing using the private key of the KeyPair object produced by generateKeyPair(). It then updates the signature via the update() method and creates the final signature via the sign() method. This signature is returned as the result of performSigning().

The performVertification() method verifies the signature that was returned by performSigning(). It uses the public key of the KeyPair object created by generateKeyPair().

This method creates a Signature object that uses DSA and initializes it for verification using the public key. It invokes the update() method of Signature to create a new signature and the verify() method to perform the signature verification.

LISTING 7.4   The `SignApp` Program

```
package com.jaworski.security.handbook;

import java.security.*;

public class SignApp {
 static String errorMessage =
  "Usage: com.jaworski.security.handbook.SignApp testString";
 public static void main(String[] args) {
  if(args.length < 1)
   System.out.println(errorMessage);
  else{
   String alg = "DSA";
   KeyPair keyPair = generateKeyPair(alg);
   byte[] signature = performSigning(args[0],alg,keyPair);
   performVerification(args[0],alg,signature,keyPair.getPublic());
  }
 }
 static KeyPair generateKeyPair(String alg) {
  try {
   KeyPairGenerator kg = KeyPairGenerator.getInstance(alg);
   System.out.println("Generating key pair ...");
   KeyPair keyPair = kg.genKeyPair();
   return keyPair;
  }catch(Exception e) {
   System.out.println(e);
   System.exit(0);
  }
  return null;
 }
 static byte[] performSigning(String s,String alg,KeyPair keyPair) {
  try {
   Signature sign = Signature.getInstance(alg);
   PrivateKey privateKey = keyPair.getPrivate();
   PublicKey publicKey = keyPair.getPublic();
   sign.initSign(privateKey);
   System.out.println("Generating signature ...");
   sign.update(s.getBytes());
   byte[] b = sign.sign();
   System.out.println("\nMessage: "+s);
   System.out.println("Private key:\n"+
    Conversion.byteArrayToBase64String(privateKey.getEncoded()));
   System.out.println("Public key:\n"+
    Conversion.byteArrayToBase64String(publicKey.getEncoded()));
   System.out.println("Signature:\n"+
```

LISTING 7.4 Continued

```
      Conversion.byteArrayToBase64String(b));
    return b;
  }catch(Exception e) {
    System.out.println(e);
    System.exit(0);
  }
  return null;
}
static void performVerification(String s, String alg,
    byte[] signature, PublicKey publicKey) {
  try {
    Signature sign = Signature.getInstance(alg);
    System.out.println("\nVerifying signature ...");
    sign.initVerify(publicKey);
    sign.update(s.getBytes());
    if(sign.verify(signature))
      System.out.println("Signature verified!");
    else
      System.out.println("Signature NOT verified!");
  }catch(Exception e){
    System.out.println(e);
    System.exit(0);
  }
 }
}
}
```

SignedObject

The `SignedObject` class provides the capability to create signed objects whose integrity can be verified. It provides a copy of a `Serializable` object and a signature of the serialized form of the object. The signature is created from a `Signature` object and signing (private) key that is provided to the `SignedObject` constructor:

```
Signature sign = Signature.getInstance("SHA1withDSA ");
SignedObject so = new SignedObject(objectToBeSigned, privatekey, sign);
```

The object's signature is verified using the `verify()` method. This method takes a `PublicKey` and `Signature` object as arguments. The `getObject()` method returns the original object that was signed:

```
Signature sign = Signature.getInstance("SHA1withDSA ");
if(so.verify(publickey, sign)) myObject = so.getObject();
```

The methods of `SignedObject` are summarized as follows:

- `boolean verify(PublicKey verificationKey, Signature verificationSignature)`—Verifies that the signature in the `SignedObject` is valid for the object stored inside. It bases verification on the verification key and verification signature object.
- `String getAlgorithm()`—Returns the name of the signature algorithm.
- `Object getObject()`—Returns the object that was signed.
- `byte[] getSignature()`—Returns the signature on the signed object as a `byte` array.

An example of using `SignedObject` is provided in the following section.

Using `SignedObject`

The `SignedObjectApp` program of Listing 7.5 shows how `SignedObjects` are created and verified. It produces the following output:

```
Generating key pair ...
Creating signed object ...

Verifying signature ...
Signature verified!
```

The key pair generation can take some time on a slow computer.

The `SignedObjectApp` program creates a DSA `KeyPair` object and a `Vector` that serves as the object that is signed. These objects are passed to `createSignedObject()`, which creates and returns a `SignedObject` based on the `Vector` that is signed using the private key of the `KeyPair`. The `performVerification()` method then verifies the signature of the `SignedObject`.

The `createSignedObject()` method creates a `Signature` object and passes the `Vector`, private key, and `Signature` object to the `SignedObject` constructor. The `SignedObject` instance that is created is then returned.

The `performVerification()` method creates a `Signature` object for verification purposes and passes this object and the public key of the key pair to the `verify()` method of `SignedObject`. The `verify()` method verifies the `Signature` using the public key.

LISTING 7.5   The `SignedObjectApp` Program

```
package com.jaworski.security.handbook;

import java.security.*;
import java.util.*;

public class SignedObjectApp {
  public static void main(String[] args) {
```

LISTING 7.5 Continued

```
  String alg = "DSA";
  KeyPair keyPair = generateKeyPair(alg);
  Vector v = new Vector();
  v.add("This is a test!");
  SignedObject so = createSignedObject(v,alg,keyPair);
  performVerification(so,alg,keyPair.getPublic());
 }
 static KeyPair generateKeyPair(String alg) {
  try {
   KeyPairGenerator kg = KeyPairGenerator.getInstance(alg);
   System.out.println("Generating key pair ...");
   KeyPair keyPair = kg.genKeyPair();
   return keyPair;
  }catch(Exception e) {
   System.out.println(e);
   System.exit(0);
  }
  return null;
 }
 static SignedObject createSignedObject(Vector v,String alg,KeyPair keyPair) {
  try {
   Signature sign = Signature.getInstance(alg);
   System.out.println("Creating signed object ...");
   SignedObject so =
    new SignedObject(v, keyPair.getPrivate(), sign);
   return so;
  }catch(Exception e) {
   System.out.println(e);
   System.exit(0);
  }
  return null;
 }
 static void performVerification(SignedObject so, String alg,
  PublicKey publicKey) {
  try {
   System.out.println("\nVerifying signature ...");
   Signature sign = Signature.getInstance(alg);
   if(so.verify(publicKey, sign))
    System.out.println("Signature verified!");
   else
    System.out.println("Signature NOT verified!");
  }catch(Exception e){
   System. out.println(e);
   System.exit(0);
  }
 }
}
```

Signer

The Signer class, a deprecated subclass of Identity, was used to support JDK 1.1 signatures. This class has been replaced by the Keystore class in JDK 1.2. Both Signer and KeyStore are covered in Chapter 6.

SignatureException

The SignatureException class is a subclass of GeneralSecurityException. SignatureException is used to represent exceptions that occur during signature generation and verification. This class is thrown by methods and constructors of Signature, SignatureSpi, and SignedObject.

Summary

This chapter covered the classes used to create message digests, MACs, and digital signatures. It also provided practical examples of using the classes to create and verify these objects. In the next chapter, "The Java Cryptography Extension," you'll cover the details of the Java Cryptography Extension (JCE) and learn how to develop a service provider.

The Java Cryptography Extension

You've been working with the JCE since Chapter 5, "An Introduction to Cryptography." However, you haven't focused specifically on the capabilities provided by the JCE. In this chapter, you'll take a high-level view of the JCE. I'll describe its organization and capabilities and introduce any special classes and interfaces that were not covered in earlier chapters. You'll also take a look at the Cryptix JCE, another JCE implementation that is internationally available via the Web. Finally, you'll look at how cryptographic providers are developed and develop a small provider of your own.

Inside the JCE

United States export control laws restrict the exporting of certain types of cryptographic software outside the United States and Canada. If the JCE 1.2 were a part of the JDK, the JDK, as a whole, would fall under these export control laws. This would severely limit Java's world-wide popularity. Although the JCE was not developed specifically to deal with U.S. export control laws, you can think of it as a set of packages that contains the implementations of security-sensitive cryptographic algorithms that would otherwise be restricted. These packages are as follows:

- `javax.crypto`—Provides the 14 classes, one interface, and four exceptions that support basic cryptographic algorithms.

- `javax.crypto.interfaces`—Provides three interfaces that support Diffie-Hellman keys.
- `javax.crypto.spec`—Provides 12 classes that define key specifications and algorithm parameter specifications.

With only three packages, 26 classes, four interfaces, and four exceptions, the JCE is rather small.

> **NOTE**
>
> ## Downloading and Installing the JCE
> Appendix E, "Downloading and Installing the JCE 1.2," covers all that you need to know to obtain the JCE 1.2 and get it working on your system.

The `javax.crypto` package is the heart of the JCE. It defines the `SecretKey` interface, which extends `java.security.Key` to provide support for symmetric, secret-key cryptography. The classes defined by `javax.crypto` also define fundamental cryptographic objects. They are summarized as follows:

- `Cipher`—Encapsulates the notion of a cipher and provides support for cipher selection, encryption, and decryption.
- `CipherSpi`—The service provider interface for the `Cipher` class.
- `NullCipher`—A subclass of `Cipher` that maps plaintext to ciphertext without performing any transformation. It is referred to as an *identity cipher* and is typically used for testing purposes.
- `CipherInputStream`—The combination of an `InputStream` and a `Cipher` that supports the decryption of data that is read from the `InputStream` using the `Cipher`.
- `CipherOutputStream`—The combination of an `OutputStream` and a `Cipher` that supports the encryption of data that is written to the `OutputStream` using the `Cipher`.
- `SealedObject`—Provides the capability to work with objects that have been serialized and encrypted.
- `SecretKeyFactory`—A key factory for transforming secret keys into key specifications and vice versa.
- `SecretKeyFactorySpi`—The service provider interface for the `SecretKeyFactory` class.
- `KeyGenerator`—A key generator for symmetric (secret-key) ciphers.
- `KeyGeneratorSpi`—Theservice provider interface for the `KeyGenerator` class.

- KeyAgreement—Encapsulates a key agreement/exchange protocol.
- KeyAgreementSpi—The service provider interface for the KeyAgreement class.
- Mac—Encapsulates a message authentication code (MAC) algorithm.
- MacSpi—The service provider interface for the Mac class.

The four exceptions defined by javax.crypto are

- BadPaddingException
- IllegalBlockSizeException
- NoSuchPaddingException
- ShortBufferException

They extend java.security.GeneralSecurityException to define exceptions with the size and padding of data processed by cryptographic algorithms.

The javax.crypto.interfaces package defines the DHKey, DHPrivateKey, and DHPublicKey interfaces. DHKey provides access to a Diffie-Helman key, and DHPrivateKey and DHPublicKey provide access to the private and public key components.

The javax.crypto.spec package defines the following key and algorithm parameter specifications:

- DESedeKeySpec
- DESKeySpec
- DHGenParameterSpec
- DHParameterSpec
- DHPrivateKeySpec
- DHPublicKeySpec
- IvParameterSpec
- PBEKeySpec
- PBEParameterSpec
- RC2ParameterSpec
- RC5ParameterSpec
- SecretKeySpec

The key specifications enable keys to be defined in a provider-independent manner. The algorithm parameter specifications are used to define various parameters used with cryptographic algorithms.

The Cryptix JCE

The Cryptix Foundation Limited has developed a clean room version of the JCE 1.2, which is available over the Web at http://www.cryptix.org. It is not subject to U.S. export restrictions.

The Cryptix JCE is aimed at being 100% compatible with Sun's JCE 1.2. However, it provides support for additional cryptographic algorithms not available in Sun's implementation. The complete list of algorithms supported by the Cryptix JCE include

- Ciphers—Blowfish, CAST5, DES, IDEA, MARS, RC2, RC4, RC6, Rijndael, Serpent, SKIPJACK, Square, TripleDES, Twofish
- KeyAgreement Protocols—Diffie-Hellman
- Modes—CBC, ECB, OFB
- Hashes—MD2, MD4, MD5, RIPEMD-128, RIPEMD-160, SHA-0, SHA-1, Tiger
- MACs—HMAC-MD2, HMAC-MD4, HMAC-MD5, HMAC-RIPEMD-128, HMAC-RIPEMD-160, HMAC-SHA-0, HMAC-SHA-1, HMAC-Tiger
- Signatures—RawDSA, RSA
- Assymetric ciphers —ElGamal, RSA

Even if you currently have Sun's JCE installed, you might want to download and install the Cryptix JCE because of the additional capabilities that it provides.

> **NOTE**
>
> ## The Cryptix JCE
> If you are outside the United States and Canada and cannot obtain a copy of Sun's JCE, you should download and install the Cryptix JCE, as described in Appendix E.

Security Providers and Algorithm Independence

One of the design features of the Java Security API and JCE is their support for cryptographic package providers. This support enables software developers to provide an independent implementation of specific cryptographic algorithms. A provider takes the form of a set of packages that implement a subset of the JCE or Java Security API.

The advantage of the Java Security API's cryptographic package provider support is that it provides a common framework for extending the API with additional algorithms, as well as with faster or more secure implementations of existing algorithms. For example, some packages might be implemented in hardware or native code to speed up algorithm response times, whereas others might be implemented in a platform-independent manner to ensure widespread availability. The end result is that the developers of cryptographic applications are able to select the algorithms and providers that best fit their needs.

Cryptographic applications can query the Java runtime environment to determine which providers have been statically installed and then dynamically install any new providers that are needed by the applications. In addition, providers can be installed in a preference order. This enables applications to choose one provider over another when a particular algorithm is supported by multiple providers.

The standard provider that is installed with the JCE 1.2 is SunJCE. SunJCE provides popular algorithms that implement the cryptographic classes of the JCE 1.2.

How a Security Provider Is Organized

The Java Security API and JCE support security providers through the use of engine, SPI, and provider classes.

Engine Classes

Engine classes define general types of cryptographic objects and the API for accessing those objects. Examples of engine classes are as follows:

- `javax.crypto`
    - `Cipher`
    - `KeyAgreement`
    - `KeyGenerator`
    - `Mac`
    - `SecretKeyFactory`
- `java.security`
    - `AlgorithmParameterGenerator`
    - `AlgorithmParameters`
    - `KeyFactory`
    - `KeyPairGenerator`
    - `KeyStore`
    - `MessageDigest`
    - `SecureRandom`
    - `Signature`

- `java.security.cert`
  - `CertificateFactory`

To use an engine class, invoke its static `getInstance()` method with the name of a specific algorithm and (optionally) a provider name.

SPI Classes

The SPI classes are abstract classes that provide a mechanism by which service providers can define their own implementations of the objects represented by and algorithms used by the engine classes. Each SPI class is used with a unique engine class. The SPI class has the same name as the corresponding engine class with `Spi` appended to it.

For example, to create a custom cipher algorithm for use with the `Cipher` engine class, you extend `CipherSpi` and override its abstract methods with the implementation of your custom cipher algorithm.

Provider Classes

The provider classes extend the `java.security.Provider` class. These classes supply the name, version number, and general information about the service provider. They also set properties that map algorithm names to the classes that implement those algorithms.

You'll see examples of the relationship between engine classes, SPI classes, and provider classes in the next section. You'll also develop a custom provider that supports a variation of the rot13 cipher.

Creating a New Provider

To show you how providers are developed and organized, you'll develop a provider that supplies a custom implementation of the rot13 cipher. The rot13 cipher is a very simple, keyless cipher that has been around since the time of Caesar. In fact, it is the Caesar cipher with a rotation of 13. The section, "A Short History of Secret Writing," in Chapter 5 covers the Caesar cipher and rot13.

Instead of limiting rot13 to the letters of the alphabet, you'll apply it to all 256 possible byte values. That is the byte value of n (between 0 and 255 inclusive) will be mapped to

`(n + 13) % 256`

To decrypt an encrypted byte value m, map it to

`(m + 243) % 256`

You'll encrypt using ECB mode and without padding (refer to Chapter 5).

Because you're developing an encryption algorithm, you'll work with the `Cipher` (the engine) and `CipherSpi` (the corresponding SPI class) classes of `javax.crypto`. You'll also extend the `java.security.Provider` class with a custom provider class that supports rot13.

Extending the SPI Class

Listing 8.1 provides the `Rot13Cipher` class, which extends `CipherSpi` to provide a rot13 implementation. When extending an SPI class, it is important to provide a `public`, parameterless constructor. This constructor is invoked by the `newInstance()` method of the `Class` class when a instance of the class is created. Other than the `public`, parameterless constructor, all you do is provide an implementation of all `abstract` methods inherited from the SPI class.

In the case of `CipherSpi`, there are 13 methods that require implementation. The three forms of `engineInit()` are used to initialize the cryptographic algorithm. Our rot13 implementation only needs to set the mode (`Ciper.ENCRYPT_MODE` or `Cipher.DECRYPT_MODE`) in which the algorithm is to operate. All other arguments are ignored.

The two forms of `engineUpdate()` perform the actual encryption/decryption operations. These methods use the `cipher()` method to apply the cipher. The second form of `engineUpdate()` checks the size of the output buffer before applying the cipher.

The two forms of `engineDoFinal()` perform the same processing as `engineUpdate()`. The `engineUpdate()` method is intended for intermediate cryptographic processing, and the `engineDoFinal()` method is used to perform the final operation on a `byte` sequence. As such, `doFinal()` would incorporate operations such as padding. However, rot13 does not require any specific finalization processing.

The `engineGetBlockSize()` method returns a value of 1 because rot13 operates on one byte at a time. The `engineGetOutputSize()` method maps input length to output length because rot13 provides a byte-for-byte transformation.

The `engineSetMode()` and `engineSetPadding()` methods support the `ECB` and `NoPadding` options.

The `engineGetParameters()` and `engineGetIV()` methods return null because rot13 does not require any special parameters or an initialization vector.

LISTING 8.1 The `Rot13Cipher` Class

```
package com.jaworski.security.handbook;

import java.security.*;
import java.security.spec.*;
import javax.crypto.*;
```

LISTING 8.1   Continued

```java
public class Rot13Cipher extends CipherSpi {
 private int opmode = Cipher.ENCRYPT_MODE;
 private int encryptionKey = 13;
 private int decryptionKey = 243;
 // Default constructor.
 public Rot13Cipher() {
 }
 // Implement the cipher
 private byte cipher(byte b) {
  int key = encryptionKey;
  if(opmode == Cipher.DECRYPT_MODE)
   key = decryptionKey;
  return (byte) ((b + key) % 256);
 }
 // CipherSpi that must be implemented.
 protected void engineInit(int opmode, Key key,
   AlgorithmParameterSpec params, SecureRandom random) {
  this.opmode = opmode;
 }
 protected void engineInit(int opmode, Key key,
   AlgorithmParameters params, SecureRandom random) {
  this.opmode = opmode;
 }
 protected void engineInit(int opmode, Key key, SecureRandom random) {
  this.opmode = opmode;
 }
 protected byte[] engineUpdate(byte[] input, int inputOffset,
   int inputLen) {
  byte[] b = new byte[inputLen];
  for(int i=0; i<inputLen; ++i)
   b[i] = cipher(input[inputOffset + i]);
  return b;
 }
 protected int engineUpdate(byte[] input, int inputOffset,
   int inputLen, byte[] output, int outputOffset)
   throws ShortBufferException {
  String msg = "Not enough room in output buffer.";
  if((output.length - outputOffset) < inputLen)
   throw new ShortBufferException(msg);
  for(int i=0; i<inputLen; ++i)
   output[outputOffset + i] = cipher(input[inputOffset + i]);
  return inputLen;
 }
 protected byte[] engineDoFinal(byte[] input, int inputOffset,
```

LISTING 8.1 Continued

```java
   int inputLen) {
  byte[] b = new byte[inputLen];
  for(int i=0; i<inputLen; ++i)
   b[i] = cipher(input[inputOffset + i]);
  return b;
 }
 protected int engineDoFinal(byte[] input, int inputOffset,
   int inputLen, byte[] output, int outputOffset)
   throws ShortBufferException {
  String msg = "Not enough room in output buffer.";
  if((output.length - outputOffset) < inputLen)
   throw new ShortBufferException(msg);
  for(int i=0; i<inputLen; ++i)
   output[outputOffset + i] = cipher(input[inputOffset + i]);
  return inputLen;
 }
 protected int engineGetBlockSize() {
  return 1;
 }
 protected int engineGetOutputSize(int inputLen) {
  return inputLen;
 }
 protected void engineSetMode(String mode)
   throws NoSuchAlgorithmException {
  String msg = "ROT13 only supports ECB mode.";
  if(!mode.toUpperCase().equals("ECB"))
   throw new NoSuchAlgorithmException(msg);
 }
 protected void engineSetPadding(String padding)
   throws NoSuchPaddingException {
  String msg = "ROT13 only supports the NoPadding option.";
  if(!padding.toUpperCase().equals("NOPADDING"))
   throw new NoSuchPaddingException(msg);
 }
 protected AlgorithmParameters engineGetParameters() {
  return null;
 }
 protected byte[] engineGetIV() {
  return null;
 }
}
```

Extending the Provider Class

Having implemented `Rot13Cipher` as a concrete subclass of `CipherSpi`, you now extend `java.security.Provider` to define a provider class. Listing 8.2 contains the `Rot13Provider` extension of `Provider`.

The `Rot13Provider()` constructor invokes the superclass constructor to pass the provider name, version number, and descriptive information to the `Provider` constructor. This information is used to register the provider. It also uses the `put()` method (inherited from `Provider`) to associate the ROT13 cipher with the `com.jaworski.security.handbook.Rot13Cipher` class.

The `put()` method takes two arguments: One is in the form *engine.algorithm,* and the second is the name of the class that implements the algorithm for the specific provider. Because you are working with the `Cipher` engine (through `CipherSpi`), and you're implementing an algorithm named ROT13, the first argument is `"Cipher.ROT13"`. The second argument is simply the name of the class resulting from Listing 8.1.

Cipher algorithm names can include the encryption mode and padding into the algorithm name. These are written in the form `"algorithmName/mode/padding"`. For example, you can use `"ROT13/ECB/NoPadding"`. If you supported cipher block chaining with PKCS 5 padding, you can use `"ROT13/CBC/PKCS5Padding"`. Multiple `put()` invocations can be used to associate multiple algorithm/mode/padding combinations with their implementation classes.

LISTING 8.2   The `Rot13Provider` Class

```
package com.jaworski.security.handbook;

import java.security.*;

public final class Rot13Provider extends Provider {
 public Rot13Provider() {
  // Pass info to superclass constructor
  super("Rot13Provider", 1.0,
   "Rot13Provider 1.0 provides a custom ROT13 implementation.");
  // Set provider properties
  put("Cipher.ROT13","com.jaworski.security.handbook. Rot13Cipher");
 }
}
```

Installing Provider Classes

Having developed the rot13 cipher's implementation and provider classes, all that's left is to install these classes. This amounts to putting them in your CLASSPATH and configuring them in the `java.security` file. Typically, provider classes are distributed as a JAR file, and the JAR file is placed in the CLASSPATH. Because the Rot13Cipher and Rot13Provider classes depend on the JCE, the JCE must be installed in order for them to work.

Editing the java.security file enables the provider class to be statically added to the set of known, approved providers. Edit C:\jdk1.2.2\jre\lib\security\java.security and look for the following:

```
#
# List of providers and their preference orders (see above):
#
security.provider.1=sun.security.provider.Sun
security.provider.2=com.sun.crypto.provider.SunJCE
```

Then add the following line:

```
security.provider.3=com.jaworski.security.handbook.Rot13Provider
```

You can also add a provider dynamically via the addProvider() and insertProviderAt() methods of the java.security.Security class.

NOTE

Install the Rot13Provider

Make sure that you install the Rot13Provider before going on to the next section.

Using the Provider

Having developed and installed the Rot13Provider, we'll write a test program that loads the provider, verifies its properties, and performs a sample encryption. The ProviderTest program of Listing 8.3 is this program. It displays the following results:

```
Provider name: Rot13Provider
Provider version: 1.0
Provider information: Rot13Provider 1.0 provides a custom ROT13 implementation.
Cipher: ROT13
Data to be encrypted: This is a test!
Encrypted data: 617576802d76802d6e2d817280812e
Decrypted data: 546869732069732061207465737421
Decrypted data as a String: This is a test!
```

The ProviderTest program invokes two methods, listProviderInfo() and testCipher(), that perform these tests. The listProviderInfo() method loads the Rot13Provider and displays the information returned by the getName(), getVersion(), and getInfo() methods inherited from Provider.

The testCipher() method creates a Cipher object that implements the rot13 algorithm as supplied by the Rot13Provider:

```
Cipher cipher = Cipher.getInstance("ROT13", "Rot13Provider");
```

It then initializes this object and puts it in the encryption mode:

```
cipher.init(Cipher.ENCRYPT_MODE,null,new SecureRandom());
```

A SecureRandom object is provided with init() so that the compiler can tell which form of init() to use. However, the SecureRandom object is not used by Rot13Cipher.

The test string is encrypted via the doFinal() method of Cipher:

```
byte[] b1 = cipher.doFinal(testString.getBytes());
```

The cipher is then reinitialized in decryption mode, and the encrypted data is decrypted:

```
cipher.init(Cipher.DECRYPT_MODE,null,new SecureRandom());
byte[] b2 = cipher.doFinal(b1);
```

The results of these operations are then displayed to the console.

LISTING 8.3   The ProviderTest Program

```
package com.jaworski.security.handbook;

import java.security.*;
import javax.crypto.*;

public final class ProviderTest {
 String providerName = "Rot13Provider";
 String algorithmName ="ROT13";
 public static void main(String[] args) {
  listProviderInfo();
  testCipher();
 }
 static void listProviderInfo() {
  Provider p = Security.getProvider("Rot13Provider");
  System.out.println("Provider name: " + p.getName());
  System.out.println("Provider version: " + p.getVersion());
  System.out.println("Provider information: " + p.getInfo());
 }
 static void testCipher() {
  try {
   Cipher cipher = Cipher.getInstance("ROT13", "Rot13Provider");
   System.out.println("Cipher: " + cipher.getAlgorithm());
   String testString = "This is a test!";
```

LISTING 8.3   Continued

```
  cipher.init(Cipher.ENCRYPT_MODE,null,new SecureRandom());
  byte[] b1 = cipher.doFinal(testString.getBytes());
  cipher.init(Cipher.DECRYPT_MODE,null,new SecureRandom());
  byte[] b2 = cipher.doFinal(b1);
  System.out.println("Data to be encrypted: " + testString);
  System.out.println("Encrypted data: " +
   Conversion.byteArrayToHexString(b1));
  System.out.println("Decrypted data: " +
   Conversion.byteArrayToHexString(b2));
  System.out.println("Decrypted data as a String: " + new String(b2));
 }catch(Exception e) {
  e.printStackTrace();
  System. exit(0);
 }
 }
}
```

Summary

In this chapter, you took a high-level view of the JCE and learned its organization and capabilities. You also looked at the Cryptix JCE. You learned how cryptographic providers are organized in terms of engine, SPI, and provider classes. Then you developed and tested a provider that implements the rot13 cipher. In the next chapter, you'll learn how the Java Authentication and Authorization Service (JAAS) is used to support strong authentication and user authorization.

8

THE JAVA
CRYPTOGRAPHY
EXTENSION

SSL and JSSE

The Secure Socket Layer (SSL) provides a standard protocol operating over TCP/IP through which encrypted traffic can be exchanged between a client and a server. The Java Secure Socket Extension (JSSE) provides a standard Java-based API to SSL. Underlying SSL provider implementations can be used with JSSE, while a standard and stable API is provided for JSSE clients. In this chapter, we will briefly explore the SSL standard and JSSE API mechanisms used by clients and servers.

In this chapter, you will learn

- The basics of the SSL protocol
- The basic architecture of the JSSE API
- The means by which JSSE provider implementations are used with the JSSE API
- The basic approach for building SSL servers using JSSE
- The basic approach for building SSL clients using JSSE
- The concepts behind SSL sessions and JSSE APIs being available to encapsulate such concepts

SSL Overview

SSL is a communications protocol layer created by the Netscape Communications Corporation. It rests atop the TCP/IP protocol stack. SSL provides secure services over TCP/IP, such as confidentiality through data encryption, integrity via a MAC algorithm, and optional authenticity and nonrepudiation of both a socket client and a socket server. Although operating over TCP/IP, SSL can also operate under other TCP/IP-based protocols such as HTTP and IIOP. Thus, SSL can be viewed as a layer that operates between TCP/IP and higher-level communications protocols, such as HTTP and IIOP, to provide a secure communications solution. Note that although SSL most typically operates above TCP/IP, it can also operate above other reliable transport protocols.

SSL v1 was never publicly used, but Netscape introduced SSL v2 with version 1 of Netscape Navigator. SSL v3 represents the most current SSL standard in wide use. The Transport Layer Security (TLS) protocol developed by the Internet Engineering Task Force (IETF) extends the SSL v3 protocol with enhancements to the authentication aspects of the SSL algorithm. The Wireless Transport Layer Security (WTLS) protocol, as its name implies, is a version of TLS used in wireless communications.

The SSL v3 behavior follows the basic algorithmic sequence described here:

1. An SSL Client connects to an SSL Server.
2. The SSL Client sends a client hello message to the SSL Server containing the SSL version number, any crypto methods supported by the client, and a random byte stream.
3. The SSL Server sends a server hello message to the SSL Client containing the SSL version number, the selected crypto method, a session ID, and a random byte stream.
4. The SSL Server sends a server X.509 certificate to the SSL Client.
5. (Optional Client Authentication) The SSL Server sends a certificate request to the SSL Client.
6. The SSL Client authenticates the SSL Server using the server certificate by checking the validity date on the certificate, determining whether the signing CA is trusted, verifying the signature, and possibly determining whether the domain name of the server certificate matches the domain name of the server.
7. The SSL Client generates a premaster secret key and encrypts it with the server public key.
8. The SSL Client sends the encrypted premaster secret key to the SSL Server.
9. (Optional Client Authentication) The SSL Client sends a client X.509 certificate and another signed piece of data to the SSL Server.

10. (Optional Client Authentication) The SSL Server authenticates the SSL Client using the client certificate by checking the validity date on the certificate, determining whether the signing CA is trusted, and verifying the signature.

11. The SSL Client and SSL Server both use the premaster secret to generate a master secret.

12. The SSL Client and SSL Server both independently generate a secret session key from the master key.

13. The SSL Client and SSL Server exchange cipher specification messages indicating that any subsequent messages should be encrypted using the secret session key.

14. The SSL Client and SSL Server exchange a handshake-finished message encrypted with the session key indicating that the SSL Session can now begin.

In addition to this basic handshaking protocol, messages can be sent between SSL client and server to indicate certain warning and error conditions. A protocol for changing the crypto algorithm used by the SSL session is also provided by SSL.

It is the SSL handshaking protocol, however, that provides the most insight into the utility of SSL. While the server can authenticate a client by validating the client's public certificate, this does not provide a complete authentication solution. Rather, the fact that key exchange messages are generated by the client using the client's private key enables the server to successfully decrypt information sent by the client to the server. The server thus authenticates that the actual client sent such information based on use of the client's public certificate. The same authentication process applies to the client's authentication of the server. Thus, the server-side SSL process must have a means to access the key store for the server private key during server authentication, and the client must have a means to access the key store for the client private key during client authentication.

A full description of SSL is beyond the scope of this book. But it does help to have a basic understanding of the SSL handshaking protocol as described above. This will enable you to better understand how to construct Java applications that utilize an API to SSL. Such an understanding can help you understand what SSL can and cannot do for you when providing confidential communications between a client and server. For example, based on the basic algorithmic SSL handshaking sequence described earlier, it may be apparent to you how difficult delegation of client identity is via SSL. That is, when using client authentication with SSL, the client's private key, retrieved from a key store, is used on the client-side in the process of generating the key exchange information. Thus, if the SSL client process is acting on behalf of another actual user process, the SSL client would have to have the private key of the actual user process. This is of course unacceptable in many situations.

Thus, while most people think of authentication as the means by which users authenticate themselves with a server process in order to perform security-critical operations, intermediate processes that must present themselves to the server on behalf of the end user may find it difficult to do so using SSL. More often than not, when using SSL for providing confidentiality between a client and server, the authentication that takes place is to authenticate the two end processes involved with the SSL session. A higher-level authentication process may actually be implemented above SSL in order for an SSL client to delegate end user process identity to the SSL server. For more information on SSL, check out `http://www.assuredtech.com/resources/ssl`.

Java Secure Socket Extension Overview

The Java Secure Socket Extension (JSSE) provides a standard API to secure socket protocols such as SSL. The JSSE also supports an API to the Transport Layer Security (TLS) secure socket protocol. These are the specific protocol versions that are supported:

- SSL version 2 and 3
- TLS version 1

These versions are supported only by virtue of the JSSE API. At the time of this writing, Sun provided a reference implementation for only a subset of these protocols (SSL v3 and TLS v1). As with the other security extensions, the JSSE architecture follows the same adapter model of providing an API and a service provider interface for different underlying implementations to plug into the JSSE. The JSSE v1.0 download is available at `http://java.sun.com/products/jsse/`.

JSSE Package and Class Overview

The following packages compose the JSSE v1.0 architecture:

- `javax.net.ssl`: This package contains the set of core classes and interfaces for the JSSE APIs.
- `javax.net`: This package is not specific to the JSSE, but it is needed to support basic client socket and server socket factory functionality.
- `javax.security.cert`: This package is also not specific to the JSSE, but it is needed to support basic certificate management functionality.

The JSSE class architecture is primarily useful for its encapsulation of SSL socket and SSL server socket objects and factories. SSL session handles can also be useful. Finally, the SSL binding and handshake event and listener APIs are also provided. Figure 9.1 depicts this core architecture of the JSSE. Note that, in order to keep the overview discussion brief, overloaded methods or method signatures are not shown in this diagram. The following list describes the role of each major API class or interface in the JSSE architecture:

- SSLSocket: A socket that supports SSL, TLS, and WTLS secure socket protocols
- SocketFactory: A factory for Socket objects
- SSLSocketFactory: A factory for SSLSocket objects
- SSLServerSocket: A server socket that supports SSL, TLS, and WTLS secure socket protocols
- ServerSocketFactory: A factory for ServerSocket objects
- SSLServerSocketFactory: A factory for SSLServerSocket objects
- SSLSession: An interface to an object encapsulating an SSL session
- SSLSessionContext: An interface to an object encapsulating a collection of SSL sessions identified with a session ID
- SSLBindingEvent: An event class encapsulating SSL session binding and unbinding events
- SSLBindingListener: A listener interface implemented by objects wanting to be made aware of SSL session binding and unbinding events
- HandshakeCompletedEvent: An event class encapsulating the fact that an SSL handshake has completed
- HandshakeCompletedListener: A listener interface implemented by objects wanting to be made aware of SSL handshake completion events

Thus, as you can see, the basic JSSE architecture is rather simple and yet provides a core suite of API abstractions necessary for tapping the functionality of SSL from within Java applications. The remainder of this chapter will describe the most important JSSE API abstractions in more detail and demonstrate how to use them in your applications. Note however that at the time of this writing, the JSSE API was still fairly young in its version 1.0 release form. Thus, the chapter discussion focuses on the core JSSE APIs and most commonly used interfaces for immediate practical API usage. Additional vendor-specific SSL library interfaces may still be utilized by Java JSSE API developers in actual real-world implementations.

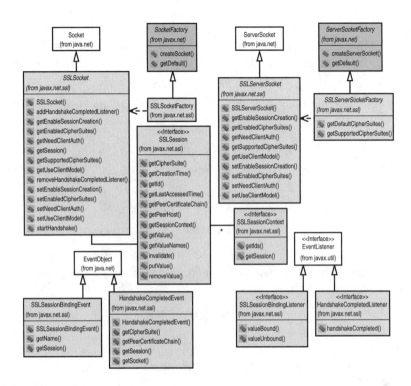

FIGURE 9.1
The JSSE architecture.

JSSE Providers

As with other Java 2 security and JCA means for configuring security module providers for use by a particular JVM instance, the JSSE follows the same provider configuration scheme. That is, a JSSE provider can be configured for use with a JVM instance by configuring an entry in the [JRE_HOME]\lib\security\java.security file. A security.provider.x entry in that file can be modified or added to reference a particular security provider. For example, you might have

```
security.provider.1=com.assuredtech.security.SSLProvider
```

Similarly, a security provider might also be configured for use with a JVM instance from within a static method call to the java.security.Security class as exemplified here:

```
// Add new instance of a JSSE provider
java.security.Provider provider
        = new com.sun.net.ssl.internal.ssl.Provider();
java.security.Security.addProvider(provider);
```

The provider class name used for this example is simply the default SSL provider that comes equipped with the downloaded JSSE reference implementation. The end-to-end SSL client and server example that is built up throughout this chapter in fact assumes that your SSL client and SSL server have established the default security provider during startup as shown above. The default provider implementation packaged with the JSSE reference implementation provides support for SSL v3 and TLS v1. The default implementation also provides support for RSA encryption used in generating signatures, support for PKCS12 key stores, X.509 key management functionality for loading authentication keys from a key store, and X.509 trust management functionality for chaining of certificates.

JSSE SSL Server Sockets

Creating SSL server sockets can be as simple as creating regular Java TCP/IP server sockets. SSL server socket abstractions provide additional hooks, however, to manipulate the security and SSL-related operation characteristics of SSL socket connections. SSL cipher parameters, authentication properties, and handshaking management are also exposed by the SSL abstractions. Although standard APIs exist for creating SSL server sockets using standard SSL server socket factories, the means by which handles to SSL server socket factories are obtained can be JSSE provider-specific.

In this section, we explore the most basic steps for creating JSSE SSL server socket factories, creating SSL server sockets, and blocking for SSL client socket requests in the context of an example SSL server. Manipulation of such sockets is then most often implemented just as regular java.net TCP/IP sockets are manipulated.

Obtaining an SSL Server Socket Factory

The JSSE uses the concept of socket factories to create handles to SSL sockets. The javax.net.ServerSocketFactory class is an abstract class used to create generic server sockets. It is subclassed by the javax.net.ssl.SSLServerSocketFactory abstract class to create SSL server socket handles. A handle to a default server socket provided by the JSSE provider can be yielded with the following static method call:

```
javax.net.ssl.SSLServerSocketFactory sslServerSocket
    = SSLServerSocketFactory.getDefault();
```

The default server socket factory class name is identified in the [JRE_HOME]\lib\
security\java.security file for your Java runtime environment using the
ssl.ServerSocketFactory.provider property name as exemplified here:

```
ssl.ServerSocketFactory.provider=com.assuredtech.ssl.ServerSocketFactory
```

Additionally, JSSE providers will often provide vendor-specific ways to obtain handles to SSLServerSocketFactory objects so that server authentication information can be provided.

9

SSL AND JSSE

For example, the JSSE reference implementation provides a `com.sun.net.ssl.SSLContext` class that can be used to obtain handles to concrete `SSLServerSocketFactory` implementation objects after proper initialization. Before you can use the reference implementation's `SSLContext` object to obtain such an SSL server socket factory, you must take a number of steps to configure the SSL server socket with particular security and operational properties.

The standard JCA `java.security.KeyStore` object is first used to obtain a handle to a stored collection of server certificates and keys. For example, a `KeyStore` object is created using the JCA-provided JKS key store type with a `samplestore` key store file name, and it is loaded using a SAMPLESTOREPASS password via the following sample block of code:

```
// Get and load standard KeyStore
java.security.KeyStore keyStore = null;
try{
  // Get key store instance
  String keyStoreType = "JKS";
  keyStore = KeyStore.getInstance(keyStoreType);
  // Create key store file stream
  String keyStoreFileName = "samplestore";
  FileInputStream fileInputStream
    = new FileInputStream(keyStoreFileName);
  // Load keys store from file stream given a password
  String keyStorePassword = "SAMPLESTOREPASS";
  char[] keyStorePassordInChars = keyStorePassword.toCharArray();
  keyStore.load(fileInputStream, keyStorePassordInChars);
}
catch(NoSuchAlgorithmException noAlgorithmEx){
  noAlgorithmEx.printStackTrace();
}
catch(FileNotFoundException fileNotFoundException){
  fileNotFoundException.printStackTrace();
}
catch(IOException ioException){
  ioException.printStackTrace();
}
catch(KeyStoreException keyStoreException){
  keyStoreException.printStackTrace();
}
catch(CertificateException certificateException){
  certificateException.printStackTrace();
}
```

A special JSSE reference implementation-specific collection of key managers is then created using the JCA `KeyStore` object. This object is used to manage the keys employed during the SSL authentication process. For example, a collection of X509-based key managers is created using the `com.sun.net.ssl.KeyManager` class as shown here:

```
// Get reference implementation key managers given key store
com.sun.net.ssl.KeyManager[] keyManagers = null;
try{
  // Create a key manager factory given an algorithm
  String keyManagerAlgorithm = "SunX509";
  com.sun.net.ssl.KeyManagerFactory keyManagerFactory =
  KeyManagerFactory.getInstance(keyManagerAlgorithm);
  // Initialize key manager factory with password and key store
  String keyManagerPassword = "SAMPLEKEYPASS";
  keyManagerFactory.init(keyStore , keyManagerPassword.toCharArray());
  // Get key managers from the factory
  keyManagers = keyManagerFactory.getKeyManagers();
}
catch(NoSuchAlgorithmException noAlgorithmEx){
  noAlgorithmEx.printStackTrace();
}
catch(UnrecoverableKeyException unrecoverableKeyException){
  unrecoverableKeyException.printStackTrace();
}
catch(KeyStoreException keyStoreException){
  keyStoreException.printStackTrace();
}
```

The JSSE reference implementation also uses trust manager objects to implement trusted remote process decisions employed during SSL authentication. For example, a collection of com.sun.net.ssl.TrustManager objects can be created as follows:

```
// Get reference implementation trust managers
com.sun.net.ssl.TrustManager[] trustedManagers = null;
try{
  // Create trust manager factory
  String trustManagerAlgorithm = "SunX509";
  com.sun.net.ssl.TrustManagerFactory trustManagerFactory
    = TrustManagerFactory.getInstance(trustManagerAlgorithm);
  // Initialize trust manager factory
  trustManagerFactory.init(keyStore);
  // Get trust managers
  trustedManagers = trustManagerFactory.getTrustManagers();
}
catch(NoSuchAlgorithmException noAlgorithmEx){
  noAlgorithmEx.printStackTrace();
}
catch(KeyStoreException keyStoreException){
  keyStoreException. printStackTrace();
}
```

The standard JCA `java.security.SecureRandom` class for generating random seed values is also utilized during initialization of the JSSE's reference implementation `SSLContext` object. A `SecureRandom` object can be created as follows:

```
// Get secure random value
java.security.SecureRandom secureRandom = null;
try{
  // Create secure random instance given an algorithm and provider
  String secureRandomAlgorithm = "SHA1PRNG";
  String secureRandomProvider = "SUN";
  secureRandom = SecureRandom.getInstance(secureRandomAlgorithm,
                                          secureRandomProvider);
}
catch(NoSuchProviderException noProviderEx){
  noProviderEx.printStackTrace();
}
catch(NoSuchAlgorithmException noAlgorithmEx){
  noAlgorithmEx.printStackTrace();
}
```

Now that we have handles to `KeyManager` objects, `TrustManager` objects, and a `SecureRandom` object, the `SSLContext` object can be created and initialized. Such objects used during initialization of the `SSLContext` object will also be used subsequently to initialize the security and operational qualities of the `SSLServerSocketFactory`. The creation and initialization of the JSSE reference implementation specific `SSLContext` object are demonstrated here:

```
// Get and initialize reference implementation SSL context
//   given key managers, trust managers, and a secure random value
com.sun.net.ssl.SSLContext sslContext = null;
try{
  // Create an SSL context given a context provider
  String sslContextProvider = "SUN";
  sslContext = SSLContext.getInstance(sslContextProvider);
  // Initialize SSL context
  sslContext.init(keyManagers, trustedManagers, secureRandom);
}
catch(NoSuchAlgorithmException noAlgorithmEx){
  noAlgorithmEx.printStackTrace();
}
catch(KeyManagementException keyManagementEx){
  keyManagementEx. printStackTrace();
}
```

We can now obtain a handle to the standard JSSE `SSLServerSocketFactory` object. Using `SSLContext`, the `SSLServerSocketFactory` handle is obtained as follows:

```
// Obtain handle to SSLServerSocketFactory using reference
//    implementation specific SSLContext
```

```
javax.net.ssl. SSLServerSocketFactory  sslServerSocketFactory
  = sslContext.getServerSocketFactory();
```

Creating SSL Server Sockets

Creating handles to SSL server sockets using the SSLServerSocketFactory object can be performed in one of three ways. The SSLServerSocketFactory object's base ServerSocketFactory class has three standard createServerSocket() methods defined. These return handles to java.net.ServerSocket objects. When you are using a SSLServerSocketFactory subclass, the returned server sockets will actually be subclasses of the abstract javax.net.ssl.SSLServerSocket class.

The three types of createServerSocket() method can take one of the following:

- An SSL port number, returning server sockets on the local host
- An SSL port number and connection backlog number
- A port number, backlog number, and specified network interface InetAddress

For example, to create a handle to an SSLServerSocket using a port number of 9000 on the local host, use

```
// Create SSL server socket using SSL server socket factory
try{
  int serverPort = 9000;
  javax.net.ssl.SSLServerSocket sslServerSocket = (SSLServerSocket)
      sslServerSocketFactory.createServerSocket(serverPort);
}
catch(IOException ioEx){
  ioEx. printStackTrace();
}
```

SSL Server Socket Listening

After an SSL server socket has been created, SSL server sockets listen for SSL client requests in the same way that regular server sockets listen for socket client requests. That is, the SSLServerSocket class's accept() method is used to block for client requests and returns an instance of a java.net.Socket object representing the socket connection with the requesting client. By casting this object to the javax.net.ssl.SSLSocket abstract subclass of Socket, special SSL-related socket manipulation operations will be exposed to the SSL server socket.

For example, if you use the SSLServerSocket object created earlier to block for client requests and hand off returned SSLSocket objects to a special thread handler, you might utilize the following code:

```
try{
  // Enter server loop to wait for client requests and then
```

9

SSL AND JSSE

```
  // hand off client sockets handles to special handler threads
  while(true){
    // Block waiting for client requests
    javax.net.ssl.SSLSocket clientSocket
      = (SSLSocket) sslServerSocket.accept();
    // Hand off SSLSocket to special runnable handler thread
    MyHandler handlerThread = new MyHandler(clientSocket);
    // Start the special handler thread
    handlerThread.start();
  }
}
catch(IOException ioEx){
  ioEx.printStackTrace();
  System.exit(0);
}
```

The thread handler may then handle client requests using socket calls from the `java.net` package and I/O stream handling from the `java.io` package as usual without any cognizance of SSL specifics. As an example, the `MyHandler` thread class may implement its `run()` method as follows:

```
public class MyHandler extends Thread
{
  private Socket sslSocket;
  private InputStream remoteInStream;
  private OutputStream remoteOutStream ;

    ...

  public MyHandler(SSLSocket sslSocket) throws IOException
  {
    // Set client socket handle and get IO streams
    this.sslSocket = sslSocket;
    this.remoteOutStream = sslSocket.getOutputStream();
    this.remoteInStream = sslSocket.getInputStream();
  }

  public void run()
  {
      try {
        ...
      // Create a data input stream
      DataInputStream inputStream = new DataInputStream(remoteInStream);

      // Read a line from the input stream
      String readLine = null;
```

```
      while( (readLine = inputStream.readLine()) == null){
         System.out.println(readLine);
      };

      // Read another line
      readLine = inputStream.readLine();
      System.out.println(readLine);
        ...
   }
   catch (IOException ioException) {
      ioException. printStackTrace();
   }
}
```

JSSE and HTTPS

Because SSL became popular due to its use on the Internet over HTTP, it is natural to think about how JSSE can be used with web-enabled applications. On the web client-side, the built-in SSL functionality of your web browser will most likely be utilized when the need for web-enabled SSL clients arises. However, signed Java applets may also take advantage of JSSE. Home-grown web clients may also utilize the standard Java URL, java.net, and java.io libraries to implement web based clients over HTTPS. However, if you use the standard Java URL libraries, a vendor must provide a java.net.URLStreamHandler implementation and you must configure such an implementation with your JVM using the java.protocol.handler.pkgs system property. The JSSE reference implementation in fact provides a URLStreamHandler implementation for HTTPS.

Use of an SSL-enabled commercial off-the-shelf web server may obviate the need to implement SSL on the web server-side, but JSSE-based SSL servers can also be implemented over HTTPS in order to communicate with web clients. The same SSL server-side development procedure described earlier is used to implement such functionality. Of course, the server implementation must know how to process HTTP request data and generate HTTP response data above the TCP/IP protocol using the java.net and java.io libraries.

9

Client Authentication

The need for clients to authenticate themselves to SSL servers can also be established on the server side. The SSLServerSocket.setNeedClientAuth(boolean flag) method call is used by SSL servers to indicate whether clients must supply certificates during the creation of new connections with the server. The SSLServerSocket.getNeedClientAuth() call returns a boolean value indicating whether client authentication is required after such a value has been set.

If client authentication is required, the SSL client will have to provide certificate information to the SSL server. When using JSSE on the client-side, the client authentication steps are accomplished primarily using vendor-specific means. The vendor-specific means for providing such information will most likely be similar to the means that JSSE SSL servers use to obtain handles to JSSE SSL server socket factories. (That method is shown earlier in this section).

JSSE SSL Client Sockets

The creation of SSL sockets from client to server is also a very simple task using JSSE. Clients must first obtain handles to SSL socket factories. These handles are obtained in the same way as SSL servers obtain handles to SSL server socket factories. Creation of SSL client sockets is then accomplished using one of a few very simple socket-creation calls. SSL sockets are then used much as regular Java `Socket` objects are used to communicate with a remote server. This section describes how to obtain SSL socket factory objects and how to create SSL socket objects using JSSE.

Obtaining an SSL Socket Factory

Akin to the way in which SSL servers obtain handles to SSL server socket factories, SSL clients obtain handles to SSL socket factories. The abstract `javax.net.ssl.SSLSocketFactory` class extends the `javax.net.SocketFactory` class to return SSL socket handles for clients. JSSE providers might provide vendor-specific mechanisms for obtaining `SSLSocketFactory` handles, or a client might obtain a handle to the default `SSLSocketFactory` configured for that client's environment.

The vendor-specific means for obtaining an `SSLSocketFactory` handle using the JSSE reference implementation is nearly identical to the creation of `SSLServerSocketFactory` handles. The only key difference is that the following sample `SSLContext` call is made after establishing all security and operational parameters:

```
SSLContext sslContext = SSLContext.getInstance("SUN");;
    ...
    // Establish parameters and initialize SSLContext
    ...
SSLSocketFactory  sslSocketFactory = sslContext.getSocketFactory();
```

Alternatively, a default `SSLSocketFactory` can be configured for the client's environment in the [*JRE_HOME*]\lib\security\java.security file's `ssl.SocketFactory.provider` property as follows:

```
ssl.ServerFactory.provider=com.assuredtech.ssl.SocketFactory
```

From within the client code, the following standard JSSE call can then be made:

```
// Get default SSL Socket Factory
SSLSocketFactory sslSocketFactory
        = (SSLSocketFactory) SSLSocketFactory.getDefault();
```

Creating SSL Client Sockets

After an SSLSocketFactory is obtained, a client can then use one of a few simple means for creating a handle to an javax.net.ssl.SSLSocket object. A java.net.Socket object is returned using one of four calls defined at the base SocketFactory level:

- createSocket(String host, int port): Creates a Socket given a remote host and port number.

- createSocket(InetAddress host, int port): Creates a Socket given a remote host and port number.

- createSocket(String host, int port, InetAddress clientHost, int clientPort): Creates a Socket given a remote host and port number in addition to a client-side host and port number.

- createSocket(InetAddress host, int port, InetAddress clientHost, int clientPort): Creates a Socket given a remote host and port number in addition to a client-side host and port number.

Additionally, the SSLSocketFactory subclass of SocketFactory defines another createSocket() method that creates a Socket wrapped around an existing Socket. In addition to an existing Socket handle, a remote server host String, a remote port number, and a boolean value are provided to indicate whether to close the wrapped socket when the newly created Socket is closed. The signature of this method is createSocket(Socket wrappedSocket, String host, int portNumber, boolean autoClose).

As a final note, when you are creating SSLSocket objects, they must be cast from the signature java.net.Socket type as exemplified here:

```
// Set remote host and port number
String host = "111.111.111.111";
String portNumber = 9000;
// Create an SSLSocket to a remote server
SSLSocket sslSocket
    = (SSLSocket) sslSocketFactory.createSocket(host, portNumber);
```

Use of SSLSocket objects on the client side then proceeds as usual with the base Socket class. All encryption and decryption via SSL occur transparently to the client when InputStream and OutputStream objects are used to receive and send data respectively.

JSSE SSL Sessions

An SSL session represents a communications session between two threads. Data communicated between such entities engaged in an SSL session can be exchanged over different physical connections during the lifetime of the session. Likewise, an SSL connection might allow more than one session to utilize the established SSL connection.

On the server side, the capability to create SSL sessions associated with an SSL server socket can be established using the SSLServerSocket.setEnableSessionCreation(boolean flag) method. The boolean value passed into such a method of course indicates true if SSL sessions are allowed to be created on the server socket connection. The SSLServerSocket.getEnableSessionCreation() method call returns a boolean value to determine if the SSL server socket enables session creation. The same two methods exist on the SSLSocket object as well. In addition to such methods, the SSLSocket object also provides a getSession() method to return an SSLSession object used by the current connection. The SSLSession.invalidate() method is used to invalidate sessions and, thus, prevent other connections from using the current SSL session.

The javax.net.ssl.SSLSession interface provides a means by which objects can be bound to a session using a String name and for removing and retrieving such objects via the following methods:

- void putValue(String name, Object value): Binds the named object to the session.
- void removeValue(String name): Removes the bound named object from the session.
- Object getValue(String name): Returns a handle to an object bound with an associated name to this session.
- String[] getValueNames(): Returns a collection of String names for those objects bound to this session.

Additionally, SSLSession defines a number of other getters related to attributes of the SSL session:

- byte[] getID(): Returns the session ID.
- String getPeerHost(): Returns the host name for the remote session peer.
- X509Certificate[] getPeerCertificateChain(): Returns a chain of certificates associated with the remote peer of this session.
- String getCipherSuite(): Returns a name for the SSL cipher suite used by this session.
- long getCreationTime(): Returns a long value representation of when the session was created, measured in milliseconds since January 1, 1970.

- long getLastAccessedTime(): Returns a long value representation of when the session was last used, measured in milliseconds since January 1, 1970.

- SSLSessionContext getSessionContext(): Returns a handle to the context for the session.

The javax.net.ssl.SSLSessionContext interface simply serves as a collection of SSLSession objects that are associated with a particular entity. The SSLSessionContext interface defines a getIds() method to return an Enumeration of all session IDs associated with the SSL context. The SSLSessionContext interface also defines a getSession (byte[] sessionID) method to return an SSLSession identified by the session ID byte array.

Summary

SSL is a popular means for encrypting traffic between clients and servers. SSL sessions are encrypted using server-side certificate information and can also, optionally, require clients to authenticate themselves. JSSE provides a standard API for encapsulating the SSL protocol for use by SSL clients and servers. JSSE providers plug their specific SSL implementations beneath the JSSE standard API. By using JSSE in your Java applications, you can better insulate your applications to vendor-specific SSL API mechanisms. Although this is generally true, a vendor-specific method for configuring socket factories and authentication information is still required for JSSE v1.0.

Distributed System Security

PART

III

IN THIS PART

Distributed Enterprise Security Overview

Enterprise systems are very often large-scale, distributed computing environments implementing functionality critical to the operation of a corporation or organization. Securing the distributed enterprise system is, thus, a key concern for corporations and organizations that want to maintain assurance for their business-critical operations. Many Java enterprise system technologies and the Java 2 Platform, Enterprise Edition (J2EE) are employed today within enterprise systems for rapidly data enabling, communications enabling, Web enabling, and scalable-applications enabling an enterprise. A collection of standard enterprise security mechanisms to complement such technologies is also provided for both standalone Java enterprise and J2EE environments.

In this chapter, you will be given

- A basic overview of the key Java enterprise system technologies
- An overview of security provisioning for Java enterprise database connectivity
- An overview of security provisioning for Java enterprise communication paradigms
- An overview of security provisioning for common Java enterprise communication services
- An overview of security provisioning for Java enterprise container-based Web and EJB components

Distributed Enterprise System Technology

Enterprise systems encompass those distributed, scalable, multiuser, and business-critical systems that are intimately related to enhancing the productivity of a corporate or organizational enterprise via information technology. More and more, corporations and organizations are tying themselves into a complex informational network in an effort to enhance the productivity of their operations for competitive and cost-reduction reasons. E-commerce, Internet/Web enabling, business-to-business (B2B) connectivity, enterprise aplication itegration (EAI), and data mining are just a few requirements that must be satisfied by enterprise system designs. Java enterprise technologies and the Java 2 Platform, Enterprise Edition (J2EE), in particular, provide an approach for more rapidly and effectively building enterprise systems that can produce reusable, scalable, distributable, maintainable, secure, reliable, and available enterprise software.

I briefly cover the core Java enterprise system technologies in this section so that you can better understand the specific security mechanisms provided for such technologies. These are discussed throughout the remainder of this chapter and this book. A much more thorough discussion of such technologies and how to build enterprise systems using these technologies can be found in *Building Java Enterprise Systems with J2EE* (Perrone/Chaganti; SAMS; ISBN 0672317958; `http://www.assuredtech.com/books/j2ee`).

In this chapter, I partition the distributed enterprise system problem into four main categories:

- *Enterprise Database Connectivity*: Provides a means for accessing data stored in a database.
- *Enterprise Communications*: Provide a means for communicating data between distributed processes over a network.
- *Enterprise Communication Services*: Provide common services built atop a distributed communications paradigm employed by enterprise applications regardless of the application domain.
- *Enterprise Container-based Components*: Provide server-side programming paradigms that enable developers to focus on application-specific component development tasks while utilizing a container/server infrastructure to manage the life cycle and configuration of such components.

Enterprise Database Connectivity

Access to warehouses of enterprise data is extremely important to building useful enterprise systems. There are a variety of ways to connect enterprise Java applications with enterprise data stored in databases, but the Java Database Connectivity (JDBC) API is the most common and feature-rich Java-based enterprise data enabling framework. JDBC is a core part of the

J2EE and has most often been used by organizations in its JDBC 1.x flavor shipped with the JDK v1.1. JDBC 2.0 offers new core functionality in the J2SE and a few important enterprise-specific extensions in the J2EE.

Basic JDBC development involves using the JDBC API with an associated underlying JDBC driver that handles connecting to your particular database of interest. The JDBC API is used to request a handle to a database connection from the JDBC driver. The JDBC connection can then be used to create regular SQL statements, prepared statements, or stored procedure calls. When querying for data, a JDBC resultset is returned and can be used to obtain database row data. JDBC 2.0 advanced features allow you to scroll around such resultsets in a more flexible manner, perform updates directly from the resultset, and perform batch updates to the database. Furthermore, a wide array of advanced SQL types can now be manipulated with JDBC 2.0. Finally, the JDBC 2.0 specification defines standards for middleware vendors for database connection pooling and distributed transaction resource management.

Enterprise Communications

The transfer and reception of enterprise information to and from computers strewn throughout the enterprise is a consideration for any enterprise system development task. Providing an enterprise computing solution frequently means providing a solution in which a heterogeneous and often widely dispersed array of computing platforms and devices can interoperate and communicate over various communication networks connecting the enterprise. Furthermore, as more computing platforms and devices are added to the enterprise, enterprise communications, as well as applications software systems, must scale to meet increasing demand on the network.

Standard Java-based support exists for three key distributed enterprise communication paradigms:

- *Basic TCP/IP Networking*: Network communications in enterprise systems *is* TCP/IP (Transmission Control Protocol/Internet Protocol). TCP/IP represents the fundamental communications protocol utilized by most enterprise Java communications paradigms. Socket programming offers an API to the TCP/IP protocol stacks. The Java platform comes with a set of Java-based standard socket programming APIs in the java.net package. A Socket class encapsulates a basic handle to a TCP/IP socket, whereas a ServerSocket class is used to create TCP/IP server sockets. The Java socket libraries can even be customized to modularly implement protocols above TCP/IP using classes and interfaces such as SocketImplFactory.

- *RMI*: The Remote Method Invocation (RMI) platform is a Java-centric distributed object communications model. By using the RMI packages and infrastructure, RMI-based Java clients can remotely invoke methods on RMI-based Java server objects. RMI enables clients and servers to pass objects as method parameters and return values either by value or by reference. If a class type used in a method parameter or return type is unknown to either the client or the server, it can be dynamically loaded using RMI codebase specifications. Although server objects can be explicitly constructed and bound on the server side to a lookup service, server objects can also be automatically activated upon client request without any prior server-side object instantiation. RMI can operate over TCP/IP via a Java-specific protocol known as Java Remote Method Protocol (JRMP) or via an open standards protocol known as Internet Inter-ORB Protocol (IIOP).

- *CORBA*: The Common Object Request Broker Architecture (CORBA) is a language- and platform-neutral body of specifications for building distributed object applications created by the Object Management Group (OMG) consortium of companies. CORBA applications are built to be largely isolated from the details of communications code. The Common Object Services Specification (CORBAservices), the Common Facilities Architecture (CORBAfacilities), and CORBA business objects are all standards built atop CORBA to provide an even richer suite of distributed communication services and frameworks. The CORBA Interface Definition Language (IDL) offers up a language-neutral mechanism for defining distributed object interfaces with standards that exist for mapping IDL to Java, as well as for mapping Java to IDL. Finally, CORBA objects now have the capability to be passed either by reference or by value. The main open-standard, TCP/IP-based protocol for communication via CORBA is General Inter-ORB Protocol (GIOP) operating above Internet Inter-ORB Protocol (IIOP).

Enterprise Communication Services

In addition to underlying distributed communication paradigms, many services are built on top of or augment those communication models to make distributed enterprise communications more immediately useful to enterprise applications. Naming services provide a means for mapping between distributed object references and human-readable object names. Enterprise systems also often employ directory and trading services for locating and discovering distributed objects on a network using both descriptive attributes and type information about those objects. Asynchronous messages sent between message producers and consumers are also often encapsulated within one of many messaging service options available to the Java enterprise system developer. Such services are common to many distributed enterprise communications-based applications and are also fundamental components of an integrated Java enterprise solution.

Standard Java-based support exists for four key common enterprise communication service APIs:

- *Java Naming and Directory Interface (JNDI)*: A naming service is the principal mechanism used in distributed systems for referring to objects from within your applications via a name identifying that object. Directory services provide a means for looking up objects in different naming contexts given a set of object attributes. JNDI provides the primary means for hooking into naming and directory systems from enterprise Java applications. JNDI defines a standard API to interact with such services and allows different service types and providers to be plugged into the framework under the hood via a service provider interface.

- *Jini*: Trading services provide a framework for objects to identify themselves in a distributed system, facilities for looking up and discovering other services, and services to remote objects. Sun's Jini technology is essentially a trading service in which descriptive information about remote processes or devices is registered with a lookup service. Jini clients can then search for such services using a service template description and obtain a set of matching service items from such a search. Proxy objects returned from these searches can represent handles to remote processes or devices. Jini also adds a mechanism for Jini services and clients to dynamically discover Jini lookup services used for trading.

- *Java Message Service (JMS)*: JMS is a Java API that defines how applications can interface with underlying asynchronous messaging service providers in a standard fashion. JMS also provides an interface that underlying messaging service providers implement to provide JMS services to clients. JMS provides both a point-to-point and a publish-subscribe model of messaging. *Point-to-point messaging* is accomplished by the implementation of message queues to which a producer writes a message to be received by a consumer. *Publish-subscribe messaging* is accomplished by the implementation of a hierarchy of topical nodes to which producers publish messages and to which consumers can subscribe. JMS provides a core abstract messaging architecture that is extended by both the point-to-point message queuing model and the publish-subscribe model.

- *JavaMail*: Email messaging systems have a very important, albeit application-specific role in the enterprise. JavaMail provides a way to interact with an email messaging system. Using JavaMail, enterprise applications can both send and receive email messages via the Internet. Thus, JavaMail provides APIs for interfacing with remote message stores used to receive email messages and for interfacing with remote message transports used to deliver email messages.

Enterprise Container-Based Components

The J2EE container/component model of modern enterprise applications development involves the use of a third-party container environment in which enterprise components can operate. Containers offer various service APIs and implementations, as do standalone application environments. However, container environments also offer management and configuration services. Management services provide infrastructure implementations to manage the life cycle, thread handling, communications handling, resource pooling, and systems assurance provisioning for the components operating within their confines. J2EE containers also provide a standard way for configuring the state and service parameters to be provided for components using standard

XML-based deployment descriptors. Two major classes of enterprise server-side components and their containers are defined within the J2EE specification and described here:

- *Web Components*: Web components are defined using either Java Servlets or JavaServer Pages (JSPs). Web components represent application-specific handling of requests received by a Web server and generate Web responses. From the container's management perspective, Java Servlets and JSPs are treated in an almost identical fashion. In fact, although Web-based Java Servlets are Java components that utilize standard Web request and response APIs, JSPs get compiled into Java Servlets. However, JSPs can be defined in a way that is more familiar to Web developers. For example, HTML template data can be directly embedded into the JSP.

- *Enterprise JavaBeans (EJB) Components*: EJB provides a model for developing server-side enterprise application components that can make building portable and distributed enterprise applications an easier task than building standalone enterprise applications. EJB containers/servers provide distributed communications-enabling services, data-enabling services, common distributed communication services, and systems assurance services for EJB components. In addition, minimal effort is required on the part of a developer to utilize these services.

  Currently, four types of EJBs can be developed. *Stateless session beans* serve as stateless input/output engines that receive EJB client requests and generate responses. *Stateful session beans* maintain state between successive calls on the bean by the same EJB client. *Bean-managed persistence entity beans* are beans that encapsulate persisted data and require that the data access code be written by the bean developer (most likely using JDBC). *Container-managed persistence entity beans* are beans that encapsulate persisted data and enable the data access code to be automatically generated by the container provider.

Enterprise Database Connectivity Security

The data that flows between a database client and database server may have a sensitive and security-critical nature. Such data may be confidential and require that only particular intended users see such data. Furthermore, a database connectivity security solution may also require a means to limit user access to particular types of data. In such cases, a means for database clients to authenticate themselves with the database server is often required.

Since Java enterprise applications connect to databases primarily via JDBC, some means for providing secure JDBC connections must be considered. When JDBC is used in a standalone enterprise application environment (that is, sans J2EE), a mechanism for authenticating yourself and establishing confidential data access must be provided via JDBC. In container-based J2EE EJB environments, bean-managed persistence entity bean developers might consider similar security-critical requirements if they are using JDBC as a database access mechanism.

Container-managed persistence entity bean developers must consider how the J2EE container will provide such services for them. In Chapter 11, "Databases and Database Security," I will provide much more detail about the problems and solutions behind Java enterprise database connectivity security.

Enterprise Communications Security

Because use of distributed communication paradigms is so common in distributed enterprise environments, you must consider a means to secure such a paradigm. Unfortunately, the basic means for providing enterprise communications security for Java-based applications is limited. The primary consideration when providing enterprise communications security in Java-based environments has been the security-critical nature of mobile Java code. Because of this, the means for limiting access to trusted resources by downloaded code or for performing basic network operations are almost the exclusive focus of TCP/IP- and RMI-based network security. Other extensions for authentication and confidentiality are sometimes used to augment such models. Java-based CORBA applications can take advantage of the much more comprehensive, albeit complex CORBA security model. This section explores the basic options for securing such distributed Java-based enterprise communications paradigms.

Basic Network Security

Providing basic network security with Java revolves around use of the fine-grained, permissions-based Java 2 security-access control model. Network permissions have names referring to a network resource for which permission is to be granted or denied. Network socket permissions also have a series of actions that scope the set of socket operations that can be performed.

Three `java.security.Permission` subclasses serve to define the primary set of Java 2 security permissions that can be used to provide secure access control for network security. These network-related permission classes are the `java.net.SocketPermission`, `java.net.NetPermission`, and `java.lang.Runtime` classes. Although permissions to access network resources from a JVM are encapsulated by the Java API hierarchy forpermissions, the management of such permissions in a configurable fashion is encapsulated by the Java 2 security-policy infrastructure. Access control in Java 2 is then managed by the `java.security.AccessController` and `java.security.AccessControlContext` classes.

The `SocketPermission` class encapsulates permissions for a network socket. A `SocketPermission` is constructed with a host name and a set of actions as illustrated in Table 10.1.

TABLE 10.1 Socket Permission Types

Socket Permission Name and Action	Description
```SocketPermission sp = new SocketPermission("www.assuredtech.com", "accept");```	Gives permission to accept connection from a single domain name.
```SocketPermission sp = new SocketPermission("205.277.44.44", "accept, connect");```	Gives permission to accept connection from and connect to a particular IP address.
```SocketPermission sp = new SocketPermission("*.com", "accept, connect");```	Gives permission to accept/connect for any domain name that ends with .com.
```SocketPermission sp = new SocketPermission("*.assuredtech.com:80", "accept, connect");```	Gives permission to accept/connect on port 80 under assuredtech.com domain.
```SocketPermission sp = new SocketPermission("*.assuredtech.com:1024-", "accept, connect");```	Accepts/connects on the unreserved ports.
```SocketPermission sp = new SocketPermission("*.assuredtech.com:-1023", "accept, connect");```	Accepts/connects on the reserved ports.
```SocketPermission sp = new SocketPermission("www.assuredtech.com:4000:4020", "accept, connect");```	Accepts/connects on ports 4000 to 4020.
```SocketPermission sp = new SocketPermission("*", "accept, connect");```	Accepts/connects every machine on every port.
```SocketPermission sp = new SocketPermission("", "accept, listen, connect");```	Accepts/connects/listens only on localhost.
```SocketPermission sp = new SocketPermission("localhost", "accept, listen, connect");```	Accepts/connects/listens only on localhost.

The target host name and actions specified in a Java 2 security policy file takes on the form

```
grant
{
 permission java.io.SocketPermission
                    "localhost", "accept, listen, connect";
 permission java.net.SocketPermission
                    "www.assuredtech.com", "accept";
};
```

Network permissions defined via the NetPermission class have only a target name with no actions defined. A NetPermission is constructed with one of the target names as illustrated in Table 10.2.

TABLE 10.2 Networking Permission Types

Networking Permission Name	Description
NetPermission np = new NetPermission("requestPasswordAuthentication");	Gives permission to get password from registered java.net. Password Authentication.
NetPermission np = new NetPermission("setDefaultAuthenticator");	Gives permission to register java.net. Authenticator used to get authentication information.
NetPermission np = new NetPermission("specifyStreamHandler");	Gives permission to designate a stream handler when creating URL.

You'll note that the use of the java.net.Authenticator and java.net. PasswordAuthentication classes is affected by the first two rows in Table 10.2. The java.net.Authenticator class provides a means for obtaining authentication information from a network connection. Subclasses of this class are registered with the JVM process by a Java application via a call to the static Authenticator.setDefault(Authenticator) method. If the "setDefaultAuthenticator" permission is granted, this method call will be allowed.

Otherwise, a `SecurityException` will be thrown. The `getPasswordAuthentication()` method is invoked on the `Authenticator` subclass during password-based authentication. A returned `PasswordAuthentication` object can be used to return a username `String` and a password `char[]` array.

A static `Authenticator.requestPasswordAuthentication()` call can be made if the `"requestPasswordAuthentication"` permission is established for the JVM process. The `requestPasswordAuthentication()` method asks the `Authenticator` that has been registered with the system for a `PasswordAuthentication` object. An `InetAddress` object specifying the authorization requesting address, a port number, a protocol `String`, a user prompt `String`, and a protocol scheme `String` are provided as input to the `requestPasswordAuthentication()` method.

Finally, in addition to the `SocketPermission` and `NetPermission` types, a target name of `"setFactory"` affiliated with a `RuntimePermission` can be used to allow an application to establish a different socket factory via the `java.net.Socket` and `java.net.ServerSocket` classes. The capability to set a URL stream handler factory via the `java.net.URL` class is also affected by this permission.

All these basic Java network security mechanisms allow for only the provisioning of basic access control for trusted networking operations. No standard means for authenticating network clients and servers or for providing confidential sessions are explicitly provided. For such services, one might use the separately packaged Java Authentication and Authorization Service (JAAS) and Java Secure Socket Extension (JSSE) APIs.

RMI Security

The default means by which security can be provided for RMI-based applications is the `java.rmi.RMISecurityManager`. The `RMISecurityManager` can be used to define security parameters governing the downloading of code given RMI's dynamic code download features. When a security manager is not established for an RMI-based application, no RMI code will be downloaded from remote codebase locations. During the startup of an RMI-based application, you will typically establish use of the `RMISecurityManager` via a call as follows:

```
java.lang.System.setSecurityManager( new java.rmi.RMISecurityManager() );
```

The standard means by which Java 2 security policies are established for certain codebase locations can then be used to control permission levels for RMI-based applications.

Such mechanisms only grant or deny access to certain JVM resources for RMI code downloaded from a remote location. The broader topics of providing authentication and confidentiality for RMI client/server sessions are not addressed by the current RMI model. The JAAS can be used in conjunction with RMI and the Java 2 security model to limit access based on a particular subject in addition to the downloaded codebase location. SSL socket extensions can also be used to provide a means to secure the communications session over which RMI traffic travels. Other chapters in this book address such topics independent of RMI.

Additionally, at the time of this writing, a specification for enhancing RMI's security capabilities was in working draft form (`http://java.sun.com/products/jdk/rmi/rmisec-doc/intro.html`). The specification outlines means for authenticating client and server subjects involved with remote method invocations, means for delegation of the client's subject such that remote server invocations can execute on behalf of the subject, and means for providing integrity and confidentiality of data when invoking remote methods.

Because the specification was in draft form at the time of this writing, I won't go into the details of this new RMI security model here. You should take note, however, of a new `java.rmi.constraint` package defined by the new RMI security specification. This new package contains classes that enable clients and servers to impose security constraints on remote method invocations. Constraints for specifying required integrity and confidentiality of data sent via remote method invocations are encapsulated by classes in such a package. Constraints for server and client authentication and identity association with remote method calls are also encapsulated by classes in this package. Finally, a delegation constraint is defined in the new package for allowing servers to execute as a client's identity.

CORBA Security

CORBA-based applications also require a means for securing the distributed CORBA object paradigm. The CORBA Security Service is an OMG CORBAservice component that relates to distributed object security for CORBA-based applications. The CORBA Security Service is defined to function primarily atop the ORB layer, but also defines some changes to the ORB layer. By using components that implement the Security Service Specification, CORBA-based enterprise applications gain the advantages of standards-based security protection including protection for identity, authenticity, nonrepudiation, authorization, auditing, integrity, and confidentiality. I address the CORBA security topic in much more detail in Chapter 13, "CORBA Security."

Enterprise Communications Service Security

Above and beyond basic distributed communications security, those common services built atop such distributed paradigms might also require a certain degree of augmented security. Because such services primarily manifest themselves as distributed servers, means for clients to authenticate themselves with such servers are the primary mechanisms needed for secure usage. Confidentiality of sessions with such services is most often provided underneath the hood at the transport layer by the service provider. In this section, you briefly explore those security services exposed via standard Java mechanisms for common distributed communication services such as naming services, directory services, trading services, and messaging services. Thus, you briefly explore the standard security mechanisms provided by JNDI, Jini, JMS, and JavaMail.

JNDI Security

In order to tap the services of a naming or directory service, JNDI client API users first create a reference to an initial context of the naming or directory service of interest. This initial context-creation process establishes a connection with the service when constructed with a set of properties describing the specific naming or directory service provider library to use, the URL of the naming or directory service process, and perhaps a username and user credentials. Other properties can also be set whose names are defined as static public attributes in the javax.naming.Context interface. A javax.naming.InitialContext class implementing the Context interface can be used to create an actual handle to a particular naming service. By passing a Properties object set with elements using the java.naming.*XXX* key names defined in the Context interface to the constructor of InitialContext, any necessary Context.*XXX* static public properties will be set and used during initialization of the InitialContext. A few key initial connection-related and security-related static public properties are defined in Table 10.3.

TABLE 10.3   Context Properties

Context Property	Description
INITIAL_CONTEXT_FACTORY	Fully qualified package and classname of provider's class used to create a JNDI context.
PROVIDER_URL	URL specifying the protocol, host, and port on which the naming or directory service is running. That is: `<protocol>://<host>:<port>`.
SECURITY_PRINCIPAL	Principal name (for example, username) to be checked by the naming or directory service if authentication is required for use.
SECURITY_CREDENTIALS	Principal's credentials (for example, a password) to be checked by the naming or directory service if authentication is required for use.
SECURITY_PROTOCOL	Specifies security protocol to use (for example, SSL).
SECURITY_AUTHENTICATION	Specifies security level to use such as none, simple, or strong.
AUTHORITATIVE	Value of true indicates that service access is for the most authoritative source.

Of all properties defined in Table 10.3, the first two properties (INITIAL_CONTEXT_FACTORY and PROVIDER_URL) will probably be the most commonly used in your JNDI programs. The SECURITY_PRINCIPAL and SECURITY_CREDENTIALS properties are very often used for basic authentication. If any property is left undefined, a default value is usually assumed, which is fine for many situations encountered. The creation of an InitialContext is, therefore, typically straightforward, as shown in this sample:

```
Properties properties = new Properties();
properties.setProperty(Context.INITIAL_CONTEXT_FACTORY,
                       "com.assuredtech.MyJNDIFactory");
properties.setProperty(Context.PROVIDER_URL,
                       "protocol:\\123.456.789.000:7002");
properties.setProperty(Context.SECURITY_PRINCIPAL, "tomhagan");
properties.setProperty(Context.SECURITY_CREDENTIALS, "yamiout");
properties.setProperty(Context.SECURITY_PROTOCOL, "SSL");
properties.setProperty(Context.SECURITY_AUTHENTICATION, "strong");
Context context = new InitialContext(properties);
Object myDistributedObject = context.lookup("MyObjectName");
```

Jini Security

The dynamic networking environment of Jini can result in a significant amount of mobile code being exchanged between distributed processes. Therefore, access to resources and permissions for such downloaded code must be controlled in some fashion. Unfortunately, the extent of security considerations employed by the dynamic networking model of Jini is very limited. Jini security is, by and large, derived from the basic Java 2 security model and use of an RMI security manager. In fact, during the Jini discovery process, the set of groups that can be joined by a Jini service or a Jini client can be limited via Java 2 security mechanisms.

The net.jini.discovery.DiscoveryPermission class encapsulates a type of Java 2 permission for limiting access to resources by particular Jini network groups. When a Jini client, Jini service, or Jini lookup service attempts to discover other lookup services on the network, it invokes the net.jini.discovery.LookupDiscovery constructor with a list of group String names. Those Jini networks belonging to one of the specified groups can be discovered via this process. If the LookupDiscovery user (Jini client, Jini service, or Jini lookup service) does not have permission to access a particular group, the discovery process for Jini lookup services in that group will result in a security exception being thrown.

The DiscoveryPermission class and associated policy file representation can be related to a target discovery group name. This group name can be defined according to one of the following forms:

- "*name*": A specified target name identifies a particular Jini network group.
- "public" or "": The "public" or empty String can be used to designate a public group accessible by all applications.

- "*": An asterisk identifies all groups.
- "*.*mygroups*.com": An asterisk prefix can be used to wildcard groups within a particular domain of groups.

Thus, a `DiscoveryPermission` can be specified in a standard Java 2 policy file as exemplified here:

```
grant SignedBy "AssuredTech" CodeBase "http://trusted.assuredtech.com/-"
{
  permission net.jini.discovery.DiscoveryPermission "tcb";
};
```

In the preceding example, code loaded by the Jini application affected via this policy file will grant discovery permissions with a target group of "tcb" for code loaded from `http://trusted.assuredtech.com` and signed by "AssuredTech".

Thus, Jini client, Jini service, and Jini lookup service JVM processes must be associated with a Java 2 security policy during startup. Additionally, Jini applications should set a security manager during initialization using an RMI security manager, such as the `RMISecurityManager` described previously.

Although such constructs indicate what lookup groups your applications can discover, you might be wondering how such groups are authenticated by the Jini infrastructure. That is, if you configure your application to allow discovery of lookup services belonging to the "xyz" group, what mechanisms guarantee that the lookup service actually belongs to such a group? The simple answer is that there is no sufficient guarantee currently provided. Code signing and codebase location specification are the only real options for providing any level of code identity assurance. It is anticipated that Jini will be extended with more rigorous security provisioning mechanisms in the future. In particular, the Jini security model will capitalize on the new RMI security model being developed.

JMS Security

Security for messaging systems will be largely dependent on the underlying middleware vendor. However, JMS does provide a few hooks for enabling simple password-based client authentication with the middleware message server. JMS accomplishes this by enabling JMS clients to provide the message server with a username and password when the initial connection to the server is created.

A `javax.jms.QueueConnectionFactory` class can be used to create an initial `javax.jms.QueueConnection` object. The `QueueConnection` represents the client connection to the JMS middleware point-to-point message queue server. The static `QueueConnectionFactory.createQueueConnection()` method can take username and password `String` parameters used to authenticate the JMS client with the middleware server. If client authentication fails, a `javax.jms.JMSSecurityException` will be thrown.

The process is similar for publish-subscribe messaging. A `javax.jms.TopicConnectionFactory` class can be used to create an initial `javax.jms.TopicConnection` object. The `TopicConnection` represents the client connection to the JMS middleware publish-subscribe message topic server. The static `TopicConnectionFactory.createTopicConnection()` method can then take the username and password `String` as parameters to authenticate the JMS client with the middleware server. If client authentication fails, a `javax.jms.JMSSecurityException` will be thrown.

JavaMail Security

The JavaMail API also exposes a means for enabling clients to authenticate with a remote messaging server. In this case, the messaging server is an email server. Before a JavaMail client can interact with an email messaging system, it must establish a mail session with a mail server. The `javax.mail.Session` class encapsulates a session with a mail server. Two static methods on the `Session` class can be used to obtain a `Session` instance. The `getDefaultInstance()` method is used to return an instance of a mail session that can be shared by other applications running on the same platform. The `getInstance()` method can be used to create a mail session that is unique and not shared with other applications. Both methods take a `javax.util.Properties` object as an argument that can have values set with standard property elements.

The creation of a `Session` object also involves the use of a `javax.mail.Authenticator` parameter to such static methods. The abstract `Authenticator` class is subclassed by service providers to implement objects that know how to authenticate a user with a mail server. If a null `Authenticator` is used to create a `Session` object using a static `Session.getDefaultInstance()` method and the default instance was already created, the `Authenticator` object must match the instance used to create the original session.

The `Authenticator` is primarily utilized by the mail messaging service environment as a callback to request user authentication information. The `javax.mail.PasswordAuthentication` class is used to encapsulate a username and password, which can be set in the `Session` object using `setPasswordAuthentication(URLName, PasswordAuthentication)` for later use in the session or by other applications. The `URLName` encapsulates the data elements of a URL that, in this case, is used to associate a mail server URL with the password authentication information. However, the `Authenticator` and `PasswordAuthentication` class and associated methods on the `Session` object are utilized, by and large, by an email transport or message store provider.

The primary means by which authentication information is provided to the mail system by the JavaMail application client is via a `javax.mail.Store` or `javax.mail.Transport` object. Such objects are obtained from the `Session` object. The `Store` object encapsulates a handle to an email message store (POP server or IMAP server) for retrieving email messages. The `Transport` object encapsulates a handle to an email transport mechanism (SMTP server) for sending email messages. The `Store` and `Transport` classes both inherit from the `javax.mail.Service` class. The `Service` class defines a collection of `connect()` methods to enable a JavaMail user to connect to the particular email service (email message store or transport service). Two of the `connect()` methods accept a username and password for authentication of a user with the remote email server. Using such methods, a JavaMail API client can thus authenticate itself with an SMTP, POP, or IMAP server when connecting with such servers.

Enterprise Container-Based Component Security

J2EE-based components, such as Java Servlets, JSPs, and EJBs, employ higher-level security mechanisms built atop the basic Java 2 security model. These mechanisms free the Web and EJB component developer from the need to know much about the underlying Java 2 security model. Rather, developers focus on specifying the security roles and associating roles with component access privileges. This section will describe the basic security provisions for Web and EJB component security.

Web Component Security

The Java Servlet and JSP frameworks are integrated with many Java 2.0 security features and also augment the Java 2.0 security framework to provide for the security of Web components. Servlet and JSP (Java Web component) security deals with identity and authentication, authorization, integrity, and confidentiality. In particular, the J2EE Web component framework provides a means to declaratively define security attributes in a standard Web-application XML deployment descriptor that is used to configure the online operational security aspects of Web components. Alternatively, certain features of the security framework are also exposed to Web components via APIs that enable more elaborate programmatic security provisioning by Web-component application developers.

An XML data element defined within the root element of the Web application XML deployment descriptor is used to define the particular authentication configuration used by a Web application. The type of authentication to be used can be specified in one of four ways, including basic password, message digest-based, HTML forms-based, and SSL client certificate-based authentication. During runtime, certain authentication-related information associated with an HTTP request can also be extracted on the server side when needed by the servlet or JSP.

When a request is sent to a Web server using a secure protocol, a server-side method call can be used to return a `boolean` value indicating this fact. When SSL is used with HTTP, an array of X509 certificate objects can also be returned from a call to the request object.

After a user has been identified using a particular authentication mechanism, the authorization to access Web component resources identified by URLs can be determined. Web component authorization is based on a role-based access control technique. Security roles are mapped to principals or groups. When a request is made by a particular principal on a resource with an associated security role, the principal name or group to which the principal belongs is compared with the principal name or group associated with the required role to determine whether access to the resource is allowed. A collection of security roles valid for a particular J2EE Web component environment can be defined within the XML deployment descriptor for that component. Chapter 15, "Java Servlet and JSP Security," provides much more information.

EJB Security

Currently, standard security mechanisms defined for EJBs are largely focused around providing a minimal set of constructs for EJB security access control. Although a mechanism for authenticating a user is implied by the fact that a particular user must be granted access to a particular EJB method, no standard means for authenticating a user is defined in EJB v1.1 and the J2EE v1.2. Such standard mechanisms are planned for the J2EE v1.3, however, and will most likely focus on use of the JAAS. Furthermore, a combination of container-specific and user-definable security mechanisms is also currently needed to create a truly secure and practical security environment for EJBs.

Although bean-implemented security access control logic is not recommended by the EJB specification, in many practical cases, it might be inevitable. Whenever a call to a programmatic EJB security role–checking method is made from within EJB code, associated role references must be defined in an XML deployment descriptor for the EJB. Such role references and other role-specification mechanisms can be used to declaratively define what security roles embodied by EJB clients can invoke particular EJB methods. I discuss EJB security in more depth in Chapter 14, "Enterprise JavaBeans Security."

Summary

More and more, Java enterprise technologies and the J2EE are being employed within enterprise systems to rapidly enable enterprise data access, communications connectivity, Web access, and scalable-applications construction. Java complements such technologies with a few standard distributed enterprise security mechanisms. As you have seen in this chapter, the scope of such security mechanisms can range from minimal to fairly extensive, depending on the particular technology.

Although Java has a long way to go to provide a standard secure environment for some Java enterprise technologies, there is a sufficient framework for application developers to begin implementing secure distributed enterprise applications out of the box in some cases. This chapter explored the various standard distributed enterprise security mechanisms provided for use by application developers. Other chapters in this book cover, in greater depth, those enterprise security mechanisms that have more comprehensive enterprise security solutions.

Databases and Database Security

Databases are significant components of any major Web application, and database security is an important part of the application's overall security. In this chapter, you'll be introduced to JDBC and the capabilities it provides. You'll learn how to develop applications that access databases via JDBC. You'll also learn about the security issues involved with developing Web-based database applications.

What Is a Database?

A *database* is a collection of data that is organized so that it can be easily searched and updated. The most important feature of a database is its organization, which supports both ease of use and efficient data retrieval. Consider an office that is organized with numbered file cabinets containing carefully labeled folders. Office information is stored by subject in specific folders kept in designated file cabinets. In such a system, every folder has its place, and it is easy to find a particular folder.

Now consider a different environment where information is stored in folders, but the folders are haphazardly stored in boxes that are placed at seemingly random locations throughout an office building. How do you find a particular folder in such an environment? Where do you store a folder when you're finished with it?

The well-organized environment is analogous to a database. Information that is entered into a database is stored in specific locations within it. Because of the database's structure and organization (assuming the database is well designed), information can be easily retrieved. The database can be accessed remotely and is shared among many users.

The unorganized environment is analogous to a situation where information is stored in files on various users' computers. In such an environment, it is very hard to locate specific information. Which file contains the information you need? Whose computer contains that file? Where is the computer located? Where is the file located in the user's file system?

A *database server* is a software program that manages databases, keeps them organized, and provides shared access to them. Database servers manage and organize databases at both a physical level and at a logical level. At a *physical level*, database servers store database information in specific locations within the particular files, directories, and disk volumes used by the server. The server keeps track of what information goes where so that you don't have to keep track. The server is like a trusty office assistant. You can turn to it and say, "Get me the file on...," and the assistant immediately retrieves the information you need and places it on your desk.

As previously mentioned, database servers also manage and organize information at a *logical level*. This logical level corresponds to the type of information that you store in a database. For example, you might have a database that stores the names, companies, email addresses, and phone numbers of your business contacts. The logical organization of the database might consist of a `Contacts` table with five columns: `LastName`, `FirstName`, `Company`, `Email`, and `Phone`.

Relational Databases

Although there are a number of different ways that databases can be logically organized, one particular organization, called the *relational model*, is the predominant method. The relational model was developed by E.F. Codd, a mathematician at IBM, during the late 1960s. Databases that adhere to the relational model are referred to as *relational databases*.

Relational databases are organized into tables that consist of rows and columns. The rows of the table contain specific records that have been entered in the database. The columns of the table identify what type of information is contained in each row.

A relational database can have one table or 1,000 tables. The number of tables is limited only by the relational database server software and the amount of available physical storage.

Working with Keys

Access to information contained within tables is organized by keys. A *key* is a column or group of columns that uniquely identifies a row of a table. Keys are used to find a particular row within a table and to determine whether a new row is to be added to a table or whether an existing row is to be replaced.

Structured Query Language

The *Structured Query Language*, or *SQL* (pronounced *sequel*) is a language for interacting with relational databases. It was developed by IBM during the '70s and '80s and standardized in the late '80s. The SQL standard has been updated over the years, and several versions currently exist. In addition, several database vendors have added product-specific extensions and variations to the language. The JDBC requires JDBC-compliant drivers to support the American National Standards Institute (ANSI) SQL-92 Entry Level version of the standard that was adopted in 1992.

SQL has many uses:

- When SQL is used to create or design a database, it is a *data definition language*.
- When it's used to update the data contained in a database, it is a *data maintenance language*.
- When it's used to retrieve information from a database, it is a *data query language*.

NOTE

For more information on SQL, check out Yahoo's SQL page at
`http://dir.yahoo.com/Computers_and_Internet/ Programming_Languages/SQL/`.

Remote Database Access

Most useful databases can be accessed remotely. In this way, shared access to the database can be provided to multiple users at the same time. For example, you can have a single database server that is used by all employees in an accounting department.

In order to access databases remotely, users need a *database client*. A database client communicates to the database server on the user's behalf. It provides the user with the capability to update the database with new information or to retrieve information from the database. Database clients talk to database servers using SQL statements. The database client can execute on the user's computer or on a separate computer that is directly or indirectly linked to the client. (See Figure 11.1.) In a typical Web application, the database server executes on a Web server or on an application server.

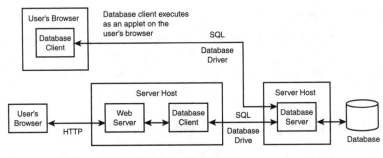

FIGURE 11.1

A database client talks to a database server on the user's behalf.

ODBC and JDBC Drivers

Database clients use database drivers to send SQL statements to database servers and to receive result sets and other responses from the servers. JDBC drivers are used by Java applications and applets to communicate with database servers. Officially, Sun says that JDBC is an acronym that does not stand for anything. However, it is associated with Java database connectivity.

Microsoft's ODBC

Because many database servers use vendor-specific protocols, a database client has to learn a new language to talk to each database server. However, Microsoft established a common standard for communicating with databases, called *Open Database Connectivity (ODBC)*. Until ODBC, most database clients were server-specific. ODBC drivers eliminate the need to deal with vendor-specific protocols, providing a common application-programming interface to database clients. By writing your database clients to the ODBC API, you enable your programs to access more database servers. (See Figure 11.2.)

Enter JDBC

So where does JDBC fit into this picture? JDBC provides a common database-programming API for Java programs. However, JDBC drivers do not yet directly communicate with as many database products as do ODBC drivers. Instead, many JDBC drivers communicate with databases using ODBC. In fact, one of the first JDBC drivers was the JDBC-ODBC bridge driver developed by JavaSoft and Intersolv.

Why did JavaSoft create JDBC? What was wrong with ODBC? There are a number of reasons why JDBC was needed. They boil down to the simple fact that JDBC is a better solution for Java applications and applets. The reasons include the following:

Databases and Database Security

CHAPTER 11

285

11

DATABASES AND
DATABASE
SECURITY

- ODBC is a C language API, not a Java API. Java is object-oriented and C is not. C uses pointers and other "dangerous" programming constructs that Java does not support. These constructs are dangerous because their use often leads to serious errors. A Java version of ODBC would require a significant rewrite of the ODBC API.

- ODBC drivers must be installed on client machines. The applet access to databases is, therefore, constrained by the requirement to download and install an ODBC driver. A pure Java solution enables JDBC drivers to be automatically downloaded and installed along with the applet. This greatly simplifies database access for applet users.

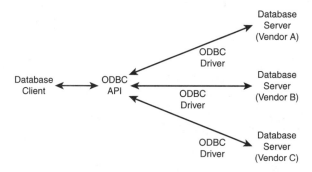

FIGURE 11.2
A database client can talk to many database servers via ODBC drivers.

JavaSoft created the JDBC-ODBC bridge driver as a temporary solution to database connectivity until suitable JDBC drivers are developed. The JDBC-ODBC bridge driver translates the JDBC API into the ODBC API and is used with an ODBC driver. The JDBC-ODBC bridge driver is not an elegant solution, but it enables Java developers to use existing ODBC drivers. (See Figure 11.3.)

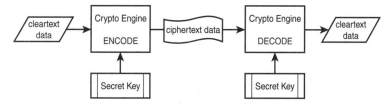

Symmetric Key Cryptography for Confidentiality

FIGURE 11.3
The JDBC-ODBC bridge lets Java database clients talk to databases via ODBC drivers.

Since the release of the JDBC API, a number of JDBC drivers have been developed. These drivers provide varying levels of capability. As a service to Java developers, JavaSoft has classified JDBC drivers into the following four driver types:

- JDBC-ODBC bridge plus ODBC driver (Type 1)—This driver category refers to the original JDBC-ODBC bridge driver. The JDBC-ODBC bridge driver uses Microsoft's ODBC driver to communicate with database servers. It is implemented in both binary code and Java and must be preinstalled on a client computer before it can be used.

- Native-API partly Java driver (Type 2)—This driver category consists of drivers that talk to database servers in the server's native protocol. For example, an Oracle driver speaks SQLNet, whereas a DB2 driver uses an IBM database protocol. These drivers are implemented in a combination of binary code and Java, and they must be installed on client machines. (See Figure 11.4.)

- JDBC-Net pure Java driver (Type 3)—This driver category consists of pure Java drivers that speak a standard network protocol (such as HTTP) to a database access server. The database access server then translates the network protocol into a vendor-specific database protocol (possibly using an ODBC driver). (See Figure 11.5.)

- Native-protocol pure Java driver (Type 4)—This driver category consists of a pure Java driver that speaks the vendor-specific database protocol of the database server with which it is designed to interface. (See Figure 11.6.)

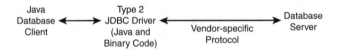

FIGURE 11.4

A Type 2 JDBC driver uses a vendor-specific protocol and must be installed on client machines.

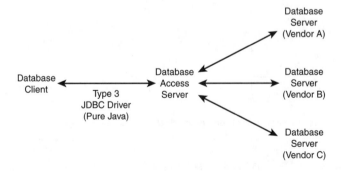

FIGURE 11.5

A Type 3 JDBC driver is a pure Java driver that uses a database access server to talk to database servers.

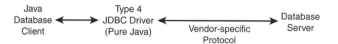

FIGURE 11.6

A Type 4 JDBC driver is a pure Java driver that uses a vendor-specific protocol to talk to database servers.

Of the four types of drivers, only Type 3 and Type 4 are pure Java drivers. This characteristic is important to support zero installation for applets. The Type 4 driver communicates with the database server using a vendor-specific protocol, such as SQLNet. The Type 3 driver makes use of a separate database access server. It communicates with the database access server using a standard network protocol, such as HTTP. The database access server communicates with database servers using vendor-specific protocols or ODBC drivers. The IDS JDBC driver that you'll use later in this chapter is an example of a Type 3 driver.

Connecting to Databases with the `java.sql` Package

One of the most powerful packages in the Java API is the `java.sql` package. This package adds database programming capabilities to Java and is referred to as the *JDBC API*. The JDBC was originally developed as a separate package from the JDK 1.02, but it is an integral part of the JDK as of JDK 1.1.

Setting Up a Database Connection

In order to use JDBC, you need a database server and a database driver. Because most readers have access to Windows 95, I'll be using Microsoft Access as my database server. You can choose to use Access or some other server. After you learn how to connect to your database, the type of server you use won't matter—JDBC provides a server-independent approach to database access. That's one of JDBC's major benefits!

You'll also need a database driver that provides the linkage between the JDBC and your database. The JDBC comes with a JDBC-ODBC bridge. This bridge enables you to access databases via Microsoft's Open Database Connectivity API. However, the JDBC-ODBC bridge is a temporary solution to database connectivity and has some significant drawbacks, such as requiring the bridge to be installed on your database users' computers.

I will use the JDBC driver of IDS Software (`http://www.idssoftware.com`). The IDS JDBC driver is a pure Java driver that supports *zero installation* for applets. Zero installation enables you to provide database access via applets to users without preinstalling any software on their computers.

NOTE

Consult the JDBC home page at `http://www.javasoft.com/products/jdbc/` for information on the JDBC drivers that will work with your database server.

11

DATABASES AND DATABASE SECURITY

Although you can use the JDBC driver of your choice for the examples in this book, I recommend the IDS driver because of its ease of use, great documentation, and zero installation feature. If you are interested in using the IDS JDBC driver, check the IDS Web page for the availability of an evaluation copy. If you intend to develop Java-based database applications, a licensed version of the IDS software is invaluable.

> **NOTE**
>
> If you use the IDS JDBC driver with Microsoft Access, make sure you have installed version 3.5 or later of Microsoft's ODBC database drivers. These drivers are available at `ftp://ftp.microsoft.com/Softlib/MSLFILES/WX1350.EXE`.

> **TIP**
>
> You can check the version of your ODBC database drivers by opening the 32-bit ODBC Control Panel applet and clicking on the ODBC Drivers tab.

The `DriverManager` Class

The `DriverManager` class of `java.sql` is used to manage the JDBC drivers that are installed on your system. These drivers can be installed by setting the `jdbc.drivers` system property or by loading the driver class using the `forName()` method of the `Class` class.

The `DriverManager` class does not provide a constructor, and all its methods are static. The `getDrivers()` method returns an enumeration of all the JDBC drivers that are installed on your system. The `getConnection()` method is used to establish a connection to a database. This method is provided in the following three forms:

```
getConnection(String url)
getConnection(String url,String userID,String password)
getConnection(String url,Properties arguments)
```

The first form takes a `String` argument that specifies the URL of the database. The second form takes two additional strings: the user ID and password required to access a database. The third form takes an additional `Properties` argument that specifies a list of connection arguments, such as user ID, password, database name, and so on. Consult your JDBC driver documentation for more information on which method to use with your drivers.

The URLs used to establish database connections vary with the JDBC drivers that you use, but they are of the following form:

```
jdbc:subprotocol:subname
```

All JDBC database protocols begin with `jdbc:`. The subprotocol is used to identify either the connection mechanism or the JDBC driver. For example, the JDBC-ODBC bridge uses protocols of the form `jdbc:odbc:subname`, and the IDS JDBC driver uses protocols of the form `jdbc:ids:subname`.

The *subname* of adatabase protocol identifies the database and provides other parameters that depend on the subprotocol and JDBC driver. For example, I use the following URL to establish a database connection to the Microsoft Access database named `DataSetName` on the host `cx122974-a.cv1.sdca.home.com` on protocol port 80:

```
jdbc:ids://cx122974-a.cv1.sdca.home.com:80/conn?dbtype=odbc&dsn=DataSetName
```

The IDS Server can be configured to support Web service and database access via the same TCP protocol port (80).

> **NOTE**
>
> Consult your JDBC driver's documentation for information on the subprotocol and subname you should use to establish a database connection.

The `Driver` Interface

The `Driver` interface is implemented by JDBC drivers. Writing a JDBC driver consists of creating a Java class that implements the `Driver` interface.

The `Connection` Interface

When a database connection is established using the `getConnection()` method of `DriverManager`, the `getConnection()` method returns an object that implements the `Connection` interface. This interface defines methods for interacting with the database via the established connection. These methods are used to manage a database connection, obtain information about a connection, roll back or commit database transactions, or prepare SQL statements for execution.

A number of methods are defined by the `Connection` interface. Consult the API documentation of the `Connection` interface for a complete description of these methods. Particular methods ofinterest include the following:

- `close()`—Closes a database connection.

- getMetaData()—Returns an object of the DatabaseMetaData interface that can be used to obtain detailed information about the structure and capabilities of a database.
- createStatement()—Creates an SQL Statement object.
- prepareStatement()—Creates an SQL PreparedStatement object using an SQL string. PreparedStatement objects are precompiled SQL statements that are more efficiently executed than statements that are not precompiled.
- prepareCall()—Creates an SQL CallableStatement object using an SQL string. CallableStatement objects are SQL-stored procedure call statements.

Executing SQL Statements

SQL is the language used to interact with database servers. SQL statements can be used to add, update, delete, or retrieve information from an existing database. The purpose of the java.sql package is to let you execute SQL statements from Java. This section discusses the JDBC API interfaces that are used to execute SQL statements.

The Statement Interface

The Statement interface defines methods that are used to interact with databases via the execution of SQL statements. These methods also support the processing of query results returned via ResultSet objects and provide control over the mechanics of query processing. The execute(), executeQuery(), and executeUpdate() methods are the primary methods of interest in the Statement interface.

The executeQuery() method executes an SQL statement (such as the SELECT statement) that queries a database and returns a ResultSet object. The executeUpdate() method executes an SQL statement (such as the INSERT, UPDATE, or DELETE statement) that updates the database and returns the integer value of the row count associated with the SQL statement or 0 if the statement did not return a result.

The execute() method executes an SQL statement that is written as a String object. It returns a boolean value indicating whether a ResultSet object was produced as the result of the statement's execution. The getResultSet() and getMoreResults() methods are used to retrieve the ResultSet object. If the statement's execution returns an update count, execute() returns false. The update count can be retrieved using the getUpdateCount() method.

The PreparedStatement and CallableStatement Interfaces

The PreparedStatement interface extends the Statement interface to define methods that are used to work with precompiled SQL statements. The use of precompiled SQL statements provides a more efficient way to execute frequently used SQL statements.

The CallableStatement interface extends the PreparedStatement interface to implement stored SQL procedures.

Databases and Database Security

CHAPTER 11

291

11

DATABASES AND
DATABASE
SECURITY

The StatementApp Program

The StatementApp program, shown in Listing 11.1, enables you to execute an SQL statement that is passed as a command-line parameter. The program uses the IDS driver to link to the IDSExamples data set (included with the IDS Server). Make sure you set up the data set as a System DSN before running the program. Also change cx122974-a.cv1.sdca.home.com to the name of the server that will host the database.

You can use the StatementApp program to brush up on your SQL. Execute the program with the "SELECT * FROM courses" SQL statement to obtain a listing of the contents of the courses table:

```
java StatementApp "SELECT * FROM courses"
SELECT * FROM courses
Course_ID | Department_ID | CourseNumber | CourseLevel | CourseName
35 | BIOL | 100 | Basic        | Physiology
37 | BIOL | 300 | Intermediate | Plant Biology
38 | BIOL | 600 | Advanced     | Microbiology
39 | BIOL | 310 | Intermediate | Neurobiology
40 | BIOL | 620 | Advanced     | Neurobiology
41 | CHEM | 100 | Basic        | General Chemistry
42 | CHEM | 300 | Intermediate | Analytical Chemistry
44 | ECON | 100 | Basic        | Financial Accounting
45 | ECON | 110 | Basic        | Business Law
51 | MATH | 100 | Basic        | Calculus I
52 | MATH | 300 | Intermediate | Calculus II
59 | MATH | 600 | Advanced     | Linear Algebra
60 | ECON | 220 | Intermediate | Microeconomics
61 | CHEM | 600 | Advanced     | Organic Chemistry
```

The economics classes don't belong with the math and science courses. Delete them by using the "DELETE FROM courses WHERE Department_ID = 'ECON'" SQL statement:

```
java StatementApp "DELETE FROM courses WHERE Department_ID
➡= 'ECON'"
DELETE FROM courses WHERE Department_ID = 'ECON'
```

Use the "SELECT * FROM courses" statement to verify that the economics classes have been deleted:

```
java StatementApp "SELECT * FROM courses"
SELECT * FROM courses
Course_ID | Department_ID | CourseNumber | CourseLevel | CourseName
35 | BIOL | 100 | Basic        | Physiology
37 | BIOL | 300 | Intermediate | Plant Biology
38 | BIOL | 600 | Advanced     | Microbiology
39 | BIOL | 310 | Intermediate | Neurobiology
```

```
40 | BIOL  | 620 | Advanced     | Neurobiology
41 | CHEM  | 100 | Basic        | General Chemistry
42 | CHEM  | 300 | Intermediate | Analytical Chemistry
51 | MATH  | 100 | Basic        | Calculus I
52 | MATH  | 300 | Intermediate | Calculus II
59 | MATH  | 600 | Advanced     | Linear Algebra
61 | CHEM  | 600 | Advanced     | Organic Chemistry
```

Which courses are missing from the list? These poor students are being deprived of a Java education. Enter the following INSERT SQL statements to round out their education:

```
java StatementApp "INSERT INTO courses VALUES ('34', 'JAVA'
➡, '999', 'Basic', 'Intro to Java')"
INSERT INTO courses VALUES ('34', 'JAVA', '999', 'Basic', 'Intro to Java')

java StatementApp "INSERT INTO courses VALUES ('43', 'JAVA'
➡, '999', 'Intermediate', 'AWT Programming')"
INSERT INTO courses VALUES ('43', 'JAVA', '999', 'Intermediate', 'AWT
Programmin
➡g')

java StatementApp "INSERT INTO courses VALUES ('62', 'JAVA'
➡, '999', 'Advanced', 'Database Programming')"
INSERT INTO courses VALUES ('62', 'JAVA', '999', 'Advanced', 'Database
Programmi
➡ng')
```

Use the "SELECT * FROM courses" statement to redisplay the courses table:

```
java StatementApp "SELECT * FROM courses"
SELECT * FROM courses
Course_ID | Department_ID | CourseNumber | CourseLevel | CourseName
35 | BIOL  | 100 | Basic        | Physiology
37 | BIOL  | 300 | Intermediate | Plant Biology
38 | BIOL  | 600 | Advanced     | Microbiology
39 | BIOL  | 310 | Intermediate | Neurobiology
40 | BIOL  | 620 | Advanced     | Neurobiology
41 | CHEM  | 100 | Basic        | General Chemistry
42 | CHEM  | 300 | Intermediate | Analytical Chemistry
51 | MATH  | 100 | Basic        | Calculus I
52 | MATH  | 300 | Intermediate | Calculus II
59 | MATH  | 600 | Advanced     | Linear Algebra
61 | CHEM  | 600 | Advanced     | Organic Chemistry
34 | JAVA  | 999 | Basic        | Intro to Java
43 | JAVA  | 999 | Intermediate | AWT Programming
62 | JAVA  | 999 | Advanced     | Database Programming
```

Databases and Database Security

CHAPTER 11

293

11

DATABASES AND
DATABASE
SECURITY

All the Java courses are appended to the end of the table. Sort the result set by the Course_ID column:

```
java StatementApp "SELECT * FROM courses ORDER BY Course_ID
➥"
SELECT * FROM courses ORDER BY Course_ID
Course_ID | Department_ID | CourseNumber | CourseLevel | CourseName
34 | JAVA | 999 | Basic        | Intro to Java
35 | BIOL | 100 | Basic        | Physiology
37 | BIOL | 300 | Intermediate | Plant Biology
38 | BIOL | 600 | Advanced     | Microbiology
39 | BIOL | 310 | Intermediate | Neurobiology
40 | BIOL | 620 | Advanced     | Neurobiology
41 | CHEM | 100 | Basic        | General Chemistry
42 | CHEM | 300 | Intermediate | Analytical Chemistry
43 | JAVA | 999 | Intermediate | AWT Programming
51 | MATH | 100 | Basic        | Calculus I
52 | MATH | 300 | Intermediate | Calculus II
59 | MATH | 600 | Advanced     | Linear Algebra
61 | CHEM | 600 | Advanced     | Organic Chemistry
62 | JAVA | 999 | Advanced     | Database Programming
```

The Database Programming course can apply to any programming language. Use the UPDATE statement to change it to Advanced JDBC:

```
java StatementApp "UPDATE courses SET CourseName = 'Advance
➥d JDBC' WHERE Department_ID = 'JAVA' AND CourseLevel = 'Advanced'"
UPDATE courses SET CourseName = 'Advanced JDBC' WHERE Department_ID = 'JAVA'
AND
➥ CourseLevel = 'Advanced'
```

Once again, display the courses table, sorted by the Course_ID column:

```
java StatementApp "SELECT * FROM courses ORDER BY Course_ID
➥"
SELECT * FROM courses ORDER BY Course_ID
Course_ID | Department_ID | CourseNumber | CourseLevel | CourseName
34 | JAVA | 999 | Basic        | Intro to Java
35 | BIOL | 100 | Basic        | Physiology
37 | BIOL | 300 | Intermediate | Plant Biology
38 | BIOL | 600 | Advanced     | Microbiology
39 | BIOL | 310 | Intermediate | Neurobiology
40 | BIOL | 620 | Advanced     | Neurobiology
41 | CHEM | 100 | Basic        | General Chemistry
42 | CHEM | 300 | Intermediate | Analytical Chemistry
43 | JAVA | 999 | Intermediate | AWT Programming
51 | MATH | 100 | Basic        | Calculus I
52 | MATH | 300 | Intermediate | Calculus II
59 | MATH | 600 | Advanced     | Linear Algebra
```

```
61 | CHEM | 600 | Advanced   | Organic Chemistry
62 | JAVA | 999 | Advanced   | Advanced JDBC
```

The StatementApp program provides a lot of capability in a few lines of code. It enables you to directly enter SQL statements into the database. It begins by loading the ids.sql.IDSDriver, connecting to the IDSExamples data set, and creating a Statement object. It then passes the program's command-line argument to the execute() method of the Statement interface. If the execute() method returns a true value, the program invokes the getResultSet() method of the Statement interface to retrieve the ResultSet object of a query operation. The program then invokes the displayResults() method to display the ResultSet.

LISTING 11.1 The StatementApp Program

```java
import java.sql.*;
import java.util.*;

class StatementApp {
 public static void main(String args[]) {
  if(args.length!=1){
   System.out.println("Usage: java StatementApp sql");
   System.exit(0);
  }
  try{
   // Load IDS driver
   Class.forName("ids.sql.IDSDriver");
   String url="jdbc:ids://cx122974-a.cv1.sdca.home.com:80/";
   url+="conn?dbtype=odbc&dsn='IDSExamples'";
   // Connect to database
   Connection connection=DriverManager.getConnection(url);
   Statement statement = connection.createStatement();
   String sql=args[0];
   System.out.println(sql);
   // Execute SQL statement
   boolean hasResults = statement.execute(sql);
   if(hasResults){
    // Retrieve result set
    ResultSet result = statement.getResultSet();
    if(result!=null) displayResults(result);
   }
   // Close database connection
   connection.close();
  }catch(Exception ex){
   System.out.println(ex);
   System.exit(0);
```

LISTING 11.1   Continued

```
 }
}
static void displayResults(ResultSet r) throws SQLException {
 // Get meta data about result set
 ResultSetMetaData rmeta = r.getMetaData();
 // Use meta data to determine the number of columns
 // in the result set
 int numColumns=rmeta.getColumnCount();
 // Display values of each column
 for(int i=1;i<=numColumns;++i) {
  if(i<numColumns)
   System.out.print(rmeta.getColumnName(i)+" | ");
  else
   System.out.println(rmeta.getColumnName(i));
 }
 while(r.next()){
  for(int i=1;i<=numColumns;++i) {
   if(i<numColumns)
    System.out.print(r.getString(i)+" | ");
   else
    System.out.println(r.getString(i). trim());
  }
 }
 }
}
```

Database Security Issues

Until now, I haven't addressed the issue of database security, which is a serious concern for most organizations. Since databases can contain sensitive information about a company's oper-ation., it is imperative that access to such information be restricted to those who are trusted to handle it in a secure manner.

The integrity of database information is also paramount. Unauthorized changes to critical data-base information might have an adverse impact on a company's capability to carry out business operations.

Finally, data availability is important. Users must be able to get access to database information when they need it. Often, this access needs to be provided 24 hours a day, seven days a week.

How does the JDBC support database security? The answer is not very comforting. The JDBC currently relies on the database server to provide security protection. You probably noticed that you didn't even need to use a password to access the sample database for this chapter. That's because you are working with a personal database product. Enterprise-wide database servers, such as Microsoft SQL Server, require a user ID and password in order to establish a database connection. However, even password protection is not very secure. If passwords are not encrypted between client and server, they can be easily intercepted and compromised.

In general, the security provided by JDBC is limited to the password used to connect to the database server. However, higher-level security issues should be considered when creating Web-based applications using JDBC. These issues are covered in the following sections.

Securing Database Connections

One of the most fundamental issues in database security is the security of the connection between the database client and the database server. Typically, the client connects to the server via an unencrypted TCP/IP connection, authenticating with the database using a reusable password. This typical case poses several significant security vulnerabilities, as shown in Figure 11.7.

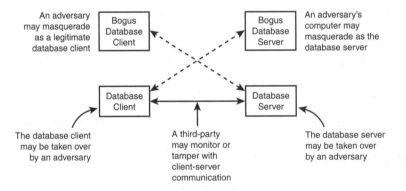

Figure 11.7

Vulnerabilities in typical database connections.

The vulnerabilities, illustrated in the preceding figure, are as follows:

- The connection from the client to the server is subject to monitoring and tampering by a third party. Both passwords and data might be disclosed as they travel between the client and the server. An adversary might insert false packets into the TCP/IP connection in order to corrupt data input to the database or to deny service to the client. If any computer that is suborned by an adversary (such as a switch, router, or packet forwarding host) lies on the path between the client and the server, the adversary can use the suborned computer to completely take over the client-server connection.

- A third party might masquerade as a database client and attempt to guess database-connection passwords or to deny service to legitimate clients.

- An adversary might take over a database client, recover any stored passwords, and use the client to disclose data that is stored in the database, insert false data into the database, or deny database access to others.

- An adversary might masquerade as the database server, causing database clients to disclose their passwords and data, retrieve false data, or fail to provide critical data to other applications.

- An adversary might take over the database server and disclose sensitive passwords and data, modify integrity-critical data, or deny database access to selected database clients.

Protecting your databases against these types of attacks is difficult but achievable by using a combination of security countermeasures.

Using a Dedicated Subnet for Client-Server Communication

One of the first steps is to protect the communication between the database client and the database server. Ideally, the client and server communicate over a dedicated subnet, as shown in Figure 11.8. The hosts on this subnet consist of the database client(s) that requires access to the database server. By limiting the number of clients that require access to the database, you can limit the overall exposure of the database. In addition, you can achieve further protection by using restricted IP addresses on the dedicated subnet. This requires an attacker to take over a client or exploit a major client vulnerability in order to obtain direct access to the database server.

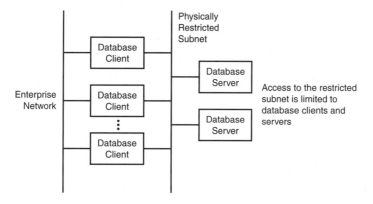

FIGURE 11.8

Using a dedicated subnet for database client-server communication.

Encrypting Communication Between the Database Client and Server

Although it is a good idea to physically restrict communication between a database client and server via a dedicated subnet, you might not always be able to do so. In these cases, it is advisable to encrypt communication between the database client and server. Encryption can be used to protect data from being disclosed or modified during transit between client and server. Encryption can also be used to authenticate the client to the server and the server to the client, as discussed in the section, "Authenticating the Client and Server," later in this chapter.

Encryption can occur at multiple levels in the communication protocol stack, as shown in Figure 11.9.

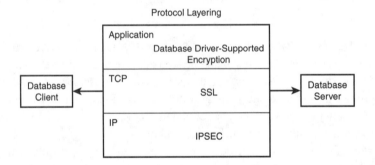

FIGURE 11.9

Encrypting client-server communication.

At the IP level, encryption can be used to protect IP packets from being disclosed as they transit from the database client to the database server. In addition, encryption can be used to verify that a packet received at a server, in fact, originated at a particular client and that a packet received at a client was sent from the database server. Verification is accomplished via the use of a virtual private network (VPN). VPNs use the IPSEC protocol for encryption and authentication over an untrusted network. Refer to Chapter 15, "Java Servlet and JSP Security," for a discussion of VPNs.

At the TCP level, encryption and mutual authentication can be accomplished using the Secure Sockets Layer (SSL). SSL is covered in Chapter 9, "SSL and JSSE." The client and server use a combination of client and server certificates to support single or mutual authentication. In addition, SSL's key agreement protocol provides the capability to set up an encrypted connection.

At an application level, client-server communication can make use of a database driver that supports encrypted communication. Major database vendors, such as Oracle (www.oracle.com), provide encryption support with their drivers. To use this encryption, you must configure its use in the client and server and provide appropriate encryption keys. In addition, you'll need to find a JDBC driver that can be made to work with the vendor's driver. This might limit the portability of your client software.

One alternative is to use database middleware, such as that provided by IDS Software (www.idssoftware.com). The middleware is physically located with the database server and mediates all client-server communication. It provides an encrypted JDBC connection between the client and the middleware. Back-end communication between the middleware and the database server is secured via a protected subnet or by other types of encryption.

There are a number of tradeoffs to consider when selecting the layer (IP, TCP, or application) with which to use encryption. Obviously, you can use encryption at each of these layers. However, encryption algorithms are computationally intensive, and three layers of encryption might have an adverse impact on application performance. IP-level encryption is supported in some network cards. These cards offload the encryption processing and minimize application performance impacts. SSL encryption can be implemented in Java (see Chapter 9) in a platform independent manner. However, because the encryption is performed in Java, performance impacts may be significant. Application-level encryption can be used with impacts on both client and server performance. If a middleware product (such as IDS Server) is used, the performance impact on the database server can be minimized. However, the hardware used with the middleware must be sufficient to handle the offloaded processing.

In general, the lower in the protocol stack that encryption is used, the more security is provided to the overall application. By employing encryption at the IP layer, you are able to prevent attacks at the TCP and application layers. By employing encryption at the TCP layer, you are able to counter application-layer vulnerabilities, but you might still be vulnerable to IP-layer attacks that can defeat TCP layer key agreement.

Protecting the Database Client and Server

Another major vulnerability area exists in the client and server platforms (refer to Figure 11.7). If an adversary takes over a database client, the adversary might use existing database connections to attack the database server. The adversary might also be able to recover any passwords that are stored on the client and use them to establish new connections to the database.

If an adversary is able to take over the database server, all is lost. Moreover, the adversary is able to provide false information to the database clients. If the database contains stored code (for example, in the form of Java objects), the adversary can modify the stored code in an attempt to take over the database clients or even the systems used by the database users.

Using Firewalls

The first step in protecting the client and server platforms is to put them behind one or more firewalls. At the very least, a firewall must be used to restrict Internet access to the enterprise intranet. All clients should be placed behind the firewall, and Internet-based communication with the database server should be prohibited. Internet access to the database client should be limited to HTTP or HTTPS if the client is located on a Web server. Otherwise, access should also be prohibited by the firewall (refer to Figure 11.10).

NOTE

Firewalls
Chapter 15 covers firewalls in more detail.

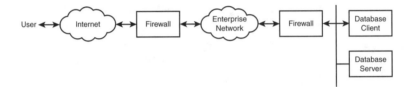

FIGURE 11.10
Protecting clients and servers using firewalls.

Limiting Internet-based access alone is not sufficient to protect the client and server. Because many network attacks are carried out by insiders, firewalls should also be used to limit intranet access to both the database client and server. Access to the database client should be limited to HTTP or HTTPS. Access to the database server should be restricted to the database clients.

Deploying Intrusion Detection Systems
Although firewalls provide a good first line of defense against network attacks, they are not infallible and can sometimes be circumvented, defeated, or disabled. Intrusion detection systems (IDS) provide a second line of defense that backs up the security provided by firewalls. In the case of database applications, intrusion detection systems can be used to detect any unauthorized access to the database clients and database servers (refer to Figure 11.11).

An IDS can be deployed between a local router and a database client to detect any unauthorized access to that client. For example, if client access is to be limited to HTTP/HTTPS, the IDS generates a security alarm if access to the client is attempted using any other application protocols.

Similarly, an IDS can be deployed on the subnet used by the database server to detect any unauthorized communication with the server. For example, if any other host beside a database client attempts to communicate with the database server, a security alarm can be generated. In addition, the IDS can be used to ensure that the client communicates with the server using only the database driver's communication ports. If a client attempts to use any other service of the database server, an alarm is generated.

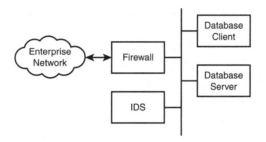

FIGURE 11.11
Protecting clients and servers using intrusion detection systems.

Hardening the Client and Server Platforms

Firewalls and intrusion-detection systems provide an enterprise-wide solution to protecting database clients and servers from takeover. Additional security can be provided by hardening the platforms upon which the clients and servers execute against network attacks. Hardening can be accomplished via the following steps:

- Use a securable OS—If at all possible, the database server should execute on a securable operating system, such as Windows NT/2000 or Linux. Avoid weak operating systems, such as Windows 95 and 98. Look for guidance on how to securely install and configure the OS that you select. Make sure that you install security-related patches and service packs.

- Remove insecure services—The default installation of an operating system might include the installation of services that are difficult to secure. For example, the Netbios services of Windows platforms and the NFS services of Unix platforms have been riddled with security vulnerabilities. By removing these services, you can remove the associated vulnerabilities.

- Minimize network services—In addition to removing insecure services, it is a good idea to remove any services that you don't need. For example, if you are deploying a client or server on a Linux platform, you might be able to remove services, such as telnet and FTP, if they are not needed as part of the application or to support the application. If you turn off a service, you can always turn it on again if necessary.

- Minimize software applications—A good rule of thumb is to install only the software you need for a particular application. Although most applications are benign, some are not. Run a recently updated virus checker to look for known viruses and Trojan horse software, such as Back Orifice.

- Securely configure applications and services—All services and applications you install should be configured in a secure manner. This means taking advantage of available security features and not configuring any features that are potential vulnerabilities. It also means minimizing the runtime privileges that are given to the software. Don't blindly install software with its default configuration and root privileges. For example, when you install database client or server software, you might want to remove any remote management features, configure encryption, and strong authentication features. You can run the software with the minimum set of privileges needed to perform its function.

- Be careful of what you share—If you do configure a file and directory sharing service, you must consider what you share and with whom you share it. For example, you might not want to put the database itself in a shared directory because doing so creates the risk that the database files might be modified directly without going through the database server. Share only the data that cannot be made accessible through more secure methods. Share the data only with systems that require direct access to the data. Never share scripts or executable files. Sharing is bidirectional. You must also be careful about the data that you receive from others. If the security of the database application depends on this data, you must make sure that access to that data is minimized.

- Minimize user access and enforce least privilege—Access to database clients and servers should be limited to those users who require such access to perform their duties. Don't increase the exposure of your application by providing blanket access to the client and server platforms. If someone needs temporary access to a client or server platform, grant the access for the time needed. Then remove the access when it is no longer required. In addition to limiting the number of users who are permitted access to a platform, you should also minimize the privileges that you grant to those who are permitted access. If a user only needs read access to a shared directory, don't grant him read and write access and don't give him login privileges. By enforcing least privilege, you minimize both the deliberate and the inadvertent damage that users can cause.

- Use strong passwords—Weak passwords are a serious vulnerability in all areas of security. It doesn't make much sense to deploy several layers of strong security countermeasures if they can be easily circumvented by someone who is able to guess or crack a password. Strong password guidelines should be established for all systems and applied to database clients and servers. These guidelines should identify the minimum password length, the restrictions on using common words, and the requirements for using digits and special characters. Strong passwords should be enforced by the operating system when possible. Systems should be checked for the use of strong passwords through the use of password checking/cracking tools.

- Audit security sensitive events—If your operating system provides the capability to audit events that affect the security of your database application, it makes sense to selectively log the occurrence of these events. I use the word *selectively* because you want to avoid auditing too many events, filling up your hard disk with audit data, and degrading system performance.

- Scan for known vulnerabilities— Whenever, possible use system scanners, such as the ISS scanner, to scan your system for known vulnerabilities. If you can find a vulnerability with a scanner, the chances are very high that someone else can also find the vulnerability. Some vendors also make database-specific security scanners. If you have access to such a scanner, by all means run it against your database application. It can point out many database server-specific vulnerabilities. Refer to the section, "Database Scanning," later in this chapter. Finally, you should periodically run a virus scanner on your system to check for known viruses.

Authenticating the Client and Server

Figure 11.7 identified two vulnerability areas related to masquerading. An adversary can masquerade as a client to gain unauthorized access to the database server. An adversary can also masquerade as the database server to spoof clients into providing it with security-sensitive information. The risk of both client and server masquerading can be minimized through the use of strong, mutual authentication.

The database client and server typically authenticate each other through the database connection login process. The client requests a connection to the server using a particular host name or IP address. If the connection is completed, it is assumed that the client connected with the correct host. However, there are a number of TCP/IP-level attacks that could result in the client connecting with the adversary's computer instead of with the intended database server. Clearly, it would be desirable for the client to be able to authenticate the database server using something other than the fact that a TCP connection was established.

The database server authenticates the client based on the fact that it connects with the correct ID and password. However, passwords can be intercepted or even guessed. Strong authentication mechanisms are needed to reduce the possibility of client masquerading.

There are several approaches to strengthening client and server authentication:

- Implement a VPN—Authentication can be simplified by implementing a VPN between the database clients and the server. Any client that is able to connect to the server via the VPN is authorized to access the server (providing that it connects with the correct ID and password).

- Use SSL—A certificate server can be set up and client and server certificates can be distributed to the database clients and the server. The clients and servers can be configured to use SSL for encryption and mutual authentication. Refer to Chapter 9 for more information on how this is accomplished.

- Use database encryption capabilities—If the database server provides drivers that support encryption between the client and the server, this encryption can also be used to support authentication. A key distribution mechanism must be set up to ensure that the clients have unique encryption keys and the database server is aware of these keys.

- Use database strong authentication capabilities—If the database server and clients can be configured to use single-use passwords, this capability can be used to reduce the exposure to attacks based on password interception or guessing.

- Use an external authentication system—If the database client and server can be configured to use an external authentication system, such as Windows NT/2000 authentication, the client-server authentication can be strengthened by adding this extra level of authentication. An alternative is to use database middleware for encryption and authentication and then support an authenticated connection from the middleware to the database server.

Of all the preceding approaches, the simplest is to use a VPN. However, this might not be a practical approach in all cases. For example, if the client is implemented as an applet that runs on the user's platform (not necessarily a good idea), a VPN must be established from the set of all possible users. This mitigates any benefits of using the VPN. SSL is a much better approach to authenticating a client that runs on a user platform. The client can authenticate the server via the server's signed certificate. The server can require a client certificate to support client authentication, or it can set up an encrypted session over which the client's ID and password are submitted.

Any database-specific encryption and authentication capabilities should be utilized provided that they are secure and do not require extensive modification to the client. One issue with using database-specific capabilities is that they might lock your application into a particular vendor's platform.

The disadvantage of using an external authentication system is that the security of the database application is dependent upon an external system, which itself might be compromised. The use of database middleware is an easy way to add encryption and authentication features to an existing application.

Securing the User Connection

In the previous sections, you considered the security issues involved with securing the connection between the database client and the database server. However, a secure application requires secure communication end-to-end security between the user and the database.

In the case where the database client runs on a Web server, the connection between the user's browser and the Web server should be secured. This is typically accomplished through the use of SSL, as shown in Figure 11.12. Figure 11.12 also covers the case where the database client

Databases and Database Security

CHAPTER 11

305

11

DATABASES AND
DATABASE
SECURITY

runs on an application server. In this case, communication between the Web and application server is secured using the approaches covered in earlier sections.

In both cases shown in Figure 11.12, the user authenticates with the Web application, and the database client separately authenticates with the database server. Authentication of the user with the Web server uses the techniques covered in Chapter 12.

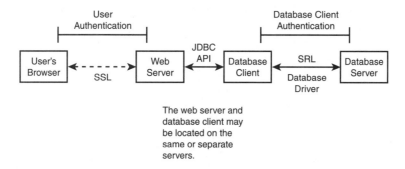

FIGURE 11.12
Securing the application front end.

In certain cases, the database client can be implemented as an applet that runs on the user's browser. This is not a very secure approach for Web applications that run over the Internet because the database server itself is opened up to Internet-based attacks. However, it might be reasonable to deploy an applet-based database client on a company's intranet.

In the case of an intranet application, a reusable database connection password should not be embedded in the applet's code. If the password is embedded, someone might be able to disassemble the applet's source code to recover the password. A custom applet could then be created to obtain general database access. Instead, users should be given individual passwords with which to access the Web application. This password can also be used to make the database connection, as shown in Figure 11.13. This approach requires that individual user accounts be established with the database server. The main advantage is that you can enforce individual accountability. The disadvantage is that additional administrative work is required of the database administrator. The following sections cover user authentication and access controls.

Authenticating the User

There are several basic approaches to authenticating users with the database. The most common approach is for the user to authenticate with a Web application, which uses a common server-side client to authenticate with the database (refer to Figure 11.12). The database connection password is typically stored with the database client on the Web or application server.

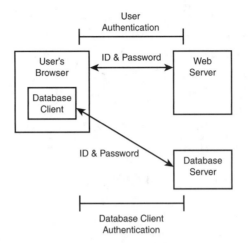

FIGURE 11.13

Authenticating individual users with the database.

This approach has the following advantages:

- The database administrator only needs to set up and manage a single account by which Web applications access the database.

- The user is not permitted direct access to the database. The user can only interact with the Web server. The database client on the server controls all access to the database.

The only problem with this approach is that any database-specific access controls or auditing features cannot be effectively put into place. The database sees only a single client, which performs all database operations on the behalf of the user.

A second approach is to give each user a separate database account and make the user's database ID and password available to the database client. The passwords can be stored in an encrypted file or made available via a directory service, such as LDAP or ActiveDirectory. When a user authenticates with the Web server, the user's database password is retrieved and is used to connect to the database (refer to Figure 11.14). The advantage of this approach is that the user is isolated from the database and the database is able to support both individual access controls and individual auditing. The disadvantage is that a unique database account has to be set up for each user. In addition, the users' database passwords need to be protected whether they are stored with the database client or made available via a directory service. One alternative is to use the same user password for authenticating with the Web application as is used with the database. However, by doing so, you risk the potential for someone to bypass the Web server and directly communicate with the database. If the database access controls are not complete or if the database server has any known vulnerabilities, this alternative might be risky.

Databases and Database Security

CHAPTER 11

307

11

DATABASES AND
DATABASE
SECURITY

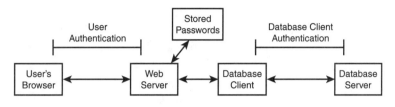

FIGURE 11.14

Using stored passwords to authenticate users with the database.

Another approach to user authentication is shown in Figure 11.13. The database client runs as an applet on the user's computer. Each user is given an individual database account. As previously mentioned, the disadvantage of this approach is that the user is given direct access to the database. For this reason, it is recommended that this approach be limited to intranet applications. The advantage of this approach is that it supports individual access controls and auditing at the database level. Its disadvantages are that it exposes the database to direct user access and that it requires individual accounts to be established with respect to the database.

Implementing Access Controls

In some database applications, every user is given equal access to the database. In other applications, some users are given more access privileges than other users. In the latter case, access controls are implemented that determine what accesses users may make of the database. These access controls can be implemented at the database server, at the database client, or at the Web server. A special case occurs when the database client executes as an applet on the user's browser. These four ways of implementing access controls are covered in the following subsections.

Implementing Access Controls at the Database Server

Although different database servers provide different access control capabilities, most implement access controls using the same basic approach. In general, database servers model basic database objects (for example: tables, views, stored procedures) and the accesses that can be made of these objects (for example: create, read, update, execute, and delete). Database access controls allow security policies to be developed and implemented that specify which objects can be accessed by which users in which ways.

Most database servers support *stored procedures*. A stored procedure is a sequence of SQL statements that is stored on the database. The database server typically optimizes the SQL so that it can be executed more efficiently. Stored procedures provide a way to define and implement common database accesses. By defining all application accesses in terms of stored procedures, access controls can be implemented that limit application access to the stored procedures. In this way, you can prevent users from directly submitting SQL statements to the database.

The main advantage of implementing access controls at the database server is that controls implemented in this way cannot be easily circumvented. If you implement them at the database client or Web server, a clever adversary might find a way to go around the access controls and communicate directly with the database. One disadvantage to implementing access controls at the database server is that your application becomes tied to that server. If you decide to port the application over to a new database server, you have to port the database specific access controls over to the new server. In some cases, the access controls supported on one server might not map to those supported on another server.

Implementing Access Controls at the Database Client

In order to develop more portable access controls, you can implement them at the database client. In this case, the client models database objects and the allowed access to those objects and performs access control decisions before generating and sending SQL statements to the database server.

To successfully implement access controls at the database client, the Web application should be organized so that access control decisions are made before SQL statements are created. In general, the higher the level at which decisions are made, the more successful the access controls will be. For example, it is much more effective to model database objects and specify which accesses are permitted than it is to parse SQL statements and determine which ones to allow.

The main advantage of implementing access controls at the server is that the access controls can be implemented in Java and, therefore, can be platform-independent. The main disadvantage is that, if the database client is circumvented, the database is left wide open.

Implementing Access Controls at the Web Server

In addition to implementing access controls on the database client and database server, it is also possible, depending on how the application is designed, to implement them at the Web server. If the user directly interacts with an application that is running on the Web server and only indirectly accesses the database client and database server, the Web server application is able to mediate all user access to the database client and server and, hence, to the database itself.

The main advantage of this approach is portability. If a user is able to circumvent the Web server and communicate directly with the database, all bets are off. This can be avoided by using different passwords for authenticating with the Web application and for accessing the database and also by not providing database passwords to the user.

Implementing Access Controls at the User's Browser

In the previous sections, we considered how database access controls can be implemented at the database and Web servers. It is also possible to implement access controls at the user's

Databases and Database Security

CHAPTER 11

309

11

DATABASES AND
DATABASE
SECURITY

browser if the database client executes as an applet on the user's browser. However, this approach is discouraged for the following reasons:

- The user can disassemble the applet's .class file and edit it to remove any access control restrictions.
- The user can reverse-engineer the applet and devise a client that talks directly to the database with no restrictions.

In both cases, the user is able to easily defeat the access controls that are enforced by the applet. The only countermeasure to this is to audit all user accesses to the database. However, auditing is reactive in that it can detect unauthorized accesses after they occur. Access controls are proactive in that they prevent unauthorized accesses from occurring.

Auditing

A major aspect of any secure application is security auditing. In the case of Web-based database applications, auditing can be performed at the Web server or at the database server. Security auditing is typically centered around the Web server's access log. Auditing at the database server is usually ineffective unless individual database accounts are utilized. In this case, auditing is typically limited to security-sensitive changes to the database, such as table creation/deletion and updates to security-sensitive tables.

More important than creating audit data is the process by which audit data is examined for potential security breaches. If the audit-trail data is not periodically reviewed, its value is negated. A series of scripts should be generated that search through the audit data and identify sets of events that indicate attempts to access the database in an unauthorized manner. For example, the scripts could look for failed connection login attempts or for SQL statements that attempt to discern the database structure.

In many cases, audit data might contain security-sensitive information, such as user passwords, financial transactions, and privacy-related data. Access to audit-trail data must be restricted to protect this information from being disclosed. In addition, access to the audit files must be restricted to prevent their being deleted to cover up unauthorized use of the database application.

Database Scanning

Database scanners, such as the provided by Internet Security Solutions Database Scanner Product, can be used to identify known database security vulnerabilities, such as insecure database configurations or weak passwords. If you have access to such tools, it is worth using them to identify and eliminate these vulnerabilities. Scanners won't help you to identify application-specific vulnerabilities, but they can ensure that database servers are securely configured.

Summary

This chapter covered the database access capabilities provided by JDBC, showed how to develop applications that access databases via JDBC, and covered general security issues related to database applications. In the next chapter, you'll cover security issues related to Java's e-commerce support.

The Java Authentication and Authorization Service

CHAPTER

12

The Java Authentication and Authorization Service (JAAS) provides a means for building Java applications that extend the standard Java 2 security model. JAAS augments the standard Java security model with the capability to authenticate subjects so that applications can be built independently of the underlying authentication mechanisms employed. JAAS also provides a means for authorizing subjects based on their authenticated identities.

In this chapter, you will learn

- The basic architecture of JAAS
- The representation of subjects in JAAS
- The means for authenticating subjects using JAAS
- The means for authorizing access to resources by subjects using JAAS

JAAS Overview

The JAAS serves as a standard extension to the Java 2 security model embodied by the J2SE v1.3. JAAS provides a standard way for limiting access to resources based on an authenticated user identity. JAAS APIs for login and logout also provide a standard technique for authenticating users. Even if different underlying authentication and authorization models are plugged into the JAAS service provider interface model, JAAS API users can continue to build their applications utilizing a stable and standard interface.

The authorization component of JAAS extends Java 2 security fine-grained access control to support access control based on identity (that is, a subject) in addition to Java 2 security access control based on a code signer and codebase. Before delving into the examples presented in this chapter, be sure that you have installed a J2SE v1.3 SDK (`http://www.javasoft.com/j2se/1.3/`). Also, you should download the JAAS v1.0 SDK from `http://java.sun.com/products/jaas/`.

The following packages compose the JAAS v1.0 architecture:

- `javax.security.auth`: Contains base classes and interfaces for authentication and authorization.
- `javax.security.auth.callback`: Contains a framework of classes and interfaces defining a contract between an application and security service that enable the security service to pass certain authentication information to the application.
- `javax.security.auth.login`: Contains classes used for login to a security domain.
- `javax.security.auth.spi`: Currently contains one interface encapsulating a login module that is implemented by JAAS service providers.

Figure 12.1 depicts the core architecture of JAAS. The following list describes the role of each major JAAS API class or interface depicted in this figure:

- `Subject`: Represents an individual or organization with multiple principal identities, along with a set of public and a set of private credentials. Authentication revolves around authenticating a subject, whereas authorization decisions are made based on an authenticated subject.
- `LoginContext`: Provides a basic API for subjects to log in and out of the system.
- `LoginModule`: Defines an interface to be implemented by authentication service providers that support JAAS.
- `Configuration`: Encapsulates an entity used to configure an application with particular login modules.
- `CallbackHandler`: Defines an interface to be implemented by applications if they want to allow the authentication service to pass them information.
- `Callback`: Specifies amarker interface implemented by objects that are passed to a `CallbackHandler` implementation. A `Callback` object contains data to be given to an application.
- `Policy`: Encapsulates the system's policy for authorization using JAAS and based on an authenticated subject.

- `AuthPermission`: Encapsulates permissions used during authentication.
- `PrivateCredentialsPermission`: Encapsulates permissions for accessing a subject's private credentials.

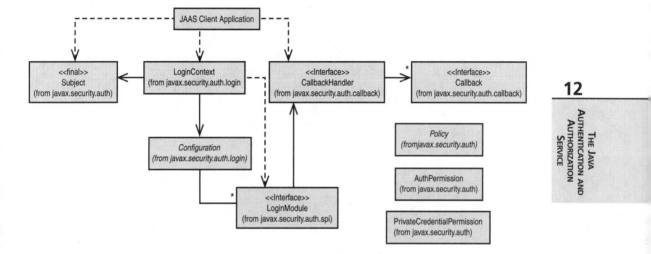

FIGURE 12.1
The JAAS architecture.

JAAS Subjects

The core abstractions involved with JAAS that are common to both authentication and authorization are depicted in Figure 12.2. An abstraction for a subject must exist to enable both the authentication of a subject with the system and the authorization of a subject's access to valued resources. Because a subject can have more than one principal name, a subject abstraction must also encapsulate a collection of principal objects. Furthermore, a subject can also have one or more public and private credentials to present to a system for authentication. Credential objects can be in any form and can implement special interfaces that signify that the credentials can be refreshed for an extended validity period or be destroyed. In what follows, I provide a more in-depth look at these very core abstractions and their basic usage.

Subject Relationships

The `javax.security.auth.Subject` class is a `Serializable` and `final` class used to encapsulate an entity that wishes to utilize some security-critical aspect of a system. Such an entity might correspond to a person, another system, or perhaps a group of people or systems. Because subjects can have multiple ways to identify themselves as a unit, the `Subject` class maintains a collection of one or more `java.security.Principal` objects in a standard java.util.Set collection. Thus, for example, if the Subject does correspond to a person, Principal objects can be associated with the Subject for that person's name, employee identification number, social security number, and so forth.

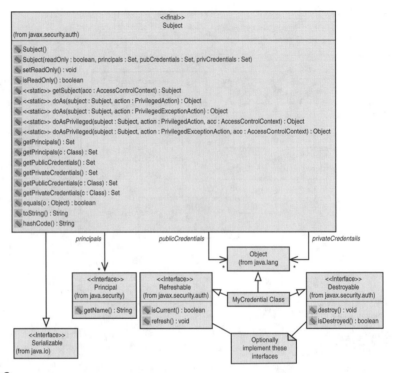

FIGURE 12.2
Core JAAS abstractions.

Subject objects can also be associated with credentials that define information used to validate such principal identities. Credential objects associated with a Subject are also stored in java.util.Set collections, but they are not required to be of any certain types except the basic java.lang.Object types. Credentials can be either public or private, and thus they are managed in different collections. Public credentials (such as public certificates) can be shared with other users of a system, whereas private credentials (such as private keys) should not be made accessible to anyone but the owning subject.

Creating Subjects

Although a default Subject constructor is provided, the Subject(boolean, Set, Set, Set) constructor is used primarily as the means to create a subject with a set of principals, a set of public credentials, and a set of private credentials. A boolean value is also passed into this constructor to indicate whether the Subject object is read-only. The following is an example:

```
// Create a principal and credentials hash sets
HashSet principals = new HashSet();
HashSet privateCredentials = new HashSet();
HashSet publicCredentials = new HashSet();

// Add initial elements to the sets
principals.add(new MyPrincipal("edison"));
publicCredentials.add("publicPassword");
privateCredentials.add("privatePassword");

// Create a Subject
Subject subject = new Subject(false, principals,
                            publicCredentials, privateCredentials);
```

Manipulating Subject Attributes

After a handle to a Subject object is either created or received, the principal objects and credential objects can be retrieved. The getPrincipals(), getPublicCredentials(), and getPrivateCredentials() methods all return a Set object containing the associated object types. Any updates performed on the Set objects from a non-read–only Subject will result in the Set object associated with the Subject being updated as well. For example

```
// Retrieve the public credential
String publicCredential =
    (String) ((subject.getPublicCredentials()).iterator()).next();
System.out.println("Public credential = " + publicCredential);

// Retrieve the private credential
String privateCredential =
    (String) ((subject.getPrivateCredentials()).iterator()).next();
System.out.println("Private credential = " + privateCredential);

// Retrieve a principal and display its value
//    and number of principals in Subject (currently has one)
MyPrincipal principal =
    (MyPrincipal) ((subject.getPrincipals()).iterator()).next();
System.out.println("Principal object in Subject = " + principal.getName());
System.out.println("Number of Principal objects in Subject = "
                    + subject.getPrincipals().size());

// Modify the principal (is OK)
principal.setName("watson");
// Modify the set (is also OK)
try{
  subject.getPrincipals().add(new MyPrincipal("joe"));
}
catch(IllegalStateException ex){
  System.out.println("This statement won't be called");
```

```
    ex.printStackTrace();
}

// See number of principals in Subject (now has two)
System.out.println("Number of Principal objects in Subject = "
                    + subject.getPrincipals().size());
```

Alternatively, the getPrincipals(Class), getPublicCredentials(Class)), and getPrivateCredentials(Class) methods all return a Set object containing the associated object types whose class type is a subclass or is the type of class specified by the Class input parameter. Because these method calls return copies of the Set objects that they return, updates made to the Set objects do not affect the state of the Subject object. However, any updates made to the individual elements within the Set object will affect the Subject object's state. For example

```
// Modify the set (only modifies the copy and not the Subject)
try{
  Set mySetCopy = subject.getPrincipals(MyPrincipal.class);
  mySetCopy.add(new MyPrincipal("bart"));
}
catch(IllegalStateException ex){
  System.out.println("This statement won't be called");
  ex.printStackTrace();
}

// See number of principals in Subject (still has two)
System.out.println("Number of Principal objects in Subject = "
                    + subject.getPrincipals().size());
```

If a Subject is set to be read-only, then attempted modifications to the Subject object's principal Set, public credentials Set, and private credentials Set are not permitted and result in the throwing of an IllegalStateException. The read-only nature of the Subject can be determined from Subject.isReadOnly(). The Subject.setReadOnly() can be used to set a Subject to be read-only, but there is no way to make a Subject writable after it has been set to read-only. For example

```
// Set the Subject to read-only
subject.setReadOnly();

// Modify the principal value (is still OK)
principal.setName("sam");
// Modify the set (is NOT OK and will throw IllegalStateException)
try{
  subject.getPrincipals().add(new MyPrincipal("marcus"));
}
catch(IllegalStateException ex2){
```

```
    System.out.println("This statement WILL be called");
    ex2.printStackTrace();
}
```

The Subject class also defines a getSubject() method, two doAs() methods, and two doAsPrivileged() methods. These methods involve authorization concepts and will be covered later in this chapter.

Specializing Subject Credentials

As a final note, two interfaces, javax.security.auth.Refreshable and javax.security.auth.Destroyable can also be used with credential objects associated with a Subject. If a particular credential class implements the Refreshable interface, such a class designates that the credential can have its validity period extended (refreshed). If a credential class implements the Destroyable interface, the credential information contained by that class can be wiped from memory.

Authentication with JAAS

Authentication in JAAS involves a client application that communicates with a login context to present any principal credential information to JAAS. It also performs login and logout operations. The login context communicates with a modular login module service-provider interface to interact with any underlying authentication-specific technologies. Such an architecture follows the pattern employed by the Pluggable Authentication Module (PAM) framework for shielding applications from the underlying authentication technologies. Login modules used by an application are configured using a special configuration abstraction that determines how to load and initialize the login modules. Figure 12.3 depicts the basic set of JAAS abstractions involved with authentication. In the next section, I expand on each of these abstractions in detail.

Login Module Configuration and Initialization

The javax.security.auth.login.LoginContext class is the primary class utilized by clients to the JAAS API. A LoginContext provides the interfaces necessary for subjects to log in and log out of the system. The LoginContext class shields JAAS clients from the underlying authentication mechanisms.

Login Context Construction

Clients first create an instance of a LoginContext object using one of four constructor options. The LoginContext(String) constructor is used to create a LoginContext for a particular named authentication configuration. The authentication configuration name is used to identify particular methodologies for logging into the application and particular parameters associated with those methodologies. All `LoginContext()` constructors require an authentication configuration name to be supplied. Because no `Subject` is associated with the `LoginContext(String)` constructor call, the `LoginContext` will create one for the user and expects to receive principal and credential information via an alternate mechanism (to be described later). The `LoginContext(String, Subject)` method creates a handle to a named authentication configuration with a particular `Subject` to be authenticated. The following is an example:

```
// Get our dummy Subject ("edison")
Subject subject = ...

// Create LoginContext
LoginContext loginContext = null;

try{
  loginContext = new LoginContext("PasswordExample", subject);
}
catch(LoginException loginException){
  loginException. printStackTrace();
  System.exit(1);
}
```

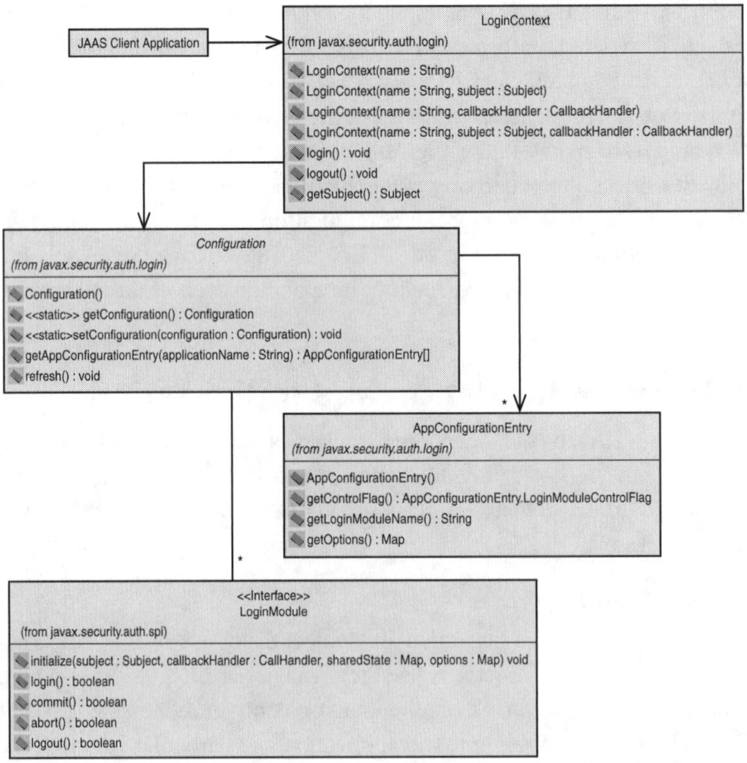

FIGURE 12.3

JAAS authentication abstractions.

Login Module Configuration

During construction time, the `LoginContext` object consults a
`javax.security.auth.login.Configuration` object to load the login modules associated
with the application. The `Configuration` object determines which login modules should be
loaded and the order in which they should be loaded. Because `Configuration` is an abstract
class, a concrete subclass must be specified somewhere for your JAAS applications to run
properly. To override the default `Configuration` implementation, you must alter your J2SE
v1.3's `<JAVA_HOME>/jre/lib/security/java.security` file so that a `login.`
`configuration.provider` property points to a fully qualified `Configuration` subclass name.
Otherwise, the default `Configuration` implementation class assumes that a special file for
configuring login modules is defined according to the form

```
AuthenticationConfigurationName
{
  ModuleName AuthenticationFlag ModuleOptions;
  ModuleName AuthenticationFlag ModuleOptions;
     ...
};

AuthenticationConfigurationName
{
  ModuleName AuthenticationFlag ModuleOptions;
  ModuleName AuthenticationFlag ModuleOptions;
     ...
};

...

other
{
  ModuleName AuthenticationFlag ModuleOptions;
  ModuleName AuthenticationFlag ModuleOptions;
     ...
};
```

Each *AuthenticationConfigurationName* identifies one or more login modules used to
authenticate users for the application that desires to use this particular configuration. Each
login module entry corresponds to a class that implements the
`javax.security.auth.spi.LoginModule` interface. The `ModuleName` entry thus relates to a
fully qualified `LoginModule` implementation class name. The default `Configuration` class
implementation will proceed down the list for the *AuthenticationConfigurationName* and
attempt any authentication with a `LoginModule` based on its ordered entry in the list. If no
AuthenticationConfigurationName is found for the application, the default `other` application
configuration will be used.

Each login module entry also defines an *AuthenticationFlag* value that specifies how authentication proceeds with the login modules configured for this authentication configuration. The basic values that can be specified for the *AuthenticationFlag* are

- Required: The associated login module must succeed with authenticating the subject for the overall authentication process to be considered successful. The authentication process still continues down the list for other login modules, however.

- Requisite: The associated login module must succeed for the overall authentication process to be considered successful. The authentication process terminates as failed if a failed login occurs.

- Sufficient: The associated login module's successful authentication is sufficient, and the authentication can terminate as successful if a successful login occurs. If a Sufficient flag is configured, only the Required and Requisite modules preceding this module must have succeeded.

- Optional: The associated login module's capability to authenticate the subject is not required. The authentication process still continues down the list for other login modules. At least one Optional or one Sufficient module must have succeeded if no Required or Requisite modules are configured.

Finally, the *ModuleOptions* entry per login module is used to define any configuration parameters that can be passed to the associated LoginModule implementation during initialization. Such parameters are defined as a series of *name=value* pairs.

For example, you might define a sample jaas.config file for your sample application as follows:

```
PasswordExample
{
    ejava.jaas.AuthenticationExampleModule Required
➥ fileName=credentials.properties;
};
```

Thus, your call to new LoginContext("PasswordExample", subject), as illustrated earlier, will induce the default Configuration implementation to configure your application to make use of the PasswordExample authentication configuration information defined in your jaas.config file. A special ejava.jaas.AuthenticationExampleModule class (to be defined soon) serves as your required login module implementation to be used for authenticating subjects. Note that your AuthenticationExampleModule class also utilizes a special fileName module option during its initialization process.

Login Module Configuration File Location

The location of your jaas.config file can be specified for your application in one of three ways. From the command line, you can set a special system property named java.security.auth.login.config to the location of your authentication configuration file. Thus if the jaas.config file is in your current directory, you might execute the example as follows:

```
java -Djava.security.auth.login.config=jaas.config
➥ ejava.jaas.AuthenticationExample
```

You can also define a series of login.config.url.*n* properties in the *<JAVA_HOME>*/jre/lib/security/java.security file to point to the location of authentication configuration files. The order in which configuration files are loaded is implied by the numeric value associated with the *n* in login.config.url.*n*. For example

```
login.config.url.1=file:C:/ejava/jaas/certificate.config
login.config.url.2=file:C:/myb2c/config/b2c.config
login.config.url.3=file:C:/myb2b/config/b2b.config
```

If no location is specified via the system property or from the java.security file, JAAS attempts to load configuration information from the default *<USER_HOME>*/.java.login.config file.

Login Module Initialization

After loading and instantiating any objects that implement the LoginModule interface, the Configuration class invokes the initialize() method on each LoginModule object. The initialize() method takes as input parameters the Subject to be authenticated, any CallbackHandler object for interacting with the end user (to be described shortly), a Map of any data shared with other LoginModule objects, and a Map of module-specific options for this LoginModule (such as those read from the *ModuleOptions* entry described earlier). Although application developers will most often utilize off-the-shelf LoginModule implementations, such as those defined at http://java.sun.com/products/jaas/, I implement a simple LoginModule here to better illustrate the authentication process involved with JAAS. The ejava.jaas.AuthenticationExampleModule class implements a simple LoginModule that you can use to authenticate users based on credential information stored in a properties file.

The AuthenticationExampleModule.initialize() method stores some basic information in addition to the name of the credential properties file. This additional information is shown here:

```
package ejava.jaas;

... // imports excluded here

public class AuthenticationExampleModule implements LoginModule
{
  private Subject subject = null;
  private String credentialFileName = null;
  private CallbackHandler callbackHandler = null;
```

```
    private Map otherState = null;
    private boolean loginSucceeded = false;

    public void initialize(Subject aSubject,
                           CallbackHandler aCallbackHandler,
                           Map sharedState, Map options) {

      // Get Subject, callback handler, and shared state
        subject = aSubject;
      callbackHandler = aCallbackHandler;
      otherState = sharedState;

      // Get file name of credential file
      credentialFileName = (String) options.get("fileName");

      // Print out info
      System.out.println("Start AuthenticationExampleModule with file "
                         + credentialFileName);
    }
    ...
}
```

The Authentication Process

After each LoginModule is initialized, user authentication can proceed. A JAAS client will
induce the authentication process to begin by invoking the LoginContext.login() method.
The LoginContext.login() method will, in turn, invoke the login() method on each
LoginModule object configured for this application. The exact nature of the login() implementation is a function of the particular authentication technique to be employed by the
LoginModule implementation. During this first phase of authentication, the
AuthenticationExampleModule implementation reads credential information from a file and
then compares it with the established credential information passed in with the Subject, as
shown here:

```
public boolean login() throws LoginException
  {
    // First dynamically load credentials file
    Properties credentialsInfo = this.loadCredentialsFile();

    // Get principal list
    Iterator principals = (subject.getPrincipals()).iterator();

    // For each principal, attempt login
    while(principals.hasNext()){
      // Get principal and print out info
      Principal principal = (Principal) principals.next();
      String name = principal.getName();
```

```
      System.out.println("Attempting login for " + name);

      // If principal is in the credentials file...
      if(credentialsInfo.containsKey(name)){
        // Get and print out password (since is just a test program)
        String password = (String) credentialsInfo.get(name);
        System.out.println(name + " password is " + password);
        Set privateCreds = subject.getPrivateCredentials();
        if(privateCreds.contains(password)){
          System.out.println("Success in login");
          loginSucceeded = true;
          return true;
        }
      }
      else{
        System.out.println("Fail in login");
        loginSucceeded = false;
        throw new LoginException("Not a valid subject");
      }
    }

    System.out.println("Fail in login");
    loginSucceeded = false;
    return false;
}

private Properties loadCredentialsFile() throws LoginException
{
    // Throw exception if no credentials file
    if(credentialFileName == null){
      System.out.println("Fail in login");
      loginSucceeded = false;
      throw new LoginException("No credentials file");
    }

    // Load the properties
    Properties properties = new Properties();
    try{
      FileInputStream fin = new FileInputStream(credentialFileName);
      properties.load(fin);
    }
    catch(Exception e){
      System.out.println("Fail in login");
      loginSucceeded = false;
      throw new LoginException("No credentials file");
    }

    return properties;
}
```

If the subject was successfully authenticated during the overall authentication process, a second phase of the authentication process results in the commit() method being invoked on each LoginModule implementation object. If a particular LoginModule successfully authenticated the subject, it should associate any Principal and credential objects with the Subject contained by this LoginModule. For your AuthenticationExampleModule, you assume that a populated Subject object will be associated with the LoginModule during initialization. Thus, there is no need to re-associate any Principal or credential information with the Subject. When a LoginContext constructor is called with no Subject, the application logic of the invoked LoginModule implementations must retrieve the principal and credential information from a user via some other mechanism (such as callbacks) and associate this information with a Subject during the call to LoginModule.commit(). If the authentication for this LoginModule failed, the LoginModule implementation must destroy any saved state. A value of true is returned from commit() if the method succeeded.

If the subject was not successfully authenticated during the overall authentication process, the second phase of the authentication process results in the abort() method being invoked on each LoginModule implementation object. This method implementation must destroy any saved state. A value of true is returned from abort() if the method succeeded.

The JAAS client application can invoke getSubject() on the LoginContext object any time after authentication succeeded and obtain a handle to the authenticated Subject object. If authentication failed, the getSubject() method returns null.

Finally, when the JAAS client application invokes logout() on a LoginContext object, the LoginContext object will invoke logout() on each LoginModule configured for this application. Each LoginModule should destroy any Principal and credential state stored. A value of true is returned from LoginModule.logout() if the method succeeded.

Callback Handling

Callbacks provide a means for JAAS application clients to be notified of certain events during the authentication process and for providing data to the authentication process. Figure 12.4 depicts the basic structure for implementing callbacks in JAAS. A special javax.security.auth.callback.CallbackHandler interface is implemented by JAAS applications that wish to be consulted during the authentication process. A CallbackHandler.handle() method is implemented by JAAS application clients to receive a collection of javax.security.auth.callback.Callback objects when a LoginModule is performing the login process. Such Callback objects contain information relevant to the particular type of authentication being performed. JAAS application clients then retrieve and provide any necessary information via Callback objects for authentication to proceed.

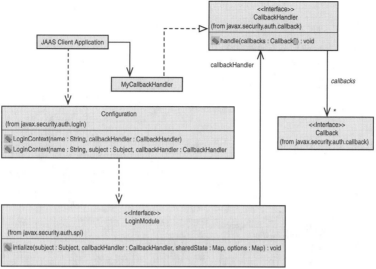

FIGURE 12.4

Basic JAAS callback handling.

CallbackHandler objects are registered with a LoginContext via one of two constructors shown in Figure 12.4. LoginModule implementations can save such CallbackHandler references for later use when a call to LoginModule.initialize() is made. A LoginModule can then invoke the services of the CallbackHandler object during the authentication process via a call to CallbackHandler.handle(). The actual Callback objects passed into the handle() method are a function of the particular type of authentication being performed. Figure 12.5 depicts the basic collection of Callback implementations equipped with JAAS v1.0.

Although I will not go into a detailed description of each Callback mechanism here, I should point out that the basic collections shown in Figure 12.5 have the following general roles:

- ChoiceCallback: Used to retrieve a list of choices available during authentication and also to enable the client application to select particular authentication options.
- ConfirmationCallback: Used to retrieve authentication confirmation information and also to enable clients to establish particular confirmation information to drive the authentication process.
- LanguageCallback: Used to get and set geographic and regional locale information during authentication.
- NameCallback: Used to get and set any username information used during authentication.
- PasswordCallback: Used to get and set any user password information used during authentication.

- `TextInputCallback`: Used to provide any general text input to the authentication process.
- `TextOutputCallback`: Usedto receive any general textual output messages from the authentication process.

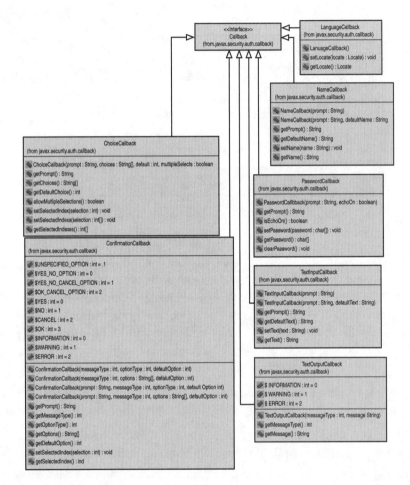

FIGURE 12.5

Standard JAAS callback implementations.

As a general example, if you want a `LoginModule` to receive username and password information from a user during authentication, you might put the following inside a `login()` method implementation of a `LoginModule`:

```
// If have no callback handler...cannot login
if (callbackHandler == null){
```

```
    throw new LoginException("No handler available");
}

// Create a user name and password callback
NameCallback nameCallback = new NameCallback(" Enter Username ");
PasswordCallback passwordCallback =
                new PasswordCallback(" Enter Password ", false);

// Create the callback array for the CallbackHandler
Callback callbacks[] = new Callback[2];
callbacks[0] = nameCallback;
callbacks[1] = passwordCallback;

// Invoke handle() on the CallbackHandler
try{
  callbackHandler.handle(callbacks);
}
catch(Exception ex){
  ex.printStackTrace();
  loginSucceeded = false;
  throw new LoginException(" Cannot login.");
}

// Now should have the user name and password
String userName = nameCallback.getName();
char [] password = passwordCallback.getPassword();
```

On the JAAS client application side, the handling of this callback will be application-specific. That is, the username and password can be obtained from a GUI, via some distributed object call or via some other mechanism. However, a basic skeleton for such a handle() implementation might follow, as shown here:

```
public void handle(Callback[] callbacks)
    throws UnsupportedCallbackException, IOException
{

    // Get callbacks
    NameCallback nameCallback = (NameCallback) callbacks[0];
    PasswordCallback passwordCallback = (PasswordCallback) callbacks[1];

    // Get user name prompt
    String prompt = nameCallback.getPrompt();
    // Get name from user (ap-specific)...
    String userName = ...
    // Now set name
    nameCallback.setName(userName);
```

```
    // Get password prompt
    passwordCallback.getPrompt();
    // Get password from user (ap-specific)...
    char [] password = ...
    // Now set password
    passwordCallback. setPassword(password);

    ...
}
```

Authorization with JAAS

After successfully authenticating a subject, the authorization features unique to JAAS can be employed to limit access to valued resources based on the authenticated subject information. Authorization with JAAS is similar to the authorization process and technique used by the Java 2 security model. In fact, JAAS authorization extends this model to include additional access control decision-making logic based on the subject requesting access.

The Subject.doAs() and Subject.doAsPrivileged() methods can be used to perform security-critical actions as a particular Subject. These static methods (as shown in Figure 12.2) have a role similar to the AccessController.doPrivileged() methods. However, these methods also require an additional Subject object input parameter. Fine-grained access control for such Subject.doXX() calls are defined in a JAAS policy file similar to the way that privileges granted for access during AccessController.doPrivileged() calls are defined in a security policy file.

An abstract javax.security.Policy class is defined for encapsulating the policy used during JAAS authentication with subjects. A default implementation class is used to define policy information in a text file akin to default implementation of the java.security.Policy class used for general Java 2 security access control.

JAAS Security Policy File Format

In the default implementation of security policy management with JAAS, a security policy is defined in an ASCII text file in much the same way as policies are defined in the default Java 2 security policy file implementation. JAAS security policy file grant entries have the following general form:

```
grant codebase "URL", SignedBy "list of names",

     Principal [principal_class_name] "principal_name",
     Principal ...
{
    permission permission_class_name [ "target name" ] [, "actions"]
                                     [, SignedBy "list of names"];
    permission ...
};
```

Each policy file entry specified for a security domain begins with the grant keyword and contains one or more permission definitions for the particular domain of protection. Each permission entry begins with the permission keyword and is followed by the fully qualified permission *class_name*. Permission target names and a comma-separated list of actions also follow a permission designation. The SignedBy field following the permission is provided with a comma-separated list of alias names that indicate who must have signed the Java code for the permissions class. Each grant entry delimiting a domain of protection can also contain a SignedBy field designating that code being executed in the JVM associated with the grant entry must be signed by the named signers. A CodeBase field can also be associated with a grant entry to relate a set of permissions with a resource location from which the code is loaded.

JAAS security policy files also associate one or more principal identification values associated with each grant entry. A fully qualified principal class name identifies the type of Principal object associated with valid principals to which the associated permissions apply. The actual principal name must also be supplied. Thus, any Subject to which the associated permissions apply must have all the specified principal values associated with the JAAS security policy entry.

The following defines a simple JAAS security file for your AuthenticationExample application:

```
grant codebase "file:authaction.jar",
      Principal ejava.jaas.MyPrincipal "edison"
{
    permission java.io.FilePermission "myLogFile.txt", "write";
};
```

Thus, your AuthenticationExample will allow only write permissions to a myLogFile.txt file for an authenticated subject containing the principal name of edison. Furthermore, the associated codebase for this permission is associated with code loaded from an authaction.jar file. You will compile and package your security-critical authorization code into this special authaction.jar file in a subsequent section.

Using JAAS Security Policy Files

Now that you know how to define policies in a JAAS security policy file, you might be wondering where to create such files and how to make your Java applications use the policies defined in such files.

There is no default JAAS security policy file assumed for JAAS applications. Therefore, you must either make your JAAS application cognizant of the JAAS security policy file via a command line system property or via setting properties in the *<JAVA_HOME>*/jre/lib/security/ java.security file.

You can define a series of auth.policy.url.*n* properties in the `<JAVA_HOME>`/jre/lib/security/java.security file to point to the location of JAAS security policy files. The order in which policy files are loaded is implied by the numeric value associated with the *n* in auth.policy.url.*n*. For example

```
auth.policy.url.1=file:C:/ejava/jaas/jaas.policy
auth.policy.url.2=file:C:/myb2c/config/b2c.policy
auth.policy.url.3=file:C:/myb2b/config/b2b.policy
```

If you want to define a policy file to be read from your own application-specific location, you can pass in the -Djava.security.auth.policy system property to the command line when starting your Java application. Such a property is used to define the location of your own JAAS security policy file as exemplified in the following code, along with other standard Java 2 security management system parameters:

```
java -Djava.security.auth.login.config=jaas.config
➡ -Djava.security.auth.policy=jaas.policy
➡ -Djava.security.manager
➡ -Djava.security.policy=java2security.policy
➡ ejava.jaas.AuthenticationExample
```

Note that you also need a custom Java 2 security policy file to be used with your application such as the java2security.policy file used in the above command. This file needs to specify the basic permissions required of your application as required by the fine-grained access control needs of any Java 2 security-based application. You will examine the contents of this file shortly, but first take a look at how to perform JAAS actions and some of the JAAS-specific policy and permission abstractions that drive the type of permissions to be inserted into this file.

Performing Security-Critical Actions

The security-critical action to be performed by your sample application attempts to write to a file named myLogFile.txt. You encapsulate this security-critical operation within a PrivilegedAction class, as you can do with other standard Java 2 security-critical actions. You then compile and insert this security-critical action class into the authaction.jar file as referenced by your jaas.policy file described above. The definition of this PrivilegedAction class is made rather simple for demonstration purposes and is encapsulated with an AuthorizationAction class as shown here:

```
package ejava.jaas;

import java.security.PrivilegedAction;
import java.io.*;
```

```
public class AuthorizationAction implements PrivilegedAction
{
  public Object run()
  {
    try{
      FileOutputStream fout = new FileOutputStream("myLogFile.txt");
      DataOutputStream dout = new DataOutputStream(fout);
      dout.writeChars("Attempted log!");
    }
    catch(Exception e){
      e.printStackTrace();
    }

    return null;
  }
}
```

The invocation of this privileged action by your `AuthenticationExample` occurs after your subject has been authenticated by the system. Thus, you might simply attempt to perform this security-critical action as follows:

```
// Get our subject after authentication
Subject mySubject = loginContext.getSubject();

// Now perform the security-critical authorization action
Subject.doAs(mySubject, new AuthorizationAction());
```

JAAS Security Authorization Abstractions

A minimalist API does exist for encapsulating JAAS security policies as shown in Figure 12.6. Here you see that a basic abstraction for JAAS policies is provided and assumes a default policy file configuration akin to the one defined for the standard Java 2 security default policies. Additionally, a few permission abstractions have been added to support authentication permission-granting and special private credential access permissions required by certain JAAS applications. The subsections that follow expand on the abstractions presented in Figure 12.6 to support authorization.

JAAS Policy Manipulation

The `javax.security.auth.Policy` abstract class implements a static `getPolicy()` method returning a handle to the current installed JAAS policy, and the static `setPolicy()` method enables one to set a new JAAS security policy. The `getPolicy()` method can be invoked if the `AuthPermission getPolicy` allows it to be, and the `setPolicy()` method can be invoked if the `AuthPermission setPolicy` allows it to be.

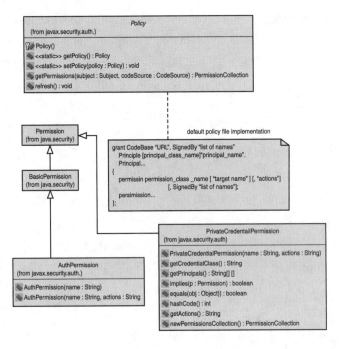

FIGURE 12.6
JAAS authorization related abstractions.

When you're setting a new security policy, the new policy must extend the JAAS `Policy` class and implement the `getPermissions()` and `refresh()` methods. The `getPermissions()` method takes a `Subject` and `CodeSource` object to be associated with those permissions granted to such principals and location. It returns the defined permissions allowed as a `PermissionCollection` object. The `refresh()` method must refresh the policy information from the underlying policy storage mechanism associated with the newly defined `Policy` implementation.

Alternatively, the default JAAS policy implementation to use with your JVM instance can be specified with an `auth.policy.provider` property in the java.security file:

```
auth.policy.provider=com.assuredtech.security.JAASPolicy
```

As a final note, if a new policy object is not set using `Policy.setPolicy()` or if the `auth.policy.provider` property is set, the default JAAS security policy provided by Sun is used. Sun's implementation of the default security policy that extends the `Policy` class and reads policy information from the previously mentioned policy files is contained in the class `com.sun.security.auth.PolicyFile`.

Authentication Permissions

The `javax.security.auth.AuthPermission` class encapsulates a JAAS authentication permission. Authentication permissions have a target name (but no action lists) that can be used to grant permissions for access to `Subject`, `LoginContext`, `Configuration`, and JAAS `Policy` objects. The target names of an `AuthPermission` can be one of the following:

- `doAs`: Allows for the invocation of `Subject.doAs()` methods.

- `doAsPrivileged`: Allows for the invocation of `Subject.doAsPrivileged()` methods.

- `getSubject`: Allows for the invocation of `Subject.getSubject()` methods to obtain a handle to a `Subject` object for the current thread.

- `getSubjectFromDomainCombiner`: Allows for the invocation of the `SubjectDomainCombiner.getSubject()` method. The `javax.security.auth.SubjectDomainCombiner` class extends the `java.security.DomainCombiner` class to update protection domains with subject permissions defined with the JAAS security policy.

- `setReadOnly`: Allows for permission to set the `Subject` to be read-only.

- `modifyPrincipals`: Allows for permission to modify a `Set` containing a `Subject` object's principals.

- `modifyPublicCredentials`: Allows for permission to modify a `Set` containing a `Subject` object's public credentials.

- `modifyPrivateCredentials`: Allows for permission to modify a `Set` containing a `Subject` object's private credentials.

- `refreshCredential`: Allows for permission to invoke the `Refreshable.refresh()` method in order to refresh a credential object's state.

- `destroyCredential`: Allows for permission to invoke the `Destroyable.destroy()` method in orderto destroy a credential object's state.

- `createLoginContext`: Allows for permission to create a `LoginContext` object.

- `getLoginConfiguration`: Allows for permission to retrieve the login `Configuration`.

- `setLoginConfiguration`: Allows for permission to set the login `Configuration`.

- `refreshLoginConfiguration`: Allows for permission to refresh the login `Configuration`.

- `getPolicy`: Allows for permission to invoke the `Policy.getPolicy()` method in order to access the JAAS policy.

- `setPolicy`: Allows for permission to invoke the `Policy.setPolicy()` method in order to set the JAAS policy.

- `refreshPolicy`: Allows for permission to invoke the `Policy.refreshPolicy()` method in order to refresh the JAAS policy.

Private Credential Permissions

The `javax.security.auth.PrivateCredentialPermission` class is used to grant or limit access to private credential objects that are associated with a `Subject`. The basic format for specifying such a permission in a standard Java 2 security file is as follows:

```
permission javax.security.auth.PrivateCredentialPermission
➥ "CredentialClassName PrincipalClassName \"principal_name\"",
➥ "read";
```

For example, you must grant permission to the principal name `edison` for access to their private credentials with `AuthenticationExample` using the following Java 2 security permission in your `java2security.policy` file:

```
permission javax.security.auth.PrivateCredentialPermission
    "java.lang.String ejava.jaas.MyPrincipal \"edison\"", "read";
```

Alternatively, an asterisk (`*`) can be used in place of the `CredentialClassName` to indicate that this permission applies to all credential class types. Furthermore, an asterisk can also be used in place of the `principal_name` to indicate that this permission applies to all principals with the associated `PrincipalClassName` as a principal class type. If the `PrincipalClassName` is also specified with an asterisk, the permission applies to any principal class type. As a final note, additional `PrincipalClassName` and `principal_name` pairs can be specified within the same permission.

Standard Java Security Policies with JAAS Permissions

As previously mentioned, your JAAS application also requires that you configure a standard Java 2 security policy in order to execute your sample application. Specifically, the `AuthenticationExample` application creates a `LoginContext` object, attempts to read private credentials for a user named `edison`, attempts to perform a privileged action associated with a `Subject`, attempts to read a properties file from the local file system, and attempts to write a security log file to the local file system. Furthermore, the downloaded JAAS extension to the J2SE must also perform a number of security-critical operations for which you must grant access. The `java2security.policy` file utilized by your application assumes the following form:

```
grant codebase "file:D:/java/downloads/jaas1_0/lib/jaas.jar"
{
    permission java.security.AllPermission;
};

grant codebase "file:example.jar"
{
    permission javax.security.auth.AuthPermission "createLoginContext";
    permission javax.security.auth.PrivateCredentialPermission
      "java.lang.String ejava.jaas.MyPrincipal \"edison\"", "read";
```

```
    permission javax.security.auth.AuthPermission "doAs";
    permission java.io.FilePermission "credentials.properties", "read";
    permission java.io.FilePermission "myLogFile.txt", "write";
};
```

As shown above, your authentication sample code is also packaged into a local `example.jar` file referenced by the codebase in this standard Java 2 security policy file. You, of course, would also need to reflect the actual location of your downloaded JAAS libraries (for instance, located in a `jaas.jar` file) in the codebase for the associated permission shown above.

You can then execute your example with the following command whereby all such referenced configuration and policy files are contained in the local directory:

```
java -Djava.security.auth.login.config=jaas.config
➡ -Djava.security.auth.policy=jaas.policy
➡ -Djava.security.manager
➡ -Djava.security.policy=java2security.policy
➡ ejava.jaas.AuthenticationExample
```

Because your `jaas.policy` file defined earlier enables `edison` to write to a log file, the example should execute with no security exceptions. If you, however, alter the `jaas.policy` file to assume a different principal name for write permission to the `myLogFile.txt` file and execute the application, a `FilePermission` failure for `edison`'s permission to write to the `myLogFile.txt` file will occur.

Summary

JAAS provides a standard means for authenticating subjects and authorizing access to valued resources based on authenticated subject identities. JAAS serves as a basic extension to the standard Java 2 security model for providing fine-grained access control. The default mechanisms for specifying JAAS access control policies are similar to the mechanisms provided by the default mechanisms of the standard Java 2 security framework.

JAAS will be particularly useful in distributed enterprise environments that provide their own custom means for specifying JAAS security policies. In fact, the J2EE specification indicates that a future version of the specification will include JAAS to manage authentication and authorization within J2EE environments. After such an integration has been performed, the primary programmatic use of JAAS will be performed by the J2EE environment vendors in order to keep their application environments independent of underlying authentication technologies.

Standard J2EE authentication and authorization mechanisms will most likely focus on declarative mechanisms utilizing JAAS underneath the hood. Application developers using J2SE environments, however, reap programmatic advantages by using JAAS to build applications that they wish to remain shielded from underlying authentication technology requirements. Furthermore, such standalone applications will also enjoy the richer level of access-control support offered by JAAS's authorization capabilities based on authenticated subjects.

CORBA Security

13

The Common Object Request Broker Architecture
(CORBA) is a language- and platform-neutral body of
specifications for building distributed object applications.
CORBA applications are designed to be largely isolated
from the details of communications code. The CORBA
Interface Definition Language (IDL) offers a language-
neutral mechanism for defining distributed object interfaces
with standards that exist for mapping IDL to Java, as well
as for mapping Java to IDL. At the lowest level, CORBA
specifications that deal with the Object Request Broker
(ORB) define exactly how distributed clients can remotely
utilize the services of distributed servers in a language- and
platform-independent fashion. They also describe the underlying communications protocol over which such service
utilization occurs. Above the layer of the ORB,
CORBAservice (Common Object Services) specifications
define those distributable CORBA services that CORBA-
based applications commonly rely upon, such as providing
human-readable object names to object reference mappings
and querying for objects using some search criteria.The
CORBA Security Service is an OMG CORBAservice
component that relates to distributed object security for
CORBA-based applications. The CORBA Security Service,
like other CORBA services, is defined to function primarily
atop the ORB layer.

However, CORBA Security also defines some changes to the ORB layer, as well as enables interoperability and enhanced security. The CORBA Security Service is defined in the OMG Security Service Specification. By using components that implement the Security Service Specification, CORBA-based enterprise applications gain the advantages of standards-based security protection including protection for identity, authenticity, nonrepudiation, authorization, auditing, integrity, and confidentiality.

In this chapter, you will learn about

- The CORBA Security Service Specification and architecture.
- Authentication using the CORBA Security Service.
- The CORBA Security Service's delegation of credentials.
- The means for authorizing users and access control in the CORBA Security model.
- The means for auditing security-sensitive activities under the CORBA Security model.
- CORBA Security Service nonrepudiation mechanisms.
- Support for integrating underlying data encryption for CORBA Security.
- The mechanisms for defining specific CORBA Security policies.
- Current support for the administration of CORBA Security.

CORBA Security Overview

CORBA Security defines standard interfaces to services that operate on top of and, to a certain extent, are part of an ORB that provides security protection for your CORBA objects. CORBA Security provides security protection for identity, authenticity, nonrepudiation, authorization, auditing, integrity, and confidentiality. CORBA Security is defined in the CORBA Security Service Specification.

Interoperability with CORBA is a fundamental consideration to be undertaken by the Java 2 Platform, Enterprise Edition (J2EE) road map. Although CORBA Security interoperability is not defined in version 1.2 of the J2EE specification, the specification alludes to the fact that future versions will define more rigid interoperability requirements. An auxiliary Enterprise JavaBeans (EJB) to CORBA Mapping specification currently defines a few minimal guidelines for providing interoperability (including security interoperability) between J2EE EJB environments and other non-J2EE client/server environments. Of course, an independent CORBA Security Service implementation can also be used with an ORB and Java 2 Platform, Standard Edition (J2SE) environment.

Digesting the CORBA Security Service Specification

The latest CORBA Security Service Specification (CSSS), December 1998, is a very complex specification that is 386 pages in length. Because the specification is part of its parent CORBAservices specification, it has its own chapter number of 15. The following is a breakdown of the CORBA Security Service Specification (ftp://ftp.omg.org/pub/docs/formal/98-12-10.pdf) with notes indicating those sections that might be of interest to you, as well as the sections that probably will not be as interesting:

- *Section 15.1:* This is an introduction to security in general.

- *Section 15.2:* This section offers a specification overview that includes different specification packaging options for levels of compliance.

- *Section 15.3:* This section provides a reference model defining those elements of a system that need to be secured. That is, the CORBA security assurance problem model is presented.

- *Section 15.4:* This section covers the architecture of CORBA Security. This section provides the big picture of how security is provided. That is, the CORBA security risk reduction model is presented.

- *Section 15.5:* This section presents the security API. This is perhaps the most useful section for you to examine because it discusses the API available for CORBA security interfacing.

- *Section 15.6:* This section describes the administration interface. It is of some interest, but most COTS vendors do not provide much in the way of administration support.

- *Section 15.7:* This section describes the service provider interface. This section will be of almost no interest to you as an enterprise developer.

- *Sections 15.8–15.15:* These sections describe security protocol interoperability. These will most likely not be of interest because they discuss ORB-to-ORB interoperability issues for security protocols.

- *Appendixes A–I:* The IDL interfaces defined in Appendix A are of interest. The guidelines for implementing CORBA Security solutions in Appendix G might also be of interest to architects.

13

CORBA SECURITY

CORBA Security Packages

Because the CSSS is a fairly complicated work, vendors might be able to implement only certain pieces of the specification at a time. The CSSS describes a standard set of security specification packages that group certain features of the specification so that vendors can claim incremental compliance using a standard terminology. The CORBA Security packages are defined here:

- *Security Functionality Level 1 Package:* Defines minimal security interfaces for applications that are largely security unaware.

- *Security Functionality Level 2 Package:* Defines application and administrative programming interfaces for building security-aware applications. It also defines much of the functionality of interest to enterprise developers.

- *Nonrepudiation Package:* Defines interfaces for providing nonrepudiation services for your application.

- *Security Replaceability Package:* Defines interfaces for supporting plug-in security services using CORBA interceptors and plug-in security service interfaces.

- *Common Secure Interoperability (CSI) Packages:* Defines three levels of support describing how one Orb is interoperable with another ORB for security interaction. CSI Level 0 defines an interoperable secure identity-passing scheme with no delegation allowed. CSI Level 1 allows delegation. CSI Level 2 signifies that the ORB supports all Security Service functionality.

- *SECIOP Package:* Indicates the information an ORB can generate and use that is passed in an IOR via GIOP and IIOP for security with SECIOP enhancements.

- *Security Mechanism Packages:* Defines which underlying identity, authenticity, and confidentiality mechanisms are relevant to ORB interoperability. For example, Kerberos and SSL are two security mechanisms used for passing around secure identity and ensuring confidentiality via encryption.

- *SECIOP and DCE-CIOP:* This package is of interest only if you are using DCE security services and the DCE-CIOP protocol.

CORBA Security Architecture

Many of the security packages defined in the CSSS actually map closely to IDL modules and, therefore, to packages in the Java binding for CORBA Security. For example, the following CORBA Security IDL modules and an explanation of how they map to associated Java packages (listed next in the form of *IDL_Module ~ Java_Package*) are important to our discussion throughout this chapter:

- `org::omg::Security` ~ `org.omg.Security`: Contains core and common CORBA Security types as needed by various security packages.

- `org::omg::SecurityLevel1` ~ `org.omg.SecurityLevel1`: Contains an interface defined for minimal CORBA Security support for application interfacing as defined by the Security Functionality Level 1 security package.

- `org::omg::SecurityLevel2` ~ `org.omg.SecurityLevel2`: Contains the large majority of interfaces relevant to CORBA Security Service application interfacing as defined by the Security Functionality Level 2 security package.

- `org::omg::NRService` ~ `org.omg.NRService`: Contains the interfaces used for nonrepudiation application interfacing as defined by the Nonrepudiation security package.

- `org::omg::SecurityReplaceable` ~ `org.omg.SecurityReplaceable`: Contains the interfaces for enhancing vendor interoperability used for service-provider interfacing as defined by the Security Replaceability security package.

- `org::omg::SecurityAdmin` ~ `org.omg.SecurityAdmin`: Contains system administration and security-policy–related interfaces used for administrative interfacing as defined by the Security Functionality Level 2 security package.

The core interfaces depicted in the UML diagram in Figure 13.1 scope the CORBA Security architecture presented in our discussion throughout the remainder of this chapter. Security features supported by the architecture of Figure 13.1 that are discussed further in subsequent sections include the following:

- Support for authenticating a client proxy with a CORBA Security domain using a principal authenticator (`PrincipalAuthenticator`) and obtaining credentials (`Credentials`) for that object.

- Support for transparent transmission of credentials from a current secure execution context (`Current`) via a security context (`SecurityContext`) over the wire from client-side secure invocation (`SecClientSecureInvocation` and `Vault`) to server-side secure invocation (`SecTargetSecureInvocation`) with delegation of credentials as an option.

- Support for access-control decision making (`AccessDecision`) based on the required rights (`RequiredRights`) for authorized access.

- Support for nonrepudiation of messages sent or received from a principal by generating tokens and verifying evidence associated with that principal's credentials (`NRCredentials`).

- Support for determining whether certain events should be audited (`AuditDecision`) and then potentially logging the event to an audit log (`AuditChannel`).

- Support for configuring cryptographic quality of protection levels (`QOPPolicy`) according to integrity and confidentiality.

- Support for the configuration of various security policy types (`Policy` subinterfaces).

> **NOTE**
>
> Throughout this chapter, I present a series of UML diagrams and code snippets that utilize CORBA Security types and interfaces in terms of their Java mappings from CORBA IDL. Whereas the CSSS describes such CORBA Security entities in terms of IDL, I felt that it would be more appropriate and intuitive for Java programmers to understand CORBA Security in terms of how they would use it in a Java application. Thus, the figures and code snippets in this chapter reference classes and interfaces that have been generated from the IDL-to-Java mapping of the CORBA Security Service IDL.

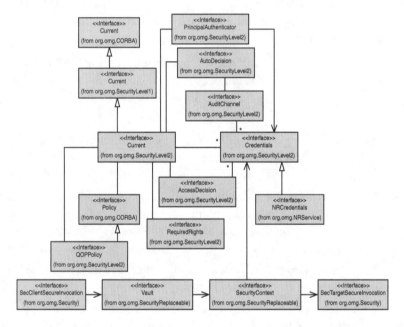

FIGURE 13.1
CORBA Security architecture.

Core CORBA Security Interfacing

Before you delve into any specific interfaces describing how security protection is provided for CORBA applications, quickly examine some of the core structures and types on which the actual security interfaces depend. Many types are defined in the general org::omg::Security IDL module. Aside from core CORBA IDL dependence, the Security IDL module also minimally depends on the TimeBase IDL module.

Table 13.1 depicts a few of the most important core security types utilized by the rest of the CSSS interfaces. All these types are encapsulated in the `org::omg::Security` module, which means that Java mappings of these types belong to the `org.omg.Security` package. The table presents each IDL entity, giving a brief description of the entity and stating what the entity looks like in its mapped Java form.

TABLE 13.1 Core Security Types

	IDL Entity	*Description*	*Java Mapping*
Basic Types	`typedef string` `    SecurityName;`	A security name used for various purposes	`java.lang.String`
	`typedef sequence<octet>` `    Opaque;`	Secures block of bytes	`byte[]`

Extensible Families	`struct ExtensibleFamily {`
	`  unsigned short family_definer;`
	`  unsigned short family;`
	`};`
		Saves information about whether a particular data type is extensible	`final public class`
			`ExtensibleFamily{`
			`    public short`
			`      family_definer;`
			`    public short`
			`      family;`
			`    ...`
			`}`

Mechanism Types	`typedef string MechanismType;`	Mechanism type name	`java.lang.String`

	`struct  SecurityMechandName{`
	`  MechanismType  mech_type;`
	`  SecurityName security_name;`
	`};`
		Associates a mechanism name with a security name	`final public class`
			`SecurityMechand`
			`Name{`
			`    public String`
			`mech_type;`
			`public String`
			`    security_name;`
			`    ...`
			`}`

	`typedef sequence`
	`<MechanismType>`
	`MechanismTypeList;`
		A collection of mechanism types	`final public class`
			`MechanismTypeList`
			`Holder{`
			`public String[]`
			`    value;`
			`    ...`
			`}`

TABLE 13.1 Continued

	IDL Entity	Description	Java Mapping
	```typedef sequence <SecurityMechandName> SecurityMechandNameList;```	A collection of security mechanism names	```final public class SecurityMechand NameListHolder { public org.omg. Security. ➥SecurityMechand Name[] value; ... }```
Security Attribute Types	```typedef unsigned long SecurityAttributeType;```	Identifies different security attributes with a set of constants also defined for various security attributes	int
	```struct AttributeType { ExtensibleFamily attribute_family; SecurityAttributeType attribute_type; };```	Associates an extensible family and security attribute	```final public class AttributeType { public org.omg. Security. ➥ExtensibleFamily attribute_ family; public int attribute_type; ... }```

TABLE 13.1 Continued

	IDL Entity	Description	Java Mapping
	```struct SecAttribute { AttributeType Attribute_type; Opaque defining_ authority; Opaque value; };```	Associates a value and authority with security attribute	```final public class SecAttribute { public org.omg. Security.Attribute Type attribute_type; public byte[] defining_ authority; public byte[] value; ... }```
	```typedef sequence <SecAttribute> AttributeList;```	Collection of security attributes	```Final public class AttributeList Holder { Public org.omg.Security. SecAttribute value[]; ... }```
Timebase Types	```// from TimeBase typedef unsigned long long TimeT; // from Security typedef TimeBase:: TimeT TimeT;```	Stores time in long form	```long```
	```// from TimeBase struct IntervalT { TimeT lower_bound; TimeT upper_bound; };```	Stores time interval	```final public class IntervalT { public long lower_bound; public long upper_bound;```

13

CORBA SECURITY

TABLE 13.1 Continued

IDL Entity	Description	Java Mapping

`// from Security`
`typedef TimeBase::`
`IntervalT`
`    IntervalT;`
		`...`
		
		`}`

`// from TimeBase`
`typedef short TdfT;`
`struct UtcT {`
 	
`  TimeT time;`
 	
`  unsigned long`
`  inacclo;`
`  unsigned short`
 	
`  inacchi;`
`  TdfT  tdf;`
`};`
	Stores
	universal
	time
		`final public class`
		`    UtcT {`
		`    public long`
		`    time;`
		`    public int`
		`    inacclo;`
		`    public short`
		`    inacchi;`
		`    public short`
		`    tdf;`
		`    ...`
		`    }`

`// from Security` `typedef TimeBase::UtcT UtcT;`		

Authentication

Authentication APIs using the CORBA Security model utilize components from the `Security`, `SecurityLevel1`, and `SecurityLevel2` security packages. A principal authenticator represents a frontline interface for CORBA clients to use when authenticating themselves with the CORBA Security Service. After authenticating themselves, clients are given a set of credentials that are stored along with their current security context. When the client makes a remote invocation on a CORBA server, its security context is passed along with the marshaled call parameters to the server-side ORB. The target server's Security Service can use this information to determine whether the client should be allowed to make the call and, optionally, to allow the server object to obtain access to the client's credential information that was passed along with the security context. Figure 13.2 depicts the core architecture of the Java-mapped CORBA entities that have relevance to such a CORBA Security authentication process.

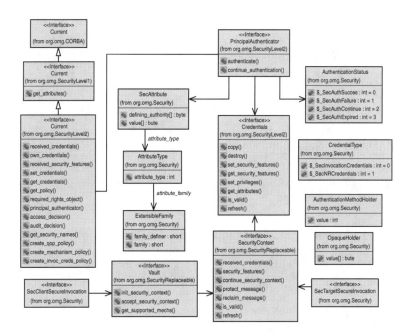

FIGURE 13.2
CORBA Security authentication.

In addition to using a few of the aforementioned core Security types, CORBA Security for authentication requires a few additional types from the org::omg::Security module:

```
// The vendor will define the values for AuthenticationMethod, with
// respect to what orb supports...e.g. password or certificate, etc.
// Maps to a Java int. Showing Holder value in Figure 13.2.
typedef unsigned long AuthenticationMethod;

// Maps to AuthenticationStatus class in Figure 13.2.
enum AuthenticationStatus {...};

// Maps to CredentialType class in Figure 13.2.
enum CredentialType {...};
```

Such types are utilized by the org::omg::SecurityLevel2::PrincipalAuthenticator interface's authenticate() and continue_authenticate() methods. The continue_ authenticate() call is a variation of authenticate() when a multistep authentication process is required. The authenticate() call is the primary interface needed for CORBA authentication. The IDL interface for this call looks like the following:

```
Security::AuthenticationStatus authenticate (
  in Security::AuthenticationMethod method,
  in Security::SecurityName security_name,
```

```
    in Security::Opaque auth_data,

    in Security::AttributeList privileges,

    out Credentials creds,

    out Security::Opaque continuation_data,

    out Security::Opaque auth_specific_data
);
```

The Java mapping (including a description of each input and output parameter added by us) for this call looks like the following:

```
// Returns status of authentication
org.omg.Security.AuthenticationStatus authenticate(

    // Designates type of authentication (e.g. password-based)
    int method,

    // Principal ID name
    java.lang.String security_name,

    // Authentication data (e.g. a password)
    byte[] auth_data,

    // Requested privileges
    org.omg.Security.SecAttribute[] privileges,

    // Returned credentials
    org.omg.SecurityLevel2.CredentialsHolder creds,

    // Returned information needed for continue_authenticate() calls
    org.omg.Security.OpaqueHolder continuation_data,

    // Returned info specific to authentication method
    org.omg.Security.OpaqueHolder auth_specific_data
);
```

The org::omg::SecurityLevel2::Current object contains security-related state information associated with the current thread execution context (that is, a security context). The org::omg::SecurityLevel1::Current interface is a parent interface for org::omg::SecurityLevel2::Current containing minimal security context information useful for security-unaware applications that can utilize a SecurityLevel1-compliant ORB. The org:::omg::SecurityLevel2::Credentials object encapsulates the credentials returned from authentication and associated with the Current object.

The basic sequence of events for authentication via CORBA Security using such objects follows these general lines, with conceptual snippets of code given to illustrate each point:

1. Obtain a reference to the `SecurityCurrent` object representing the current security execution context:

```
ORB orb = ORB.init(args, null);
org.omg.CORBA.Object currentReference =
    orb.resolve_initial_references("SecurityCurrent");
org.omg.SecurityLevel2.Current current
    = org.omg.SecurityLevel2.CurrentHelper.narrow(currentReference);
```

2. Obtain a reference to `PrincipalAuthenticator`:

```
org.omg.SecurityLevel2.PrincipalAuthenticator principalAuthenticator
    = current.principal_authenticator();
```

3. Create the data needed for authentication and holders for the output of authentication:

```
// Create security name (principal and domain example here)
String securityName = "sam@assuredtech.com";
// Specify authentication method using vendor-specific
// identifiers. For example, ORB Vendor may define
// password-based authentication as constant value 1.
int authenticationMethod = 1;
// Set password value
String passwordValue = "MyPassword";
byte[] authorizationData = passwordValue.getBytes();
// Define requested privileges (some methods may not support)
org.omg.Security.SecAttribute[] privileges
    = new org.omg.Security.SecAttribute[0];
// Create holders for output values
org.omg.SecurityLevel2.CredentialsHolder credentials
    = new org.omg.SecurityLevel2.CredentialsHolder();
org.omg.Security.OpaqueHolder continuationData
    = new org.omg.Security.OpaqueHolder();
org.omg.Security.OpaqueHolder authSpecificData
    = new org.omg.Security.OpaqueHolder();
```

4. The CORBA client now authenticates itself with a `PrincipalAuthenticator` object:

```
org.omg.Security.AuthenticationStatus status
    = principalAuthenticator.authenticate(
        authenticationMethod, securityName, authorizationData,
        privileges,credentials,continuationData, authSpecificData);
```

5. The authentication process returns a `Credentials` object and is associated with the client's `Current` object, as well as returned in a `CredentialsHolder` object parameter to the `authenticate()` method.

6. The client then makes remote invocations on security-sensitive target CORBA servers.

13

CORBA SECURITY

So how is authentication information used and communicated under the hood during such invocations? The following basic steps highlight just such a process during remote invocations on security-sensitive servers:

1. An `org::omg::Security::SecClientSecureInvocation` object handles secure invocations by a security-aware ORB on the client side.

2. An `org::omg::SecurityReplaceable::Vault` object is called by the `SecClientSecureInvocation` object.

3. The `Vault` creates a `org::omg::SecurityReplaceable::SecurityContext` object used to encapsulate a security context with a read-only collection of `Credential` objects and a `Current` object.

4. The `org::omg::SecurityReplaceable::SecurityContext` objects have methods enabling them to be serialized and sent over the wire.

5. An `org::omg::Security::SecTargetSecureInvocation` on the target server-side ORB deserializes `SecurityContext` and retrieves the credentials associated with the client.

6. The target server side now has the necessary credentials that were created during principal authentication to identify the client object. Based on such client identity from the credentials, the target can use some policy to determine whether the client has permission to perform the invocation (per the authorization discussion later in this chapter).

7. Server objects running in secure mode can also retrieve and access the credentials associated with the invocation.

Delegation

CORBA Security supports three modes of operation for delegation of credentials during security-sensitive object invocations, as illustrated in Figure 13.3. Delegation pertains to issues regarding how some Object A's credentials propagate during a call to some Object C by some Object B when Object A first calls Object B. A *No Delegation* mode of CORBA Security means that the client's identity is not delegated, and thus an Object A's credentials do not propagate to Object C in this example. With a *Simple Delegation* mode, Object A's credentials get propagated to Object C. *Composite Delegation* means both Object B's and Object A's credentials propagate to Object C.

Object A can turn delegation on by calling `set_credentials()` on a `Current` object reference using the `org::omg::Security::DelegationMode` enum `Delegate` value. Thus, Object A would let Object B use Object A's credentials during delegation:

```
org.omg.SecurityLevel2.Current current
  = org.omg.SecurityLevel2.CurrentHelper.narrow(
      orb.resolve_initial_references("SecurityCurrent"));
```

```
org.omg.SecurityLevel2.Credentials[] ownCredentials
  = current.own_credentials();

org.omg.Security.CredentialType credentialType
  = org.omg.Security.CredentialType.SecInvocationCredentials;

org.omg.SecurityLevel2.DelegationMode delegationMode
  = org.omg.SecurityLevel2.DelegationMode.Delegate;

current.set_credentials(credentialType, ownCredentials, delegationMode);
```

The `DelegationMode` enum `NoDelegate` value can be used to turn off delegation for Object A. In such a mode, Object A would not let Object B use Object A's credentials during delegation:

```
org.omg.SecurityLevel2.DelegationMode delegationMode
  = org.omg.SecurityLevel2.DelegationMode.NoDelegate;

current.set_credentials( credentialType, ownCredentials, delegationMode);
```

As a final note, the particular mode of delegation for the set of credentials can also be established via the `Credentials.set_security_feature()` interface. Here, a `SecurityFeature` value defined according to the direction of invocation (that is, `request`, `reply`, or `both`) can be set on a particular `Credentials` object to establish whether no delegation, simple delegation, or composite delegation is supported.

13

CORBA SECURITY

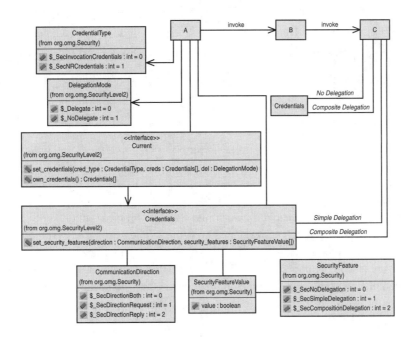

FIGURE 13.3

CORBA Security delegation.

Authorization

Authorization in CORBA follows a role-based, access-control model in which ACLs are maintained that describe which rights are required for particular operations, which roles are assigned to which principal identities, and which rights get associated with which roles. For particular calls on the server side, a target invocation might use the received client credential information and information about the operation being invoked to consult a CORBA Security access decision-making object for a *yes* or *no* answer regarding whether the operation is to be permitted. The required rights for such operations can also be determined prior to using the CORBA Security Service. Figure 13.4 shows some key objects involved in CORBA Security authorization.

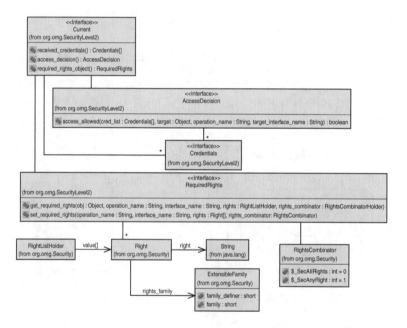

FIGURE 13.4

CORBA Security authorization.

On the target object side of a particular invocation, a target server asks the `Current` object for an `org::omg::SecurityLevel2::AccessDecision` object. The `AccessDecision` object can be used to determine whether access should be allowed for a particular operation. To accomplish this task, the `AccessDecision` object needs the credentials associated with the invoking client object that contains the privilege information it needs to make the decision. The received client credentials can be obtained from a call to the `Current.received_credentials()` call. For example

```
org.omg.SecurityLevel2.AccessDecision accessDecision
  = current.access_decision();

org.omg.SecurityLevel2.Credentials[] credentialsList
  = current.received_credentials();

boolean  allowed =
  accessDecision.access_allowed(credentialsList,
    targetObject, "someOperationName, "TargetServer" );
```

If you desire prior knowledge of the required rights level associated with such an operation, you can use the `org::omg::SecurityLevel2::RequiredRights` object to return a set of rights required for performing a particular operation. After a `RequiredRights` reference is retrieved from the `Current` object, a `required_rights()` call can be made on the `RequiredRights` object specifying the target object, the target object name, and the name of the target object interface. The `required_rights()` call returns a list of `Right` objects via a `RightsListHolder` object and a `RightsCombinator` object via a `RightsCombinatorHolder` object. These two objects can then be used to determine the particular rights information required for an operation.

```
org.omg.SecurityLevel2.RequiredRights
  requiredRights  = current.required_rights_object();

org.omg.Security.RightsListHolder  assignedRights
  = new org.omg.Security.RightsListHolder();
org.omg.Security.RightsCombinatorHolder rightsCombinator
  = new org.omg.Security.RightsCombinatorHolder();

requiredRights.get_required_rights(targetObject, "someOperationName",
  "TargetServer", assignedRights, rightsCombinator);
```

Auditing

Auditing of security-critical operations under the CORBA Security Service requires an audit decision. This determines whether an audit is needed based on a particular audit event. If an audit is needed, the audit event data, the invoking principal's credentials, and the time are all written to an audit channel. Figure 13.5 depicts the CORBA interface constructs that implement such auditing functionality.

An `org::omg::SecurityLevel2::AuditDecision` object must first be obtained on the target server side from the `Current` object using `Current.audit_decision()`. The received client

13

CORBA SECURITY

credentials must also be obtained from the Current object. An org::omg::Security:: AuditEventType object is then constructed to encapsulate a particular event type that can be logged. This event type, along with an array of event type selectors, is passed to the AuditDecision.audit_needed() call. Here's a conceptual example:

```
// Get Current object as did in Authentication section of chapter
org.omg.SecurityLevel2.Current current = // Get "SecurityCurrent"
org.omg.SecurityLevel2.AuditDecision auditDecision
  = current.audit_decision();
org.omg.SecurityLevel2.Credentials[] receivedCredentials
  = current.received_credentials();

org.omg.Security.ExtensibleFamily eventFamily
  = new  org.omg.Security.ExtensibleFamily(0, 0);
short eventType = org.omg.Security.AuditAll.value;
org.omg.Security.AuditEventType auditEventType
  = new  org.omg.Security.AuditEventType(eventFamily, eventType);
org.omg.Security.SelectorValue[]  selectors
  = new org.omg.Security.SelectorValue[1];

boolean auditNeeded
  = auditDecision.audit_needed(auditEventType,selectors);
```

If the returned value from an AuditDecision.audit_needed() call indicates that an audit should be performed, an AuditChannel object should be obtained from the AuditDecision object. This AuditChannel object's audit_write() call is then called with the audit event, the received client credentials, the timestamp, event selectors, and other event-specific information. The audit_write() call then writes such information to the specific audit log. For example

```
if(auditNeeded){
  org.omg.SecurityLevel2.AuditChannel currentAuditChannel
    = auditDecision.audit_channel();
  int currentAuditChannelID = currentAuditChannel.audit_channel_id();
  String data = "called someOperationName";
  byte[] eventSpecificData = data.getBytes();
  org.omg.TimeBase.UtcT time =
    new  org.omg.TimeBase.UtcT();

  currentAuditChannel.audit_write(auditEventType,
    receivedCredentials, time, selectors, eventSpecificData);
}
```

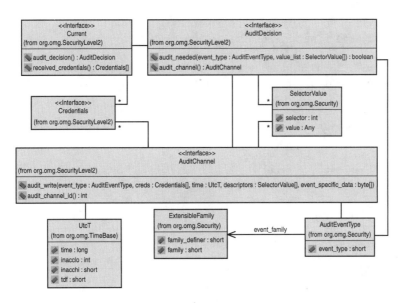

FIGURE 13.5
CORBA Security auditing.

Nonrepudiation

CORBA Security also provides a set of interfaces for performing nonrepudiation (NR) of operation invocations. The generation of an NR token associated with received data from some principal can be used later to prove that that the principal sent such data (in case of a dispute). NR can also be used to prove that some principal received data. Figure 13.6 shows the core CORBA Security objects involved with providing an NR service.

An org::omg::NRService::NRCredentials object can be used to generate and verify NR tokens. The NRCredentials object inherits from the regular Credentials object. A returned set of credentials from the Current object can be narrowed to a NRCredentials object when NR support is in place. The NRCredentials.generate_token() call generates an NR token associated with a block of data passed to it and including principal identity information extracted from the NRCredentials object. The block of data is some message that one side of the NR process says it received or sent. Evidence received by the generate_token() call can be used later with the NR token to verify that the data was sent or received. This following is an example of token generation using the NRCredentials.generate_token() call:

```
org.omg.NRService.NRCredentials[] receivedCredentials
    = (org.omg.NRService.NRCredentials[])current.received_credentials();

org.omg.NRService.NRPolicyFeatures[] nrPolicyFeatures
    = receivedCredentials[0].get_NR_features();

org.omg.NRService.EvidenceType evidenceType
    = org.omg.NRService.EvidenceType.SecProofofReceipt;

boolean includeDataInToken = true;
boolean generateRequest = true;
boolean inputBufferComplete = true;

// request everything
org.omg.NRService.RequestFeatures requestFeatures
    = new org.omg.NRService.RequestFeatures();
// data for which evidence is generated.
String received = "Hi There";
byte[] receivedData = received.getBytes();

// nrToken will be filled by the call
org.omg.Security.OpaqueHolder nrToken
            = new    org.omg.Security.OpaqueHolder();
// evidenceCheck will be filled by the call
org.omg.Security.OpaqueHolder evidenceCheck
            = new org.omg.Security.OpaqueHolder();

// generate token:
//      during token generation it uses credential information
receivedCredentials[0].generate_token( receivedData, evidenceType,
        includeDataInToken, generateRequest, requestFeatures,
        inputBufferComplete, nrToken,  evidenceCheck);
```

The return nrToken and evidenceCheck values in the preceding snippet are returned in an Opaque object stored in the OpaqueHolder. The identity information of the principal associated with the received NRCredentials is also used during the creation of the NR token so that the principal identity can be bound to the received data.

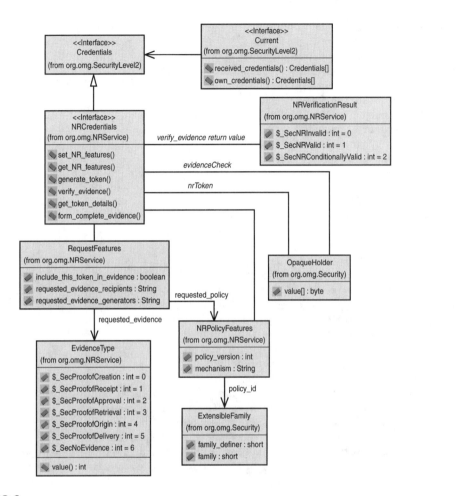

FIGURE 13.6

CORBA Security nonrepudiation.

Verification of evidence assumes that you have an NR token and evidence to verify that a particular action previously occurred. The `NRCredentials.verify_evidence()` call takes both the NR token and the evidence check value created during a prior `generate_token()` call. A returned `NRVerificationResult` object can then be used to determine whether the NR token was considered valid, invalid, or conditionally valid by the partner object. The following is an example of verification:

```
boolean checkGeneratedEvidence = true; // to check evidence
boolean formCompleteEvidence = true; // complete evidence requested
boolean tokenBufferComplete = true; // token buffer complete
```

```
// use token you got during generate token
byte[] inputToken = nrToken.value;
// use check value you got during generate token
byte[] evidenceCheckValue = evidenceCheck.value;

// All the following values are output values...
// output token
org.omg.Security.OpaqueHolder outputToken
        = new org.omg.Security.OpaqueHolder();
// data associated with evidence
org.omg.Security.OpaqueHolder dataIncludedInEvidence
        = new org.omg.Security.OpaqueHolder();
// evidence complete
org.omg.CORBA.BooleanHolder evidenceComplete
        = new org.omg.CORBA.BooleanHolder();
// is Trusted time used
org.omg.CORBA.BooleanHolder trusedTimeUsed
        = new org.omg.CORBA.BooleanHolder();
// complete evidence before time
org.omg.CORBA.LongHolder completeEvidenceBefore
        = new org.omg.CORBA.LongHolder();
// complete evidence after time
org.omg.CORBA.LongHolder compleEvidenceAfter
        = new org.omg.CORBA.LongHolder();

// All of that for the following evidence verification call
org.omg.NRService.NRVerificationResult verificationResult
        = receivedCredentials[0].verify_evidence(
            inputToken, evidenceCheckValue, formCompleteEvidence,
            tokenBufferComplete, outputToken, dataIncludedInEvidence,
            evidenceComplete, trusedTimeUsed,  completeEvidenceBefore,
            compleEvidenceAfter);
```

In the case of a dispute, the CSSS discusses the concept of arbitration, as well as evidence storage and retrieval, but has not defined any clear specification for such services. In fact, the whole NR interface suite is very difficult to understand and even has many holes (meaning support that is lacking). Such holes lead to application developer hand-coded solutions and nonstandard vendor solutions to fulfill undefined interface needs. These, in turn, lead to a lack of interoperability.

Encryption

CORBA objects need cryptographic support for both integrity and confidentiality. Integrity protection means the use of something like message digests, whereas confidentiality protection includes the use of key-based encryption. A quality of protection (QOP) level can be set for both requests and responses, indicating whether no protection, integrity protection, confidentiality protection, or both integrity and confidentiality protection are assumed. The underlying interfacing that takes place for providing a requested QOP is transparent to the API developer. Figure 13.7 depicts such QOP specification interfaces for defining the QOP in a particular current execution context.

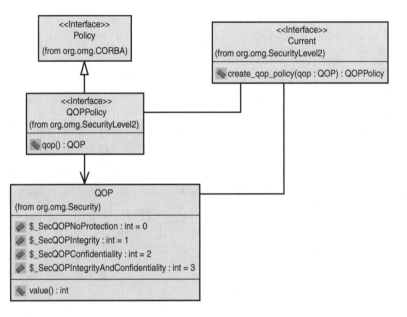

FIGURE 13.7
CORBA Security encryption protection.

Various underlying protocols that operate below the CORBA Security Service layer (for example, SSL) are by and large utilized transparently to the applications developer. Various common security interface protocols supported by the CSSS are SSL, Kereberos, SPKM, ECMA, and DCE-IOP (Distributed Computing Environment Inter-ORB Protocol). However, specifications for the use of such secure protocols in the CSSS are defined at the ORB-to-ORB level to ensure interoperability between ORBs supporting such protocols. Thus an ORB from vendor A using SSL can theoretically talk to an ORB from vendor B using SSL.

The level of ORB-to-ORB interoperability is defined according to a Common Secure Interoperability (CSI) level. CSI Level 0 defines an interoperable secure-identity–passing scheme with no delegation allowed. CSI Level 1 allows delegation of identity for the principal that initiated an operation. CSI Level 2 signifies that the ORB supports all Security Service functionality. Thus, all the information that can be passed along with a security context, such as privileges, is also communicated between ORBs.

13

CORBA SECURITY

No standard API for configuring and initializing secure protocols for use with an application is described in the CSSS. Although the QOP interfaces can be used to specify some abstract distinction between integrity and confidentiality, the particular initialization of SSL, for example, is vendor specific. For instance, to configure your server-side CORBA environment for SSL using the Inprise Visigenics SSL solution, you follow these steps:

1. Establish an `ORBServices` property during ORB initialization to select the vendor-specific SSL libraries.
2. Obtain a handle to a vendor-specific SSL certificate manager.
3. Use a proprietary certificate manager interface to configure the SSL protocol.
4. Initialize the BOA or POA to use connections pulled from an SSL pool for invocation requests.
5. When an SSL Client connection is made and client authentication is required, use an `SSLCurrent` object to obtain client certificate information used for authentication.

Clients of such a server can then make invocations on the server with invocation requests and replies being encrypted via SSL. The following is an example of configuring your client-side CORBA environment for SSL using the Inprise Visigenics SSL solution:

1. Establish an `ORBServices` property during ORB initialization to select the vendor-specific SSL libraries.
2. Obtain a handle to a vendor-specific SSL certificate manager if client authentication is required.
3. Use a proprietary certificate manager interface to configure the SSL protocol.
4. Bind to the CORBA server.
5. Use an `SSLCurrent` object to obtain server certificate information for server authentication.

Security Policies

The CSSS security domain is defined according to which security policy governs that domain. Security policies for the various protection mechanisms of CORBA Security can be defined using a standard set of CORBA Security policy interfaces that inherit from the base `org::omg::CORBA::Policy` interface. The basic policy architecture used in establishing policies for different CORBA Security protection schemes is shown in Figure 13.8.

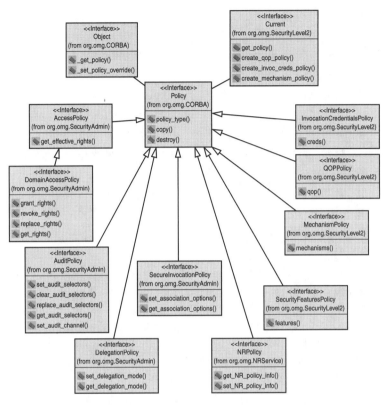

FIGURE 13.8

CORBA Security policies.

The CORBA policy interface serves as the base interface from which all other security-policy–related interfaces extend. Policies for a particular distributed CORBA object can be retrieved and set onto that object using the `get_policy()` and `set_override_policy()` methods inherited from the `org::omg::CORBA::Object` interface. Policies from a current execution context can be obtained using `get_policy()` on the `Current` object. The suite of currently defined security related policy types includes the following:

- `org::omg::SecurityAdmin::AccessPolicy` is used for access control policies by returning a list of rights giving some credential information.

- `org::omg::SecurityAdmin::DomainAccessPolicy` extends `AccessPolicy` and is used for granting, revoking, and replacing rights in a particular security domain.

- `org::omg::SecurityAdmin::AuditPolicy` is used for auditing policies.

- `org::omg::SecurityAdmin::DelegationPolicy` is used for establishing delegation policies.

- `org::omg::SecurityAdmin::SecureInvocationPolicy` is used for establishing policies related to secure invocations.

- `org::omg::NRService::NRPolicy` is used for establishing nonrepudiation policies.

- `org::omg::SecurityLevel2::SecurityFeaturesPolicy` is used for security feature policies.

- `org::omg::SecurityLevel2::MechanismPolicy` is used for establishing specific security mechanism policies and for using `Current.create_mechanism_policy()`.

- `org::omg::SecurityLevel2::QOPPolicy` is used for quality of protection policy information and for using `Current.create_qop_policy()`.

- `org::omg::SecurityLevel2::InvocationCredentialsPolicy` is used for invocation credentials requirement policies and for using `Current.create_invoc_creds_policy()`.

Security Administration

Support for administration of security policies in a domain can take advantage of the base class inheritance from the `org::omg::CORBA::Policy` interface. Thus, any generic interface defined for administering the `Policy` interface can apply to the CORBA Security policies. The problem is that standard support for even generic policy administration is lacking. The `org::omg::CORBA::DomainManager` interface can be used to retrieve security policies for access of their information, but it is of little use beyond that. It seems that support for any significant policy administration interfaces was deferred to the CORBA facilities layer.

A System Management Common Facilities specification has an expressed goal of providing support for such common system functions. The Policy and Security Management components of that specification in particular apply. However, pursuit of the System Management Common Facilities specification has been minimal. Thus, the only practical solution for many companies interested in managing the security policies encapsulated by the `SecurityAdmin` package and the `Policy` interfaces, as shown in Figure 13.8, is to develop their own interface support.

Summary

The CORBA Security Service Specification is very complex. This has led to minimal levels of support by vendors. Of course, even when such vendor products are provided, the method signatures and other aspects about the CORBA Security API are difficult for enterprise developers to adopt. The CORBA Security Service Specification needs some improvement and is being improved to make it a more palatable enterprise object security solution.

Nevertheless, it is a fairly well-rounded solution. Security for identity, authenticity, authorization, nonrepudiation, and auditing have all been considered. Interoperability among vendor solutions to provide encryption support has also been considered. However, configuration of such encryption support tends to be vendor specific. Furthermore, although the specification defines the concept of security administration, actual standard security administration interfaces are few and far between.

It is true that CORBA Security is defined with a complicated specification and currently forces application developers to comprehend some extremely complex API method signatures. However, CORBA Security is currently required by a CORBA-EJB mapping and can be incorporated into the Java 2 Platform, Enterprise Edition for enhanced server interoperability. At the very least, enterprise security architects and developers should understand the concepts and architecture of CORBA Security described in this chapter.

Enterprise JavaBeans Security

Java 2 Platform, Enterprise Edition (J2EE)-compliant Enterprise JavaBeans (EJB) provides a model for developing server-side enterprise application components that can make building portable and distributed enterprise applications easier than building standalone enterprise applications. EJB containers/servers provide distributed communications services, data-enabling services, and systems assurance services for EJB components. These services require minimal effort on the part of a developer.

Standard security assurance is primarily provided in the form of role-based access control to EJBs. Vendor-specific support is also needed to map the roles defined using standard mechanisms to principals managed by a particular EJB container/server vendor's operational environment. Additionally, vendor-specific and/or hand-coded mechanisms are needed to provide any necessary authentication, identity delegation policy selection, secure communications, and auditing. This chapter will describe the standard mechanisms provided for J2EE-compliant EJBs and outline those vendor-specific or hand-coded mechanisms that must be provided to fully secure your EJBs.

In this chapter, you will learn

- A basic overview of the options available for securing your EJBs
- The standard programmatic access control mechanisms available for EJBs
- The standard declarative access control mechanisms available for EJBs
- The most common vendor-specific access control mechanisms available for EJBs
- The most common vendor-specific identity and authentication mechanisms available for EJBs
- A basic overview of the additional vendor-specific mechanisms available for providing secure EJB communications, principal delegation, and auditing

EJB Security Overview

As with any distributed object used in security-critical enterprise applications, EJBs must be secured. However, EJB components operate inside a container environment and rely on the container to provide distributed connectivity to an EJB, to create and destroy EJB instances, to passivate and activate EJB instances, to invoke business methods on EJBs, and to generally manage the life cycle of an EJB. Because such control is relinquished to an EJB container/server environment, securing the EJB also relies heavily on the support provided by the EJB container environment. Security mechanisms can distinguish between standard mechanisms required by the J2EE and EJB specifications, mechanisms that are EJB container/server vendor-specific, and mechanisms that can be hand-coded by the EJB developer.

Figure 14.1 illustrates the basic architecture required for securing EJBs. Standard security mechanisms defined for EJBs are currently focused around providing a minimal set of constructs for role-based EJB access control. Standard mechanisms for determining role-based permissions to access EJB methods can be tapped by EJB components programmatically via a few interfaces to the EJB container context, as exposed by the EJB API. Standard EJB method access control mechanisms can also be defined declaratively via a set of standard XML elements contained in a standard EJB deployment descriptor. Additionally, a few vendor-specific access control features are needed to support the mapping of security roles defined in standard deployment descriptors to principal identities managed by the operational environment.

Although a mechanism for authenticating a user is implied by the fact that a particular user must be granted access to a particular EJB method, no standard means for authenticating a user is defined in the EJB v1.1 and the J2EE v1.2 specifications. Such standard mechanisms are planned for the J2EE v1.3 and EJB 2.0, however. It is anticipated that the Java Authentication and Authorization Standard (JAAS) will play a key role in determining how principals are authenticated. Nevertheless, some form of identity propagation from client to server, and principal authentication with an identity repository must be provided by an EJB container/server vendor for practical EJB enterprise security. The policy for delegating principal identity between EJBs must also be defined by an EJB container/server vendor. Furthermore, the security of the communications session between EJB client and server must be provided by a vendor for practical enterprise deployment scenarios. Vendors can also provide a means for auditing security-critical EJB events.

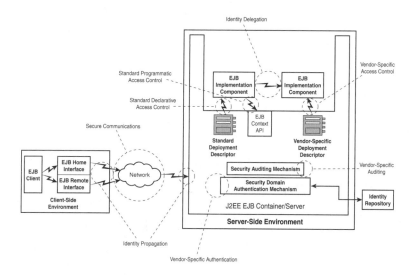

FIGURE 14.1

EJB security architecture.

Standard Programmatic EJB Access Controls

Although the programmatic implementation of security access control logic within EJB components is not recommended by the EJB specification, in many practical cases, it is inevitable. A minimal set of standard methods is provided by the EJB API to enable programmatic access control from within your EJB. As illustrated in Figure 14.2, two primary EJB v1.1 hooks for obtaining security information from the EJB container environment are provided by the javax.ejb.EJBContext object (and two other EJB v1.0 methods are deprecated). Other non-security related EJBContext methods are not shown in this diagram.

A handle to an EJBContext object is available to an EJB implementation object when the EJB container sets the context object onto a bean instance after the bean instance has been created by the container. For session bean implementations, such as MySessionBean shown in Figure 14.2, the EJB container calls setSessionContext() on the bean with a javax.ejb.SessionContext object. For entity bean implementations, such as MyEntityBean shown in Figure 14.2, the EJB container calls setEntityContext() on the bean with a javax.ejb.EntityContext object. After a context is set onto a bean, security-related calls to the EJBContext object are callable only from within the context of a business-specific method on the EJB. Otherwise, a java.lang.IllegalStateException will be thrown by the container to indicate that no security context exists.

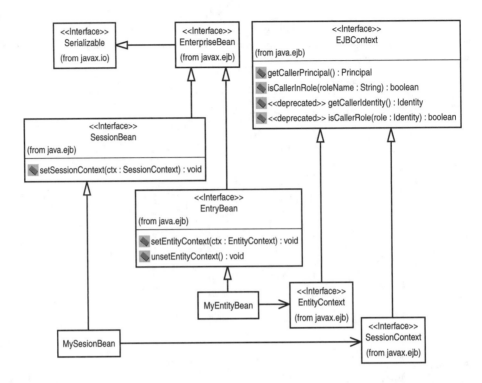

EJB security APIs.

The EJBContext.getCallerPrincipal() method is invoked by an EJB to obtain a handle to a java.security.Principal object. The Principal represents the particular principal identity on behalf of which the invoking EJB client is acting. A call to Principal.getName() by the bean can return a String object that can be used for implementing business-specific security-checking logic. The deprecated EJBContext.getCallerIdentity() method might still be supported by your container, but a vendor might choose to throw an exception or return null from this method.

The EJBContext.isCallerInRole(String) method is used to ask the EJB environment whether the current principal associated with this security context is a member of the role passed in as a String to this method. A Boolean return value indicates whether the caller is indeed in this role. The deprecated EJBContext.isCallerInRole(Identity) method might still be supported by your container, but a vendor might choose to throw an exception from this method.

For example, you might have an EJB that allows a client to retrieve sensitive customer-order data given a customer ID. You might restrict such access only to authorized users in the admin role or to the particular customer having that customer ID as a principal name, as shown here:

```
public Order getOrder(String customerID) throws OrderException
{
    // Declare some application-specific Order object to return
    Order returnOrder = null;

    // Get principal from context and principal name
    java.security.Principal caller = ejbContext.getCallerPrincipal();
    String callerID = caller.getName();

    // If not in admin role and not the user associated with
    //   this order, then deny access...
    if(   (ejbContext.isCallerInRole("admin") == true)
        ||(callerID.equalsIgnoreCase(customerID)      ))
    {
        // Allow access to do security-critical stuff here...
        ...
    }
    else
    {
        // Access denied. Audit this event and return...
        ...
        // Throw some application-specific OrderException
        throw new OrderException("Order retrieval access denied.");
    }

    // Return the application-specific Order object
    return returnOrder;
}
```

Whenever a call to EJBContext.isCallerInRole() is made from within EJB code, an associated <security-role-ref> should be identified in the EJB's standard deployment descriptor for that bean. The <security-role-ref> element is defined within an <entity> element for entity beans and within a <session> element for session beans. The <entity> and <session> elements are defined within an <enterprise-beans> element that, in turn, is defined within an outer most <ejb-jar> element inside of the standard ejb-jar.xml file.

For example, you might define a standard ejb-jar.xml file for an OrderManager session bean that implements the getOrder() method defined earlier. Next, you define a <security-role-ref> entry for the referenced admin role as follows:

```
<?xml version="1.0" encoding="UTF-8"?>

<!DOCTYPE ejb-jar PUBLIC '-//Sun Microsystems, Inc.//
➡DTD Enterprise JavaBeans 1.1//EN'
➡ 'http://java.sun.com/j2ee/dtds/ejb-jar_1_1.dtd'>
```

```
<ejb-jar>
  ...
  <enterprise-beans>
    <session>
      ...
      <!-- EJB Reference name for our bean -->
      <ejb-name>OrderManager</ejb-name>
      <!-- Class name for our EJB Home interface -->
      <home>ejava.ejbsecurity.OrderManagerHome</home>
      <!-- Class name for our EJB Remote interface -->
      <remote>ejava.ejbsecurity.OrderManager</remote>
      <!-- Class name for our EJB implementation -->
      <ejb-class>ejava.ejbsecurity.OrderManagerBean</ejb-class>

      ...
      <!-- Identifies a security role reference for this EJB.-->
      <security-role-ref>

        <!-- Describes this security role. -->
        <description> Bean references admin role. </description>

        <!-- Identifies a logical role name that this EJB uses. -->
        <role-name>admin</role-name>

      </security-role-ref>

    </session>

  </enterprise-beans>
</ejb-jar>
```

It is the responsibility of EJB developers to define, in a deployment descriptor, those security roles that their EJB implementations programmatically reference. However, it is up to the EJB assembler and deployer to map such roles to security roles and users in the deployment environment. The next section illustrates how such a mapping occurs in the context of standard declarative EJB access controls.

Standard Declarative EJB Access Controls

Standard declarative EJB access control mechanisms are defined as XML elements in a standard EJB deployment descriptor file. In addition to the `<role-name>` element, a `<role-link>` element can also be defined within an EJB's `<security-role-ref>` element. This element value is defined during EJB assembly to reference a role name specified by an individual (an EJB assembler) cognizant of the security roles assumed by a particular deployment environment. Thus, an EJB assembler might modify the standard `ejb-jar.xml` file to map a programmatic role name identified by the `<role-name>` element to an assembly-specific role name identified by a `<role-link>` element.

You can, for example, modify the `OrderManager` deployment descriptor to incorporate an
assembly-specific `<role-link>` element as follows:

```
<?xml version="1.0" encoding="UTF-8"?>
  ...
<ejb-jar>
  ...
  <enterprise-beans>
    <session>
      ...
      <!-- Identifies a security role reference for this EJB.-->
      <security-role-ref>

        <!-- Describes this security role. -->
        <description> Bean references admin role. </description>

        <!-- Identifies a logical role name that this EJB uses. -->
        <role-name>admin</role-name>

        <!-- Identifies a role to map to during assembly. -->
        <role-link>Administrator</role-link>

      </security-role-ref>

    </session>

  </enterprise-beans>
</ejb-jar>
```

The `<role-link>` element must refer to a `<role-name>` defined within a special `<security-role>` element defined by an EJB assembler in the standard `ejb-jar.xml` file. All logical security roles defined for a particular EJB module are identified by `<security-role>` elements that sit within an `<assembly-descriptor>` element that is defined within the root `<ejb-jar>` element for an EJB module.

For example, an EJB assembler might define a `<security-role>` element for the
`Administrator` role linked by the `OrderManager` bean as well as a `RegisteredCustomer` and
`UnregisteredCustomer` role as follows:

```
<?xml version="1.0" encoding="UTF-8"?>
  ...
<ejb-jar>
  ...
  <enterprise-beans>
    ...
  </enterprise-beans>
```

14

ENTERPRISE
JAVABEANS
SECURITY

```
<assembly-descriptor>
  <!-- Identifies those security roles defined for an EJB module.-->
  <security-role>
    <!-- Describes a security role. -->
    <description> Administrator role for bean. </description>
    <!-- Identifies a logical role name that this EJB module uses. -->
    <role-name>Administrator</role-name>
  </security-role>

  <!-- Identifies those security roles defined for an EJB module.-->
  <security-role>
    <!-- Describes a security role. -->
    <description> Registered customer role for bean. </description>
    <!-- Identifies a logical role name that this EJB module uses. -->
    <role-name>RegisteredCustomer</role-name>
  </security-role>

  <!-- Identifies those security roles defined for an EJB module.-->
  <security-role>
    <!-- Describes a security role. -->
    <description> Unregistered customer role for bean. </description>
    <!-- Identifies a logical role name that this EJB module uses. -->
    <role-name>UnregisteredCustomer</role-name>
  </security-role>
    ...
</assembly-descriptor>

</ejb-jar>
```

Special deployment descriptor elements can also be defined that dictate those security roles that can access particular methods on an EJB. Zero or more <method-permission> elements defined within an <assembly-descriptor> element are used to provide such role-to-method access control mappings. A <method-permission> element can contain a <description> element, one or more <role-name> elements, and one or more <method> elements. The <role-name> elements simply contain role name values that have been defined in a <role-name> element contained by the <security-role> elements defined previously. The <method> element identifies particular EJB method(s) for which this access control specification applies. A <method> element in turn can contain the following elements:

- <description>: The <description> element can optionally be used to describe the EJB method access control mapping.

- <ejb-name>: The <ejb-name> element identifies the EJB reference name to which this specification applies.

- `<method-intf>`: The `<method-intf>` element optionally specifies if the home or remote interface applies to this particular method specification. The values of `Home` or `Remote` are used. This element is of use when EJB home and remote interfaces have identical method names, and you need to differentiate between the two types.

- `<method-name>`: The `<method-name>` element identifies the EJB method(s) to which this mapping applies. A name can be used here to define a specific method name. Alternatively, if an asterisk (*) is used, this particular mapping applies to all methods on the EJB.

- `<method-params>`: The `<method-params>` element is used to specify fully qualified parameter types associated with an EJB method to which this mapping applies. The `<method-params>` element can contain zero or more `<method-param>` elements that are associated with fully qualified class type names. The `<method-params>` element information uniquely identifies a particular EJB method according to its parameter types and overrides any generic specification for a particular group of overloaded methods or for the whole EJB.

For example, you might have defined the following additional methods on an `OrderManager` bean for which you want a container to manage secure access control:

```
public void makeOrder(String orderID)
    { /* Do something...*/ }
public void makeOrder(String orderID, String customerID)
    { /* Do something...*/ }
public void makeOrder(String orderID, String customerID, Vector items)
    {/* Do something...*/ }

public void cancelOrders(String customerID)
    { /* Do something...*/  }
public void cancelOrders(String customerID, Vector items)
    { /* Do something...*/ }
```

Now suppose that during assembly time, you decide the following about this bean's secure access control semantics:

- All remote methods should allow `Administrator` role access by default.
- The previously defined `getOrder()` method should also allow `RegisteredCustomer` role access.
- Both remote `cancelOrders()` methods should also allow `RegisteredCustomer` role access.
- The remote `makeOrder(String, String)` and `makeOrder(String, String, Vector)` method should also allow `UnregisteredCustomer` and `RegisteredCustomer` role access.

Given such security access role semantics, you can define your `ejb-jar.xml` file for this bean using the `<method-permission>` elements shown here:

```xml
<?xml version="1.0" encoding="UTF-8"?>
  ...
<ejb-jar>
  ...
  <enterprise-beans>
    <session>
        ...
      <!-- EJB Reference name for our bean -->
      <ejb-name>OrderManager</ejb-name>
      <!-- Class name for our EJB Home interface -->
      <home>ejava.ejbsecurity.OrderManagerHome</home>
      <!-- Class name for our EJB Remote interface -->
      <remote>ejava.ejbsecurity.OrderManager</remote>
      <!-- Class name for our EJB implementation -->
      <ejb-class>ejava.ejbsecurity.OrderManagerBean</ejb-class>
        ...
    </session>
      ...
  </enterprise-beans>

  <assembly-descriptor>
      ...
    <!-- Define Administrator access. -->
    <method-permission>
      <description>
        Administrator access control for the OrderManager bean.
        Will allow access to all methods on OrderManager.
      </description>
      <role-name>Administrator</role-name>
      <method>
        <ejb-name>OrderManager</ejb-name>
        <method-name>*</method-name>
      </method>
    </method-permission>

    <!-- Add access on getOrder to RegisteredCustomer. -->
    <method-permission>
      <description>
        RegisteredCustomer access control for access to the
        OrderManager getOrder() method.
      </description>
      <role-name>RegisteredCustomer</role-name>
      <method>
```

```
      <ejb-name>OrderManager</ejb-name>
      <method-intf>Remote</method-intf>
      <method-name>getOrder</method-name>
    </method>
</method-permission>

<!-- Add access on cancelOrders to RegisteredCustomer. -->
<method-permission>
  <description>
    RegisteredCustomer access control for access to the
    OrderManager cancelOrders() methods.
  </description>
  <role-name>RegisteredCustomer</role-name>
  <method>
      <ejb-name>OrderManager</ejb-name>
      <method-intf>Remote</method-intf>
      <method-name>cancelOrders</method-name>
  </method>
</method-permission>

<!-- Add access to specific makeOrder methods. -->
<method-permission>
  <description>
    RegisteredCustomer access control for access to the
    OrderManager makeOrder(String, String) and the
    makeOrder(String, String, Vector) methods.
  </description>
  <role-name>UnregisteredCustomer</role-name>
  <role-name>RegisteredCustomer</role-name>
  <method>
      <ejb-name>OrderManager</ejb-name>
      <method-intf>Remote</method-intf>
      <method-name>makeOrder</method-name>
      <method-params>
        <method-param>java.lang. String</method-param>
        <method-param>java.lang.String</method-param>
      </method-params>
  </method>
  <method>
      <ejb-name>OrderManager</ejb-name>
      <method-intf>Remote</method-intf>
      <method-name>makeOrder</method-name>
      <method-params>
        <method-param>java.lang.String</method-param>
        <method-param>java.lang.String</method-param>
```

```
      <method-param>java.util.Vector</method-param>
    </method-params>
  </method>
</method-permission>

</assembly-descriptor>

</ejb-jar>
```

Vendor-Specific EJB Access Controls

Although the roles specified by an assembler in the `<security-role>` elements of an
`ejb-jar.xml` file define logical roles assumed by an EJB application, the container and EJB
deployers must map these roles to actual user groups and/or to users in the operational system.
Additionally, the container and EJB deployers must manage how these roles relate to particular
security domains from the operational system. Vendor-specific mappings from logical security
role to operational environment groups/users can be performed in an automated fashion without requiring the development of vendor-specific code.

An example of a vendor-specific mapping tool is the `DeployerTool`, a GUI tool that comes
with the BEA WebLogic Server. The `DeployerTool` can be used to map standard J2EE EJB
defined role names to principal names that have meaning in an operational BEA WebLogic
Server environment. After selecting a particular WebLogic Server, an EJB deployer loads a particular EJB module stored in a JAR file. After selecting the particular bean whose security profile will be mapped, you select a Security item in the GUI for that bean. The standard EJB
security application roles that were stored in `<security-role>` elements for that module are
then be displayed. The GUI also displays those principal names available to the BEA
WebLogic Server environment. (Exactly how such principal names are made available will be
described in the next section.) The GUI tool then allows you to see what principal names are
currently mapped to those standard roles. You can also add and delete principal associations
with those roles.

When performing such a mapping, the `DeployerTool` populates a vendor-specific
`weblogic-ejb-jar.xml` file. The `weblogic-ejb-jar.xml` file contains zero or more
`<security-role-assignment>` elements containing a standard EJB `<role-name>` element that
maps to one or more WebLogic-specific `<principal-name>` elements. For example, you might
specify that your standard `Administrator` role name maps to a `root` and `sysop` user in an
operational WebLogic Server environment and yields the following `weblogic-ejb-jar.xml`
file:

```
<?xml version="1.0"?>

<!DOCTYPE weblogic-ejb-jar PUBLIC '-//BEA Systems, Inc.//
➥DTD WebLogic 5.1.0 EJB//EN'
```

```
➠ 'http://www.beasys.com/j2ee/dtds/weblogic-ejb-jar.dtd'>

<weblogic-ejb-jar>
  <weblogic-enterprise-bean>
    ...
  </weblogic-enterprise-bean>
  ...
  <security-role-assignment>
    <role-name>Administrator</role-name>
    <principal-name>root</principal-name>
    <principal-name>sysop</principal-name>
  </security-role-assignment>
  ...
</weblogic-ejb-jar>
```

Such declarative EJB security access control checking mechanisms provide a codeless way for determining whether a particular user in a particular role is allowed access to a particular method on a particular EJB. However, some enterprise applications might need to provide access control checking functionality in which access to a particular EJB method is allowed based on some business-specific state and logic of the system associated with that user. For example, it might not be valid to say that all users belonging to a particular `employee` role have access or do not have access to particular getter and setter methods on some `TimeSheet` EJB that encapsulates employee timesheets in an enterprise human resource management application. Rather, you might implement a security-checking mechanism that provides access control to such `TimeSheet` EJB getter and setter methods based on whether the identity of the invoking client matches some `employeeID` field state of the `TimeSheet` EJB. Although bean developers can use the standard programmatic EJB access control checking mechanisms to implement the needed logic, some EJB container vendors provide additional access control mechanisms to implement such features.

Vendor-Specific EJB Identity and Authentication

Vendor-specific mappings, from logical security role to operational environment groups/users, might not require any vendor-specific code, but the exact means by which your container manages the access, addition, and removal of the operational groups/users within its auspices might indeed require vendor-specific code. You saw the vendor-specific means for mapping standard EJB security roles to principal names in the last section. But how do you customize your vendor's server environment to be cognizant of such valid principal names? For example, if your enterprise manages principal information in a database, a vendor-specific means to access that information via custom JDBC calls might be required. However, you might also decide to use whatever means are provided by your particular vendor to automatically manage such

14

ENTERPRISE
JAVABEANS
SECURITY

information, which might not require specialized coding. Such methods might, instead, include a means to specify principal information in a simple text file, an XML file, or an LDAP structure.

The BEA WebLogic Server, in fact, uses a text-based configuration file (that is, its `weblogic.properties` file) as the default means for storing usernames and passwords. User information is added to this file in the form of name/value entries as follows:

```
weblogic.password.userName=userPassword
```

Similarly, groups can be added to the file in the following form:

```
weblogic.security.group.groupName=userName1,userName2,userName3,...
```

Configuring principal information using static configuration files, however, is infeasible for most medium-to-large-scale applications. Thus, BEA WebLogic also provides a means to manage identities stored in alternative principal identification repositories (security domains or realms). An alternate realm is designated in the `weblogic.properties` file by setting a special `weblogic.security.RealmClass` property equal to a fully qualified class name encapsulating the alternative realm. Such classes implement WebLogic-specific interfaces that enable the WebLogic server environment to invoke operations on such class instances during operational processing of security-related events. The available alternative BEA WebLogic v5.1 realm types include

- *LDAP Realm*: Enables the authentication of principals managed in a Lightweight Directory Access Protocol (LDAP) server. The `weblogic.security.ldaprealm.LDAPRealm` class must be referenced in the `weblogic.properties` file by the `weblogic.security.RealmClass` property. You must also edit a special WebLogic `ldaprealm.properties` file containing a number of LDAP-specific properties that must be edited for your environment.

- *Windows NT Realm*: Enables the authentication of principals managed in a Windows NT security domain. The `weblogic.security.ntrealm.NTRealm` class must be referenced in the `weblogic.properties` file by the `weblogic.security.RealmClass` property. A special WebLogic `ntrealm.properties` file's `weblogic.security.ntrealm.domain` property must also contain a reference to the primary Windows NT domain controller host name.

- *UNIX Realm*: Enables the authentication of principals managed in a UNIX security domain. The `weblogic.security.unixrealm.UnixRealm` class must be referenced in the `weblogic.properties` file by the `weblogic.security.RealmClass` property. You must also configure your system for use of a special WebLogic `wlauth` program that looks up users and groups from the UNIX security domain.

- *Database Realm*: Enables the authentication of principals whose information is stored in a database. WebLogic supplies an `examples.security.rdbmsrealm.RDBMSRealm` class that can be used as a template for your database-specific custom-realm management. The sample class can also be referenced directly in the `weblogic.properties` file by the `weblogic.security.RealmClass` property. A special `rdbmsrealm.properties` file can then be configured with your RDBMS's particular database connection information and principal-management-related database SQL queries.

If none of the principal information management realms that come equipped with BEA WebLogic satisfy your needs out of the box, you can create your own custom realm following the pattern of the `RDBMSRealm` class described earlier. A custom extendable identity management realm, however, involves the implementation of vendor-specific interfaces to support interoperation with the WebLogic security-checking environment. The basic approach is to create a special realm class that implements methods to retrieve and modify user, group, and access control information. Thus, user profile information can be stored in a repository of your choice and managed in a business-specific fashion by these interface implementations. Your operational environment-specific implementations of these interfaces are based entirely on vendor-specific interfaces. However, such built-in support provides a lot of flexibility for managing your specific operational user profiles. Furthermore, a proper design pattern implementation can be used to isolate vendor-specific library dependencies from your business-specific logic.

Future EJB and J2EE specifications will most likely incorporate JAAS for standard authentication within EJB servers. In the meantime, you'll have to rely on utilizing vendor-specific means for authenticating clients in EJB server environments. A principal identity name and set of credentials must somehow propagate from EJB client to EJB server for authentication to occur. BEA WebLogic accomplishes this by setting the `javax.naming.Context.SECURITY_PRINCIPAL` and `javax.naming.Context.SECURITY_CREDENTIALS` properties onto a `javax.naming.InitialContext` during initial connectivity with the EJB server from the client.

For example, the EJB client using the BEA WebLogic Server wishes access to the previously secured `OrderManager` EJB. The client passes username and credential information to the EJB server when obtaining an initial Java Naming and Directory Interface (JNDI) context as follows (excluding exception handling):

```
// Create properties that we'll use to connect with EJB server
Hashtable props = new Hashtable();
props.put(javax.naming.Context.PROVIDER_URL, "t3://localhost:7001/");
props.put(javax.naming.Context.INITIAL_CONTEXT_FACTORY,
          "weblogic.jndi.WLInitialContextFactory");
```

```
props.put(javax.naming.Context.SECURITY_PRINCIPAL, "root");
props.put(javax.naming.Context.SECURITY_CREDENTIALS, "turnthetheta");

// Get initial context for standalone client using properties
Context context = new InitialContext(props);
```

On the BEA WebLogic server side, if a custom realm is being used, special callbacks onto the custom realm implementation class are made to pass such principal and credential information enabling your code to provide custom authentication of such users with the system. A vendor-specific object (weblogic.security.acl.User) returned by your custom realm code to the WebLogic container representing an authenticated user of the system is then associated with a server-side thread handler for the client. When subsequent requests are made from that same client associated with the thread, the client's credentials from its thread handler can be used in the process of providing access control for EJBs.

Thus, if the EJB client previously authenticated during an initial JNDI context creation operation can access the system, it might attempt to lookup EJB home references and invoke operations on those EJBs as usual. If an EJB's methods have been restricted using the standard and vendor-specific access control mechanisms defined previously, the security-critical EJB operations will be checked by the server during runtime operation. For example, if your EJB client now wishes to make a security-critical getOrder() call onto your OrderManager EJB defined earlier, you might have the following code (excluding exception handling):

```
// Look up server reference using raw JNDI name
Object object = context.lookup("OrderManagerHome");

// Narrow to order manager reference
OrderManagerHome orderManagerHome = (OrderManagerHome)
    PortableRemoteObject.narrow(object,
        ejava.ejbsecurity.OrderManagerHome.class);

// Create handle to server object now using home factory
OrderManager mgr = orderManagerHome.create();

// Now make a security-critical EJB call
Order order = mgr.getOrder("joeShmoe");
```

The OrderManager.getOrder() call can be successfully invoked in the preceding example because this EJB client logged in as a root user, you have mapped the root user to the Administrator role, and the Administrator role has been granted access to this EJB method.

EJB Security Authentication Model Limitations

Herein lies the rub with the current EJB framework: EJB designs with minimal or no security requirements might be portable, but implementation of commercially-viable and practical security mechanisms into your EJB-based designs can lead you down the path to creating non-portable, server-side code without proper designs. Furthermore, if you do not consider this model carefully during EJB design, a particular vendor's model for associating principal and credential information with a particular EJB invocation can lead to unforeseen problems with your EJB implementations. For example, associating the security context with server-side thread representatives for EJB clients is somewhat disjoint with the EJB component and client modeling assumptions.

From my (that is, Paul Perrone's) own experience with designing and implementing EJB security mechanisms using EJB-compliant servers, I've had to create many vendor-specific design workarounds in practice and have made suggestions directly to EJB vendors regarding how to better support security that suits EJB application serving models. The BEA WebLogic Server v5.1 release seems to have actually incorporated a few of these suggestions. Nevertheless, this issue is something to be cognizant of and plan for, if you must incorporate enterprise security mechanisms into your EJB designs.

EJB Secure Communications, Delegation, and Auditing

Thus far, I have covered EJB access control, secure identity propagation, and authentication. You must consider a few additional issues, however, before deploying your security-critical EJBs into an operational enterprise environment. For one, the connection between your EJB clients and servers must often be secured in some fashion. The means by which principal identity is delegated and the mechanisms for auditing security-critical events must also be taken into consideration. This section closes the chapter with a discussion of those vendor-specific mechanisms that must be provided to support such concerns.

EJB Connection Security

The EJB client authentication sequence defined in the previous section passes user credential information into a JNDI context object with no guarantee about the secured nature of the client-to-server connection. Thus, the client's credential information might very well have been transferred to the server in the clear. For certain types of EJB clients and application scenarios, this might be acceptable. For example, if the EJB client is a Java Servlet or JavaServer Page, and if the Web server sits behind the same trusted computing base and firewall as the EJB application server, this situation might be acceptable. However, for most enterprise applications, the connection between EJB client and EJB server needs to operate over some secured socket mechanism.

The J2EE v1.2 and EJB v1.1 specifications do not specify any standard means for securing such connections. Securing the EJB client-to-server connection is left up to your particular vendor's product implementation. The BEA WebLogic Server uses SSL with certificate credentials passed over the initial connection made with the server via JNDI. Although X509 certificates can be put into the Hashtable object passed to an InitialContext object constructor, you must also pass a username and optional password into the Hashtable. As described previously, the username will enable the WebLogic Server to identify the principal name associated with the certificate.

Such vendor-specific mechanisms also require additional identification and authentication handling logic to enable you to map between certificates and principal identity on the server side. Again, this logic might be provided to you in a vendor-specific fashion, or you can elect to implement your own hand-coded mechanisms (which will inevitably require hooking into vendor-specific features). Future EJB and J2EE specifications are expected to define more rigorous identity and authentication standard mechanisms, which will naturally incorporate standard means for ensuring secure EJB client-to-server communications.

EJB Principal Delegation

The default means for propagating principal identity should allow principal identity to propagate from one EJB to another. Thus, in a chain of calls made from one EJB to another, the principal identity associated with the original EJB client that initiated the call sequence will be propagated. Exactly how principal identity is propagated from the initial EJB client to the EJB server is left up to the vendor. If more than one option is provided, the vendor, of course, should provide a means during deployment for selecting the identity propagation policy to be employed. As a minimum requirement, the EJB client's principal identity used to connect to the EJB server can be used as the principal identity to be delegated to other EJBs within the EJB server environment.

EJB Security Auditing

EJB server vendors can also provide a means for auditing security-critical events. Security-critical events include logging the generation of any java.security.Exception exceptions, successful and failed authentication attempts, and failed EJB access attempts. The BEA WebLogic Server, for example, enables you to implement a vendor-specific AuditProvider auditing class. A special weblogic.security.audit.AuditProvider property in the `weblogic.properties` file must then be set to this class name. The WebLogic server will invoke methods on this class when an attempted authentication occurs, an authorization request is made, or an invalid user certificate is propagated to the server.

Summary

The standard provisions for EJB security focus on minimal programmatic and declarative access control mechanisms. Such mechanisms provide role-based access control for your EJBs. Nevertheless, a particular EJB container/server vendor must still provide a means to map such roles to principal names managed by a particular operational environment. Support for authentication, identity propagation, and identity delegation must be provided by your particular EJB container/server vendor. Furthermore, a vendor must also provide any means for secure communications between EJB client and server, as well as any means for security auditing. Thus, the J2EE v1.2 and EJB v1.2 specifications provide EJB developers with minimal, standard security-provisioning options. Future J2EE and EJB specifications are expected to incorporate JAAS into the mix for securing EJBs with authentication and authorization provided in a standards-based fashion.

Java Servlet and JSP Security

This chapter covers security issues associated with Web applications developed using Java servlets and JavaServer Pages (JSP). It summarizes the operation of the Common Gateway Interface and discusses CGI and other Web-related security issues. It explains how servlets are developed and deployed and how a Web application's web.xml file can be configured to specify user authentication and access controls. JSP is introduced, and the relationship between JSP and servlet security is discussed.

The Common Gateway Interface

The Common Gateway Interface was adopted early on in the Web's formation as a standard for interfacing external programs to Web servers. The CGI enables these external programs, referred to as CGI programs or CGI scripts, to be written so that they are not dependent on the use of a particular Web server. The CGI specification describes a standard interface for a Web server to send browser requests to the CGI program and for the CGI program to return response data to the browser via the Web server. These interfaces are summarized in the following sections.

Web Server-to-CGI Program Communication

Web servers communicate with CGI programs using environment variables, command-line arguments, and the standard input stream. These three communication methods are used as follows:

- Environment variables—This method is the most common way that a Web server passes information to a CGI program. Environment variables are variables that are defined outside a program, but in the program's execution context or environment. The CGI defines a number of environment variables for communicating with a CGI program. These variables are described in Table 15.1. The capability of a program to read environment variables is important for CGI programming. Unfortunately, the Java API does not support this capability well.

- Command-line arguments—Certain types of browser requests, such as HTTP ISINDEX queries, cause the Web server to pass information to CGI programs using the command-line arguments of the CGI program. For example, in the following Java program invocation, v1, v2, and v3 are command-line arguments:

```
java ProgramName v1 v2 v3
```

A Java program reads the command-line variables via the args parameter of its main() function.

- Standard input—Browser requests that are submitted using the POST method are sent to the CGI program via its standard input stream. This enables the CGI program to read the data using its standard I/O capabilities. Java programs use the classes and interfaces of the java.io and other packages to read data via an input stream.

CGI Program-to-Web Server Communication

Although there are three ways that information is provided to a CGI program, there is only one way that the CGI program returns information to the Web server (and on to the browser). CGI program output is written to the standard output stream. Java programs use the classes and interfaces of the java.io package to write data to an output stream.

There are some additions to the CGI, such as the use of nonparsed headers, but these are not significant for Java programming.

TABLE 15.1   Environment Variables Used with the CGI

Variable	Description
AUTH_TYPE	The authentication scheme used with the request
CONTENT_LENGTH	The length of standard input in bytes
CONTENT_TYPE	The MIME type of the standard input

TABLE 15.1   Continued

Variable	Description
GATEWAY_INTERFACE	The version of the CGI in use by the server
PATH_INFO	Extra path information added to the URL of the CGI program
PATH_TRANSLATED	The full path name of the CGI program
QUERY_STRING	The query string appended to the request URL
REMOTE_ADDR	The IP address of the requestor
REMOTE_HOST	The host name of the requestor
REMOTE_IDENT	The verified host name of the requestor
REMOTE_USER	The name of the user making the request
REQUEST_METHOD	The HTTP method used to make the request
SCRIPT_NAME	The name of the CGI program
SERVER_NAME	The host name of the server
SERVER_PORT	The TCP port used by the Web server
SERVER_PROTOCOL	The protocol used to submit the request
SERVER_SOFTWARE	The name and version of the Web server software

Session State Maintenance

The hypertext transport protocol (HTTP) is a stateless protocol. This means that every browser request and server response is independent of every other. HTTP does not provide any mechanism by which multiple browser requests can be organized into a single user session.

A number of mechanisms are available to the Web application designer to overcome the fact that HTTP is stateless. These include the use of cookies, URL rewriting, and hidden form fields.

Cookies

Cookies are the predominant mechanism used to maintain state in Web applications. Cookies were developed by Netscape as a means to store state information in a persistent manner. Cookies enable information to be stored on the user's browser for time spans ranging from a few minutes to several years. A cookie consists of information that is sent by a server-side script to a browser as the result of processing a particular URL request. The information is organized as a name-value pair and associated with a particular URL. The cookie is stored by the browser in a cookie file.

15

Whenever a cookie-enabled browser requests a URL from a Web server, it first checks to see if any cookies are associated with the URL. If so, the browser sends the cookie information to the server as part of the URL request.

Cookies enable application designers to store information on the user's browser that spans multiple URL requests. This information might consist of session ID information that enables the designer to associate multiple requests with a single user session.

URL Rewriting

URL rewriting is another technique that is used by Web application designers to maintain session state information. URL rewriting consists of rewriting the URLs of the links of a Web page to contain extra information in the form a query string and extra path information. For example, suppose a user named Bill Jones has logged in to a Web application (with session ID = 1234) and has loaded page 1 (page1.cgi) of that application. Also suppose that page1.cgi generates a Web page that contains a link to page2.cgi, the second page of the application. URL rewriting can be used to inform the page2.cgi CGI program of the username and session ID of the current user by appending the username and session ID of the URL used to request page2.cgi. Consider the following URL:

```
http://yourserver.com/page2.cgi?fname=Bill&lname=Jones&sessionid=1234
```

When the Web server receives the preceding request, it launches the page2.cgi program and passes it a QUERY_STRING environment variable fname=Bill&lname=Jones&sessionid=1234. The CGI program can then decode this query string to obtain the username and session ID. In this way, state information can be passed from page1.cgi to page2.cgi.

> **NOTE**
>
> CGI programs aren't required to end in a .cgi extension. I just used this extension to identify that a particular request is for a CGI program, rather than for an HTML Web page.

Hidden Form Fields

Hidden form fields are a third technique that can be used by application designers to maintain the state of Web applications. They consist of form fields that use the <INPUT TYPE= "HIDDEN"> HTML tags. These fields are typically contained in forms that are placed in a common frame of a frameset and accessed using client-side JavaScript. When a JavaScript script executes in one page of an application (in a separate frame from the hidden form fields), it stores values (such as session ID) in the hidden form fields. When subsequent pages are loaded and other scripts execute, they are able to read the hidden form values to keep track of the session state.

Server-Side Programming Security Issues

Web applications don't fall prey to vulnerabilities—vulnerabilities make them more likely to fall prey to attackers. Because every Web application is somewhat unique, I cannot list them all here. Instead, I'll describe some of the more general ones that Web application designers face.

Interception of Session State Information

The mechanisms used to maintain session state are susceptible to attack. Depending on how session state information is maintained, if an adversary is able to intercept that information through the use of a sniffer or by other means, the adversary might be able to hijack the browser session and masquerade as the user. Depending on the application, this can lead to a number of undesirable consequences.

Cookies are especially vulnerable to interception because they are sent back and forth between the browser and the server with every request and response. They can also be read from the user's cookie file if the user shares a computer with other users. This is a significant vulnerability in the Internet café environment.

URL rewriting is also vulnerable to interception. The URLs requested by the browser and rewritten by the browser are passed back and forth between the browser and server. If intercepted, they can be used to take over a user's session.

Hidden form fields are vulnerable to interception to the extent that they are sent between the browser and server. Because hidden form fields are typically used with client-side scripts, the amount of browser-server communication might be less than with cookies and URL rewriting.

The best safeguard against interception is to encrypt communication between the browser and server. This is typically accomplished through the use of Secure Sockets Layer (SSL). (SSL is discussed in detail in Chapter 9, "SSL and JSSE.")

Forgery of Session State Information

In some cases, an adversary might be able to take over a user's session without having to intercept communication between the browser and server. This is possible if the adversary is able to predict or guess the session state information. For example, suppose the user's session is tracked using an integer value that is incremented with each new session. If an adversary logs into a Web application and receives a session ID of 123456, the adversary can forge the cookie or rewritten URL of other users by using session ID values of 123454, 123455, and 123457.

This can be accomplished even if the Web application uses SSL to encrypt browser-server communication.

The countermeasure to the forgery of session state information is to use large session ID values that are randomized. The goal is to make session information as difficult as possible to predict. In addition, session information may be encrypted on the server.

Buffer Overflow

Buffer overflow vulnerabilities are common to Web applications. A buffer overflow vulnerability occurs when a program accepts more input data than it is able to store in an input buffer. When a buffer overflows, the overflow data overwrites other program data, and sometimes, instruction or stack information. In a case when program instructions are overwritten, the adversary can supply code that executes on the Web server. This generally leads to takeover of the Web application and the Web server as a whole.

The countermeasure to buffer overflows is simple: Don't put more data into a buffer than it can hold. That is, validate the data that is received from a browser before using it in a Web application.

Data Validation

The buffer overflow problem is a special case of a more general problem: failing to validate data that is received from the user. In many cases, data validation problems stem from the fact that the Web application designer makes an assumption about what a user will or will not do. This type of assumption is often fatal. An attacker exploits the designer's assumption to provide data that causes the sever-side program to malfunction, sometimes leading to a security compromise.

For example, suppose that a Web application solicits input from a user via a text field that is stored in a database and later displayed to other users. If the user types in a SCRIPT tag and a JavaScript script into the text field and the SCRIPT is later executed on another user's browser, it might be possible for one user to attack the other.

Attackers can carry out many types of attacks related to data validation. They can rewrite URLs or modify hidden form fields to contain unexpected values, enter numeric values that result in numeric overflows, or fail to provide information resulting in operations on null values. The possibilities are endless.

The countermeasure to data validation attacks is to validate all data that is received from the browser. In addition, the validation should be performed on the server. Although it is tempting to use an applet or client-side script to take the load off the Web server and validate user input, client-side data validation isn't reliable. A clever adversary will simply circumvent the client-side validation and send invalid data directly to the Web application.

Page Sequencing

Web application designers often erroneously assume that if they have a multipage application, users will proceed through the pages of the application in the sequence designed into the application's links. This is not the case. Users will enter custom URLs, copy mid-application URLs and email them to their friends, and jump backward and forward through application pages in near-random order. Attackers will do the same in the hope of finding security holes in the assumptions of Web developers. For example, consider the situation in which the first page of a Web application requires a user to login, but the user bypasses the login page and goes directly to the page he needs. To prevent this situation, each page of the application must verify that the user has logged in.

Session Timeout

When does a user's session terminate? In most applications, this is a difficult question to answer. If a user logs in to an application, browses some other pages, and then comes back, should the user still be logged into the application? Most applications provide two means for a user to end a session: by explicitly clicking a link to terminate the application and by using session timeouts.

A session timeout is implemented by keeping track of the last time that a user's browser makes a request of the Web server. If a new request is not made within a certain time (the timeout time), the user's session is terminated, and the user is required to log in again.

The problem with timeouts is that there can be a gap between the user's last action and the timeout. For example, a user can be at work interacting with his online banking application, close his browser, and then get up to get a cup of coffee. In the meantime, someone else can open his browser, go through the browser's history list, and possibly use it to gain continued access to the user's bank account.

Setting the duration of a session timeout involves tough tradeoffs. If the timeout is too short, users are forced to repeatedly log in. If the timeout is too long, the user's session may be vulnerable to takeover. Timeouts are typically set between 10 and 45 minutes, with 20 minutes being a common value.

Information Reporting

Web servers and Web applications typically provide too much information to an adversary. For example, a Web server might announce its name and version number to a Web browser. If a vulnerability (such as a buffer overrun) is discovered with a particular version of the Web server, the attacker can immediately identify servers that are susceptible to this vulnerability. Some Web servers provide the capability to obtain listings of the directories served by the Web server. An attacker can sometimes use this capability to download files that provide access to the source code of compiled applications and other information that can be used to uncover Webapplication vulnerabilities.

Browser Residue

The user's browser stores all kinds of information related to the user's interaction with a Web application. The files that are loaded by the browser are stored in the browser's cache. The most recent URLs that are accessed by the browser are stored in the browser's history list. The Web application's cookies are stored in cookie files. Each of these stored values can provide useful information to an attacker. For example, cookies and the history list can be used to gain access to session state information. Cached files can contain private user data.

User Authentication

Security-sensitive Web applications typically require users to log in. Logging in enables users to identify themselves to the application and allows the application to authenticate users' identities. Identification and authentication (I&A) is a major area of information security. The stronger the I&A mechanism, the more secure the Web application. Weak I&A diminishes the overall security of the Web application.

One of the weakest and widely used forms of I&A is reusable passwords. Passwords can be intercepted during transmission between the browser and Web server. Passwords can also be guessed or cracked using password cracking tools. The use of SSL prevents password interception, but it does not reduce the vulnerability of easily guessed passwords. User education and password screening help to reduce this vulnerability.

One difficult tradeoff faced by application designers is whether to implement application lockouts. A lockout occurs when a user fails to correctly log into an application after a specified number of attempts. The locked-out user is required to take special steps to reopen his account. Lockouts provide a way to discourage attackers from guessing user passwords. On the other hand, lockouts can be used by attackers to cause denial of service. For example, if an attacker is able to determine the IDs of an application's users, the attacker can make multiple bad login attempts to lock out these users.

Logging of Sensitive Information

Web servers typically provide the capability to log all URLs requested by browsers. Because sensitive user information can be encoded in URLs, the logging data itself is security sensitive and needs to be protected. For this reason, online access to log data should be prohibited. In addition, log data should not be sent over the Internet without being encrypted.

Least Privilege

Web applications typically execute with privileges that allow them to read and write from the server's file system, access databases and application servers, and communicate using sockets.

These privileges are restricted, to a certain extent, by the identity with which the applications execute. Because the programs and scripts that compose a Web application can contain exploitable security flaws, it is important to limit the privileges associated with this identity to the minimum set needed to perform the application's processing. This limitation is referred to as *least privilege*.

Most Web application programming environments do not provide any additional restrictions beside those supported by the underlying operating system. However, as you'll learn later in this chapter, Java servlets can be executed in a server sandbox, and least privilege can be enforced via an application security policy.

Java Servlets

Java servlets are the server-side analog to applets and provide a CGI-like programming capability for Java. They provide the capability to execute Java code in response to browser requests. Servlets are executed via server-side Java Virtual Machines (JVMs), which run in servlet containers. Servlet containers are implemented via the Web server's extension API. Servlet containers provide support for CGI programming via the Servlet API. At the time of this writing, the latest version of the Servlet API is 2.2. Servlet containers are available for all major Web servers.

> **NOTE**
>
> The Java servlets home page is located at `http://java.sun.com/products/servlet/index.html`. It provides pointers to servlet documentation and servlet-related products.

A servlet container can execute on the same computer as the Web server or as an independent application server running on a separate computer. It translates browser requests, the CGI, and cookies to objects that can be accessed via the Servlet API. The container also provides the capability to enforce security restrictions on servlet execution.

Servlets have the advantage of being able to use the extensive Java API to create platform-independent Web applications that support security, scalability, clustering, and reliability. In addition, servlet containers can be designed to support execution environments that provide higher performance than those typically achieved by CGI programs.

15

JAVA SERVLET
AND JSP
SECURITY

Why Servlets?

The Java Development Kit (JDK), by itself, is not a good programming environment in which to write raw CGI programs for two reasons: It doesn't support environment variables well, and the loading of the Java interpreter adds quite a bit of overhead to CGI processing.

Java's inability to read environment variables is an API problem. The preJDK 1.0 API supported the getenv() method of the System class for obtaining access to environment variables. However, this method was deprecated and is no longer supported. Instead, the preferred solution is to use the getProperties() and getProperty() methods of the system class to access the environment properties of the Java program. When the Java interpreter is loaded and executed by a Web server, the server sets the CGI-standard environment variables in the interpreter's environment. However, the Java interpreter does not pass these variables on to the Java program as properties. This makes Java unsuitable for writing standard CGI programs.

Even if Java programs could read the environment variables of the Java interpreter, the overhead of loading the Java interpreter for every CGI program is prohibitive. This is not a show-stopper, but it is a serious performance limitation.

Because Java is a popular programming language and many people want to develop server-side programs in Java, there has been a concerted effort to develop an API and environment for Java server-side programming. The Servlet API is a major result of this effort.

The Servlet API

The Servlet API is a standard extension API that consists of the following four packages:

- javax.servlet—Defines the basic interfaces, classes, and exceptions of the servlet API.
- javax.servlet.http—Extends the basic servlet interfaces, classes, and exceptions to provide support for HTTP.
- javax.servlet.jsp—Provides support for JavaServer Pages.
- javax.servlet.jsp.tagext—Provides an extension mechanism for JavaServer Pages.

These packages are covered in the following sections.

The javax.servlet Package

The javax.servlet package consists of seven interfaces, three classes, and two exceptions that provide the foundation for the servlet API.

Interfaces

The javax.servlet package's interfaces are as follows:

- RequestDispatcher—Provides the capability to forward a request or a response from one servlet to another.

- `Servlet`—The basic interface that is implemented by all servlets. It provides methods for initializing, executing, and destroying servlets and for obtaining information about the servlet and its configuration. The `Servlet` interface is implemented by the `GenericServlet` class.

- `ServletConfig`—Provides a standard mechanism for passing initialization and configuration information to a servlet instance. This information is passed via a list of name-value pairs. In addition, the `getServletContext()` method returns a `ServletContext` object that provides access to the servlet container and the overall application supported by the servlet. The `ServletConfig` interface is implemented by the `GenericServlet` class.

- `ServletContext`—Defines methods by which a servlet can obtain information about the underlying servlet container and information that is common to all servlets of a Web application.

- `ServletRequest`—Encapsulates a client request in a protocol-independent manner. It is extended by `HttpServletRequest` to provide support for HTTP request processing.

- `ServletResponse`—Encapsulates a response to a client request in a protocol-independent manner. It is extended by `HttpServletResponse` to provide support for HTTP response processing.

- `SingleThreadModel`—Implemented by servlets to indicate to the servlet container that a servlet instance should only process one client request at a time in a serialized manner.

Classes

The `javax.servlet` package's classes are as follows:

- `GenericServlet`—Provides a basic implementation of the `Servlet` interface in a protocol-independent manner. The `javax.http.HttpServlet` class extends `GenericServlet` to provide an HTTP-specific implementation.

- `ServletInputStream`—Provides an input stream that can be used to read binary data associated with a client request. A `ServletInputStream` object is obtained via the `getInputStream()` method of the `ServletRequest` class.

- `ServletOutputStream`—Provides an output stream for sending binary data to a client. A `ServletOutputStream` object is obtained via the `getOutputStream()` method of the `ServletResponse` class.

Exceptions

The `javax.servlet` package's exceptions are as follows:

- `ServletException`—Extends `java.lang.Exception` to provide a common class for servlet-specific exceptions.

15

JAVA SERVLET
AND JSP
SECURITY

- UnavailableException—Extends ServletException to signal that a servlet is unavailable and should not be loaded.

The `javax.servlet.http` Package

The javax.servlet.http package provides five interfaces and four classes that provide direct support for HTTP.

Interfaces

The javax.servlet.http package's interfaces are as follows:

- HttpServletRequest—Extends ServletRequest to provide support for handling HTTP requests. Defines numerous methods for accessing the details of an HTTP request and any associated cookies.

- HttpServletResponse—Extends ServletResponse to provide support for responding to HTTP requests. Provides methods for sending information back to the requesting browser and for setting cookie values.

- HttpSession—Provides a basic mechanism for tracking session state that uses either cookies or URL rewriting. HttpSession also supports the binding and unbinding of objects with a particular session.

- HttpSessionBindingListener—Used to notify an object that it is bound or unbound from a particular HttpSession.

- HttpSessionContext—This interface was deprecated as of version 2.1 of the Servlet API and is no longer supported.

Classes

The javax.servlet.http package's classes are as follows:

- Cookie—Encapsulates an HTTP cookie. Allows cookies to be created, exchanged with browsers, accessed, and updated.

- HttpServlet—Extends the GenericServlet class to provide HTTP-specific protocol support.

- HttpSessionBindingEvent—Used to notify HttpSessionBindingListener objects that they are bound to or unbound from a user session.

- HttpUtils—Provides a collection of static utility methods for working with URLs, query strings, and posted form data.

The `javax.servlet.jsp` Package

The javax.servlet.jsp package contains two interfaces, four classes, and two exceptions that provide support for JavaServer Pages.

Interfaces

The javax.servlet.jsp package's interfaces are as follows:

- HttpJspPage—Extends the JspPage interface to provide support for the hypertext transfer protocol. JspPage extends the Servlet interface.
- JspPage—This interface is implemented by all compiled JavaServer Pages. It provides methods for initializing, processing, and destroying a page object.

Classes

The javax.servlet.jsp package's classes are as follows:

- JspEngineInfo—Abstract class that provides information about the underlying JSP engine.
- JspFactory—An abstract class that provides methods for accessing PageContext, JspEngineInfo, and JspFactory objects.
- JspWriter—Extends java.io.Writer to provide support for writing the output of a Web page.
- PageContext—Provides access to the execution context of a JSP page. This includes the JSPWriter object, namespaces, and session information.

Exceptions

The javax.servlet.jsp package's exceptions are as follows:

- JspException—Extends java.lang.Exception to provide support for exceptions that occur during the execution of a JSP page.
- JspTagException—Extends JspException to provide exception support for tag handlers.

The javax.servlet.jsp.tagext Package

The javax.servlet.jsp.tagext package contains two interfaces and nine classes that provide support for JSP tag extensions.

Interfaces

The javax.servlet.jsp.tagext package's interfaces are as follows:

- BodyTag—Extends Tag to provide methods for accessing the body of a tag.
- Tag—Defines basic methods that are implemented by all tag handlers.

Classes

The javax.servlet.jsp.tagext package's classes are as follows:

- BodyContent—Extends JspWriter to support buffered writing of body content.
- BodyTagSupport—Provides a default implementation of the BodyTag interface.

- `TagAttributeInfo`—Provides information about the attributes of a tag.
- `TagData`—Provides access to the attributes of a tag.
- `TagExtraInfo`—Provides extra tag information related to scripting.
- `TagInfo`—Provides basic information about a tag.
- `TagLibraryInfo`—Provides basic information about a tag library.
- `TagSupport`—Provides utility methods that support tag processing.
- `VariableInfo`—Provides information about scripting variables.

How Servlets Work

A servlet is a class that implements the `javax.servlet.Servlet` interface. Servlets, JavaServer Pages, HTML files, and other resources are deployed as Web applications by making them available to the servlet container in a particular directory structure. The servlet container maps this directory structure to a set of URLs. When a browser requests these URLs, the servlet classes of the Web application are executed.

> **NOTE**
>
> Servlets can be distributed in a compressed Web application archive format. Web application archive files have the `.war` extension and are created by the JAR (Java archive) tool. The compressed files are deployed by uncompressing them into the correct directory structure.

The application's root directory is the highest-level directory in the application directory structure. A subdirectory, named WEB-INF, under the root directory structure is used to hold all supporting files, such as servlet classes, that are not served to the user's browser. The WEB-INF directory also contains a file named `web.xml` that describes how the Web application should be configured and deployed. The `web.xml` file contains the following types of information:

- `ServletContext` initialization parameters
- Session configuration information
- Servlet/JSP definitions and mappings
- Mime type mappings
- Welcome file list
- Error pages
- Security configuration information

These features are specified using the XML syntax defined by the Data Type Definition (DTD) shown in Listing 15.1. If you are unfamiliar with XML, check out the links to tutorials at http://www.xml.org.

LISTING 15.1   The Web-App DTD

```
<!--
The web-app element is the root of the deployment descriptor for
a web application
-->
<!ELEMENT web-app (icon?, display-name?, description?, distributable?,
context-param*, servlet*, servlet-mapping*, session-config?,
mime-mapping*, welcome-file-list?, error-page*, taglib*,
resource-ref*, security-constraint*, login-config?, security-role*,
env-entry*, ejb-ref*)>
<!--
The icon element contains a small-icon and a large-icon element
which specify the location within the web application for a small and
large image used to represent the web application in a GUI tool. At a
minimum, tools must accept GIF and JPEG format images.
-->
<!ELEMENT icon (small-icon?, large-icon?)>
<!--
The small-icon element contains the location within the web
application of a file containing a small (16x16 pixel) icon image.
-->
<!ELEMENT small-icon (#PCDATA)>
<!--
The large-icon element contains the location within the web
application of a file containing a large (32x32 pixel) icon image.
-->
<!ELEMENT large-icon (#PCDATA)>
<!--
The display-name element contains a short name that is intended
to be displayed by GUI tools
-->
<!ELEMENT display-name (#PCDATA)>
<!--
The description element is used to provide descriptive text about
the parent element.
-->
<!ELEMENT description (#PCDATA)>
<!--
The distributable element, by its presence in a web application
deployment descriptor, indicates that this web application is
programmed appropriately to be deployed a distributed servlet
```

LISTING 15.1 Continued

```
container
-->
<!ELEMENT distributable EMPTY>
<!--
The context-param element contains the declaration of a web
application's servlet context initialization parameters.
-->
<!ELEMENT context-param (param-name, param-value, description?)>
<!--
The param-name element contains the name of a parameter.
-->
<!ELEMENT param-name (#PCDATA)>
<!--
The param-value element contains the value of a parameter.
-->
<!ELEMENT param-value (#PCDATA)>
<!--
The servlet element contains the declarative data of a
servlet. If a jsp-file is specified and the load-on-startup element is
present, then the JSP should be precompiled and loaded.
-->
<!ELEMENT servlet (icon?, servlet-name, display-name?, description?,
(servlet-class|jsp-file), init-param*, load-on-startup?, security-role-ref*)>
<!--
The servlet-name element contains the canonical name of the
servlet.
-->
<!ELEMENT servlet-name (#PCDATA)>
<!--
The servlet-class element contains the fully qualified class name
of the servlet.
-->
<!ELEMENT servlet-class (#PCDATA)>
<!--
The jsp-file element contains the full path to a JSP file within
the web application.
-->
<!ELEMENT jsp-file (#PCDATA)>
<!--
The init-param element contains a name/value pair as an
initialization param of the servlet
-->
<!ELEMENT init-param (param-name, param-value, description?)>
<!--
```

LISTING 15.1   Continued

```
The load-on-startup element indicates that this servlet should be
loaded on the startup of the web application. The optional contents of
these element must be a positive integer indicating the order in which
the servlet should be loaded. Lower integers are loaded before higher
integers. If no value is specified, or if the value specified is not a
positive integer, the container is free to load it at any time in the
startup sequence.
-->
<!ELEMENT load-on-startup (#PCDATA)>
<!--
The servlet-mapping element defines a mapping between a servlet
and a url pattern
-->
<!ELEMENT servlet-mapping (servlet-name,  url-pattern)>
<!--
The url-pattern element contains the url pattern of the
mapping. Must follow the rules specified in Section 10 of the Servlet
API Specification.
-->
<!ELEMENT url-pattern (#PCDATA)>
<!--
The session-config element defines the session parameters for
this web application.
-->
<!ELEMENT session-config (session-timeout?)>
<!--
The session-timeout element defines the default session timeout
interval for all sessions created in this web application. The
specified timeout must be expressed in a whole number of minutes.
-->
<!ELEMENT session-timeout (#PCDATA)>
<!--
The mime-mapping element defines a mapping between an extension
and a mime type.
-->
<!ELEMENT mime-mapping (extension, mime-type)>
<!--
The extension element contains a string describing an
extension. example: "txt"
-->
<!ELEMENT extension (#PCDATA)>
<!--
The mime-type element contains a defined mime type. example:
"text/plain"
```

15

LISTING 15.1 Continued

```
-->
<!ELEMENT mime-type (#PCDATA)>
<!--
The welcome-file-list contains an ordered list of welcome file
elements.
-->
<!ELEMENT welcome-file-list (welcome-file+)>
<!--
The welcome-file element contains file name to use as a default
welcome file, such as index.html
-->
<!ELEMENT welcome-file (#PCDATA)>
<!--
The taglib element is used to describe a JSP tag library.
-->
<!ELEMENT taglib (taglib-uri, taglib-location)>
<!--
The taglib-uri element describes a URI, relative to the location
of the web.xml document, identifying a Tag Library used in the Web
Application.
-->
<!ELEMENT taglib-uri (#PCDATA)>
<!--
the taglib-location element contains the location (as a resource
relative to the root of the web application) where to find the Tag
Libary Description file for the tag library.
-->
<!ELEMENT taglib-location (#PCDATA)>
<!--
The error-page element contains a mapping between an error code
or exception type to the path of a resource in the web application
-->
<!ELEMENT error-page ((error-code | exception-type), location)>
<!--
The error-code contains an HTTP error code, ex: 404
-->
<!ELEMENT error-code (#PCDATA)>
<!--
The exception type contains a fully qualified class name of a
Java exception type.
-->
<!ELEMENT exception-type (#PCDATA)>
<!--
The location element contains the location of the resource in the
web application
```

LISTING 15.1 Continued

```
-->
<!ELEMENT location (#PCDATA)>
<!--
The resource-ref element contains a declaration of a Web
Application's reference to an external resource.
-->
<!ELEMENT resource-ref (description?, res-ref-name, res-type, res-auth)>
<!--
The res-ref-name element specifies the name of the resource
factory reference name.
-->
<!ELEMENT res-ref-name (#PCDATA)>
<!--
The res-type element specifies the (Java class) type of the data
source.
-->
<!ELEMENT res-type (#PCDATA)>
<!--
The res-auth element indicates whether the application component
code performs resource signon programmatically or whether the
container signs onto the resource based on the principle mapping
information supplied by the deployer. Must be CONTAINER or SERVLET
-->
<!ELEMENT res-auth (#PCDATA)>
<!--
The security-constraint element is used to associate security
constraints with one or more web resource collections
-->
<!ELEMENT security-constraint (web-resource-collection+,
auth-constraint?, user-data-constraint?)>
<!--
The web-resource-collection element is used to identify a subset
of the resources and HTTP methods on those resources within a web
application to which a security constraint applies. If no HTTP methods
are specified, then the security constraint applies to all HTTP
methods.
-->
<!ELEMENT web-resource-collection (web-resource-name, description?,
url-pattern*, http-method*)>
<!--
The web-resource-name contains the name of this web resource
collection
-->
<!ELEMENT web-resource-name (#PCDATA)>
```

15

LISTING 15.1   Continued

```
<!--
The http-method contains an HTTP method (GET | POST |...)
-->
<!ELEMENT http-method (#PCDATA)>
<!--
The user-data-constraint element is used to indicate how data
communicated between the client and container should be protected
-->
<!ELEMENT user-data-constraint (description?, transport-guarantee)>
<!--
The transport-guarantee element specifies that the communication
between client and server should be NONE, INTEGRAL, or
CONFIDENTIAL. NONE means that the application does not require any
transport guarantees. A value of INTEGRAL means that the application
requires that the data sent between the client and server be sent in
such a way that it can't be changed in transit. CONFIDENTIAL means
that the application requires that the data be transmitted in a
fashion that prevents other entities from observing the contents of
the transmission. In most cases, the presence of the INTEGRAL or
CONFIDENTIAL flag will indicate that the use of SSL is required.
-->
<!ELEMENT transport-guarantee (#PCDATA)>
<!--
The auth-constraint element indicates the user roles that should
be permitted access to this resource collection. The role used here
must appear in a security-role-ref element.
-->
<!ELEMENT auth-constraint (description?, role-name*)>
<!--
The role-name element contains the name of a security role.
-->
<!ELEMENT role-name (#PCDATA)>
<!--
The login-config element is used to configure the authentication
method that should be used, the realm name that should be used for
this application, and the attributes that are needed by the form login
mechanism.
-->
<!ELEMENT login-config (auth-method?, realm-name?, form-login-config?)>
<!--
The realm name element specifies the realm name to use in HTTP
Basic authorization
-->
<!ELEMENT realm-name (#PCDATA)>
```

LISTING 15.1 Continued

```
<!--
The form-login-config element specifies the login and error pages
that should be used in form based login. If form based authentication
is not used, these elements are ignored.
-->
<!ELEMENT form-login-config (form-login-page, form-error-page)>
<!--
The form-login-page element defines the location in the web app
where the page that can be used for login can be found
-->
<!ELEMENT form-login-page (#PCDATA)>
<!--
The form-error-page element defines the location in the web app
where the error page that is displayed when login is not successful
can be found
-->
<!ELEMENT form-error-page (#PCDATA)>
<!--
The auth-method element is used to configure the authentication
mechanism for the web application. As a prerequisite to gaining access
to any web resources that are protected by an authorization
constraint, a user must have authenticated using the configured
mechanism. Legal values for this element are "BASIC", "DIGEST",
"FORM", or "CLIENT-CERT".
-->
<!ELEMENT auth-method (#PCDATA)>
<!--
The security-role element contains the declaration of a security
Role, which is used in the security-constraints placed on the web
application.
-->
<!ELEMENT security-role (description?, role-name)>
<!--
The role-name element contains the name of a role. This element
must contain a non-empty string.
-->
<!ELEMENT security-role-ref (description?, role-name, role-link)>
<!--
The role-link element is used to link a security role reference
to a defined security role. The role-link element must contain the
name of one of the security roles defined in the security-role
elements.
-->
<!ELEMENT role-link (#PCDATA)>
```

LISTING 15.1   Continued

```
<!--
The env-entry element contains the declaration of an
application's environment entry. This element is required to be
honored on in J2EE compliant servlet containers.
-->
<!ELEMENT env-entry (description?, env-entry-name, env-entry-value?,
env-entry-type)>
<!--
The env-entry-name contains the name of an application's
environment entry
-->
<!ELEMENT env-entry-name (#PCDATA)>
<!--
The env-entry-value element contains the value of an
application's environment entry
-->
<!ELEMENT env-entry-value (#PCDATA)>
<!--
The env-entry-type element contains the fully qualified Java type
of the environment entry value that is expected by the application
code. The following are the legal values of env-entry-type:
java.lang.Boolean, java.lang.String, java.lang.Integer,
java.lang.Double, java.lang.Float.
-->
<!ELEMENT env-entry-type (#PCDATA)>
<!--
The ejb-ref element is used to declare a reference to an
enterprise bean.
-->
<!ELEMENT ejb-ref (description?, ejb-ref-name, ejb-ref-type, home,
remote,
ejb-link?)>
<!--
The ejb-ref-name element contains the name of an EJB
reference. This is the JNDI name that the servlet code uses to get a
reference to the enterprise bean.
-->
<!ELEMENT ejb-ref-name (#PCDATA)>
<!--
The ejb-ref-type element contains the expected java class type of
the referenced EJB.
-->
<!ELEMENT ejb-ref-type (#PCDATA)>
<!--
The ejb-home element contains the fully qualified name of the
EJB's home interface
```

LISTING 15.1   Continued

```
-->
<!ELEMENT home (#PCDATA)>
<!--
The ejb-remote element contains the fully qualified name of the
EJB's remote interface
-->
<!ELEMENT remote (#PCDATA)>
<!--
The ejb-link element is used in the ejb-ref element to specify
that an EJB reference is linked to an EJB in an encompassing Java2
Enterprise Edition (J2EE) application package. The value of the
ejb-link element must be the ejb-name of an EJB in the J2EE
application package.
-->
<!ELEMENT ejb-link (#PCDATA)>
<!--
The ID mechanism is to allow tools to easily make tool-specific
references to the elements of the deployment descriptor. This allows
tools that produce additional deployment information (information
beyond the standard deployment descriptor information) to store the
non-standard information in a separate file, and easily refer from
these tools-specific files to the information in the standard web-app
deployment descriptor.
-->
<!ATTLIST web-app id ID #IMPLIED>
<!ATTLIST icon id ID #IMPLIED>
<!ATTLIST small-icon id ID #IMPLIED>
<!ATTLIST large-icon id ID #IMPLIED>
<!ATTLIST display-name id ID #IMPLIED>
<!ATTLIST description id ID #IMPLIED>
<!ATTLIST distributable id ID #IMPLIED>
<!ATTLIST context-param id ID #IMPLIED>
<!ATTLIST param-name id ID #IMPLIED>
<!ATTLIST param-value id ID #IMPLIED>
<!ATTLIST servlet id ID #IMPLIED>
<!ATTLIST servlet-name id ID #IMPLIED>
<!ATTLIST servlet-class id ID #IMPLIED>
<!ATTLIST jsp-file id ID #IMPLIED>
<!ATTLIST init-param id ID #IMPLIED>
<!ATTLIST load-on-startup id ID #IMPLIED>
<!ATTLIST servlet-mapping id ID #IMPLIED>
<!ATTLIST url-pattern id ID #IMPLIED>
<!ATTLIST session-config id ID #IMPLIED>
<!ATTLIST session-timeout id ID #IMPLIED>
<!ATTLIST mime-mapping id ID #IMPLIED>
<!ATTLIST extension id ID #IMPLIED>
<!ATTLIST mime-type id ID #IMPLIED>
```

15

LISTING 15.1 Continued

```
<!ATTLIST welcome-file-list id ID #IMPLIED>
<!ATTLIST welcome-file id ID #IMPLIED>
<!ATTLIST taglib id ID #IMPLIED>
<!ATTLIST taglib-uri id ID #IMPLIED>
<!ATTLIST taglib-location id ID #IMPLIED>
<!ATTLIST error-page id ID #IMPLIED>
<!ATTLIST error-code id ID #IMPLIED>
<!ATTLIST exception-type id ID #IMPLIED>
<!ATTLIST location id ID #IMPLIED>
<!ATTLIST resource-ref id ID #IMPLIED>
<!ATTLIST res-ref-name id ID #IMPLIED>
<!ATTLIST res-type id ID #IMPLIED>
<!ATTLIST res-auth id ID #IMPLIED>
<!ATTLIST security-constraint id ID #IMPLIED>
<!ATTLIST web-resource-collection id ID #IMPLIED>
<!ATTLIST web-resource-name id ID #IMPLIED>
<!ATTLIST http-method id ID #IMPLIED>
<!ATTLIST user-data-constraint id ID #IMPLIED>
<!ATTLIST transport-guarantee id ID #IMPLIED>
<!ATTLIST auth-constraint id ID #IMPLIED>
<!ATTLIST role-name id ID #IMPLIED>
<!ATTLIST login-config id ID #IMPLIED>
<!ATTLIST realm-name id ID #IMPLIED>
<!ATTLIST form-login-config id ID #IMPLIED>
<!ATTLIST form-login-page id ID #IMPLIED>
<!ATTLIST form-error-page id ID #IMPLIED>
<!ATTLIST auth-method id ID #IMPLIED>
<!ATTLIST security-role id ID #IMPLIED>
<!ATTLIST security-role-ref id ID #IMPLIED>
<!ATTLIST role-link id ID #IMPLIED>
<!ATTLIST env-entry id ID #IMPLIED>
<!ATTLIST env-entry-name id ID #IMPLIED>
<!ATTLIST env-entry-value id ID #IMPLIED>
<!ATTLIST env-entry-type id ID #IMPLIED>
<!ATTLIST ejb-ref id ID #IMPLIED>
<!ATTLIST ejb-ref-name id ID #IMPLIED>
<!ATTLIST ejb-ref-type id ID #IMPLIED>
<!ATTLIST home id ID #IMPLIED>
<!ATTLIST remote id ID #IMPLIED>
<!ATTLIST ejb-link id ID #IMPLIED>
```

Servlet Examples

To give you a better feel for how servlets work, I'll show you a few basic examples. You can compile these examples and add them to the default Web application that is installed with your servlet container. If you do so, you won't have to edit the web.xml file.

Listing 15.2 shows the source code for the HelloWorldServlet. This servlet simply generates a Web page that displays the text *Hello World!* as shown in Figure 15.1.

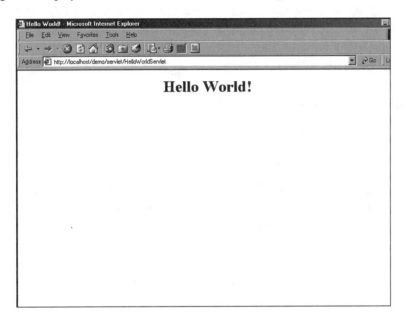

FIGURE 15.1

The output of the HelloWorldServlet.

LISTING 15.2   HelloWorldServlet.java

```java
import javax. servlet.*;
import javax.servlet.http.*;

import java.io.*;

public class HelloWorldServlet extends HttpServlet {
 public void doGet(HttpServletRequest req, HttpServletResponse resp)
   throws ServletException, java.io.IOException {
  resp.setContentType("text/html");
  PrintWriter out = resp.getWriter();
  out.println("<HTML><HEAD><TITLE>Hello World!</TITLE></HEAD>");
  out.println("<BODY><H1 ALIGN='CENTER'>Hello World!</BODY></HTML>");
 }
}
```

This simple servlet illustrates the basic structure of a servlet. The HelloWorldServlet class extends HttpServlet (which implements the Servlet interface). The doGet() method is overridden to handle HTTP GET requests. The servlet container invokes doGet() when it encounters a GET request for the servlet's URL. The servlet container supplies HttpServletRequest and HttpServletResponse objects as arguments to doGet(). (The doPut() method is overridden to handle PUT requests.)

The setContentType() method of the HttpServletResponse object is invoked to set the MIME type of the response to text/html. A PrintWriter object is obtained via the getWriter() method of the HttpServletResponse object. The PrintWriter object is used to write output to the requesting browser as part of the Web server's response.

Listing 15.3 provides a servlet example (DisplayRequestServlet) that illustrates the methods of the HttpServletRequest object. It returns detailed information about the request that was received. Figure 15.2 shows the output that it produces.

The DisplayRequestServlet class extends HttpServlet and overrides the doGet() method. The setContentType() method is used to set the MIME type of the response to text/html. A PrintWriter object is obtained via the getWriter() method of HttpServletResponse. The displayHead() method is used to generate the head of the output response. The openBody() method displays the opening body tag. The displayRequest() method displays detailed information about the HttpServletRequest object. The closeBody() method closes the BODY and HTML tags of the response output.

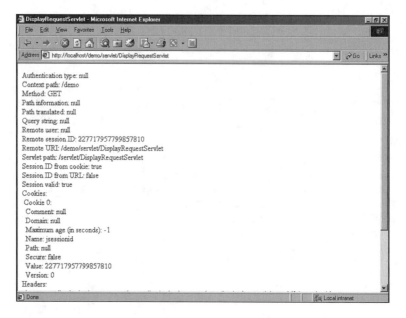

FIGURE 15.2

The output of the DisplayRequestServlet.

LISTING 15.3   The `DisplayRequestServlet` Servlet

```java
import javax.servlet.*;
import javax.servlet.http.*;

import java.io.*;
import java.util.*;

public class DisplayRequestServlet extends HttpServlet {
 public void doGet(HttpServletRequest req, HttpServletResponse resp)
   throws ServletException, java.io.IOException {
  resp.setContentType("text/html");
  PrintWriter out = resp.getWriter();
  displayHead(out,"DisplayRequestServlet");
  openBody(out);
  displayRequest(out,req);
  closeBody(out);
 }
 public void displayHead(PrintWriter out, String title) {
   out.println("<HTML><HEAD><TITLE>"+title+"</TITLE></HEAD>");
 }
 public void openBody(PrintWriter out) {
  out.println("<BODY>");
 }
 public void closeBody(PrintWriter out) {
  out.println("</BODY></HTML>");
 }
 public void displayRequest(PrintWriter out, HttpServletRequest req) {
  displayLine(out,"Authentication type: "+req.getAuthType());
  displayLine(out,"Context path: "+req.getContextPath());
  displayLine(out,"Method: "+req.getMethod());
  displayLine(out,"Path information: "+req.getPathInfo());
  displayLine(out,"Path translated: "+req.getPathTranslated());
  displayLine(out,"Query string: "+req.getQueryString());
  displayLine(out,"Remote user: "+req.getRemoteUser());
  displayLine(out,"Remote session ID: "+req.getRequestedSessionId());
  displayLine(out,"Remote URI: "+req.getRequestURI());
  displayLine(out,"Servlet path: "+req.getServletPath());
  String s = "Session ID from cookie: "+req.isRequestedSessionIdFromCookie();
  displayLine(out,s);
  displayLine(out,"Session ID from URL: "+req.isRequestedSessionIdFromURL());
  displayLine(out,"Session valid: "+req.isRequestedSessionIdValid());
  displayCookies(out,req);
  displayHeaders(out,req);
 }
 public void displayLine(PrintWriter out, String s) {
  out.println(s+"<BR>");
 }
```

LISTING 15.3   Continued

```java
public void displayCookies(PrintWriter out, HttpServletRequest req) {
 Cookie[] cookies = req.getCookies();
 if(cookies != null) {
  displayLine(out,"Cookies:");
  for(int i=0;i<cookies.length;++i) {
   displayLine(out," Cookie "+i+": ");
   displayLine(out,"  Comment: "+cookies[i].getComment());
   displayLine(out,"  Domain: "+cookies[i].getDomain());
   String s = "  Maximum age (in seconds): "+cookies[i].getMaxAge();
   displayLine(out,s);
   displayLine(out,"  Name: "+cookies[i].getName());
   displayLine(out,"  Path: "+cookies[i].getPath());
   displayLine(out,"  Secure: "+cookies[i].getSecure());
   displayLine(out,"  Value: "+cookies[i].getValue());
   displayLine(out,"  Version: "+cookies[i].getVersion());
  }
 }
}
public void displayHeaders(PrintWriter out, HttpServletRequest req) {
 Enumeration headerNames = req.getHeaderNames();
 if(headerNames != null) {
  displayLine(out,"Headers:");
  while(headerNames.hasMoreElements()) {
   String headerName = (String) headerNames.nextElement();
   displayLine(out," "+headerName+": "+req.getHeader(headerName));
  }
 }
}
}
```

Servlet Security

One of the most attractive capabilities of the Servlet 2.2 API specification is the security support that it requires from the servlet container. This support consists of flexible user authentication, role-based access controls, transmission security, and programmatic security. This support is covered in the following sections.

> **NOTE**
>
> The Servlet API 2.2 specification is available from Sun's Web site at http://www.javasoft.com/.

User Authentication

The Servlet 2.2 API specification requires the servlet container to authenticate users for Web applications. The res-auth element (refer to Listing 15.1) of the web.xml can be used to specify whether authentication is performed by the container (the default) or the servlet. Unless you've come up with your own high-security authentication mechanism, you're much better off using that of your servlet container.

Four different types of authentication are called for by the servlet spec:

- HTTP basic authentication —Supports basic client authentication as specified by the HTTP 1.1 specification. This consists of a user ID and reusable password. The password is base64-encoded, but transmitted in the clear. As such, it is subject to interception and should be used in conjunction with SSL or IPSec.

- HTTP digest authentication—In digest authentication, the password is hashed by the browser before it is sent to the server. This protects the password from being disclosed during transmission. Digest authentication is stronger than basic encryption, but it can be vulnerable to replay or cryptographic attacks.

- HTTPS client authentication—HTTPS client authentication uses SSL to authenticate the user. It requires the user to possess a compatible certificate. Only J2EE-compliant servlet containers are required to support HTTPS client authentication.

- Form-based authentication—Form-based authentication enables the Web application designer to present his own custom login form (and error page) to the user. User authentication is still performed by the servlet container. The user's name and password are transmitted in the clear as in HTTP basic authentication. For that reason, it is wise to use form-based authentication with SSL or IPSec.

The Web application designer selects an authentication method using the login-conf element of web.xml. The syntax of this element is defined in Listing 15.1 and summarized as follows:

```
<login-conf>
<auth-method>method_type</auth-method>
<realm-name>realm_string</realm-name>
<form-login-config>
<form-login-page>url<form-login-page>
<form-error-page>url<form-error-page>
</form-login-config>
</login-conf>
```

The auth-method element should be supplied. The realm-name and form-login-config elements are optional.

The allowed method types are BASIC, DIGEST, CLIENT-CERT, and FORM.

The realm name is a string that identifies the security realm in which the user is logging in. It is used with HTTP basic identification in the login prompt. You can supply any value that you like.

The `form-login-config` element should be used only with form-based login. It provides the URLs of the login form and error page. The error page is displayed if the user fails to log in with a valid username and password.

The login form must name the username and password fields as `j_username` and `j_password` and must have its `ACTION` attribute set to `j_security_check`.

> **NOTE**
>
> The usernames and passwords that are used to authenticate users are outside the scope of the Servlet 2.2 API. They are provided to the servlet container using the container-specific conventions.

Role-based Access Controls

After you've authenticated a user, the next step is authorization/access control; that is, you decide which resources the user should or should not have. The servlet specification supports role-based access controls, which are defined via the security-role element of `web.xml`. Role-based access controls map individual users and groups of users to roles. Access to resources is then limited to a specific set of roles.

The `security-role` element defines a Web application security role as follows:

```
<security-role>
<description>Description of the role.</description>
<role-name>name of the role</role-name>
</security-role>
```

The `description` element is optional.

Roles are mapped to application resources via the `security-constraint` element of `web.xml`. This element consists of a `web-resource-collection` element and optional `auth-constraint` and `user-data-constraint` elements:

```
<security-constraint>
<web-resource-collection> ... </web-resource-collection>
<auth-constraint> ... </auth-constraint>
<user-data-constraint> ... </user-data-constraint>
<security-constraint>
```

The `web-resource-collection` element identifies a collection of application resources to which the security constraint applies:

```
<web-resource-collection>
<web-resource-name>The name of the resource.</web-resource-name>
<description>A description of the resource.</description>
<url-pattern>A partial URL with optional wildcard characters</url-pattern>
<http-method>A valid HTTP method, such as GET or PUT</http-method>
</web-resource-collection>
```

The Web resources requiring authentication are identified by zero or more URL patterns and HTTP methods. The URL patterns are of the form

```
/applicationpath/file name
/applicationpath/*
```

The first requires authenticated access to a particular file. The second requires authenticated access to all files in `/applicationpath`. To authenticate all resources of an application, use `*` as the URL pattern.

The HTTP methods specify the methods requiring authentication (for example, `GET` and `POST`). If these are omitted, all methods will be authenticated.

The `auth-constraint` element identifies the roles that are allowed to access the resource. Its syntax is as follows:

```
<auth-constraint>
<description>A text description of the constraint.<description>
<role-name>security role</role-name>
</auth-constraint>
```

Zero or more role-name elements may be supplied. If no role names are identified, no one is allowed to access the resource.

Transmission Security

The `user-data-constraint` element is optional. It is used to require confidential or high integrity communication with the user's browser. The servlet container typically satisfies this requirement through the use of SSL. The syntax of the `user-data-constraint` element follows:

```
<user-data-constraint>
<description>A description of the requirement.</description>
<transport-guarantee>NONE, INTEGRAL, or CONFIDENTIAL</transport-guarantee>
</user-data-constraint>
```

`INTEGRAL` and `CONFIDENTIAL` imply the use of SSL.

15

Adding Security to the Sample Servlets

It's easy to add user authentication and role-based access controls to the `HelloWorldServlet` and `DisplayRequestServlet` using the security features of the Servlet 2.2 specification. Add HTTP basic authentication and control access to these servlets based on security role. Listing 15.4 shows the `web.xml` file that you'll use to do this.

The `web.xml` configures basic authentication using the `login-config` element:

```
<login-config>
  <auth-method>BASIC</auth-method>
  <realm-name>Security test realm</realm-name>
</login-config>
```

It defines the user and superuser security roles using the `security-role` element:

```
<security-role>
  <role-name>user</role-name>
</security-role>
<security-role>
  <role-name>superuser</role-name>
</security-role>
```

It limits access to the `DisplayRequestServlet` to users who are authenticated in the superuser role. This is accomplished via the following `security-constraint` element.

```
<security-constraint>
  <web-resource-collection>
   <web-resource-name>DisplayRequestServlet</web-resource-name>
   <url-pattern>/myapp/servlet/DisplayRequestServlet</url-pattern>
  </web-resource-collection>
  <auth-constraint>
   <role-name>superuser</role-name>
  </auth-constraint>
</security-constraint>
```

Another `security-constraint` element is used to limit access to the `HelloWorldServlet` to those who authenticate with the user role:

```
<security-constraint>
  <web-resource-collection>
   <web-resource-name>HelloWorldServlet</web-resource-name>
   <url-pattern>/myapp/servlet/HelloWorldServlet</url-pattern>
  </web-resource-collection>
  <auth-constraint>
   <role-name>user</role-name>
  </auth-constraint>
</security-constraint>
```

When a user browses a servlet's URL, he or she is confronted with the login prompt shown in Figure 15.3. The user enters his username and password. If the user fails to authenticate, the page shown in Figure 15.4 is displayed. If the user authenticates, the servlet is requested on behalf of the user.

FIGURE 15.3

The login prompt.

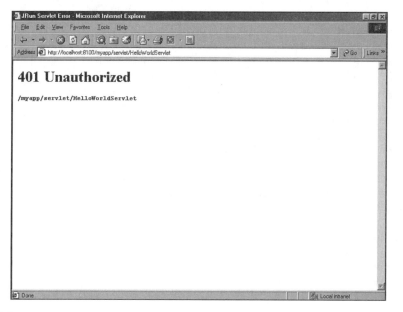

FIGURE 15.4

A failed login.

LISTING 15.4   Adding Security Via `web.xml`

```
<!DOCTYPE web-app PUBLIC "-//Sun Microsystems, Inc.// DTD Web Application
➥1.2//EN"
"http://java.sun.com/j2ee/dtds/web-app_2_2.dtd">
<web-app>
 <display-name>My Secure Application</display-name>
 <description>Example of an application that uses authentication</description>
 <session-config>
  <session-timeout>20</session-timeout>
 </session-config>
 <mime-mapping>
  <extension>html</extension>
  <mime-type>text/html</mime-type>
 </mime-mapping>
 <security-constraint>
  <web-resource-collection>
   <web-resource-name>DisplayRequestServlet</web-resource-name>
   <url-pattern>/myapp/servlet/DisplayRequestServlet</url-pattern>
  </web-resource-collection>
  <auth-constraint>
   <role-name>superuser</role-name>
  </auth-constraint>
 </security-constraint>
 <security-constraint>
  <web-resource-collection>
   <web-resource-name>HelloWorldServlet</web-resource-name>
   <url-pattern>/myapp/servlet/HelloWorldServlet</url-pattern>
  </web-resource-collection>
  <auth-constraint>
   <role-name>user</role-name>
  </auth-constraint>
 </security-constraint>
 <login-config>
  <auth-method>BASIC</auth-method>
  <realm-name>Security test realm</realm-name>
 </login-config>
 <security-role>
  <role-name>user</role-name>
 </security-role>
 <security-role>
  <role-name>superuser</role-name>
 </security-role>
</web-app>
```

Container Security Requirements

In the previous example, users were authenticated by the servlet container as belonging to a particular security role. In order to accomplish this, the servlet container must maintain a list of usernames and passwords (hopefully hashed or encrypted) and the security roles to which these users have been assigned. Typically, users are organized into groups, and groups are assigned to security roles. The specific implementation of the mechanism used to track users, their passwords, groups, and security roles is left to the servlet container.

Programmatic Security

The previous servlet security example used the `web.xml` file to configure the application's security external to the applet being protected. It is also possible to implement security access controls internal to the servlet (although this is not recommended). The `getRemoteUser()`, `getUserPrincipal()`, and `isUserInRole()` methods of `HttpServletRequest` provide information about the user, the `Principal` object associated with the user, and the security role associated with the user. The servlet can use this information to make internal access control decisions.

In some cases, a servlet that implements internal access controls might use role names that differ from those used in the application's `web.xml` file. For example, the servlet could have been purchased from a servlet vendor. The `security-role-ref` element of the `web.xml` file can be used to map a Web application's security role to one that is used internal to a servlet. Its definition follows:

```
<!ELEMENT security-role-ref (description?, role-name, role-link)>
<!ELEMENT role-link (#PCDATA)>
```

The `role-name` element refers to the servlet's internal name and the `role-link` element refers to the Web application's role name.

JavaServer Pages

JavaServer Pages are a server-side scripting technique supported through servlets. JSP pages are written using a combination of HTML, JSP tags, and embedded code. These elements are compiled into servlets and supporting classes and executed within the context of a servlet container. JSP pages are deployed in the same manner as servlets and use the security mechanisms that are configured via the `web.xml` file.

Summary

In this chapter, you covered security issues commonly faced by Web application developers. You learned how the Common Gateway Interface works and about the session state maintenance problems associated with the hypertext transport protocol. You also learned about common Web application vulnerabilities. You learned how Java servlets work and how security is added to servlet-based Web applications. Finally, you were introduced to JSP and learned about the relationship between JSP and servlet security.

15

Appendixes

PART

IV

IN THIS PART

Past Java Security Flaws

This appendix summarizes the Java security flaws that have been discovered as of April 2000. These flaws are arranged in chronological order. Sun maintains a chronology of Java security bugs at `http://java.sun.com/sfaq/ chronology.html`. This appendix is based on Sun's chronology, but it provides additional information not found at the Sun site. The dates listed are the dates that the bugs were corrected.

JavaScript (February, 1996)

The earliest item (chronologically) in Sun's list is a commentary on JavaScript and Java. This commentary dates back to Navigator 2, which does not support Netscape's LiveConnect technology. LiveConnect is used by Navigator 3.0, Internet Explorer 4.0, and to support communication between JavaScript and Java. Sun's comment is that JavaScript cannot be used to invoke Java applets. This is no longer true for LiveConnect-enabled browsers. Under certain conditions, JavaScript scripts can invoke the public methods of Java applets.

DNS Attack (February, 1996)

This attack, discovered by Drew Dean, Ed Felten, and Dan Wallach from Princeton and independently by Steve Gibbons, is covered by CERT Advisory CA-96.05. It concerns Navigator 2.0 and JDK 1.0 and involves the use of bogus DNS information. The attack is summarized as follows:

1. A user browses an attacker's Web site (`www.attacker.org`) using Navigator 2.0.

2. The user's browser loads and runs an applet from the attacker's Web site.

3. The applet tries to open up a connection to a host in the attacker's domain. The applet queries the attacker's DNS for the IP address of the host. The attacker's DNS returns a pair of IP addresses. The first address is to a host (let's call it unauthorized.com) with which the applet is NOT permitted to connect. The second address is the address of the Web server (`www.attacker.org`) from which the applet was loaded. The applet security manager matches the second address (any matching address in the list is sufficient) with the address of the server from which the applet was loaded and allows the connection.

4. When the connection is established, the first IP address is used. As a result, a connection is established from the applet to unauthorized.com, a violation of the applet security policy.

The vulnerability lies in the fact that the applet security manager checks all addresses in the list and gives the go-ahead if one address is that of the server from which the applet is loaded. This vulnerability is combined with bogus DNS information from the attacker's domain. The effect is that the attacker can use the applet to establish connections with other Internet hosts. In particular, the applet can be used to circumvent firewall security measures and probe hosts that are on the same side of the firewall as the user.

The fix to this problem was incorporated into Navigator 2.01 and JDK 1.01. The fix restricts applets to opening connections to the IP address of the servers from which they are loaded.

The risk associated with this vulnerability is eliminated in Navigator 2.01 and later. Internet Explorer does not have this vulnerability.

Class Loader Implementation Bug (March, 1996)

David Hopwood of Oxford University discovered a flaw in the class loader that allows an attacker to load an untrusted class file and have it masquerade as trusted code. The flaw applies to Navigator 2.01 and JDK 1.01, which allow a fully-qualified class name to begin with a backslash. It is exploited as follows:

1. A user browses an attacker's Web site (www.attacker.org) using Navigator 2.0.1.

2. The user's browser loads and runs an applet from the attacker's Web site.

3. The applet loads a file into the browser's cache.

4. The applet references the file in the browser's cache as a class file.

5. The browser loads the class(es) from the file and treats it (them) as trusted. This releases the classes from the restrictions of the applet security policy.

Navigator and Internet Explorer treat classes that are loaded from the user's hard disk as trusted. However, class-naming conventions (the use of relative path names) are used to prevent applets from loading files outside a restricted directory path. These naming conventions prevent the use of a period, slash, or backslash as the first character of a fully qualified class name. However, Hopwood discovered that Navigator 2.01 allows the use of a backslash character as the first character of the fully qualified class name. This gives applets the capability to reference files in the browser's cache.

The fix to this problem is incorporated into Navigator 2.02 and JDK 1.02. The fix removes the bug that allows fully qualified class names to identify an absolute path.

The risk associated with this vulnerability is eliminated in Navigator 2.02 and later. Internet Explorer does not have this vulnerability.

Verifier Implementation Bug (March, 1996)

The Princeton Java security team found a flaw in the bytecode verifier that allows an applet to create an instance of a subclass of java.lang.ClassLoader. This capability enables applets to load classes and report them as being of different class types. This can enable an untrusted class to be loaded as a trusted class.

The vulnerability is that an instance of a ClassLoader subclass can be constructed. This vulnerability appears in Navigator 2.01 and JDK 1.01. The fix to this vulnerability allows ClassLoader instances to be created, but it adds an initialized property that can only be set by a trusted ClassLoader. Unless the initialized property is set to true, the ClassLoader object is prevented from loading other classes. The fix went into effect in JDK 1.0.2 and in Netscape Navigator 2.02. (This countermeasure was circumvented in the May 18, 1996 attack.) Navigator 2.02 remains vulnerable to class loader attacks.

URL Name Resolution Attack (April, 1996)

A software engineer from Sprint reported an attack in which an applet that is loaded from within a firewall is able to connect to another (unauthorized) host that is also behind the firewall. The attack requires that the firewall-internal network use the same domain name as the attacker's network. This is a far-fetched scenario, and the best solution is to not use someone else's domain name. The vulnerability occurs in Navigator 2.01 and JDK 1.01. It is fixed in Navigator 2.02 and JDK 1.02.

Hostile Applets (April, 1996)

A number of hostile applets were identified in April, 1996. These applets tie up browser resources in denial of service attacks. Some applets try to con users into revealing their user IDs and passwords. Others try to cause browsers to run out of resources and lock up. The applet security policy does not contain safeguards against such attacks. Users are still vulnerable to denial of service attacks when they execute Java applets.

Classloader Attack Variant (May 18, 1996)

Tom Cargill, a Java software consultant, discovered a flaw in the way `private` methods are protected. Under Navigator 2.02, if a class A implements an interface and a `private` method of the class implements a non-`private`, non-`protected` method of the interface, a subclass B of class A is able to invoke the `private` method (under certain conditions). This flaw was used to circumvent the fix for the March 1996 verifier bug, which used a `private` method to set the value of the `initialized` property.

Netscape fixed the vulnerability by revising the implementation of the `ClassLoader` class in its JVM and by removing the flaw that circumvents the `private` method protection mechanisms. This change took effect in Navigator 3.0 beta 3. Navigator 2.02 is still vulnerable to this attack.

Illegal Type Cast Attack (June 2, 1996)

David Hopwood, a Java researcher, discovered a flaw that allows applets to create two classes of the same name with objects of one class being referenced as if they belonged to the other class. The flaw is that under JDK 1.02, Navigator 2.02, and Internet Explorer 4.0 beta 1, classes are compared by name without consideration of the name space to which they belong. This allows an applet A to create a class C, and an applet B to create a different class C. Applet A is then able to create an instance of class C and pass it to applet B. Applet B is then able to access the object as if it belonged to its local class C. By doing so, B is able to use the object in a way that circumvents the applet security policy.

The flaw was fixed in Navigator 3.0, Internet Explorer 4.0, and JDK 1.1. Navigator 2.02 and JDK 1.02 remain vulnerable.

Inconsistency in `javakey` (December 13, 1996)

The first beta of JDK 1.1 contained an implementation of `javakey` that incorrectly signed JAR files. This caused the JAR files to run as untrusted. This was not a security vulnerability—just a security-related bug. It was fixed in JDK 1.1 beta 2.

Web Spoofing (December, 1996)

The Princeton team identified an obvious attack, known as Web spoofing, in which an attacker interposes his Web site between a user and a legitimate Web site. The attacker makes a duplicate of the legitimate Web site's pages and intercepts all user communication between the user and the legitimate Web site. By doing so, the attacker is able to access any sensitive data that the user sends to the legitimate Web site.

This attack has nothing to do with Java security. It exploits a general vulnerability of the Web.

Java Versus ActiveX (February 25, 1997)

Sun seized upon a series of attacks on ActiveX to highlight the strengths of Java versus ActiveX. The information contained in this bug report is factual, but is of a marketing nature.

Virtual Machine Bug (March 5, 1997)

Sun discovered this flaw on March 5, 1999 in the JVM. It describes the flaw as complex and difficult to exploit. The bug allows malicious byte code to be slipped by the Java byte code verifier. The details of the bug are not released to the public. The JDK 1.02 was updated to include the bug fix.

Disclosure of IP Addresses (March 17, 1997)

Ben Laurie and Major Malfunction (a pen name) discovered a flaw in Navigator 3.x and 4.0 that allows an applet to find the IP address of the client machine. This is not a significant vulnerability because browsers typically disclose this address when they connect to a Web server. It is only a problem when the client is behind a firewall, and the client's address is hidden by a firewall proxy.

The problem is that the `getLocalHost()` method of the applet class returns the local IP address. Netscape (and Sun) fixed the problem by having this method return the localhost (127.0.0.1) address. This problem does not occur in Internet Explorer.

At the same time, Laurie and Malfunction reported a more serious flaw in Internet Explorer (http://www.alcrypto.co.uk/java/) that is not addressed in Sun's security bug chronology. This flaw allows an applet to perform TCP port scans of firewall-protected hosts. It is accomplished by loading the scanning code from a file that is in the browser's cache. The flaw occurred in Internet Explorer 3.0 and 3.01 and was fixed by Microsoft in Internet Explorer 3.02.

Signing Flaw (April 29, 1997)

The Princeton Java security team found a flaw in the Java code-signing scheme. The flaw was manifested in JDK 1.1 and the HotJava browser. (Navigator and Internet Explorer have a different implementation of code signing.) The flaw allowed a signed applet to change its list of signers to gain more privileges. The getSigners() method of the java.lang.Class class returns an array of signers that can be modified by an applet. A malicious (but signed) applet can add a trusted principal to its list of signers in order to acquire the privileges of the trusted principal. The flaw was fixed in JDK 1.1.2 and a subsequent release of HotJava.

Verifier Bugs (May 16, 1997)

The Kimera Project at the University of Washington developed a code verifier known as the Kimera Verifier. The verifier was tested by running it against the verifiers of JDK 1.1, JDK 1.02, Internet Explorer 4.0, and Internet Explorer 3.02. The verifier (initially) found 24 flaws in the Sun verifiers and 17 flaws in the Microsoft verifiers. The most lethal flaw in the Sun verifiers also existed in Navigator 3.01 Gold. This flaw allowed numbers to be converted to object references (*pointers* in the C vernacular). The flaw was exploited to cause complete takeover of the browser.

Ten of the Internet Explorer flaws coincided with flaws in the Sun verifiers. In particular, the number to object reference conversion flaw was also found to exist in Internet Explorer.

Sun, Netscape, and Microsoft havereleased patches for the most serious security flaws.

Another Verifier Bug (June 23, 1997)

The Kimera Verifier identified another verifier flaw in June, 1997 that resulted in type mismatches. The flaw was identified in JDK 1.1.1, 1.1.2, and HotJava. The Kimera team showed how the flaw could be exploited by an applet to disclose sensitive information. The flaw was fixed in JDK 1.1.3.

RSA PKCS1 Risk in SSL (June 26, 1998)

Sun refers to a flaw in SSL Web servers that was identified by RSA Data Security, Inc. The flaw applies to all Web servers that use SSL, including the Java Web Server. However, it has nothing to do with Java.

Princeton Classloader Attack (July 22, 1998)

The Princeton Classloader Attack is a famous Java security exploitation developed by the Princeton Java security team. This attack, as you might guess from its name, involves the misuse of Java class loaders. The flaw existed in all Java implementations of the time, but it was only exploitable in Navigator 4.0x versions.

Navigator allows applets to create instances of subclasses of the `AppletClassLoader` class. In addition, Sun, Microsoft, and Netscape Java implementations allow class loaders to overwrite the definitions of built-in classes. If these two flaws are combined under Navigator 4.0x, it is possible to create a malicious subclass of `AppletClassLoader` that overwrites built-in classes. This provides the attacker with complete control over the JVM and browser.

Navigator 4.5 corrected the vulnerability.

Execution of Unverified Code (March 26, 1999)

Karsten Sohr of the University of Marburg in Germany discovered a flaw that allows applets to execute unverified code. The bug affects JDK 1.1, JDK 1.2, Navigator 4.x, and Internet Explorer 4.x and 5. The details of the bug have not been made public. Fixes to the bug were distributed by Sun, Netscape, and Microsoft.

Construction of Unverified Classes (April 14, 1999)

Paul Haahr of Jive Technologies discovered a bug that allows unverified classes to be constructed. This bug affects JDK 1.1 through JDK 1.1.7 and was corrected in JDK 1.1.8.

Locally Installed Applet Classes (February 2, 2000)

This item is a plug for the security capabilities of the Java 2 platform instead of a description of a security flaw. Under JDK 1.1.x, Java classes that are locally installed are fully trusted. Any flaws in these classes are subject to exploitation by applets. There is a tradeoff between performance (loading local classes is much faster) and security (local classes may have too much trust). This issue is resolved in JDK 1.2, which allows locally installed classes to be subject to Java security policy.

Under JDK 1.2, JAR files can be placed in the Java Plug-in's lib/applet/ directory. They can be quickly loaded but still be restricted by the applet security policy.

The Mathematics of RSA

This appendix covers the mathematics used in the Rivest, Shamir, Adelman (RSA) public-key encryption algorithm and provides algorithms for setting up an RSA system, performing encryption and decryption, and computing/verifying signatures.

The Math Behind RSA

In an RSA cryptosystem, two prime numbers, p and q, are generated whose product is n. The encryption key (that is, the public key), e, is a number that is relatively prime to $(p-1)(q-1)$. The decryption key (private key), d, is calculated so that ed mod $((p-1)(q-1))$ is 1. The values of p and q are critical to the security of RSA and should be securely discarded after an RSA system is set up.

At this point, you might have a few questions relative to prime numbers, relatively prime numbers, and the computation of d from n:

- How many prime numbers are there?
- How can I tell whether a number is prime?
- How can I generate a large prime number?
- Is it always possible to find an e that is relatively prime to $(p-1)(q-1)$?
- How does one find e?

- Is it always possible to find d, such that ed mod $((p-1)(q-1))$ is 1?
- How does one find d?
- How difficult is it for someone to compute d, knowing only e and n?

I'll answer each of these questions in the following sections.

The Prime Numbers Are Infinite

It is easy to show that there are an infinite number of prime numbers. Suppose that there were a finite number of prime numbers, with the largest being n. Then the number $n!+1 = 1 \times 2 \times 3 \times ... \times n + 1$ would not be divisible by 2 through n, and would, therefore, be prime. This contradicts the assumption that n is the largest prime number.

Primality Testing

For small numbers (32 bits or less), the easiest way to tell if a number is prime is to try and factor it. If the number does not have any factors other than one and itself, it is, by definition, prime. Typically, primality tests are used for larger numbers. These tests determine the probability that a number is prime. One popular test is described in Federal Information Processing Standard 186-1 and is implemented as the isProbablePrime() method of the java.math.BigInteger class. This method takes a certainty value as an argument and returns true if the likelihood of a BigInteger being a prime number is greater than $1-2^{-n}$, where n is the certainty value. A value of n equal to 10 produces a prime number with likelihood 99.9%. A value of n equal to 20 produces a prime number with likelihood 99.9999%.

The PrimeTest program of Listing B.1 shows how to use the isProbablePrime() method of BigInteger to test a BigInteger for primality. The program takes two arguments: the value of the certainty value (a positive integer value) and the number to be tested. It then displays a message that identifies whether or not the number is probably prime with respect to the certainty value. For example, executing

```
java com.jaworski.security.handbook.PrimeTest 50 1234567890133
```

produces the following output:

```
1234567890133 IS probably prime with certainty 50.
```

LISTING B.1   The Primetest Program

```
package com.jaworski.security.handbook
import java.math.BigInteger;

public class PrimeTest {
  public static void main(String[] args) {
```

The Mathematics of RSA

APPENDIX B

433

B

THE
MATHEMATICS OF
RSA

LISTING B.1   Continued

```java
  if(args.length != 2) {
    String err = "Usage: java ";
    err += "com.jaworski.security.handbook.PrimeTest ";
    err += "certainty numberToBeTested";
    System.out.println(err);
    System.exit(0);
  }
  int arg = 0;
  try {
    int c = (new Integer(args[0])).intValue();
    ++arg;
    BigInteger n = new BigInteger(args[1]);
    boolean result = n.isProbablePrime(c);
    String resultString = ""+args[1]+" IS ";
    if(!result) resultString += "NOT ";
    resultString += "probably prime with certainty "+c+".";
    System.out.println(resultString);
  }catch(NumberFormatException e) {
    String err = "Error: arg["+arg+"] is invalid.";
    System.out.println (err);
  }
 }
}
```

Prime Number Generation

There are a number of different ways to generate prime numbers. However, the trial and error method is usually sufficient. In this approach, you generate a random sequence of digits of the desired number size. If the last digit is even, add 1. Then you test for primality, plugging the desired certainty level into the test. If the test is positive, you've found your number. Otherwise, add 2 to the number and retest. Repeat this process until you find a number that passes the primality test.

Fortunately, you don't have to go through the trouble of implementing a prime number generation algorithm, because one is provided with the BigInteger class. One of the BigInteger constructors takes three arguments, an int bit length argument, an int certainty argument, and a java.util.Random random number generator argument. You can construct a 100-bit prime number with a certainty of 50 as follows:

```java
Random rnd = new Random();
BigInteger n = new BigInteger(100, 50, rnd);
```

However, if you are planning on using the prime number for cryptography (as in RSA), you should generate the prime number using a secure random number generator. Secure prime number generation consists of generating random numbers in a way that is difficult to repeat. The java.security.SecureRandom class is a subclass of java.util.Random that implements a cryptographically strong pseudo-random number generator. It uses a secure random number generation algorithm that is provided by the highest priority security provider. Listing B.2 provides an example of its use.

The program takes two arguments, the bit length and certainty values, and produces a prime number of the required length with the specified certainty. For example, the following generates a 100-bit prime number with a certainty of 50:

```
java com.jaworski.security.handbook.PrimeGeneration 100 50
1197225550526631298316060432467
```

LISTING B.2 The PrimeGeneration Program

```
package com.jaworski.security.handbook

import java.math.BigInteger;
import java.security.SecureRandom;

public class PrimeGeneration {
 public static void main(String[] args) {
  if(args.length != 2) {
   String err = "Usage: java ";
   err += "com.jaworski.security.handbook.PrimeGeneration ";
   err += "bitLength certainty";
   System.out.println(err);
   System.exit(0);
  }
  int arg = 0;
  try {
   int bitLength = (new Integer(args[0])).intValue();
   ++arg;
   int certainty = (new Integer(args[1])).intValue();
   SecureRandom rnd = new SecureRandom();
   BigInteger n = new BigInteger(bitLength,certainty,rnd);
   System.out.println(n);
  }catch(NumberFormatException e) {
   String err = "Error: arg["+arg+"] is invalid.";
   System.out.println(err);
  }
 }
}
```

The Mathematics of RSA

APPENDIX B

435

B

THE
MATHEMATICS OF
RSA

Finding an Encryption Key

The RSA encryption key, e, is a positive integer that is relatively prime to $(p-1)(q-1)$. Given primes p and q, is it always possible to find such an e? The answer is yes when $(p-1)(q-1)$ is greater than 2. However, it involves some math, which I'll summarize in the following subsections.

Reduced Set of Residues

For a given number n, the reduced set of residues mod n is the subset of $\{0, 1, 2, \ldots, n-1\}$ (consisting of those numbers that are relatively prime to n). For example, the reduced set of residues mod 5 is $\{1, 2, 3, 4\}$, the reduced set of residues mod 6 is $\{1, 5\}$, and the reduced set of residues mod 10 is $\{1, 3, 7, 9\}$. When n is a prime number the reduced set of residues mod n is $\{1, 2, \ldots, n-1\}$.

> **NOTE**
>
> ### Reduced Set of Residues
> The number 0 is never included in the reduced set of residues.

The Euler totient function or Euler phi function is defined as the number of numbers in the reduced set of residues mod n. Table B.1 lists the values of totient(n) for n between 2 and 10.

TABLE B.1   Values of the Euler Totient Function

n	totient(n)
2	1
3	2
4	2
5	4
6	2
7	6
8	4
9	6
10	4

For any *n* that is greater than 2, *n* is either of the form 2^k (where *k* is greater than 1) or has a prime factor $p > 2$. In the first case, totient(*n*) is 2^k-1, which is 2 or greater. In the second case, totient(*n*) is greater than or equal to $(p-1)$, which is also 2 or greater. Because totient(*n*) is 2 or greater, the reduced set of residues always contains another number besides 1. Hence, there will always be an *e*, such that *e* is relatively prime to $(p-1)(q-1)$ when $(p-1)(q-1)$ is greater than 2.

How do you go about finding *e*? This turns out to be fairly straightforward. Two numbers are relatively prime if their greatest common divisor is 1. The `BigInteger` class provides the `gcd()` method to calculate the greatest common divisor of two `BigInteger` objects.

To find a number that is relatively prime to *n*, I recommend that you generate a secure random number between 1 and *n* and test whether their greatest common denominator is 1. If not, try again. There are approaches that will find *e* more quickly. However, they tend to be more predictable—the last thing that you want when generating an encryption key. Listing B.3 provides a program for finding a number that is relatively prime to another number *n* using this approach. The argument to the program is *n*. The program produces a number greater than 1 that is relatively prime to *n*. For example, the following generates a number that is relatively prime to 1234567890:

```
java com.jaworski.security.handbook.FindRelativelyPrime 1234567890
Trying 245294505 ...
Trying 289784754 ...
Trying 846132246 ...
Trying 977301996 ...
Trying 407939981 ...
```

407939981 is relatively prime to 1234567890.

LISTING B.3   The `FindRelativelyPrime` Program

```
package com.jaworski.security.handbook
import java.math.BigInteger;
import java.security.SecureRandom;

public class FindRelativelyPrime {
  public static void main(String[] args) {
   if(args.length != 1) {
    String err = "Usage: java ";
    err += "com.jaworski.security.handbook.FindRelativelyPrime ";
    err += "number";
    System.out.println(err);
    System.exit(0);
   }
```

LISTING B.3 Continued

```
try {
  BigInteger n = new BigInteger(args[0]);
  int len = n.bitLength();
  SecureRandom rnd = new SecureRandom();
  BigInteger one = new BigInteger("1");
  BigInteger i;
  do {
   i = new BigInteger(len,rnd);
   i = i.mod(n);
   System.out.println("Trying "+i+" ...");
  } while(!n.gcd(i).equals(one));
  System.out.println(""+i+" is relatively prime to "+n+".");
 }catch(NumberFormatException e) {
  String err = "Error: arg[0] is invalid.";
  System.out. println(err);
 }
 }
}
```

Calculating *d* from *e*, *p*, and *q*

Given *e*, relatively prime to $(p-1)(q-1)$, it is always possible to find *d*, such that *ed* mod $((p-1)(q-1))$ is 1. This results from the fact that *ek* is relatively prime to $(p-1)(q-1)$ for all $k > 0$. Because the set $\{0, 1, 2, ..., (p-1)(q-1)-1\}$ is finite, for some *i* and $j > 0$, with $i > j$, *ei* mod $(p-1)(q-1) = ej$ mod$(p-1)(q-1)$. From this, we find that $ei-j$ mod $(p-1)(q-1) = 1$. This leads to *e* $ei-j-1$ mod $(p-1)(q-1) = 1$ or $d = ei-j-1$. The value $i-j$ turns out to be totient$((p-1)(q-1))$.

The BigInteger class provides the modInverse() method for calculating *d* from *e* and $(p-1)(q-1)$. For example, if $m = (p-1)(q-1)$, then e.modInverse(m) yields *d*.

Listing B.4 shows the FindInverse program, which takes *e* and *k* as parameters. For example:

```
java com.jaworski.security.handbook.FindInverse 407939981  1234567890
```

produces the value 20024381. You can check this by calculating 407939981×20024381 mod 1234567890, which is 1.

LISTING B.4 The FindInverse Program

```
package com.jaworski.security.handbook
import java.math.BigInteger;

public class FindInverse {
 public static void main (String[] args) {
```

LISTING B.4   Continued

```
if(args.length != 2) {
  String err = "Usage: java ";
  err += "com.jaworski.security.handbook.FindInverse ";
  err += "e modulous";
  System.out.println(err);
  System.exit(0);
}
int arg = 0;
try {
  BigInteger e = new BigInteger(args[0]);
  ++arg;
  BigInteger m = new BigInteger(args[1]);
  BigInteger d = e.modInverse(m);
  System.out.println(d);
}catch(NumberFormatException ex) {
  String err = "Error: arg["+arg+"] is invalid.";
  System.out.println (err);
}
}
}
```

Calculating *d*, Knowing Only *e* and *n*

The strength of RSA lies in the difficulty of factoring *n* into *p* and *q*. If *p* and *q* are known, then *d* can be readily calculated, as demonstrated in the previous section. How difficult is it to factor a large number? The answer is that it is currently difficult because mathematicians do not currently have a factoring approach that is much better than controlled trial and error. This means that factoring an *n*-bit number is usually as difficult as picking values from a set of $2n–2$ values. I add the qualifier *usually*, because *n* can simply be a one-digit prime times some large prime number, or the analyst might simply guess one of the factors in a few tries.

The good news about RSA is that it has been around for 25 years and has successfully held up to public cryptanalysis.

Cryptix and RSA

The remaining sections of this appendix provide algorithms for performing encryption and signing using the BigInteger class. These algorithms illustrate the basic principles of RSA. If you want to implement RSA cryptography using Java, don't use these algorithms. Instead, install the Cryptix 3.1 or later JCE software, which provides direct support for RSA. Appendix E, "Downloading and Installing the Cryptix JCE 1.2," shows how to download and install the Cryptix software.

Encryption and Decryption

RSA encryption involves converting plaintext to an integer modulo n and then raising the integer to the power of the encryption key modulo n. For example, if m represents the value of the plaintext, then $c = me$ mod n is the ciphertext corresponding to m, e, and n.

Decryption is accomplished by raising c to the value of d mod n. That is, $m = cd$ mod n.

In this section, we'll provide a program, RSAEncrypt, that shows how RSA encryption can be implemented using the `BigInteger` class. However, before we get to RSAEncrypt, we'll tie together everything that we've covered so far and introduce the RSASetup program (Listing B.5), which generates private and public key values and the modulus n.

The RSASetup program generates n, e, and d. You can run it as follows:

```
java com.jaworski.security.handbook.RSASetup
p is 794985534913
q is 585775438511
n is 465683000323564475234543
e is 117391087578288537201631
d is 406866821874449771625631
```

These values are generated using the `SecureRandom` class. When you run the program, it will generate a different set of values. It also displays the values of p and q for informational purposes. Only n, e, and d are needed for an RSA cryptosystem.

The RSAEncrypt program of Listing B.6 can be used to perform RSA encryption and decryption on numeric values. It takes the values of n, e, and the number to be encrypted as its arguments. It then encrypts the number and displays the resulting ciphertext. For example, the following encrypts 1234567890:

```
java com.jaworski.security.handbook.RSAEncrypt
→465683000323564475234543 117391087578288537201631 1234567890
```

and displays the following ciphertext:

```
201021538530068786561204
```

You can also use RSAEncrypt to decrypt ciphertext into plaintext. Just substitute d for e and the ciphertext for the plaintext. For example, the following:

```
java com.jaworski.security.handbook.RSAEncrypt
→465683000323564475234543 406866821874449771625631 201021538530068786561204
```

decrypts 201021538530068786561204 to produce the original 1234567890.

Use RSASetup to generate n, e, and d.

LISTING B.5 The RSASetup Program

```
package com.jaworski.security.handbook
import java.math.BigInteger;
import java.security.SecureRandom;

public class RSASetup {
 public static void main(String[] args) {
  int bitLength = 40;
  int certainty = 50;
  SecureRandom rnd = new SecureRandom();
  BigInteger p = new BigInteger(bitLength,certainty,rnd);
  System.out.println("p is "+p);
  BigInteger q = new BigInteger(bitLength,certainty,rnd);
  System.out.println("q is "+q);
  BigInteger n = p.multiply(q);
  System.out.println("n is "+n);
  BigInteger one = new BigInteger("1");
  BigInteger m = p.subtract(one).multiply(q.subtract(one));
  BigInteger e;
  do {
   e = new BigInteger(m.bitLength(),rnd);
   e = e.mod(m);
  } while(!m.gcd(e).equals (one));
  System.out.println("e is "+e);
  BigInteger d = e.modInverse(m);
  System.out.println("d is "+d);
 }
}
```

LISTING B.6 The RSAEncrypt Program

```
package com.jaworski.security.handbook
import java.math.BigInteger;

public class RSAEncrypt {
 public static void main(String[] args) {
  if(args.length != 3) {
   String err = "Usage: java ";
   err += "com.jaworski.security.handbook.RSAEncrypt ";
   err += "modulous key plaintext";
   System.out.println(err);
   System.exit(0);
  }
  int arg = 0;
```

The Mathematics of RSA

APPENDIX B

441

B

THE
MATHEMATICS OF
RSA

LISTING B.6   Continued

```
try {
 BigInteger n = new BigInteger(args[0]);
 ++arg;
 BigInteger e = new BigInteger(args[1]);
 ++arg;
 BigInteger plaintext = new BigInteger(args[2]);
 BigInteger ciphertext = plaintext.modPow(e,n);
 System.out.println(ciphertext);
 }catch(Exception ex1) {
 String err = "Error: arg["+arg+"] is invalid.";
 System.out.println(err);
 }
 }
}
```

Computing and Verifying Signatures

Signatures are computed by encrypting using d (the private key). Signatures are verified by decrypting using e (the public key). You can use the RSAEncrypt program to experiment with signature creation and verification. For example, you can sign the number 1234567890 by encrypting using d:

```
java com.jaworski.security.handbook.RSAEncrypt
➡465683000323564475234543 40686682187444977625631 1234567890
```

The signature that is produced is 383253315545282423605846.

You can verify the signature with:

```
java com.jaworski.security.handbook.RSAEncrypt

465683000323564475234543 117391087578288537201631
➡383253315545282423605846
```

which produces 1234567890.

Downloading and Installing the JCE

This appendix shows how to download and install version 1.2 of the Java Cryptography Extension (JCE).

Downloading the JCE

The JCE is a standard extension API that provides a base implementation of several cryptographic algorithms, including DES. It is available from Sun for download to users in the United States and Canada. If you do not reside in the U.S. or Canada, you can download and install the Cryptix version of the JCE 1.2. Refer to Appendix E, "Downloading and Installing the Cryptix JCE 1.2."

To download the JCE 1.2, go to Sun's Web site at `http://www.javasoft.com/products/jce/index.html`. You'll be prompted with selection lists for downloading the JCE 1.2 software and documentation or the JCE 1.2 API specification. Because the API specification is included with the JCE software, you need only register and download the software.

In order to download the JCE 1.2 software, you must select a format that is compatible with your operating system and then fill out a form that verifies your eligibility to receive the software. Answer Yes to each question and then click the Verify button.

After clicking the Verify button, you will be presented with a license agreement. After you have read the agreement, click Accept to accept it. At this point, you will be presented with buttons to download the software via FTP or HTTP. If your computer is behind a firewall, HTTP might be a better solution than FTP. Next, download the software to your computer.

Installing the JCE

The JCE software should be in an archived and/or compressed format that is appropriate for your operating system. For example, Windows users should select the ZIP format, and UNIX/Linux users should select either compressed TAR or GZIP TAR formats. Installing the JCE begins with uncompressing or unarchiving the downloaded file. For Windows users, I recommend using the WinZip program (http://www.winzip.com). UNIX/Linux users should use the UNIX tar command or tar and gunzip.

> **NOTE**
>
> ### JCE Version Compatibility
>
> Because the JCE is written entirely in Java, the UNIX and Windows versions are equivalent. The only difference between these versions is in the way that they are packaged.

The directory to which you unzip or extract the files does not matter. Under Windows 98, I unzipped the files to my C:\ directory. This results in the JCE being located at C:\jce1.2.

In order to use the JCE 1.2, you must have the JDK 1.2 (Java 2 SDK) installed (Java 2 Platform). Other than that, all you have to do is put the JCE .jar file in your CLASSPATH and edit your java.security file. For example, because I installed the JCE as C:\jce1.2, the .jar file is in the C:\jce1.2\lib directory. I simply add C:\jce1.2\lib\jce1_2-do.jar to my CLASSPATH:

```
set CLASSPATH=.;c:\jdk1.2.2\lib\classes.zip;C:\jce1.2\lib\jce1_2-do.jar;
```

Windows users, be sure that you have a semicolon at the end of your CLASSPATH. Failure to do so can result in the last CLASSPATH item being ignored.

The java.security file is located in the lib\security subdirectory of your java-home directory. In the standard Java 2 Windows installation, it is located at C:\jdk1.2.2\jre\lib\security\java.security. If you are using an earlier or later version of the Java 2 platform, adjust the beginning of this path to the directory where Java is installed.

Open java.security with a text editor and scroll down until you see the following line:

```
security.provider.1=sun.security.provider.Sun
```

This line installs the default Java 2 cryptography provider. To install the JCE 1.2 as an additional provider, simply add the following line as the next line in java.security:

```
security.provider.2=com.sun.crypto.provider.SunJCE
```

This line tells the JRE that the JCE is the next provider that should be used after the default provider.

Testing Your Installation

After you've set up your CLASSPATH and edited your java.security file, you can compile and run the program shown in Listing C.1. It will verify whether or not the JCE has been correctly installed. If you've correctly installed the JCE, the program will display JCE Installed! Otherwise, it will display JCE Installation Failure! If there is a CLASSPATH problem, you will probably find out when you compile the program because a bad CLASSPATH will result in the javax.crypto package not being found by the Java compiler. If the program compiles, but displays JCE Installation Failure!, you should check your java.security file to make sure that you added the JCE as described earlier in this appendix.

LISTING C.1   JCE Installation Test Program

```
import javax.crypto.*;
public class JCEInstallationTest {
 public static void main(String[] args) {
  // Create a cipher to test the JCE
  Cipher cipher = null;
  try {
   cipher = Cipher.getInstance("DES");
   System.out.println("JCE Installed!");
  }catch(Exception e) {
   System.out.println("JCE Installation Failure!");
  }
 }
}
```

The Java 2 Security API

This appendix summarizes the classes and interfaces of the java.security packages included with the Java 2 platform and classes and interfaces of the javax.crypto packages of the JCE 1.2.

The java.security Package

The java.security package contains 39 classes and 8 interfaces that provide the foundation for the Java Security API. It also defines 15 security-related exceptions.

Interfaces

Certificate

The Certificate interface has been deprecated (as of JAVA 2 SDK) and is replaced by the java.security.cert.Certificate class. In JDK 1.1, it was used to provide a common set of methods for accessing digital certificates.

Guard

The Guard interface defines an object that is used to guard access to another object. The checkGuard() method throws a SecurityException if access to the object being guarded is not permitted.

Key

The `Key` interface is the top-level interface that defines methods for accessing `Key` objects. A key has three main characteristics: an algorithm (such as RSA or DSA), an encoded form, and a format. The corresponding se methods are `getAlgorithm()`, `getEncoded()`, and `getFormat()`. The `getAlgorithm()` method returns the name of the algorithm used with the key. The `getEncoded()` method returns the external encoded form of the key (that is, the form used while transporting/transmitting the key, such as the X.509 format). The `getFormat()` method returns the name of the format of the encoded key.

The Key interface implements `java.io.Serializable`.

Principal

The `Principal` interface defines methods for accessing a representation of a *principal* (which is an entity, such as a person, or organization). The `getName()` method returns the name of the principal. Other methods are used to compare or create a `String` representation of the principal.

PrivateKey

The `PrivateKey` interface extends `Key` to identify a key as a private key (as opposed to a public key). This interface does not define any methods or constants.

PrivilegedAction

The `PrivilegedAction` interface provides access to an operation that is performed with privileges enabled. These operations result from invoking the `doPrivileged()` method of the `AccessController` class. The `run()` method of this interface is invoked to perform the privileged action.

The `PrivilegedAction` interface is used for security-sensitive operations that do not throw checked exceptions. Privileged operations that throw checked exceptions should implement the `PrivilegeExceptionAction` interface.

PrivilegedExceptionAction

The `PrivilegedExceptionAction` interface is similar to the `PrivilegedAction` interface. There is one only difference between the two interfaces. The `run()` method of `PrivilegedExceptionAction` throws a checked exception, and the `run()` method of `PrivilegedAction` does not.

PublicKey

The `PublicKey` interface extends `Key` to identify a key as a public key (as opposed to a private key). This interface does not define any methods or constants.

Classes

AccessControlContext

The AccessControlContext class extends Object to encapsulate a context for making access control decisions. The checkPermission() method checks whether a permission is allowed within the access control context. Because the access control context can be independent of the the currently executing thread, you can make permission decisions based on a context other than the current one.

AccessController

The AccessController class extends Object to provide a framework for making access control decisions. It is used to check whether an access is permitted by the security policy that is in effect, to identify privileged code, and to create AccessControlContext objects.

AlgorithmParameterGenerator

The AlgorithmParameterGenerator class is a subclass of Object that generates parameters for use with cryptographic algorithms. The static getInstance() method is a *factory* method that creates an AlgorithmParameterGenerator instance for a particular algorithm type. The generateParameters() method generates the parameters required by a specific algorithm. Other methods are provided that can be used to initialize the parameter generator and return information about the algorithm and its provider.

AlgorithmParameterGeneratorSpi

The AlgorithmParameterGeneratorSpi class is a subclass of Object that defines a service provider interface for an AlgorithmParameterGenerator class. It defines abstract methods that are implemented by each cryptographic service provider that provides a parameter generation capability for a particular algorithm.

AlgorithmParameters

The AlgorithmParameters class is a subclass of Object that encapsulates parameters used with cryptographic algorithms. The init() method is used to initialize the algorithm parameters. A variety of get methods are provided to return information about the algorithm parameters. This class represents the opaque representation—that is, you cannot inspect the individual parameter values.

AlgorithmParametersSpi

The AlgorithmParametersSpi class is a subclass of Object that provides a service provider interface for an AlgorithmParameters class. The abstract methods of this class are implemented by a service provider that supports a parameter management capability for a cryptographic algorithm.

AllPermission

The `AllPermission` class is a subclass of `Permission` that is used to represent all other permissions. This permission is used to effectively disable security permission checking.

BasicPermission

The `BasicPermission` class is a subclass of `Permission` that provides a base class for implementing permissions that use a standard naming convention. It implements the `java.io.Serializable` interface.

CodeSource

The `CodeSource` class is a subclass of `Object` that identifies the location from which code is loaded and the certificate(s) that were used to verify signed code originating from that location. It implements the `java.io.Serializable` interface.

DigestInputStream

The `DigestInputStream` class is a subclass of `java.io.FilterInputStream` that is used to compute a message digest from the data that is read from the stream.

DigestOutputStream

The `DigestOutputStream` class is a subclass of `java.io.FilterOutputStream` that is used to compute a message digest from the data that is written to the stream.

GuardedObject

The `GuardedObject` class is a subclass of `Object` that is used to protect other objects. An object that implements the `Guard` interface determines whether access to the object being guarded is allowed. If access is allowed, the `getObject()` method of `GuardedObject` returns the object being guarded.

`GuardedObject` implements the `java.io.Serializable` interface.

Identity

The `Identity` class is a subclass of `Object` that provides an identity used for making access control decisions. It implements the `Principal` and `java.io.Serializable` interfaces. The `Identity` class is no longer used as of the Java 2 SDK. It is replaced by the `KeyStore` class and the `Principal` interface.

IdentityScope

The `IdentityScope` class is a subclass of `Identity` that defines the scope of an identity. This scope may contain one or more identities. The `IdentityScope` class is no longer used as of the Java 2 SDK. It is replaced by the `KeyStore` class and the `Principal` interface.

KeyFactory

The KeyFactory class is a subclass of Object that is used to transform Key objects into KeySpec objects and vice versa. KeySpec objects provide external representations of Key objects.

KeyFactorySpi

The KeyFactorySpi class is a subclass of Object that provides a service provider interface to a KeyFactory class. It provides abstract methods that are implemented by service providers that support KeyFactory classes.

KeyPair

The KeyPair class is a subclass of Object that encapsulates a public-private key pair. It implements the java.lang.Serializable interface.

KeyPairGenerator

The KeyPairGenerator classis a subclass of KeyPairGeneratorSpi that is used to create public-private key pairs. The static getInstance() method returns a KeyPairGenerator object for a specific algorithm type. The genKeyPair() method is then used to generate a KeyPair object for that algorithm.

KeyPairGeneratorSpi

The KeyPairGeneratorSpi class is a subclass of Object that provides a service provider interface to a KeyPairGenerator object.

KeyStore

The KeyStore class is a subclass of Object that supports the management of cryptographic keys and digital certificates. The getInstance() method is used to create a KeyStore object. Several methods are provided for adding, retrieving, and managing keys and certificates.

KeyStoreSpi

The KeyStoreSpi class extends Object to provide a service provider interface for the KeyStore class.

MessageDigest

The MessageDigest class is a subclass of MessageDigestSpi that encapsulates a message digest. The getInstance() method returns a MessageDigest object for a particular algorithm type. The update() method is used to update a message digest based on new data. The digest() method returns the final value of the computed message digest.

MessageDigestSpi

The MessageDigestSpi class is a subclass of Object that provides a service provider interface to a MessageDigest class.

Permission

The Permission class is a subclass of Object that defines a permission to access a protected resource. It implements the Guard and java.io.Serializable interfaces. The implies() method provides the capability to determine whether one type of permission implies another permission.

PermissionCollection

The PermissionCollection class is a subclass of Object that implements a collection of Permission objects. It implements the java.io.Serializable interface. The add() method may be used to add Permission objects to a PermissionCollection. See the Permissions class for a PermissionCollection that can be used to organize permissions of different types.

Permissions

The Permissions class is a subclass of PermissionCollection that supports a mixed collection of Permission objects. It implements the java.io.Serializable interface. The Permiissions class differs from the PermissionCollection class in that PermissionCollection objects organize Permission objects of the same type (such as FilePermission) and Permissions objects can be used with Permission objects of different types (such as FilePermission and RuntimePermission).

Policy

The Policy class is a subclass of Object that implements a Java security policy. The Policy class is an abstract class that is extended by subclasses that specify the details of a security policy in terms of the permissions that are provided to code from different sources and signers.

ProtectionDomain

The ProtectionDomain class is a subclass of Object that identifies a set of classes with the same permissions from the same CodeSource. Every class belongs to one and only one protection domain. This protection domain identifies the class's CodeSource and permissions.

Provider

The Provider class is a subclass of java.util.Properties that encapsulates a service provider. A provider is a set of packages that provide an implementation of one or more cryptographic algorithms or support (such as key generation) for the alogorithms. The getInfo() method provides a human-readable description of a provider and the services it provides.

SecureClassLoader

The SecureClassLoader class is a subclass of java.lang.ClassLoader that supports secure class loading. It provides support for class creation, and it associates permissions with the class and its CodeSource.

SecureRandom

The SecureRandom class is a subclass of java.util.Random that provides secure random-number-generation capabilities. A secure random number generator generates random numbers in a way that is difficult to predict or duplicate. The getInstance() method is used to create a SecureRandom object, and the next() method is used to generate random int values.

SecureRandomSpi

The SecureRandomSpi class extends Object and implements Serializable to provide a service provider interface for the SecureRandom class.

Security

The Security class is a subclass of Object that provides common access to security-related objects, properties, and methods. The getProperty() method is used to access security properties. The getProvider() and getProviders() methods are used to access installed security providers.

SecurityPermission

The SecurityPermission class is a subclass of BasicPermission that defines security-related permissions, such as those needed to access security policies, properties, and providers.

Signature

The Signature class is a subclass of SignatureSpi that provides digital signature support. The getInstance() method creates a Signature object for a particular type of signature algorithm. The sign() and verify() methods perform signature computation and verification. Data is fed into the object using the update() method.

SignatureSpi

The SignatureSpi class is a subclass of Object that provides a service provider interface to a Signature class.

SignedObject

The SignedObject class is a subclass of Object that represents an object that has been signed. It implements the java.io.Serializable interface. It provides methods for accessing the object that is signed, its signature, and the signature algorithm. The verify() method is used to verify the signature of the signed object.

Signer

The Signer class is a subclass of Identity that is capable of signing an object. It is deprecated and has been replaced by the KeyStore class and the Principal interface.

D

UnresolvedPermission

The UnresolvedPermission class is a subclass of Permission that is used to identify permissions that are not loaded when a security Policy object is initialized. It implements the java.io.Serializable interface.

Exceptions

AccessControlException

The AccessControlException class is a subclass of SecurityException that indicates access to a protected object is denied.

DigestException

The DigestException class is a subclass of GeneralSecurityException that is thrown as the result of errors in message digest calculation.

GeneralSecurityException

The GeneralSecurityException class is a subclass of java.lang.Exception that is used as the base class for defining other security-related exceptions.

InvalidAlgorithmParameterException

The InvalidAlgorithmParameterException class is a subclass of GeneralSecurityException that indicates that an invalid parameter was supplied to a cryptographic algorithm.

InvalidKeyException

The InvalidKeyException class is a subclass of KeyException that indicates that an invalid key was supplied to a cryptographic algorithm.

InvalidParameterException

The InvalidParameterException class is a subclass of IllegalArgumentException indicating that an invalid parameter was supplied to a cryptographic algorithm.

KeyException

The KeyException class is a subclass of GeneralSecurityException that identifies an exception related to a cryptographic key.

KeyManagementException

The KeyManagementException class is a subclass of KeyException that identifies an exception in the management of keys.

KeyStoreException

The KeyStoreException class is a subclass of GeneralSecurityException that identifies an exception in the operation of a KeyStore object.

NoSuchAlgorithmException

The NoSuchAlgorithmException class is a subclass of GeneralSecurityException indicating that a requested algorithm does not exist.

NoSuchProviderException

The NoSuchProviderException class is a subclass of GeneralSecurityException indicating that a requested service provider does not exist.

PrivilegedActionException

The PrivilegedActionException class extends java.lang.Exception to indicate that the performance of a privileged action resulted in a checked exception.

ProviderException

The ProviderException class is a subclass of java.lang.RuntimeException that is generated by a service provider.

SignatureException

The SignatureException class is a subclass of GeneralSecurityException that identifies an exception occurring during signature calculation/verification.

UnrecoverableKeyException

The UnrecoverableKeyException class is a subclass of GeneralSecurityException that signals that a key cannot be recovered from a key store.

The java.security.acl Package

The java.security.acl package's five interfaces provide the basic elements for implementing security access controls. These interfaces have been replaced by the classes and interfaces of the java.security package that implement permission-based security controls. The java.security.acl package also defines three security-related exceptions.

Interfaces

Acl

The deprecated Acl interface extends the Owner interface to define methods for classes that implement access control lists. An Acl object consists of zero or more AclEntry objects.

AclEntry

The deprecated AclEntry interface defines methods for an entry in an access control list. It also manages a set of permissions for Principal objects. It extends the java.lang.Cloneable interface.

Group

The deprecated Group interface extends the java.security.Principal interface to provide methods for working with a group of Principal objects. A Group object may also contain other Group objects.

Owner

The deprecated Owner interface defines methods for working with the owners of an access control list.

Permission

The deprecated Permission interface defines methods for implementing permissions to access-protected resources.

Classes

None.

Exceptions

AclNotFoundException

The AclNotFoundException classis a subclass of java.lang.Exception that signals a reference to a nonexistent access control list.

LastOwnerException

The LastOwnerException class is a subclass of java.lang.Exception that signals an attempt to delete the last owner of an access control list.

NotOwnerException

The NotOwnerException class is a subclass of java.lang.Exception that signals an attempt to modify an access control list by an object that is not the list's owner.

The java.security.cert Package

The java.security.cert package contains seven classes and one interface that implement digital certificates. It also defines six security-related exceptions.

Interfaces

X509Extension

The X509Extension interface provides methods that encapsulate extensions defined for X.509 version 3 certificates and version 2 certificate revocation lists.

Classes

Certificate

The Certificate class is a subclass of Object that provides an abstract base class for implementing identity certificates. Identity certificates are certificates that attest to the fact that a particular Principal has a particular public key.

CertificateFactory

The CertificateFactory class extends Object to provide a factory for creating certificates and certificate revocation lists. The getInstance() method creates a CertificateFactory instance for a particular certificate type. The generateCertificate() method generates a certificate (from an input data stream) for a CertificateFactory object. The generateCRL() method generates a certificate revocation list (from an input data stream) for a CertificateFactory object.

CertificateFactorySpi

The CertificateFactorySpi class extends Object to provide a security provider interface for the CertificateFactory class.

CRL

The CRL class extends Object to provide an abstract implementation of a certificate revocation list (CRL). The getType() method returns the CRL type. The isRevoked() method is used to determine whether a particular certificate has been invoked.

X509Certificate

The X509Certificate class is a subclass of Certificate that provides an abstract base class for implementing X.509 digital certificates. It implements the X509Extension interface.

X509CRL

The X509CRL class is a subclass of Object that implements an X.509 certificate revocation list. It implements the X509Extension interface.

X509CRLEntry

The X509CRLEntry class extends Object and implements the X509Extension interface to provide an abstract class for a revoked certificate in a CRL.

Exceptions

CRLException

The CRLException class is a subclass of java.security.GeneralSecurityException that identifies an exception occurring in the processing of a certificate revocation list.

CertificateEncodingException

The CertificateEncodingException class is a subclass of CertificateException that identifies that an exception occurred during the encoding of a certificate.

CertificateException

The CertificateException class is a subclass of java.security.GeneralSecurityException that acts as a base class for other certificate-related exceptions.

CertificateExpiredException

The certificateExpiredException class is a subclass of CertificateException that identifies that an expired certificate has been encountered.

CertificateNotYetValidException

The CertificateNotYetValidException class is a subclass of CertificateException that identifies that a certificate has been processed before its valid date range.

CertificateParsingException

The CertificateParsingException class is a subclass of CertificateException that indicates an error occurred in the parsing of a certificate.

CRLException

The CRLException class is a subclass of java.security.GeneralSecurityException that identifies an exception occurring in the processing of a certificate revocation list.

The `java.security.interfaces` Package

The java.security.interfaces package contains eight interfaces that support implementation of the NIST digital signature algorithm and the RSA public key encryption algorithm.

Interfaces

DSAKey

The DSAKey interface defines the getParams() method for accessing a Digital Signature Algorithm (DSA) public or private key.

DSAKeyPairGenerator

The DSAKeyPairGenerator interface is implemented by objects that can generate DSA key pairs.

DSAParams

The DSAParams interface defines methods for accessing a set of DSA key parameters.

DSAPrivateKey

The DSAPrivateKey interface extends the DSAKey and java.security.PrivateKey interfaces to provide access to a DSA private key.

DSAPublicKey

The DSAPublicKey interface extends the DSAKey and java.security.PublicKey interfaces to provide access to a DSA public key.

RSAPrivateCrtKey

The RSAPrivateCrtKey interface extends RSAPrivateKey to provide access to the values of p and q used to create a public/private key pair and modulus using the Chinese Remainder Theorem.

RSAPrivateKey

The RSAPrivateKey interface extends PrivateKey to provide support for RSA private keys. The getModulus() method returns the modulus, and the getPrivateExponent() method returns the private key exponent value.

RSAPublicKey

The RSAPublicKey interface extends PublicKey to provide support for RSA public keys. The getModulus() method returns the modulus, and the getPublicExponent() method returns the public key exponent value.

Classes

None.

Exceptions

None.

The java.security.spec Package

The java.security.spec package contains nine classes and two interfaces that provide specifications for cryptographic keys and algorithm parameters. It also defines two security-related exceptions.

Interfaces

AlgorithmParameterSpec

The AlgorithmParameterSpec interface provides no constants or methods. It is used to identify an object that provides cryptographic algorithm parameters.

KeySpec

The KeySpec interface provides no constants or methods. It is used to identify an object that is a key for a cryptographic algorithm.

Classes

DSAParameterSpec

The DSAParameterSpec class is a subclass of Object that provides access to the parameters used in a Digital Signature Algorithm (DSA) implementation. It implements the AlgorithmParameterSpec and java.security.interfaces.DSAParams interfaces.

DSAPrivateKeySpec

The DSAPrivateKeySpec class is a subclass of Object that provides access to the values used in a private DSA key. It implements the KeySpec interface.

DSAPublicKeySpec

The DSAPublicKeySpec class is a subclass of Object that provides access to the values used in a public DSA key. It implements the KeySpec interface.

EncodedKeySpec

The EncodedKeySpec class is a subclass of Object that provides access to an encoded public or private key. It implements the KeySpec interface.

The getFormat() method returns the encoding format. The getEncoded() method returns the key in the encoded format.

PKCS8EncodedKeySpec

The PKCS8EncodedKeySpec class is a subclass of EncodedKeySpec that represents the PKCS #8 standard encoding of a private key.

RSAPrivateCrtKeySpec

The RSAPrivateCrtKeySpec class extends RSAPrivateKeySpec to specify RSA private key values that are obtained using the Chinese Remainder Theorem.

RSAPrivateKeySpec

The RSAPrivateKeySpec class extends Object and implements KeySpec to provide support for RSA private keys.

RSAPublicKeySpec

The RSAPublicKeySpec class extends Object and implements KeySpec to provide support for RSA public keys.

X509EncodedKeySpec

The X509EncodedKeySpec class is a subclass of EncodedKeySpec that represents the X.509 standard encoding of a public or private key.

Exceptions

InvalidKeySpecException

The InvalidKeySpecException class is a subclass of java.security.GeneralSecurityException that identifies an invalid key specification.

InvalidParameterSpecException

The InvalidParameterSpecException class is a subclass of java.security.GeneralSecurityException that identifies an invalid parameter specification.

The javax.crypto Package

The javax.crypto package contains 14 classes and 1 interface that are used to provide basic cryptographic support. It also defines four security-related exceptions.

Interfaces

SecretKey

The SecretKey interface extends java.security.Key to identify secret keys. It does not define any methods or constants and is used only for identification purposes.

Classes

Cipher

The Cipher class extends Object to encapsulate a cipher that is used for encryption or decryption. The getInstance() method creates a Cipher object for a particular encryption algorithm. Other methods provide access to algorithm parameters and support the actual encryption/decryption operations.

CipherInputStream

The `CipherInputStream` class extends `java.io.FilterInputStream` to support the encryption or decryption of data that is read from a stream. One of the `CipherInputStream` constructors allows a `Cipher` object to be specified. This `Cipher` object is used in the encryption/decryption operations.

CipherOutputStream

The `CipherOutputStream` class extends `java.io.FilterOutputStream` to support the encryption or decryption of data that is written to a stream. One of the `CipherOutputStream` constructors allows a `Cipher` object to be specified. This `Cipher` object is used in the encryption/decryption operations.

CipherSpi

The `CipherSpi` class extends `Object` to define a service provider interface for the `Cipher` class.

KeyAgreement

The `KeyAgreement` class extends Object to encapsulate a key agreement/exchange protocol, such as the Diffie-Hellman key exchange protocol. The `getInstance()` method creates a `KeyAgreement` object. The `generateSecret()` method is used to generate a `SecretKey` object.

KeyAgreementSpi

The `KeyAgreementSpi` class extends `Object` to define a service provider interface for the `KeyAgreement` class.

KeyGenerator

The `KeyGenerator` class extends `Object` to provide the capability to generate secret (symmetric) keys. The `getInstance()` method is used to create a `KeyGenerator` object. The `generateKey()` method is used to generate a secret key.

KeyGeneratorSpi

The `KeyGeneratorSpi` class extends `Object` to define a service provider interface for the `KeyGenerator` class.

Mac

The `Mac` class extends `Object` to encapsulate a Message Authentication Code (MAC). The `getInstance()` method creates a `Mac` object for a particular type of MAC algorithm. The `update()` and `doFinal()` methods are used to compute the MAC. The `Mac` class implements the `java.lang.Cloneable` interface.

MacSpi

The `MacSpi` class extends `Object` to define a service provider interface for the `Mac` class.

NullCipher

The NullCipher class extends Cipher to implement a cipher that does not perform any data transformation when going from plaintext to ciphertext (or vice versa). The ciphertext generated by the NullCipher is identical to the plaintext.

SealedObject

The SealedObject class extends Object to provide the capability to create encrypted (sealed) versions of serialized objects. The SealedObject constructor takes a Serializable object and Cipher object as its arguments. The getObject() method can be used to recover the original object provided that the correct Cipher or Key is provided.

SealedObject implements the java.io.Serializable interface.

SecretKeyFactory

The SecretKeyFactory class extends Object to provide the capability to generate SecretKey objects from KeySpec objects and to create KeySpec objects that correspond to SecretKey objects.

SecretKeyFactorySpi

The SecretKeyFactorySpi class extends Object to define a service provider interface for the SecretKeyFactory class.

Exceptions

BadPaddingException

The BadPaddingException class extends java.security.GeneralSecurityException to identify that a padding error was encountered.

IllegalBlockSizeException

The IllegalBlockSizeException class extends java.security.GeneralSecurityException to identify that a block of incorrect size was provided to a block cipher.

NoSuchPaddingException

The NoSuchPaddingException class extends java.security.GeneralSecurityException to identify that a particular padding algorithm is not available.

ShortBufferException

The ShortBufferException class extends java.security.GeneralSecurityException to identify that an output buffer is not large enough to hold the result of a particular operation.

The `javax.crypto.interfaces` Package

The `javax.crypto.interfaces` package includes three interfaces that support Diffie-Hellman key exchange.

Interfaces

DHKey

The `DHKey` interface provides access to the parameters of a Diffie-Hellman key. The `getParams()` method returns a `javax.crypto.spec.DHParameterSpec` object that can be used to access these parameters.

DHPrivateKey

The `DHPrivateKey` interface extends `DHKey` and `java.security.PrivateKey` to provide access to a Diffie-Hellman private key value. The `getX()` method returns this value.

DHPublicKey

The `DHPublicKey` interface extends `DHKey` and `java.security.PublicKey` to provide access to a Diffie-Hellman public key value. The `getY()` method returns this value.

Classes

None.

Exceptions

None.

The `javax.crypto.spec` Package

The `javax.crypto.spec` package contains 12 classes that provide key and algorithm parameter specifications for a variety of cryptographic algorithms.

Interfaces

None.

Classes

DESedeKeySpec

The `DESedeKeySpec` class extends `Object` and implements the `java.security.spec.KeySpec` interface to provide access to a DES-EDEede (triple-DES) key.

DESKeySpec

The DESKeySpec class extends Object and implements the java.security.spec.KeySpec interface to provide access to a DES key.

DHGenParameterSpec

The DHGenParameterSpec class extends Object and implements the java.security.spec.AlgorithmParameterSpec interface to provide access to the parameters used to create a Diffie-Hellman system for key exchange.

DHParameterSpec

The DHParameterSpec class extends Object and implements the java.security.spec.AlgorithmParameterSpec interface to provide access to the g, l, and p parameters used in a Diffie-Hellman system for key exchange.

DHPrivateKeySpec

The DHPrivateKeySpec class extends Object and implements the java.security.spec.KeySpec interface to provide access to a Diffie-Hellman private key.

DHPublicKeySpec

The DHPublicKeySpec class extends Object and implements the java.security.spec.KeySpec interface to provide access to a Diffie-Hellman public key.

IvParameterSpec

The IvParameterSpec class extends Object and implements the java.security.spec.AlgorithmParameterSpec interface to provide access to the initialization vector used in a cryptographic algorithm.

PBEKeySpec

The PBEKeySpec class extends Object and implements the java.security.spec.KeySpec interface to provide access to a password that is used for password-based encryption.

PBEParameterSpec

The PBEParameterSpec class extends Object and implements the java.security.spec.AlgorithmParameterSpec interface to provide access to the parameters used in a password-based encryption system.

RC2ParameterSpec

The RC2ParameterSpec class extends Object and implements the java.security.spec.AlgorithmParameterSpec interface to provide access to the parameters used in the RC2 cryptographic algorithm.

RC5ParameterSpec

The RC5ParameterSpec class extends Object and implements the
java.security.spec.AlgorithmParameterSpec interface to provide access to the parameters
used in the RC5 cryptographic algorithm.

SecretKeySpec

The SecretKeySpec class extends Object and implements the java.security.spec.KeySpec
and javax.crypto.SecretKey interfaces to provide the capability to generate secret keys from
byte arrays.

Exceptions

None.

Downloading and Installing the Cryptix JCE 1.2

This appendix shows how to download and install version 3.1 of the Cryptix JCE replacement.

Downloading the Cryptix 3.1

Because it is against U.S. export control laws to export the JCE outside of the U.S. or Canada, only users in these countries will be able to take advantage of Sun's JCE. However, there is a viable international JCE alternative that is provided by Cryptix, an international volunteer organization that provides open-source cryptographic software libraries. In fact, the Cryptix libraries provide additional cryptographic algorithms that are not found in the JCE 1.2, such as RSA and PGP. Whether or not you are able to obtain Sun's JCE, I still recommend that you download and install the Cryptix package.

To download Cryptix 3.1, go to the Cryptix Web site at `http://www.cryptix.org`. From there, either select the Master Site or navigate to a mirror from your native country. Follow the links to the Cryptix 3.1 (or later) package and download it to your computer.

Installing Cryptix 3.1

The Cryptix software is packaged as a zip file. Unzip it to a directory of your choosing. For example, I unzipped it to the C:\cryptix3.1 directory under Windows 98.

The Cryptix software is distributed as source Java source code. You must have a properly functioning Java 2 installation in order to compile, install, test, and use Cryptix. Also, make sure that you have the current directory included in your CLASSPATH.

To compile the Cryptix software, move to the directory where you unzipped Cryptix and run either build.bat or ./build.sh depending on whether you are running Windows or UNIX/Linux. When you build the software, you might notice some compiler warnings. Just ignore them. The following code shows the output generated by the compiler when I build Cryptix under Windows 98:

```
C:\cryptix3.1>build.bat
Note: 3 files use or override a deprecated API.  Recompile with "-deprecation"
for details.
1 warning
Note: 5 files use or override a deprecated API.  Recompile with "-deprecation"
for details.
1 warning
Note: cryptix\provider\md\HAVAL.java uses or overrides a deprecated API.
Recompile with "-deprecation" for details.
1 warning
Note: 2 files use or override a deprecated API.  Recompile with "-deprecation"
for details.
1 warning
Note: 2 files use or override a deprecated API.  Recompile with "-deprecation"
for details.
1 warning
Note: 4 files use or override a deprecated API.  Recompile with "-deprecation"
for details.
1 warning
C:\cryptix3.1>
```

Your output may differ if you are using a later version of the Cryptix package.

Next, you install the Cryptix package in your java.security file. You can do this by simply running java cryptix.provider.Install from the Cryptix directory:

```
C:\cryptix3.1>java cryptix.provider.Install
Examining the Java installation at C:\JDK1.2.2\JRE
The following lines were added to
  C:\JDK1.2.2\JRE\lib\security\java.security:

# Added by Cryptix V3 installation program:
security.provider.3=cryptix.provider.Cryptix

To uninstall Cryptix, remove these lines manually.

C:\cryptix3.1>
```

NOTE

You may have to change to the cryptix310/build/classes directory to install Cryptix under some operating systems.

In the previous example, I had already installed Sun's JCE as provider 2, so Cryptix was installed as provider 3. If this is the first cryptography provider that you're installing, it will be installed as provider 2. (Provider 1 is reserved for Sun's default provider.) Consult Appendix C, "Downloading and Installing the JCE," for more information on the java.security file.

After installing the Cryptix provider, I recommend that you run the Cryptix test suite. These tests will verify the correct operation of the Cryptix package. Their output is as follows:

```
C:\cryptix3.1>java cryptix.test.TestAll
Running tests for cryptix.test.TestAll
>>> cryptix.test.TestInstall.
>>> cryptix.test.Test3LFSR.
>>> cryptix.test.TestBase64Stream.
>>> cryptix.test.TestBR.
>>> cryptix.test.TestIJCE.
>>> cryptix.test.TestBlowfish.
>>> cryptix.test.TestCAST5.
>>> cryptix.test.TestDES.
>>> cryptix.test.TestDES_EDE3.
>>> cryptix.test.TestIDEA.
>>> cryptix.test.TestLOKI91.
>>> cryptix.test.TestRC2.
>>> cryptix.test.TestRC4.
```

```
>>> cryptix.test.TestSAFER.
>>> cryptix.test.TestSPEED.
>>> cryptix.test.TestSquare.
>>> cryptix.test.TestHAVAL.
>>> cryptix.test.TestMD2.
>>> cryptix.test.TestMD4.
>>> cryptix.test.TestMD5.
>>> cryptix.test.TestRIPEMD128.
>>> cryptix.test.TestRIPEMD160.
>>> cryptix.test.TestSHA0.
>>> cryptix.test.TestSHA1.
>>> cryptix.test.TestHMAC.
>>> cryptix.test.TestScarTestScar> Warning: Unable to delete all test files!
 .
>>> cryptix.test.TestUnixCrypt.
>>> cryptix.test.TestRSA.
>>> cryptix.test.TestElGamal.
==========================================================================
Number of passes:        29
Number of failures:      0
Expected passes:         29
```

You're almost done. To complete the installation, simply add the location of the Cryptix directory to your CLASSPATH. For example, I set my CLASSPATH as follows:

```
set CLASSPATH=.;c:\jdk1.2.2;c:\jdk1.2.2\lib\classes.zip;
 C:\jce1.2\lib\jce1_2-do.jar;C:\cryptix3.1;
```

Windows users, make sure that you put a semicolon at the end of the CLASSPATH. If you do not, the last CLASSPATH item might be ignored.

Testing Your Installation

After you've installed Cryptix and set up your CLASSPATH, you can compile and run the following program in Listing E.1, which will verify whether or not the Cryptix has been correctly installed. If you've correctly installed the Cryptix JCE, the program will display Cryptix Installed! Otherwise, it will display Cryptix Installation Failure!

If there is a CLASSPATH problem, you will probably discover it when you compile the program. A bad CLASSPATH will keep the Java compiler from finding the Cipher class. The Cipher class is provided by the java.security package of Cryptix and not by the Java 2 platform. If the program displays Cryptix Installation Failure! but still compiles, check your java.security file to make sure that you added the Cryptix provider as described above.

Listing E.1   Cryptix Installation Test Program

```java
import java.security.Cipher;

public class CryptixInstallationTest {
 public static void main(String[] args) {
  // Create a cipher to test Cryptix
  Cipher cipher = null;
  try {
   cipher = Cipher.getInstance("RSA");
   System.out.println("Cryptix Installed!");
  }catch(Exception e) {
   System.out.println("Cryptix Installation Failure!");
  }
 }
}
```

Using the Keytool

This appendix shows how to use the keytool of the Java 2 Platform SDK. It provides an overview of the keytool's operation, describes the keytool commands, and provides examples of their use.

Overview

The keytool provides the capability to manage a keystore (see Chapter 6, "Key Management and Digital Certificates"). A keystore is a container for key entries and trusted certificate entries. A key entry consists of a private key and an X.509 certificate chain that authenticates the associated public key. (The keytool does not provide support for symmetric (secret) keys.) A trusted certificate entry is a certificate that authenticates the public key of another party.

The keytool provides the following capabilities:

- Key pair generation
- Certificate generation
- Certificate signing request generation
- Management of key entries
- Management of trusted certificate entries
- Management of passwords

- Importing of JDK 1.1 identity databases
- Help

These capabilities are covered in the section "Keytool Commands," later in this appendix.

Keystore Locations

The keytool operates on a keystore (a `java.security.KeyStore` object), which is stored in a file. The default name of this file is `.keystore` and the default location is the user's home directory. This directory is defined by the setting of the `user.home` property. Use the `DisplayProperty` program of Listing F.1 to display the value of this property:

```
C:\>java com.jaworski.security.handbook.DisplayProperty user.home
C:\WINDOWS
```

The keytool commands take the `-keystore` option, which enables you to specify a different keystore file in a different path. For example, the `-keystore ./mykeystore` option, can be used to specify the keystore as the `mykeystore` file in the current directory.

LISTING F.1   The `DisplayProperty` Program

```
package com.jaworski.security.handbook;

public class DisplayProperty {
 public static void main(String[] args) {
  System.out.println (System.getProperty(args[0]));
 }
}
```

Keytool Commands

The keytool supports the following commands:

- `-certreq`—Generates a Certificate Signing Request (CSR), in the PKCS#10 format.
- `-delete`—Deletes an entry from the keystore.
- `-export`—Exports a certificate to a file.
- `-genkey`—Generates a key pair and an X.509 v1 self-signed certificate for the public key.
- `-help`—Provides help information on the keystore commands.
- `-identitydb`—Imports a JDK 1.1 identity database into the keystore.
- `-import`—Imports a certificate or certificate chain into the keystore.
- `-keyclone`—Creates a copy of a key entry under a new alias.
- `-keypasswd`—Changes the password associated with the private key of a key entry.

- `-list`—Lists the contents of the keystore.
- `-printcert`—Prints a certificate contained in a file or from the standard input stream (stdin).
- `-selfcert`—Generates an X.509 v1 self-signed certificate.
- `-storepasswd`—Sets the password used to protect the integrity of the keystore.

A keystore organizes its entries using aliases. Each of the entries in a keystore is associated with a unique alias. This alias is a string that identifies the use of a key entry or the name of the entity with which a trusted certificate is associated.

Aliases are case insensitive.

Most of the keytool commands take several options. These options are summarized in Table F.1 and described below.

- `-Jjavaoption`—Passes the option to the Java interpreter.
- `-alias alias`—Specifies the alias of the entry to which the command applies. The default value is `mykey`.
- `-dest dest_alias`—Specifies the alias that is the destination of the command.
- `-dname dname`—Specifies the X.500 Distinguished Name to be associated with the alias.
- `-file filename`—Specifies the name of a file to be used with the command.
- `-keyalg keyalg`—Identifies the name of a key-generation algorithm. The default value is DSA.
- `-keypass keypass`—Provides the password used to protect the private key of a key entry.
- `-keysize keysize`—Specifies the size of the key to be generated. The default value is 1024.
- `-keystore keystore`—Specifies the keystore file to be used. The default value is the file named .keystore in the user's home directory.
- `-new new_keypass`—Identifies a new password to be used to protect the private key of a key entry.
- `-noprompt`—Turns off program interaction with the user.
- `-rfc`—Specifies the use of the RFC 1421 printable encoding format.
- `-sigalg sigalg`—Identifies the signature algorithm to be used. The value is derived from the algorithm of the underlying private key. If the underlying private key is of type DSA, the option defaults to SHA1withDSA. If the private key is of type RSA, the option defaults to MD5withRSA.

- -storepass storepass—Specifies the password that is used to protect the integrity of the keystore. The password must be at least six characters. The password must be supplied with all keytool commands.

- -storetype storetype—Identifies the type of keystore to be used. The default value is specified by the keystore.type property of the java.security file located in the \lib\security path off of the directory identified by the java.home property. This value is java.security.KeyStore. (You can use the DisplayProperty program of Listing F.1 to display the value of java.home.)

- -trustcacerts—Specifies that certificates in the cacerts keystore file should be used in addition to those in the keystore. The cacerts file is located in the \lib\security subdirectory of java.home.

- -v—Causes verbose output mode to be used.

- -validity valDays—Specifies the number of days for which the certificate should be considered valid.

TABLE F.1 Command Options

Option	-certreq	-delete	-export
-Jjavaoption	The option is passed to the Java interpreter.	The option is passed to the Java interpreter.	The option is passed to the Java interpreter.
-alias alias	Uses the key entry specified by alias.	Deletes the entry Specified by alias.	Exports the certificate specified by alias.
-dest dest_alias -dname dname -file filename	Specifies the name of the file in which to store the CSR.		Specifies the name of the file in which to store the certificate.
-keyalg keyalg -keypass keypass	Specifies the password of the private key.		

TABLE F.1   Continued

Option	-certreq	-delete	-export
-keysize keysize -keystore keystore	Specifies the location of the The keystore.	Specifies the location of keystore.	Specifies the location of the key-keystore.
-new new_keypass -noprompt -rfc			Uses the RFC 1421 printable encoding format.
-sigalg sigalg	Specifies the signature algorithm to be used.		
-storepass storepass	Specifies the password that is used to protect the integrity of the keystore.	Specifies the password that is used to protect the integrity of the keystore.	Specifies the password that is used to protect the integrity of the keystore.
-storetype storetype	Specifies the type of keystore to use.	Specifies the type of keystore to use.	Specifies the type of keystore to use.
-trustcacerts -v -validity valDays	Uses verbose mode.	Uses verbose mode.	Uses verbose mode.

Option	-genkey	-help	-identitydb
-Jjavaoption	The option is passed to the Java interpreter.		The option is passed to the Java interpreter.
-alias alias	Saves the generated key entry as alias.		

TABLE F.1   Continued

Option	-genkey	-help	-identitydb
-dest dest_alias			
-dname dname	Specifies the X.500 Distinguished Name to be associated with the alias.		
-file filename			Specifies the name of the file containing the database to be imported.
-keyalg keyalg	Specifies the algorithm to be used to generate the key pair.		
-keypass keypass	Specifies the password used to protect the private key.		
-keysize keysize	Specifies the size of the keys to generate.		
-keystore keystore	Specifies the location of the keystore.		Specifies the location of the keystore.
-new new_keypass -noprompt -rfc -sigalg sigalg	Specifies the signature algorithm to be used.		
-storepass storepass	Specifies the password that is used to protect the integrity of the keystore.		Specifies the password that is used to protect the integrity of the keystore.

TABLE F.1   Continued

Option	-genkey	-help	-identitydb
-storetype storetype	Specifies the type of keystore to use.		Specifies the type of keystore to use.
-trustcacerts -v	Uses verbose mode.		Uses verbose mode.
-validity valDays	Specifies the number of days for which the certificate should be considered valid.		

Option	-import	-keyclone	-keypasswd
-Jjavaoption	The option is passed to the Java interpreter.	The option is passed to the Java interpreter.	The option is passed through directly to the Java interpreter.
-alias alias	Stores the imported certificate as alias.	Clones the entry specified by alias.	Changes the password for the private key of the entry identified by alias.
-dest dest_alias		Specifies the alias of the cloned entry.	
-dname dname -file filename	Specifies the name of the file containing the certificate to be imported.		

TABLE F.1   Continued

Option	-import	-keyclone	-keypasswd
-keyalg keyalg -keypass keypass	Specifies the password used to protect the private key.	Specifies the current password used to protect the private key.	Specifies the current (old) password used to protect the private key.
-keysize keysize -keystore keystore	Specifies the location of the keystore.	Specifies the location of the keystore.	Specifies the location of the keystore.
-new new_keypass		Specifies the password used to protect the cloned entry.	Specifies the new password.
-noprompt	Suppresses interaction with the user.		
-rfc -sigalg sigalg -storepass storepass	Specifies the password that is used to protect the integrity of the keystore.	Specifies the password that is used to protect the integrity of the keystore.	Specifies the password that is used to protect the integrity of the keystore.
-storetype storetype	Specifies the type of keystore to use.	Specifies the type of keystore to use.	Specifies the type of keystore to use.
-trustcacerts	Uses certificates specified in the cacerts keystore file in addition to those in the keystore upon which the command is being invoked.		

TABLE F.1   Continued

Option	-import	-keyclone	-keypasswd
-v	Uses verbose mode.	Uses verbose mode.	Uses verbose mode.
-validity valDays			

Option	-list	-printcert	-selfcert
-Jjavaoption	The option is passed to the Java interpreter.	The option is passed to the Java interpreter.	The option is passed to the Java interpreter.
-alias alias	Lists the contents of the entry identified by alias.		Generates an X.509 v1 self-signed certificate using the key entry specified by alias.
-dest dest_alias			
-dname dname			Specifies the X.500 Distinguished Name to be used as both the issuer and subject of the certificate.
-file filename		Specifies the file containing the certificate to be printed.	
-keyalg keyalg			
-keypass keypass			Specifies the password used to protect the private key.
-keysize keysize			
-keystore keystore	Specifies the location of the keystore.		Specifies the location of the keystore.

Table F.1   Continued

Option	-list	-printcert	-selfcert
-new new_keypass -noprompt -rfc	Uses the RFC 1421 printable encoding format.		
-sigalg sigalg			Specifies the signature algorithm to be used.
-storepass storepass	Specifies the password that is used to protect the integrity of the keystore.		Specifies the password that is used to protect the integrity of the keystore.
-storetype storetype	Specifies the type of keystore to use.		Specifies the type of keystore to use.
-trustcacerts -v	Uses verbose mode. Only one of -v and -rfc may be specified.	Uses verbose mode.	Uses verbose mode.
-validity valDays			Specifies the number of days for which the certificate should be considered valid.

Option	-storepasswd
-Jjavaoption -alias alias -dest dest_alias -dname dname	The option is passed to the Java interpreter.

TABLE F.1   Continued

Option	-storepasswd
-file filename	
-keyalg keyalg	
-keypass keypass	
-keysize keysize	
-keystore keystore	Specifies the location of the keystore.
-new new_keypass	Specifies the new password used to protect the keystore.
-noprompt	
-rfc	
-sigalg sigalg	
-storepass	Specifies the password that is used to protect storepass the integrity of the keystore.
-storetype storetype	Specifies the type of keystore to use.
-trustcacerts	
-v	Uses verbose mode.
-validity valDays	

The following subsections cover each of the keytool commands.

NOTE

stdin and stdout

The terms, stdin and stdout, refer to the standard input stream and the standard output stream. These terms are a carryover from the UNIX operating system and the C programming language. The standard input stream is usually associated with the user's keyboard. The standard output stream is usually a console window. However, both may be redirected to other streams.

The -certreq Command

The -certreq command generates a CSR in the PKCS#10 format. A CSR is an file that is sent to a certification authority when applying for a certificate (or certificate chain) that is signed by the CA. The -alias option specifies the key entry to be used to sign the certificate. The -keypass option specifies the password used to protect the key entry's private key. The -sigalg option identifies the signature algorithm to be used. In most cases, this option should not be specified because the algorithm is derived from the algorithm that is internally associated with the key entry's private key. The -file option identifies the file to which the CSR should be written. If it is not specified, the CSR is written to stdout.

The following is an example of the use of the `-certreq` command:

```
C:\>keytool -certreq -alias Signer -file csr.txt
Enter keystore password:  123456
Enter key password for <Signer>:  abcdefg
```

The preceding command generates a CSR for the key entry identified by the Signer alias. The CSR is stored in the `csr.txt` file. The contents of this file are as follows:

```
-----BEGIN NEW CERTIFICATE REQUEST-----
MIICkTCCAk8CAQAwgYsxCzAJBgNVBAYTAlVTMRMwEQYDVQQIEwpDYWxpZm9ybmlhMRIwEAYDVQQH
EwlTYW4gRGllZ28xHjAcBgNVBAoTFUphd29yc2tpICYgQXNzb2NpYXRlczEaMBgGA1UECxMRU29m
dHdhcmUgU2VjdXJpdHkxFzAVBgNVBAMTDkphbWVlIEphd29yc2tpMIIBuDCCASwGByqGSM44BAEw
ggEfAoGBAP1/U4EddRIpUt9KnC7s5Of2EbdSPO9EAMMeP4C2USZpRV1AIlH7WT2NWPq/xfW6MPbL
m1Vs14E7gB00b/JmYLdrmVClpJ+f6AR7ECLCT7up1/63xhv4O1fnxqimFQ8E+4P2O8UewwI1VBNa
FpEy9nXzrith1yrv8iIDGZ3RSAHHAhUAl2BQjxUjC8yykrmCouuEC/BYHPUCgYEA9+GghdabPd7L
vKtcNrhXuXmUr7v6OuqC+VdMCz0HgmdRWVeOutRZT+ZxBxCBgLRJFnEj6EwoFhO3zwkyjMim4TwW
eotUfI0o4KOuHiuzpnWRbqN/C/ohNWLx+2J6ASQ7zKTxvqhRkImog9/hWuWfBpKLZl6Ae1UlZAFM
O/7PSSoDgYUAAoGBAMg2pX/Zm/xdUITLdc12V0IuqQg4LCxm1wkhsvrjYiaL0Kgg/xrRHtP1XA8e
FawP6oOATnoSfUOYDmSVQntblh8kUm8t4OF//9zKWjPWK0mBAuMXpB4BSF3LeIXVju44na/S9Ecz
FTFJPxIn7jimWHEDngf9KsIZtHFqO8x37h+doAAwCwYHKoZIzjgEAwUAAy8AMCwCFERwmwjxa7z3
OXH5GuteBtnPMjBWAhQzF+X68+22mjDJvkgEh8y+FUlJ/g==
-----END NEW CERTIFICATE REQUEST-----
```

When your CA returns the signed certificate (referred to as a certificate reply), you can import it into your keystore using the `-import` command. The other `-certreq` options are generic and are covered in Table F.1.

The `-delete` Command

The `-delete` command deletes the entry specified by the `-alias` option. If you don't specify an alias, you'll be prompted to enter one. The following is an example of the `-delete` command:

```
C:\ >keytool -delete -alias Signer
Enter keystore password:  123456
```

The preceding command deletes the entry associated with the Signer alias.

The `-export` Command

The `-export` command exports the certificate specified by the `-alias` option to the file specified by the `-file` option. If the `-file` option is not specified, the certificate is exported to `stdout`. By default, the certificate is stored in binary format. If the `-rfc` option is specified, the certificate is stored in the RFC 1421 printable encoding format. If the entry's public key is associated with a certificate chain, only the first certificate in the chain is exported. An example of using the `-export` command follows:

```
C:\>keytool -export -alias Signer -file export.txt -rfc
Enter keystore password:  123456
Certificate stored in file <export.txt>
```

The command exports the certificate associated with the Signer key entry to the file
`export.txt`. The certificate is stored in the printable RFC 1421 format. The user is queried to
enter the keystore password. The contents of `export.txt` are as follows:

```
-----BEGIN CERTIFICATE-----
MIIDTTCCAwsCBDghFX4wCwYHKoZIzjgEAwUAMIGLMQswCQYDVQQGEwJVUzETMBEGA1UECBMKQ2Fs
aWZvcm5pYTESMBAGA1UEBxMJU2FuIERpZWdvMR4wHAYDVQQKExVKYXdvcnNraSBIEFzc29jaWAWF0
ZXMxGjAYBgNVBAsTEVNvZnR3YXJlIIFNlY3VyaXR5MRcwFQYDVQQDEw5KYW1pZSBKYXdvcnNraTAe
Fw05OTExMDQwNTExMjZaFw0wMDAyMDIwNTExMjZaMIGLMQswCQYDVQQGEwJVUzETMBEGA1UECBMK
Q2FsaWZvcm5pYTESMBAGA1UEBxMJU2FuIERpZWdvMR4wHAYDVQQKExVKYXdvcnNraSBIEFzc29j
aWF0ZXMxGjAYBgNVBAsTEVNvZnR3YXJlIIFNlY3VyaXR5MRcwFQYDVQQDEw5KYW1pZSBKYXdvcnNr
aTCCAbgwggEsBgcqhkjOOAQBMIIBHwKBgQD9f1OBHXUSKVLfSpwu7OTn9hG3UjzvRADDHj+AtlEm
aUVdQCJR+1k9jVj6v8X1ujD2y5tVbNeBO4AdNG/yZmC3a5lQpaSfn+gEexAiwk+7qdf+t8Yb+DtX
58aophUPBPuD9tPFHsMCNVQTWhaRMvZ1864rYdcq7/IiAxmd0UgBxwIVAJdgUI8VIwvMspK5gqLr
hAvwWBz1AoGBAPfhoIXWmz3ey7yrXDa4V7l5lK+7+jrqgvlXTAs9B4JnUVlXjrrUWU/mcQcQgYC0
SRZxI+hMKBYTt88JMozIpuE8FnqLVHyNKOCjrh4rs6Z1kW6jfwv6ITVi8ftiegEkO8yk8b6oUZCJ
qIPf4VrlnwaSi2ZegHtVJWQBTDv+z0kqA4GFAAKBgQDINqV/2Zv8XVCEy3XNdldCLqkIOCwsZtcJ
IbL642Imi9CoIP8a0R7T9VwPHhWsD+qDgE56En1DmA5klUJ7W5YfJFJvLeDhf//cyloz1itJgQLj
F6QeAUhdy3iF1Y7uOJ2v0vRHMxUxST8SJ+44plhxA54H/SrCGbRxajvMd+4fnTALBgcqhkjOOAQD
BQADLwAwLAIUZf5EiMQbVFtG2hqO5oc/IRYgin8CFGgTzecMWZI2TGGDA65A7U3VmItn
-----END CERTIFICATE-----
```

The `-genkey` Command

The `-genkey` command is used to generate a public-private key pair and store it as the key
entry identified by the `-alias` option. The public key is contained in an X.509 version 1 self-
signed certificate.

The `-keypass` option is used to specify the password to be used to protect the private key. If
this option is omitted, you are prompted to enter a password. If you do not enter a password
(hit Return at the prompt), the keystore's password is used to protect the private key. If you do
supply a password, it must be at least six characters in length.

The `-keyalg` and `-keysize` options specify the algorithm for which the key should be generated and the size of the key to be generated. The default values are DSA and 1024 bits. Valid
key sizes are between 512 and 1024 and are a multiple of 64 bits.

The `-sigalg` option identifies the algorithm that is used to sign the certificate. In most cases,
this option should not be specified because the algorithm is derived from the algorithm that is
internally associated with the key entry's private key. Valid values are `SHA1withDSA` and
`MD5withRSA`.

The -dname option specifies the X.500 Distinguished Name to be associated with the alias. It is used as the issuer and subject fields of the self-signed certificate. If you don't supply this option, you'll be prompted to enter a distinguished name.

The -validity option identifies the number of days for which the certificate is to be considered valid. The default value is 90 days.

An example of using the -genkey command follows:

```
C:\>keytool -genkey -alias Signer -keyalg DSA -keysize 1024
Enter keystore password:  123456
What is your first and last name?
  [Unknown]:  Jamie Jaworski
What is the name of your organizational unit?
  [Unknown]:  Software Security
What is the name of your organization?
  [Unknown]:  Jaworski & Associates
What is the name of your City or Locality?
  [Unknown]:  San Diego
What is the name of your State or Province?
  [Unknown]:  California
What is the two-letter country code for this unit?
  [Unknown]:  US
Is <CN=Jamie Jaworski, OU=Software Security, O=Jaworski & Associates, L=San
Dieg
o, ST=California, C=US> correct?
  [no]:  y

Enter key password for <Signer>
        (RETURN if same as keystore password):  abcdefg
```

The preceding command creates a 1024-bit DSA key entry that is stored under the alias Signer. The user is then queried for the keystore password and the distinguished name to be used with the key pair's certificate. Finally, the user is queried for the password used to protect the key entry's public key.

The -help Command

The -help command displays the following output:

```
keytool usage:

-certreq      [-v] [-alias <alias>] [-sigalg <sigalg>]
              [-file <csr_file>] [-keypass <keypass>]
              [-keystore <keystore>] [-storepass <storepass>]
              [-storetype <storetype>]
```

```
-delete        [-v] -alias <alias>
               [-keystore <keystore>] [-storepass <storepass>]
               [-storetype <storetype>]

-export        [-v] [-rfc] [-alias <alias>] [-file <cert_file>]
               [-keystore <keystore>] [-storepass <storepass>]
               [-storetype <storetype>]

-genkey        [-v] [-alias <alias>] [-keyalg <keyalg>]
               [-keysize <keysize>] [-sigalg <sigalg>]
               [-dname <dname>] [-validity <valDays>]
               [-keypass <keypass>] [-keystore <keystore>]
               [-storepass <storepass>] [-storetype <storetype>]

-help

-identitydb    [-v] [-file <idb_file>] [-keystore <keystore>]
               [-storepass <storepass>] [-storetype <storetype>]

-import        [-v] [-noprompt] [-trustcacerts] [-alias <alias>]
               [-file <cert_file>] [-keypass <keypass>]
               [-keystore <keystore>] [-storepass <storepass>]
               [-storetype <storetype>]

-keyclone      [-v] [-alias <alias>] -dest <dest_alias>
               [-keypass <keypass>] [-new <new_keypass>]
               [-keystore <keystore>] [-storepass <storepass>]
               [-storetype <storetype>]

-keypasswd     [-v] [-alias <alias>]
               [-keypass <old_keypass>] [-new <new_keypass>]
               [-keystore <keystore>] [-storepass <storepass>]
               [-storetype <storetype>]

-list          [-v | -rfc] [-alias <alias>]
               [-keystore <keystore>] [-storepass <storepass>]
               [-storetype <storetype>]

-printcert     [-v] [-file <cert_file>]

-selfcert      [-v] [-alias <alias>] [-sigalg <sigalg>]
               [-dname <dname>] [-validity <valDays>]
               [-keypass <keypass>] [-keystore <keystore>]
               [-storepass <storepass>] [-storetype <storetype>]

-storepasswd   [-v] [-new <new_storepass>]
               [-keystore <keystore>] [-storepass <storepass>]
               [-storetype <storetype>]
```

The -identitydb Command

The -identitydb command is used to import a JDK 1.1 identity database. The -file option specifies the pathname of the database to be imported. If it is not supplied then the database is read from stdin. Only trusted entities are imported. Their names are used as the alias for the entry. Private keys are protected using the keystore's password. If an identity has multiple certificates, only the first is imported (because an alias may only have a single key entry).

```
An example of using the -identitydb command follows:
C:\>keytool -identitydb -file identitydb.obj
Enter keystore password:  123456
Creating keystore entry for <Emily> ...
Creating keystore entry for <Lisa> ...
Creating keystore entry for <Jason> ...
```

The preceding command imports the certificates for Emily, Lisa, and Jason from the identity database specified by the -file option.

The -import Command

The -import command is used to import a certificate (or certificate chain) into a keystore. The -file option identifies the file containing the certificate. If it is not supplied, the certificate is imported from stdin. The certificate must be an X.509 certificate (versions 1, 2, or 3) in the PKCS #7 format. The certificate can be in binary encoding format or in RFC 1421 printable encoding format (delimited by ------BEGIN and END------).

The -alias option identifies the alias under which the certificate should be stored. If the alias refers to an existing key entry, the -keypass option specifies the password that is used to protect the private key of the key entry. If the password is correct, the key entry is replaced by the certificate (or certificate chain) being imported (assuming that it is authenticated).

The certificate being imported is authenticated in one of three ways depending on whether it is a single certificate reply (that is, reply to a CSR by a CA), a certificate reply consisting of a chain of certificates, or a trusted certificate:

1. single certificate reply—A single certificate reply is authenticated by constructing a chain of trust from the certificate to a self-signed CA certificate using the certificates in the keystore (and optionally, the cacerts file—see the -trustcacerts option). The certificate reply and the chain of certificates that are used to verify it are used as the alias's certificate chain. Any existing certificate chain for that alias is replaced with the new certificate chain.

2. chain of certificates—The chain is examined to determine whether it is a valid chain and that the chain's root CA certificate matches a certificate in the keystore (or the cacerts file if the -trustcacerts option is specified). If there is a match, the certificate chain is

imported and replaces any certificate chain that is currently specified for that alias. Otherwise, the root CA certificate is displayed, and the user is given the option to manually verify and import it.

3. trusted certificate—A trusted certificate is authenticated by constructing a chain of trust from the certificate to a self-signed CA certificate using the certificates in the keystore (and optionally, the cacerts file—see the -trustcacerts option). If the certificate being imported is not authenticated by the keystore (or the cacerts file), it is displayed for user review. A user can then verify the certificate using information received from another source. Depending on the result of the manual verification process, the user can elect to continue with or abort the importing of the certificate (unless the -noprompt option is specified—see below). A trusted certificate must be imported to an alias that does not currently exist in the keystore.

The -trustcacerts option specifies that a special common keystore, referred to as the cacerts file, should be used to augment the keystore to which the certificate is being imported. The cacerts file is covered in the section, "The Cacerts Keystore," later in this Appendix.

When a single certificate (or the root certificate of a certificate chain) fails to be authenticated, it is displayed to the user for manual review. The user can then decide whether to trust the certificate based on other information. The -noprompt option suppresses this dialog with the user. This option causes the user to implicitly accept the certificate without review.

The following is an example of using the -import command:

```
C:\ >keytool -import -file jamie.txt -alias jamie
Enter keystore password:  123456
Owner: CN=Jamie Jaworski, OU=Software Security, O=Jaworski & Associates, L=San
Diego, ST=California, C=US
Issuer: CN=Jamie Jaworski, OU=Software Security, O=Jaworski & Associates, L=San
Diego, ST=California, C=US
Serial number: 382264b3
Valid from: Thu Nov 04 21:01:39 PST 1999 until: Wed Feb 02 21:01:39 PST 2000
Certificate fingerprints:
        MD5:   5D:C9:4A:DE:E4:FD:60:8A:20:21:36:9F:C9:53:91:38
        SHA1:  2C:8D:0E:2D:1A:9C:60:8B:0A:50:B8:AB:F2:44:E7:4A:9E:62:00:40
Trust this certificate? [no]:  y
Certificate was added to keystore
```

The preceding command imports the trusted certificate contained in the jamie.txt file and stores it under the alias jamie. Because the certificate cannot be authenticated, its distinguished name, serial number, and fingerprint are displayed during the import.

The -keyclone Command

The -keyclone command creates a copy of a key entry and stores it under a new alias. The -alias option specifies the entry to be copied. Its default value is mykey. The -dest option specifies the alias to be used with the copied entry. If you do not supply this option, you'll be prompted to supply it.

The -keypass option specifies the password that is used to protect the private key of the key entry to be copied. If it is not supplied and is different than the keystore password, you'll be prompted to enter it. The -new option specifies the password to be used to protect the cloned entry. If it is not supplied, you'll be prompted to enter it.

The following is an example of using the -keyclone command:

```
C:\>keytool -keyclone -alias signer -new
mail
Enter destination alias name:
C:\jdk1.2.2\com\jaworski\security\handbook>keytool -keyclone -alias signer
➥-dest
 mail
Enter keystore password:  123456
Enter key password for <signer>:  abcdefg
Enter key password for <mail>
        (RETURN if same as for <signer>):  uvwxyz
```

The preceding command clones the signer entry and saves it as mail. The password for the new entry is set to uvwxyz.

The -keypasswd Command

The -keypasswd command is used to change the password that is used to protect the private key of a key entry. The -alias option identifies the key entry whose password is being changed. The -keypass option specifies the old password, and the -new option specifies the new password. If these options are not specified, you'll be prompted to enter them.

An example of using the -keypasswd command follows:

```
C:\>keytool -keypasswd -alias signer
Enter keystore password:  123456
Enter key password for <signer>:  abcdefg
New key password for <signer>:  gfedcba
Re-enter new key password for <signer>:  gfedcba
```

The preceding command changes the password associated with signer from abcdefg to gfedcba.

The `-list` Command

The `-list` command lists the keystore entry identified by the `-alias` option. If the `-alias` option is not supplied, the contents of the entire keystore is listed.

By default, only the MD5 fingerprint of a certificate is displayed. If the `-v` option is supplied, the contents of the certificate are displayed. If the `-rfc` option is provided, the certificate is displayed in RFC 1421 format. You cannot supply both the `-v` and `-rfc` options because they are mutually exclusive.

An example of using the `-list` command follows:

```
C:\>keytool -list
Enter keystore password:   123456

Keystore type: jks
Keystore provider: SUN

Your keystore contains 7 entries:

mail, Thu Nov 04 21:25:56 PST 1999, keyEntry,
Certificate fingerprint (MD5): 67:B6:A5:11:EC:6E:69:18:88:84:61:09:6D:57:02:6B
signer, Thu Nov 04 21:36:18 PST 1999, keyEntry,
Certificate fingerprint (MD5): 67:B6:A5:11:EC:6E:69:18:88:84:61:09:6D:57:02:6B
jason, Thu Nov 04 20:30:10 PST 1999, keyEntry,
Certificate fingerprint (MD5): 39:3B:D4:21:FD:A8:FC:C2:72:6A:A8:D8:D3:59:32:8C
jamie, Thu Nov 04 21:06:53 PST 1999, trustedCertEntry,
Certificate fingerprint (MD5): 5D:C9:4A:DE:E4:FD:60:8A:20:21:36:9F:C9:53:91:38
emily, Thu Nov 04 20:29:36 PST 1999, keyEntry,
Certificate fingerprint (MD5): 98:79:04:10:99:0F:35:A2:BC:54:2B:7C:6B:8C:AA:E6
lisa, Thu Nov 04 20:30:10 PST 1999, keyEntry,
Certificate fingerprint (MD5): 07:E6:AE:0C:F0:24:12:E1:59:62:73:B3:7F:DB:38:1E
tim, Thu Nov 04 21:20:28 PST 1999, trustedCertEntry,
Certificate fingerprint (MD5): 88:CD:33:F9:1B:06:B1:06:3A:07:26:05:40:90:03:A3
```

The command lists the preceding seven keystore entries.

The `-printcert` Command

The `-printcert` command reads the certificate contained in the file specified by the `-file` option and displays its contents. If the `-file` option is not specified, the certificate is read from `stdin`. The certificate may be stored in binary or printable encoding format. The following is an example of the `-printcert` command:

```
C:\>keytool -printcert -file jamie.txt
Owner: CN=Jamie Jaworski, OU=Software Security, O=Jaworski & Associates, L=San
```

```
Diego, ST=California, C=US
Issuer: CN=Jamie Jaworski, OU=Software Security, O=Jaworski & Associates, L=San
Diego, ST=California, C=US
Serial number: 382264b3
Valid from: Thu Nov 04 21:01:39 PST 1999 until: Wed Feb 02 21:01:39 PST 2000
Certificate fingerprints:
        MD5:  5D:C9:4A:DE:E4:FD:60:8A:20:21:36:9F:C9:53:91:38
        SHA1: 2C:8D:0E:2D:1A:9C:60:8B:0A:50:B8:AB:F2:44:E7:4A:9E:62:00:40
```

The preceding command displays the certificate stored in the `jamie.txt` file.

The `-selfcert` Command

The `-selfcert` command generates a self-signed X.509 version 1 digital certificate for the key entry specified by the `-alias` option. The X.500 distinguished name (issuer and subject) is taken from the alias unless the `-dname` option is provided. In this case, the issuer and subject are taken from the `-dname` option.

The `-validity` option specifies the number of days that the certificate should be considered valid.

The `-keypass` option supplies the password for protecting the private key of the key entry. If it is not provided and is different than the keystore password, you'll be prompted to enter it.

The `-sigalg` option identifies the signature algorithm to be used. In most cases, this option should not be specified because the algorithm is derived from the algorithm that is internally associated with the key entry's private key.

An example of using the `-selfcert` command follows:

```
C:\>keytool -selfcert -alias Mail
Enter keystore password:  123456
Enter key password for <Mail>:  uvwxyz
```

The preceding command generates a certificate for Mail and stores it in the keystore.

The `-storepasswd` Command

The `-storepasswd` command changes the password that is used to protect the integrity of a keystore. The `-storepass` option specifies the old (current) keystore password, and the `-new` option specifies the new password. The `-keystore` and `-storetype` options can be used to identify the keystore's path name and type. An example of using the `-storepasswd` command follows:

```
C:\>keytool -storepasswd -new abcdefg
Enter keystore password:  123456
```

The preceding command changes the keystore password from 123456 to abcdefg. Because the -storepass option was omitted, the user was prompted to enter the old keystore password.

The Cacerts Keystore

The cacerts (certification authority certificates) file is a keystore of CA certificates that is intended to be shared across applications and users on a single system. It typically contains root CA certificates. It is of the default type jks.

The cacerts file is located in the java.home\lib\security directory. You can use the DisplayProperty program of Listing F.1 to display the value of the java.home property.

The cacerts default file is initialized with the following 5 root CA certificates (trusted certificate entries) from VeriSign (see http://www.verisign.com). Its keystore password is changeit:

- OU=Class 1 Public Primary Certification Authority, O="VeriSign, Inc.", C=US

- OU=Class 2 Public Primary Certification Authority, O="VeriSign, Inc.", C=US

- OU=Class 3 Public Primary Certification Authority, O="VeriSign, Inc.", C=US

- OU=Class 4 Public Primary Certification Authority, O="VeriSign, Inc.", C=US

- OU=Secure Server Certification Authority, O="RSA Data Security, Inc.", C=US

The cacerts file is used to provide a core set of certificates from which certificate authentication decisions can be made. It augments the other keystores used on a system.

When the -trustcacerts option is used with the -import command, it specifies that the cacerts file should augment the keystore to which the certificate (or certificate chain) is being imported. If the certificate being imported is not authenticated by the keystore or the cacerts file, it (or the root certificate in the case of a certificate chain) is displayed for user review. A user can then verify the certificate using information received from another source. Depending on the result of the manual verification process, the user can elect to continue with or abort the importing of the certificate (unless the -noprompt option is specified, in which case the user dialog is suppressed and the certificate is imported.)

Using the `jarsigner` Tool

This appendix shows you how to use the `jarsigner` tool of the Java 2 platform to sign JAR files. It can also be used as a command-line reference for the `jarsigner` tool.

JAR Files

A JAR file is a compressed archive file that is created using the Java archive tool (`jar`), which is similar to the PKZIP program developed by Phil Katz. It combines multiple files into a single archive file that is compressed using the ZLIB compression library. Although `jar` is a general-purpose file archive and compression tool, its main purpose is to combine the files used by an applet, application, or API into a single compressed file for efficient loading by a Java-enabled Web browser.

Using JAR files with applets can greatly improve browser performance. Because all the files used by an applet are combined into a single file, a browser needs to establish only a single HTTP connection with a Web server. This reduces the communication-processing overhead on both the browser and the server. File compression reduces the time required to download an applet by 50% or more. This benefits both the applet's user and publisher.

Note

A description of the ZLIB compression format is available at the URL
`http://www.cdrom.com/pub/infozip/zlib/`.

Another feature of JAR files is that they support the capability to sign archived files. This enables browsers to differentiate between untrusted applets and those applets that can be trusted to perform sensitive processing in a secure manner (because they are signed by a reputable identity). The sensitive processing that is permitted to trusted applets is determined by the local Java security policy.

Using the `jar` Tool

The `jar` tool is easy to use. You invoke it using the following command line:

```
jar [options] [manifest] jar-file input-file(s)
```

The `jar-file` is used as an archive. The `.jar` extension should be supplied in the command line. The `input-file(s)` are written as a space-separated list of files to be placed in the archive. Filename wildcard characters may be used (for example, `*.class`).

The `manifest` is a file that contains information about the archived files. It need not be supplied—`jar` will create it automatically and store it as `META-INF\MANIFEST.INF` within the archive. Information about the manifest file can be found in the file `docs\guide\jar\manifest.html` that is included with the JDK 1.2 API documentation.

The `jar` `options` are used to control the input and output of the `jar` tool. They are described in Table G.1.

TABLE G.1 The `jar` Tool Options

Option	Description
c	Creates a new (empty) archive file.
t	Displays the archive's table of contents.
x [file(s)]	Extracts the specified `file(s)`. If no files are specified, all files are extracted.
f	Identifies the file to be created, listed, or extracted.
v	Generates verbose output.

TABLE G.1   Continued

Option	Description
i [jar-file]	Generates index information for the jar-file.
0	Stores files but does not compress them.
M	Skips creation of the manifest file.
m manifest	Uses the supplied manifest file.
U	Indicates that an existing JAR file should be updated.
-C directory	Specifies an alternate directory from which classes should be loaded.

If any of the specified files is a directory, the jar tool will process the directory recursively—that is, all class files in that package and subpackage will be included.

NOTE

The syntax of the jar tool is similar to the UNIX tar command.

NOTE

Note

The @ character may be used in a jar command, followed by a filename. When this occurs, command arguments are taken from the file (one argument per line) and inserted into the command at the position of the @ character.

Examples of using the jar tool are provided in the following sections.

Creating a JAR File

If you have ever used the UNIX tar command or the DOS PKZIP program, you will find the jar tool familiar and easy to use. In this section, you'll learn how to create a JAR file for the ReadFileApplet applet shown in Listing G.1.

I'll use the ReadFileApplet applet because it uses two .class files, which makes it a good candidate for archival and compression. Go ahead and compile it to produce ReadFileApplet.class and ReadFileApplet$ButtonHandler.class.

Listing G.1   The `ReadFileApplet` Applet

```java
import java.applet.*;
import java.awt.*;
import java.awt.event.*;
import java.io.*;

public class ReadFileApplet extends Applet {
 TextArea text = new TextArea();
 Button goButton = new Button("Read Local File");
 Panel panel = new Panel();
 String fileName = "";
 public void init() {
  fileName = getParameter("fileName");
  setLayout(new BorderLayout());
  goButton.addActionListener(new ButtonHandler());
  panel.add(goButton);
  add("North",panel);
  add("Center",text);
 }
 class ButtonHandler implements ActionListener {
  public void actionPerformed(ActionEvent e){
   String s = e.getActionCommand();
   if("Read Local File".equals(s)){
    try {
     FileInputStream inStream = new FileInputStream(fileName);
     int inBytes = inStream.available();
     byte inBuf[] = new byte[inBytes];
     int bytesRead = inStream.read(inBuf,0,inBytes);
     text.setText(new String(inBuf));
    }catch(Exception ex){
     text.setText (ex.toString());
    }
   }
  }
 }
}
```

Let's use `jar` to archive and compress the `*.class` files into a file named `rfa.jar`:

```
jar cf rfa.jar ReadFileApplet*.class
```

You can use the list option of the `jar` command to see what's inside the `rfa.jar` file:

```
jar tf rfa.jar
META-INF/
META-INF/MANIFEST.MF
```

```
ReadFileApplet$ButtonHandler.class
ReadFileApplet.class
```

The only thing that looks out of place is the META-INF/MANIFEST.MF entry. That's the file used to keep a manifest of the JAR file's contents. Go ahead and delete ReadFileApplet.class and ReadFileApplet$ButtonHandler.class. You'll recreate them later in this chapter.

Viewing a JAR File

You're probably wondering how you would include the rfa.jar file in an applet. The answer is that you add the ARCHIVE="rfa.jar" attribute to the applet tag. This attribute tells the browser to load the rfa.jar archive file to find the ReadFileApplet.class file and other related classes. Listing G.2 shows the file ReadFileApplet.htm that is used to display the ReadFileApplet applet.

LISTING G.2   The ReadFileApplet.htm File

```
<HTML>
<HEAD>
<TITLE>An Applet that reads local files</TITLE>
</HEAD>
<BODY>
<H1>An Applet that reads local files.</H1>
<APPLET CODE="ReadFileApplet.class" ARCHIVE="rfa.jar" HEIGHT=300 WIDTH=600>
<PARAM NAME="fileName" VALUE="C:\AUTOEXEC.BAT">
Text displayed by browsers that are not Java-enabled.
</APPLET>
</BODY>
</HTML>
```

You can view the ReadFileApplet applet using the appletviewer tool, as follows (see Figure G.1):

```
appletviewer ReadFileApplet.htm
```

The applet displays a text box and the Read Local File button. The applet is designed to read the AUTOEXEC.BAT file on Windows systems. However, if you click the Read Local File button, you'll receive an error message, as shown in Figure G.2. That's because the applet is not permitted to read any files. Later in this chapter, you'll use the jarsigner tool to sign the applet and modify your security policy to allow the signed applet to read the AUTOEXEC.BAT file.

> **NOTE**
>
> ### NonWindows Users
>
> If you are running Java on a nonWindows system, simply substitute another filename for AUTOEXEC.BAT in Listing G.2.

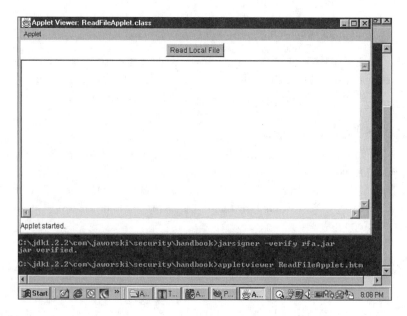

FIGURE G.1

The ReadFileApplet *applet viewed by* appletviewer.

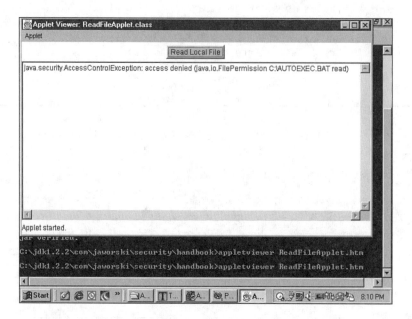

FIGURE G.2

The unsigned applet is not permitted to read AUTOEXEC.BAT.

Extracting the Contents of a JAR File

The x option of the jar tool lets you extract the file's contents. You can use it to re-create the .class files that you deleted:

```
jar xf rfa.jar
```

Note that the META-INF directory is also created. This directory contains a single manifest file named MANIFEST.MF.

Delete the .class files and the META-INF directory before going on to the next section.

Signing JAR Files

The next thing that you're going to do is to digitally sign the rfa.jar file. Before you can sign the JAR file, you need to create a public/private key pair and make it available to the jarsigner tool, in the form of a keystore entry. You'll use the keytool (see Appendix F, "Using the Keytool,") to create a keystore with the public/private key pair.

> **NOTE**
>
> The keytool and jarsigner tools of JDK 1.2 replace the javakey tool of JDK 1.1.

You can generate a public/private key pair for yourself using the -genkey command of keytool. For example, the following command generates a key pair for the alias "Jamie" in the default keystore:

```
keytool -genkey -alias "Jamie"
```

The keytool then prompts you to enter a password for the keystore:

```
Enter keystore password:  123456
```

When you enter a password, keytool prompts you for the following additional information:

```
What is your first and last name?
  [Unknown]:  Jamie Jaworski
What is the name of your organizational unit?
  [Unknown]:  Software Development
What is the name of your organization?
  [Unknown]:  Jaworski & Associates
What is the name of your City or Locality?
  [Unknown]:  San Diego
What is the name of your State or Province?
  [Unknown]:  California
```

```
What is the two-letter country code for this unit?
  [Unknown]:  US
Is <CN=Jamie Jaworski, OU=Software Development, O=Jaworski & Associates, L=San
➥Diego, ST=California, C=US> correct?
  [no]:  yes
```

Finally, you are prompted to enter a password for your private key:

```
Enter key password for <Jamie>
        (RETURN if same as keystore password):
```

I showed you how I filled in this information. You would enter your own information, of course. This information is used to associate an X.500 distinguished name with the alias.

NOTE

If the -keystore option is not supplied, keytool generates a keystore named .keystore that is stored in the directory specified by the user.home system property.

Using jarsigner to Sign a JAR File

Now that you have created a keystore with your public and private keys, you can use the jarsigner tool and your private key to sign a JAR file. The jarsigner tool is used for both signature generation and signature verification. I'll cover signature generation in this section and signature verification in the next section.

To sign a JAR file, you enter a jarsigner command in the following form:

```
jarsigner [-keystore keystore] [-storepass storePassword] -keypass keyPassword
➥JARFileName alias
```

The parameters to this command are as follows:

- *keystore*—The name of the keystore to use (for example, MyKeyStore).
- *storePassword*—The keystore password (for example, 123456).
- *keyPassword*—The private key password (for example, 123456).
- *JARFileName*—The name of the JAR file to be signed (for example, rfa.jar).
- *alias*—The alias of the signer (for example, "Jamie").

Additional command parameters are available for the jarsigner command. Use jarsigner -help to obtain a description of these parameters:

```
jarsigner -help
Usage: jarsigner [options] jar-file alias
       jarsigner -verify [options] jar-file
```

[-keystore <url>]	keystore location
[-storepass <password>]	password for keystore integrity
[-storetype <type>]	keystore type
[-keypass <password>]	password for private key (if different)
[-sigfile <file>]	name of .SF/.DSA file
[-signedjar <file>]	name of signed JAR file
[-verify]	verify a signed JAR file
[-verbose]	verbose output when signing/verifying
[-certs]	display certificates when verbose and verifying
[-internalsf]	include the .SF file inside the signature block
[-sectionsonly]	don't compute hash of entire manifest
[-provider]	name of cryptographic service provider's master class file

I used the following command to sign the rfa.jar file:

```
jarsigner rfa.jar "Jamie"
Enter Passphrase for keystore: 123456
```

If the -keystore option is not specified, the default (.keystore) keystore is used. If the keystore password is not supplied, you are prompted to enter this password.

Signing a JAR file causes the JAR file to be updated as follows:

- A signature (.SF) file is added to the META-INF directory. The name of this signature file is the first eight characters of the alias used to sign the file. This name can be changed using the -sigFile option.
- A signature block file (.DSA) file is added to the META-INF directory. The name of the signature block file is generated in the same way as the signature file.

The signature file identifies each file in the JAR file, the digest algorithm used in the signing process, and a digest value. The digest value is the digest computed from the file's entry in the manifest file. Listing G.3 provides an example signature file.

LISTING G.3   A Sample Signature File

```
Signature-Version: 1.0
SHA1-Digest-Manifest: LrVFCFftXCITdMRYZKie/E0GWBg=
Created-By: 1.2.2 (Sun Microsystems Inc.)

Name: ReadFileApplet$ButtonHandler.class
SHA1-Digest: TTx0UYjUot7EujvpWi9Ug1UdKUQ=

Name: ReadFileApplet.class
SHA1-Digest: K8SfTC5qVpG0dxTEE5hQy4K1t40=
```

The signature block file contains the signature of the signature file and a certificate that authenticates the public key corresponding to the private key used in the signature generation. The signature block file is a binary file.

> **NOTE**
>
> By default, `jarsigner` uses the SHA-1 digest and DSA signature algorithms to sign and verify JAR files. Other digest and signature algorithms can be installed and used instead of SHA-1 and DSA.

> **NOTE**
>
> A JAR file can have multiple signers. Each signer signs the JAR file in succession.

Verifying the Signature of a JAR File

The `jarsigner` tool is also used to verify the signature of a signed JAR file. This is accomplished using the `-verify` option. The following `jarsigner` command form is used:

```
jarsigner -verify JARFileName
```

For example, the following command verifies the signature of `edit.jar`:

```
jarsigner -verify edit.jar
```

If the signature is valid, `jarsigner` produces the following output:

```
jar verified.
```

If the signature is invalid, `jarsigner` responds with an exception identifying why the failure occurred:

```
jarsigner: java.util.zip.ZipException: invalid entry size (expected 900 but got
876 bytes)
```

The `jarsigner` signature verification process is optimized for performance. This process consists of the following:

- Verifying that the signature block (`.DSA`) file contains a valid signature for the signature (`.SF`) file.
- Verifying that the signature file entries are valid digests for each of the corresponding manifest (`MANIFEST.MF`) file entries.
- Verifying that the digests in the `MANIFEST.MF` file are valid for each of the files in the JAR file.

Any error encountered in the verification process results in the generation of a security exception.

Changing the Applet Security Policy

The signing of JAR files provides the basis for developing an applet security policy. JAR files that are received from trusted sources whose signatures can be verified may be given greater privileges than JAR files that are unsigned or come from an untrusted source. In this section, I'll show how to update the default applet security policy (based on digital signatures) to permit `ReadFileApplet` to read your `AUTOEXEC.BAT` file.

The default security policy is defined in the java.policy file located in the *java.home*\lib\ security directory, where *java.home* refers to the value of the `java.home` system property. To grant permission for the `ReadFileApplet` applet in `rfa.jar` to access `AUTOEXEC.BAT`, I added the following lines at the beginning of java.policy:

```
keystore "file:/C:/Windows/.keystore";

grant {
  permission java.io.FilePermission "/AUTOEXEC.BAT", "read", signedBy "Jamie";
};
```

The first line specifies that my default keystore (located at `C:\Windows\.keystore`) should be used. The grant statement specifies that permission to read `C:\AUTOEXEC.BAT` should be granted to code that is signed by Jamie.

Now use `appletviewer` to run `ReadFileApplet` with the new policy:

`appletviewer ReadFileApplet.htm`

Click the Read Local File button. The `appletviewer` displays your `AUTOEXEC.BAT` file, as shown in Figure G.3.

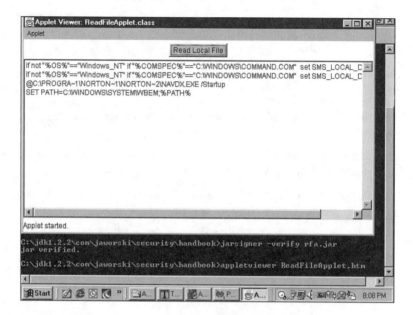

FIGURE G.3

The `ReadFileApplet` *is trusted to read your* `AUTOEXEC.BAT` *file.*

INDEX

SYMBOLS

A

C